Itineraries and Languages of Madness in the Early Modern World

Drawing on a wide range of sources, including interdiction procedures, records of criminal justice, documentation from mental hospitals, and medical literature, this book provides a comprehensive study of the spaces in which madness was recorded in Tuscany during the eighteenth century. It proposes the notion of itineraries of madness, which, intended as a heuristic device, enables us to examine records of madness across the different spaces where it was disclosed, casting light on the connections between how madness was understood and experienced, the language employed to describe it, and public and private responses devised to cope with it. Placing the emotional experience of the Tuscan families at the core of its analysis, this book stresses the central role of families in the shaping of new understandings of madness and how lay notions interacted with legal and medical knowledge. It argues that the perceptions of madness in the eighteenth century were closely connected to new cultural concerns regarding family relationships and family roles, which resulted in a shift in the meanings of and attitudes to mental disturbances.

Mariana Labarca is Assistant Professor at the History Department of the Universidad de Santiago de Chile.

Routledge Studies in Renaissance and Early Modern Worlds of Knowledge

Series Editors: Harald E. Braun
University of Liverpool, UK

Emily Michelson
University of St Andrews, UK

SRS Board Members:
Erik DeBom (KU Leuven, Belgium), Mordechai Feingold (California Institute of Technology, USA), Andrew Hadfield (Sussex), Peter Mack (University of Warwick, UK), Jennifer Richards (University of Newcastle, UK), Stefania Tutino (UCLA, USA), Richard Wistreich (Royal College of Music, UK)

This series explores Renaissance and Early Modern Worlds of Knowledge (c.1400 – c.1700) in Europe, the Americas, Asia and Africa. The volumes published in this series study the individuals, communities and networks involved in making and communicating knowledge during the first age of globalization. Authors investigate the perceptions, practices and modes of behaviour which shaped Renaissance and Early Modern intellectual endeavour and examine the ways in which they reverberated in the political, cultural, social and economic sphere.

The series is interdisciplinary, comparative and global in its outlook. We welcome submissions from new as well as existing fields of Renaissance Studies, including the history of literature (including neo-Latin, European and non-European languages), science and medicine, religion, architecture, environmental and economic history, the history of the book, art history, intellectual history and the history of music. We are particularly interested in proposals that straddle disciplines and are innovative in terms of approach and methodology.

The series includes monographs, shorter works and edited collections of essays. The Society for Renaissance Studies (www.rensoc.org.uk) provides an expert editorial board, mentoring, extensive editing and support for contributors to the series, ensuring high standards of peer-reviewed scholarship. We welcome proposals from early career researchers as well as more established colleagues.

11 Euhemerism and Its Uses
   The Mortal Gods
   Edited by Syrithe Pugh

12 Itineraries and Languages of Madness in the Early Modern World
   Family Experience, Legal Practice, and Medical Knowledge in Eighteenth-Century Tuscany
   Mariana Labarca

For more information about this series, please visit: www.routledge.com/Routledge-Studies-in-Renaissance-and-Early-Modern-Worlds-of-Knowledge/book-series/ASHSER4043

Itineraries and Languages of Madness in the Early Modern World

Family Experience, Legal Practice, and Medical Knowledge in Eighteenth-Century Tuscany

Mariana Labarca

LONDON AND NEW YORK

First published 2021
by Routledge
2 Park Square, Milton Park, Abingdon, Oxon OX14 4RN

and by Routledge
605 Third Avenue, New York, NY 10158

Routledge is an imprint of the Taylor & Francis Group, an informa business

© 2021 Mariana Labarca

The right of Mariana Labarca to be identified as author of this work has been asserted by her in accordance with sections 77 and 78 of the Copyright, Designs and Patents Act 1988.

All rights reserved. No part of this book may be reprinted or reproduced or utilised in any form or by any electronic, mechanical, or other means, now known or hereafter invented, including photocopying and recording, or in any information storage or retrieval system, without permission in writing from the publishers.

Trademark notice: Product or corporate names may be trademarks or registered trademarks, and are used only for identification and explanation without intent to infringe.

British Library Cataloguing-in-Publication Data
A catalogue record for this book is available from the British Library

Library of Congress Cataloging-in-Publication Data
A catalog record for this book has been requested

ISBN: 978-0-367-52828-7 (hbk)
ISBN: 978-0-367-52829-4 (pbk)
ISBN: 978-1-003-05855-7 (ebk)

Typeset in Sabon
by Apex CoVantage, LLC

For Matilde

Contents

List of figures viii
List of tables ix
List of abbreviations x
Acknowledgments xi

Introduction 1

1 Interdiction procedures: a context for public intervention in family life 24

2 Mad spendthrift men: prodigality as a category of mental incapacity 57

3 Beyond financial mismanagement: interdictions by reason of *demenza* 86

4 Spaces and itineraries of madness 128

5 Experts and authorities on madness 176

6 Emotional disturbances and the circulation of the languages of madness 222

Conclusion 267

Index 273

Figures

1.1 Number of interdiction procedures recorded in the Magistrato dei Pupilli between 1690 and 1774 in blocks of 5 years 28
1.2 Distribution of the categories used in interdiction procedures between 1700 and 1774 30

Tables

1.1 Distribution of interdiction petitioners according to their blood relation with the defendant, 1688–1775   41
3.1 Categories of mental incapacity used in interdiction procedures between 1700 and 1775   91
5.1 Involvement of medical opinion in interdiction procedures between 1700 and 1775   179

Abbreviations

ASF	Archivio di Stato di Firenze
BNCF	Biblioteca Nazionale Centrale di Firenze
CR	Consiglio di Reggenza
GTT	Le carte di Giovanni Targioni Tozzetti
MPAAP	Magistrato dei Pupilli et Adulti avanti il Principato
MPAP	Magistrato dei Pupilli et Adulti del Principato
MS	Magistrato Supremo
SD	Ospedale di Santa Dorotea
OGB	Otto di Guardia e Balìa
SMN	Santa Maria Nuova

Acknowledgments

I owe an immense debt of gratitude to Giulia Calvi for her insightful comments, guidance, generosity, and dedication during the years of my Ph.D. at the European University Institute. I am also indebted to Bartolomé Yun-Casalilla for his support and encouragement to transform my doctoral dissertation into a book. I am also very thankful to the examiners of my doctoral dissertation, Sandra Cavallo and John Henderson, for their valuable suggestions.

Many people have made the publication of this book possible through the process of researching and writing. I thank Lisa Roscioni for her challenging observations on my research and Elizabeth Mellyn, whom I met in the Archivio di Stato di Firenze, and was kind enough to share her book with me at that time before it was published. I am also very much indebted to colleagues and friends who have been kind enough to read and discuss parts of this book with me. I would like to thank specially Rafael Mandressi, Francisca Valenzuela, José Tomás Labarca, Marcelo Casals, Mauricio Onetto, Rafael Gaune, and Daniela Belmar. They have been keen critics, helpful advisers, and insightful readers. I am profoundly indebted to them in many ways. I am also grateful for Chet Van Duzer's close reading of the entire manuscript. Alejandro García Montón, María Soledad Zárate, Pilar Larroulet, Javiera Müller, Silvana Lozano, and Macarena Cordero also have been vital supporters throughout this journey.

I would also like to thank the staffs of Archivio di Stato di Firenze, Biblioteca Nazionale Centrale di Firenze, and the Wellcome Trust Library in London for the assistance during the process of research. The Departamento de Historia of the Universidad de Santiago de Chile let me spend precious time in the revision of the manuscript. I am grateful for that.

My most profound debt of gratitude is to my family, who has accompanied me and encouraged me during the different stages of this endeavor from the time of my doctoral research back in Florence to the period during which it was turned into a book in Santiago de Chile. I owe my deepest gratitude to my parents Rodrigo and Mariana and my siblings Elvira, Constanza, Daniel, and José Tomás. All of them in their own personal ways have been crucial to me throughout this entire process. I also thank the steady support of Jaime Ramos from the beginning of this research through its completion. My deepest gratitude also goes to my daughter Matilde, who, since her birth, has accompanied me in this process with her patience and understanding. She has encouraged and inspired me in many levels. *¡Gracias hijita querida por tanto!*

Introduction

On 5 May 1745, a petition reached the office of the Magistrato dei Pupilli, the Tuscan Court of Wards. It was sent by a certain Lorenzo Baldinotti, who requested to be freed from the interdiction that 2 years earlier had deprived him of his right to administer his patrimony and manage his affairs, placing him under the curatorship of the magistracy. In a moving narrative, he recounted all the sufferings he had experienced since his interdiction, for which he held one Marco Guerrini, his wife's maternal uncle, who had been entrusted with the administration of his patrimony, responsible. In his petition, Lorenzo asked for the Grand Duke's protection against the abuses and humiliations he had suffered at the hands of his wife's kin, with whom he had been forced to live by direct command of the court.

> Your Excellency should know that to this point the treatments that I receive in all respects from the Signore Marco Guerrini have become unbearable. Moreover, he sees fit to interfere in all my affairs against my will, acting as if he was master over myself and what is mine, even to the great detriment of my interests. He is in agreement with his sister, the mother of my wife, who also treats me badly in actions and in words, pushed by her said two relatives, and this they can do, and do so continually, because I find myself forced to cohabit with them, and be in their house.[1]

Baldinotti's petition did not refer to either the reasons for his interdiction or his past or present mental condition but focused exclusively on the emotional distress generated by his current situation. He felt that his in-laws, particularly Marco Guerrini, were only interested in his patrimony and had deprived him of his civil rights just to take advantage of him. "They consider me a man of straw," he complained, to be exploited for their purposes. His petition was intended to revoke the interdiction or at the least partially regain his rights to administer his patrimony. He also requested to be allowed to live with his wife and children, and no other relatives, in a residence of his choice.

2   *Introduction*

Lorenzo Baldinotti's case is one of the 611 interdiction procedures conducted between 1700 and 1775 that can be found in the archives of the Magistrato dei Pupilli, the Tuscan Court of Wards. A member of a traditional and wealthy Florentine family, he was denounced to the grand ducal administration as mentally afflicted early in his life and traveled the itineraries of madness from 1725 until his death in 1755. He was subject to four interdictions, alternatively imprisoned, and committed first to the Tuscan mental hospital, Santa Dorotea, and then two times to the *pazzeria* (madhouse) of the Florentine Hospital, Santa Maria Nuova. In 1729, he faced rape charges and was tried by the Tuscan criminal court, the Otto di Guardia e Balìa.[2] When he was not within the walls of the Tuscan hospitals, he was subject to a series of residential arrangements, either cared for by family members or lodged in paid accommodations, prisons, or fortresses. These venues and the responsibility for his care were the outcomes of a negotiation between various members of his family, the officials of the Magistrato dei Pupilli, the Auditore Fiscale – supervisor of criminal courts and head of police and public order – and various physicians.

Lorenzo Baldinotti's case invites us to reflect on how mental disturbances were understood, perceived, and coped with by eighteenth-century Tuscan families. As an exceptionally well-documented case, Lorenzo's story opens a window into the itineraries of madness covered by this book. His case not only is telling regarding the destinations of an allegedly mad person but also reflects the new conflicts and concerns of the eighteenth-century Tuscan families. Married twice and the father of three children, Lorenzo Baldinotti had troubled relationships with all the members of his family, including his in-laws. Although his case appears for the first time in 1725 in the records of the Pupilli, clues as to how his mental disorder was perceived by his family were only recorded more than 20 years later, when the conflicts surrounding him escalated.

Starting in May 1747, his wife's uncle petitioned the Pupilli several times requesting the officials' intervention regarding his whereabouts. This is how we learn that in February 1746 Lorenzo had been sent to the madhouse of Santa Maria Nuova because of his "unhealthy mind," a "defect" that impelled him to insult his wife and children and to perform other "imprudent and improper actions." However, only a few months later he was released after one of his brothers, the priest Zanobi Baldinotti, petitioned for his liberation, promising to guard and feed him properly. But the arrangement ended abruptly after 2 months, when Zanobi violently expelled Lorenzo from his house. According to the Pupilli officials, Zanobi was unable to endure his brother's recurrent "insolences and furious outbursts" any longer.[3]

Subsequently, following the Pupilli's suggestion, the case was placed once more in the hands of the Auditore Fiscale who after a series of unsuccessful attempts to discipline Lorenzo, concluded that the only solution was to imprison him. Although the Fiscale had "exhorted him to be wise, particularly with his wife," who had recently given birth, Lorenzo had nevertheless turned up in her residence and performed "many mad actions."[4] When more complaints arose regarding Lorenzo's behavior, this time from the Florentine prison, he was once more sent to Santa Maria Nuova in June 1747.[5] This second time, Lorenzo remained in the hospital for around 10 months, until his brother Zanobi intervened again to obtain his discharge.[6] As before, the priest tried to share his home with his brother, but the cohabitation once again proved impossible to bear after 3 years. After that, neither his blood relatives nor his in-laws were willing to take on the responsibility of caring for him. In the end, in July 1754, his wife's maternal uncle petitioned once more to liberate the Baldinotti patrimony from the authority of the Pupilli and for Lorenzo's wife to be appointed administrator. Additionally, he requested that Lorenzo should remain under the authority of the grand ducal administration and the Auditore Fiscale, while living under his brother Zanobi's care. The brother refused Guerrini's request.[7]

This new conflict gave occasion for more accurate descriptions of Lorenzo Baldinotti's mental derangements, disclosing the various terms that characterized eighteenth-century language of madness. We hear that he had been incarcerated and confined several times on account of "his extremely extravagant brain [*stravagantissimo cervello*] and long series of absurdities." His blood relatives declared it was "notorious that Lorenzo Baldinotti . . . is of an extravagant, furious and uneasy nature [*naturale stravagante, furioso, ed inquieto*], and sick in his mind." For their part, the officials of the Pupilli supported this assertion by referring to Lorenzo's mental distress with expressions such as that he was "not perfect in his judgment," had an "extravagant brain," and performed numerous "absurdities, scandals and extravagances."[8]

As the case of Lorenzo Baldinotti shows, the itineraries of madness were a series of stages that did not follow linear or preconceived courses but responded and adapted to the characteristics and necessities of each particular case. The ways in which Lorenzo Baldinotti's insanity was described in the various narratives produced throughout his life speak about the complicated interplay between the different notions, interests, concerns, and legal requirements that converged in the decisions regarding his itinerary, how to handle his behavior and cope with its familial and economic consequences. Moreover, they illuminate the reasons for the families' decision to turn to the authorities particularly well, providing valuable information regarding the profound forces that moved families to have recourse to the grand ducal administration for mediation and the ways in which the destinies of the mentally afflicted were decided.

In the chapters that follow, I examine cases similar to that of Lorenzo Baldinotti to illuminate the itineraries of madness and the family conflicts surrounding the disclosure of madness to the public administration in Tuscany during the eighteenth century. Drawing from interdiction procedures, records of criminal justice, documentation from the Tuscan mental hospitals, and medical literature, I analyze social perceptions and attitudes to mental afflictions by placing the experience of the Tuscan families at the core of the analysis. Discussing how notions about and attitudes toward madness were negotiated between families, the surrounding community, authorities, and medical practitioners, this book provides a comprehensive study of the spaces in which madness was recorded, with particular attention to the circulation of languages between lay society, medical practitioners, and state officials. To do so, it proposes the notion of the itineraries of madness, intended as a heuristic device that enables us to examine records of madness across the different spaces where it was disclosed, casting light on the connections between how madness was understood and experienced, the language employed to describe it, and public and private responses devised to cope with it.

The notion of "itinerary" in this book has various levels of meaning, both literal and figurative. The first level corresponds to the itinerary formed by the routes followed by the mentally disturbed through the different measures offered by the Tuscan state. The second level alludes to the emotional itineraries followed by Tuscan families when coping with mental afflictions in one of their members. In the end, the notion of the itineraries of madness also includes the idea of movement and flexibility that characterized the languages of madness. On the whole, the itineraries of this book are a journey across the different layers that composed the experience of madness in the eighteenth-century on a route that takes us through the homes of the mentally afflicted, civil and criminal courts, prisons, hospitals, and the office of the Auditore Fiscale. Along this journey, we are able to understand the experience of eighteenth-century families in their struggles with what they perceived as mental affliction, with their different voices, concerns, and expectations. We are able to observe them as they moved through the spaces of madness, adjusting their languages to the requirements of each institution and circumstance, negotiating with state officials and physicians, and settling their private disputes.

The itineraries of madness

Scholars on the history of madness in Early Modern Europe agree that during the eighteenth century, madness captured the attention of families, medical professionals, authorities, and the judicial administration in unprecedented ways. In Tuscany, and throughout Europe, mental afflictions acquired new visibility, leaving more abundant traces in asylum records, civil law inquiries into mental capacity, criminal procedures, registers of the poor relief system, police documents, and medical literature.[9] The visibility acquired by mental afflictions in Tuscany during the eighteenth century speaks not only of a growing concern over what to do with relatives deemed mentally afflicted, but also of families' increasing recourse to the grand ducal administration to resolve their private conflicts. During the century, Tuscan families turned to the authorities with unprecedented frequency not only to negotiate remedies for the custody and cure of the mentally afflicted, but most of all to request the mediation of state officials in their private disputes.

The different remedies available to families in the eighteenth century for the custody and care of the mentally disturbed and the possible paths they could pursue in trying to mitigate the financial, familial, and emotional repercussions of mental afflictions date back to the fourteenth century to the early stages of the Florentine Republic. Scholars have studied the different legal provisions devised between the fourteenth and seventeenth centuries by the Tuscan administration to tackle the problems caused by mental afflictions, focusing particularly on criminal procedures and guardianship suits. According to Elizabeth Mellyn, responses to madness during this period were carefully negotiated between families and the ducal administration. Rather than serving as proof of the "expanding mechanisms of control," as previous scholarship had claimed, Mellyn argues that the civil and criminal court records of this period suggest that public institutions played a limited role in the care of the mentally disabled; the decision of what to do about the public and private problems caused by madness was the outcome of a collaboration between families and authorities in which "the spirit of compromise and negotiation reigned."[10] Against this historical background, it is not only possible to identify certain continuities but also possible to observe important changes in the ways domestic and public responses to mental disturbances were negotiated during the eighteenth century.

First of all, in 1643, the foundation of the Pia Casa di Santa Dorotea dei Pazzerelli, the Florentine madhouse, provided a new alternative for the custody and cure of the mentally disturbed. Under the forceful influence of Michel Foucault's *Histoire de la folie* (1961), scholars initially studied the institution from the point of view of its normative dispositions and segregational purposes.[11] Taking issue with this approach, Lisa Roscioni, in her thorough study of mental institutions in early modern Italy, argues that the rise of mental hospitals in the Italian peninsula was the result of a long process of social and medical institutionalization of the mentally ill which began in the mid-sixteenth century.[12] Casting doubt on both the scope and chronology of the Foucauldian "Great Confinement," Roscioni has shown that asylums in early modern Italy developed as spaces increasingly destined to cure and not only to control and segregate the insane. In the particular case of Tuscany during the eighteenth century, the physicians of Santa Dorotea and the ducal administration oscillated between the need to keep the insane under custody and the desire to cure them, giving rise to a debate that brought a complicated balance between charity and public responsibility to the fore.[13]

Confinement was a solution of last resort for families regardless of their social rank, a path followed only when close relatives were unable or unwilling to take care of the mentally afflicted. According to Roscioni, the dynamics of internment show a relationship of complicity and collaboration between families and authorities, marked by short periods of confinement and relatively low number of inmates, which leads her to consider asylums during this period as a space of transit or of temporary aid in a web of institutions of assistance.[14] The emergence of the Tuscan asylum provided a new institution for the custody and cure of the mentally ill which did not change the dynamics of the collaboration and negotiation between families and authorities developed in the previous centuries over what to do with those deemed mentally disturbed.

Scholars have convincingly argued that asylums "did not *replace* the family as the central locus of care of the insane" and were not a space destined to the indiscriminate confinement of the mad, poor, and marginalized members of society.[15] What can be observed in the eighteenth century is the increasing intervention of public institutions in the lives of the mentally afflicted at request of the families, which by no means interfered with the central role played by families as the primary system of care. Historians have elaborated on the extent to which the available measures to cope with mental illness functioned as a network through which families moved in their attempts to deal with madness and control its consequences. Studies on the wide array of public and private provisions devised in early modern Europe to handle the problems posed by madness and unruly family members demonstrate that remedies were predominantly temporary and far more flexible than Michel Foucault had envisaged.[16] In this regard, scholars have identified the development of welfare institutions as a process that entailed a complex interaction between state and society, arguing that it was not imposed top down.[17] Taking care of the mentally ill was considered a shared responsibility throughout the early modern period.

In Tuscany, in 1643, the foundation of Santa Dorotea provided an unprecedented institution for the custody and care of the mentally afflicted. However, it did not replace other strategies to cope with the mentally disturbed. As can be observed in the case of Lorenzo Baldinotti, in eighteenth-century Tuscany, there were various courses of action that families could resort to when they had to deal with a mentally disturbed relative. The family-based system of care was many times accompanied by the advice and treatment of various medical practitioners. Families could also try to make different residential arrangements by turning to family networks, priests, or neighbors. Many of these arrangements, as one might expect, left no documentary trace. But there were a range of other resources available for families that did leave a mark, some of which make up the evidence upon which this book is written. Depending on the case and the conflicts caused by the mentally disturbed, families could ask a state official to visit them and try to produce a change in the patient's behavior, and they could ask the local authority or the Auditore Fiscale, in his capacity as a supervisor of public order, to issue an official reprimand. When reprimands failed to produce a change, families could combine legal admonishments with requests for temporary imprisonment or exile, or they could press criminal charges when the behavior breached the law. They could petition for their alleged mentally disturbed relatives to be committed to Santa Dorotea or the *pazzeria* of Santa Maria Nuova or, when they could not afford confinement, they could negotiate with the authorities for different custodial arrangements. Finally, families could also petition for them to be interdicted and placed under guardianship.

Inquiries into mental capacity

In this book, the itineraries of madness start with interdiction procedures, which constitute the core source of the study. Interdictions, the legal mechanism by which individuals deemed mentally or physically incapable of managing their affairs were deprived of their rights to administer their patrimonies and placed under curatorship (*curatela*), were under the jurisdiction of the Magistrato dei Pupilli. Following an interdiction, the Pupilli officials acted as universal curators, assigning an administrator or *attore* of the patrimony and supervising all matters related to the defendants' legal and personal affairs. Founded in 1393 to provide state guardianship for orphans whose fathers had died intestate or without having assigned a tutor, the Magistrato dei Pupilli was an institution with profound influence over the lives of the mentally disturbed in Tuscany. Although connected with the guardianship of mentally or physically impaired adults since its foundation, the Pupilli officially established its exclusive prerogative over the curatorship of adults in 1473, aiming to protect property and neutralize the effects of economic mismanagement.[18] I argue that by the eighteenth century, the officials of the Pupilli had come to play a crucial role in the coordination of the different institutions concerned with the mentally disturbed, working closely with the Auditore Fiscale. During that century, families placed an increasing reliance on interdiction procedures as a way to handle the economic consequences of madness and its domestic strains. During the eighteenth century, the number of interdictions grew steadily, side by side with the growing capacity of Santa Dorotea.

Studies on judicial inquiries into mental capacity have shown the extent to which these records constitute valuable sources to study both social perceptions of madness, private strategies to deal with it, and public remedies devised to alleviate some of its effects. Further, given the range of agents who participated in the discussion, from families, neighbors, medical practitioners, and priests, to procurators, judges, and state officials, they allow us to grasp the different languages and perceptions that came together in the courts of law to define what mental disturbance amounted to, as the studies of Robert Allan Houston, Akihito Suzuki, and Elizabeth Mellyn have shown.[19] The Tuscan interdiction procedures are a local variant of other European legal procedures devised to protect the patrimony and person of those deemed mentally impaired, depriving individuals of their rights to administer their assets and manage their affairs. In all of these procedures, the definitions of mental impairment we find recorded are closely connected with ideas about proper financial behavior. They also have in common that they were largely initiated at the request of family members and affected men predominantly from the propertied sorts.

8   *Introduction*

In the case of Tuscany, these sources provide a particularly interesting window into the dynamics of family relationships, in so far as interdiction procedures were employed not only to prevent or put an end to financial mismanagement, but also to request state intervention in private conflicts. I argue that during the eighteenth century, representations of and attitudes toward mental disturbance went beyond a concern over financial mismanagement. While in the previous centuries, descriptions and definitions of mental disturbance were primarily related to property and based on financial behavior, during the eighteenth century the focus shifted to emotional instability and the ways in which defendants conducted their relationships with other family members. Since the beginning of the Magistrato dei Pupilli's involvement with mental impairment in the fifteenth century, Tuscan society had concurred that mental illness was responsible for reckless spending and economic mismanagement in accordance with the principles of what Elizabeth Mellyn called "patrimonial rationality."[20] The novelty in the eighteenth century was that a new accent was placed on how public performance and financial behavior disclosed one's state of mind, revealed above all by the person's emotional reactions. Descriptions abide by the principles of "patrimonial rationality," but characterizations of mad behavior were now increasingly centered on how actions revealed emotional instability and how the allegedly mentally disturbed related to other members of the household. Furthermore, when defining mental capacity, litigants and authorities were debating new aspirations and expectations regarding filial or paternal responsibility, matrimony, and family relationships.

The extent to which an action was the outcome of madness involved less contention than which measures were to be taken to help families cope with the disorders it caused, which required more debate on the state of mind and inner disposition of the person, beyond the resultant acts themselves. More attention was paid to the person's state of mind to determine how it affected those surrounding him or her. Rather than the presence of financial mismanagement alone or of a behavior that contravened the principles of "patrimonial rationality," it was the flaring up of conflicts in relationships that propelled families to seek public intervention. Moreover, most families who requested the mediation of authorities did so only after the alleged misbehaviors had been going on for a long time.

This is predominantly a history of married men told by women, which is interesting if we remember that in both Scotland and France, for instance, judicial inquiries into mental capacity affected single men mostly.[21] The extent to which gender is a key to understand how madness was perceived and described in Tuscany is also illustrated by the constant reference to these men's position in the family structure and their expected gendered behavior. The predominance of wives petitioning for the interdiction of their husbands changes the focus compared to the previous periods, from patrimonial disputes to marital conflicts, followed by clashes between firstborns and their mothers and between old fathers and their sons. Mellyn shows that long-lasting conflicts between family lines were the mobilizing forces behind guardianship suits in the previous centuries.[22] By contrast, in eighteenth-century interdiction procedures, marital disputes, intergenerational conflicts, and the difficulties of cohabitation come to the fore as the leading forces propelling families to request interdiction.

Interdiction procedures reveal specific expectations regarding proper behavior according to age, gender, marital status, and position in the family structure. As a result, *demenza* and prodigality, the two overarching categories of mental incapacity, were defined differently for young bachelors, married middle-aged men, and elderly men. In each case, the family group was different, as was the set of conflicts inflicted on their families by their alleged mental incapacity. The few cases of women denounced for mental incapacity, on the contrary, affected mostly widows and corresponded to cases less involved in domestic divisiveness. The pattern that emerges when families came under the strain of having a mentally afflicted head of family is that a woman often took his post. In response to the disorder produced by mental affliction, state officials and families negotiated the temporary empowerment of women, who were generally appointed administrators of their husbands' or sons' patrimonies and were the most recurrent solicitors of public intervention. This shows the extent to which women were key agents in the responses and attitudes to mental incapacity in Tuscany during the eighteenth century.

Flexible categories and nuanced conceptions

Legal and institutional provisions devised to respond to the private and public challenges posed by madness configured a network by means of which authorities, medical practitioners, families, and their surrounding communities debated the meanings, indicators, and consequences of mental disturbance. Scholars have argued that perceptions of madness in the eighteenth century went beyond the medico-legal categories that structured the public provisions devised to help families to cope with mental disturbances.[23] Behind seemingly simplistic and rigid legal categories, structured according to origin and level of mental incapacity and often used interchangeably, early modern societies developed nuanced conceptions of madness, which acquired different features according to the institutional spaces in which madness was recorded.[24] In this context, this book pays particular attention to language and its circulation, examining how lay notions interacted with legal and medical knowledge. It shows that litigants, state officials, witnesses, and physicians framed their narratives of madness according to each institutional context, choosing their lexicon and adapting their descriptions according to the requirements and purposes of each institutional space.

The legal framework in Tuscany provided generic categories of madness and mental incapacity – *pazzo, prodigo, demente, mentecatto* – which derived from a long tradition and remained mostly unchanged.[25] These medico-legal categories of mental incapacity were simple and often overlapped but, in practice, gave space to a wide range of interpretations of what mental disturbance amounted to. For instance, Lisa Roscioni has shed light on the extent to which *pazzia furiosa* (raving madness), the category liable for committal, is but one facet of a much more complex social, medical, and political approach to madness in the eighteenth century. The debate between state officials, medical practitioners, families, and the community of origin over who was to be admitted to Santa Dorotea evidences conceptions of mental disturbance that go beyond the stereotypes of violent, disruptive, and suicidal madness, with overlapping definitions and subtle shades of what was considered mad behavior. Descriptions of open defiance to public decency or public order, extravagances, and scandals were combined with references to signs such as refusing to work and spending most of the time in bed, disrespect for family hierarchies, dissipation of financial resources, obscene behavior, blasphemy, dishonorable amorous affections, and mental fixations.[26]

A similar phenomenon can be observed in the records of civil and criminal courts of law. Descriptions provided to convince the authorities for the need to interdict a *prodigo* or a *demente* included the widest array of indicators of what was considered mad behavior and a perturbed state of mind. In the case of criminal procedures, the generic employment of the categories of *pazzo*, *demente*, or *mentecatto* in requests for acquittal or a mitigation of penalty on the grounds of mental incapacity or temporary mental obfuscation discloses subtle strategies to define each type of deranged behavior and alteration of mind. Slightly different are the records of the office of the Auditore Fiscale, which reveal situations and behaviors which were not necessary to describe using legal vocabulary. Requests made to the Auditore Fiscale by families seeking his help to cope with allegedly unruly, disordered, or unstable relatives show characterizations similar to those that can be found in interdiction accounts, the proceedings of criminal justice, and hospital records but without the employment of the medico-legal categories that were required by these institutions.

Beyond these differences, on the whole these records show a persistent concern over the breaching of behavioral codes, with a special focus on the incapacity to control or manage one's emotions, which was increasingly singled out as an evidence of a disease the source of which was to be found in the mind. What interdiction procedures, criminal records, and documents from Santa Dorotea show is the existence of shared cultural perceptions regarding what it meant to be mentally disturbed, its defining characteristics, and most pressing effects on social and family life. Furthermore, the itinerary through interdictions, hospitals, criminal courts, and institutions such as the office of the Auditore Fiscale illustrates the instrumental use of the languages of madness. Litigants resorted artfully to the vocabulary of madness to ground their accusations against each other and to justify their pleas for the authorities' intervention.

I argue that the perceptions of madness in the eighteenth century were closely connected to new cultural anxieties regarding family relationships and family roles. While in terms of legal vocabulary, long-term continuities seem to predominate, the eighteenth century brings new concerns and a new codification of familial conflicts to the fore, which resulted in a shift in the meanings of madness. The eighteenth century saw challenges to patriarchal authority, conflicting expectations over marriage, motherhood, fatherhood, and the responsibilities of a firstborn son, intergenerational conflicts, and new forms of affection.[27] All of these, combined with the anxieties generated by disobedience and sexual permissiveness, were the gauges of the debate around mental derangement. During the century, the narratives of madness increasingly delved into the relational dimensions of mental disturbance, paying particular attention to certain forms of emotional disruption. In contrast with the unchanged legal categories of *pazzo*, *demente*, and *prodigo*, we can observe the appearance of the culturally meaningful *stravaganza* (extravagance); *inquietudine* (uneasiness); or *carattere irregolare, volubile,* and *incerto* (irregular, changing, or uncertain character).

The Tuscan records show a relatively low incidence of medical testimonies and a preference for a lay language. Judicial narratives of mental incapacity only rarely made use of medical terminology, which allows us to generate a more nuanced account of the process of infiltration of medical terminology into the Tuscan civil and criminal courts beginning in the sixteenth century.[28] Social notions regarding the signs and consequences of insanity mattered more than determining a diagnosis or giving medical explanations for the mental disease in question, which explains why medical opinion had a limited intervention. The limited infiltration of medical terminology, nonetheless, does not entail that medical theories did not circulate among the laity, for the attention given to emotional disturbances as indicators of mental affliction across medical and judicial accounts suggests an interesting convergence between medical, legal, and lay cultures of knowledge.[29]

Throughout Europe, the medical profession played an incipient role in the legal assessment of insanity during the eighteenth century. Although we do witness a marked increase in the introduction of medical testimonies in the second half of the century, these were neither necessary nor sufficient to assess mental incapacity or criminal insanity.[30] Families continued to hold the authority to characterize mental afflictions and expose their impact on social and family life. Medical testimonies appear more frequently in the Tuscan criminal and civil courts in the eighteenth century than previously, but the vast majority of cases during the period under study here were still decided without recourse to medical opinion; and, when we do find medical testimonies, they tend to be formulated in a language similar to that of lay witnesses. A clear difference must be mentioned here from the procedure for admission to Santa Dorotea, where medical certification was compulsory from 1750 onward. Requests for admission and records of discharge, however, were framed in a largely unmedicalized language. Although the use of the ubiquitous category of *pazzia furiosa* was mandatory in the records of the hospital, and terms such as melancholic delirium or mental fixations do appear in other judicial procedures, over all, medical testimonies employed a language very similar to the one employed by litigants and state officers in criminal and civil courts.

Family and emotions

As historians have convincingly argued, madness was first identified and experienced at the core of family life. To identify mental disturbances, families had first to form an understanding of what it meant to be mentally disturbed, then to ponder how they would handle it, and eventually where they would turn if they decided to seek external help.[31] Studies have stressed the extent to which the disclosure of madness in the public realm was dependent upon the dynamics of household life and family conflicts.[32] As Robert Allan Houston puts it, cases of madness would have remained unknown to us if not for a circumstantial disturbance of family life. Drawing on Erving Goffman's *Asylums*, he has termed these as the "contingencies" which determined the appearance of madness in the records, and they may even have been disconnected from the ways in which mental derangement manifested itself and affected its sufferers.[33] Houston argues that the visibility acquired by madness during the eighteenth century suggests "changing ways of dealing with the contingencies which insane behavior produced."[34] Building on this argument, I suggest that the Tuscan records of madness point to changing attitudes toward domestic life and family relationships, making the disclosure of madness to the authorities part of an increasing recourse to the courts of law to solve family disputes.

From this point of view, the study of madness also sheds new light on some of the traditional problems of the history of the family, in particular, on the uses of justice for resolving domestic affairs. Entangled with discussions of bottom-up models of social disciplining and negotiated forms of social control, studies of justice and family litigation have taken into consideration the agency of litigants, the role of intermediaries in settling private disputes, and the range of alternative solutions for solving conflicts that did not necessarily entail following judicial procedures as the law had intended them to be followed.[35] Judicial practices were negotiated and even manipulated by family members to achieve their means. In this sense, recourse to litigation, an intrinsic part of the mechanisms for exerting social control from below,[36] enables us to study social debates about accepted behavior and about the consequences of breaching the norms, as much as they illuminate the dynamics of family relationships.

The eighteenth century witnessed an explosion of family conflicts in the administration of justice, exposing the private *désordre des familles* to the public.[37] The century was marked by a clash between generations over divergent ideals and conceptions of financial behavior, self-determination, the value of social status, and proper manifestations of affection, all of which were submitted to the judicial system for arbitration.[38] Scholars have inquired into what moved family members to denounce each other in front of a court of law, given that usually what was being described had been occurring for a long time. Early modern litigation illuminates issues as diverse as paternal and intergenerational relationships, the negotiation of behavioral norms according to age and gender, conflicting conceptions of economic management and the transmission of the patrimony, the building of strategies and alliances between and against family members, the roles of kinship, the experience of marriage, the distribution of power, and gender relations.[39] In all these aspects of familial life, the presence of madness and the ideas about and reactions to it left an indelible mark. The family disputes that are revealed in the eighteenth-century Tuscan accounts of mental derangement shed light on the relationships between family members, disclosing day-to-day mechanisms for resolving conflicts or for devising obstacles to the implementation of patriarchal power. As this book shows, litigants made instrumental use of the argument that their spouse was mad or that their son exhibited behaviors that were associated with madness. Turning to the authorities to deal with the challenges posed by madness served to address gender roles, marital, intergenerational, and parental responsibilities and to resolve family conflicts. By approaching these aspects through the lens of the itineraries of madness, we are able to grasp the connections between notions about and attitudes toward madness, family conflicts, and state–society relations, all of which enrich the study of the debates and negotiations that gave shape to a social knowledge of madness.

The study of the itineraries of madness is, thus, also a study of the relationship between families and the state. A part of the early modern process of state building, this relationship reveals the settlement of an agreement on the shared responsibility of state and families over weak members of society.[40] In a political landscape characterized by the end of the Medici dynasty and the institutional reforms brought by the Habsburg-Lorraine since 1737,[41] the changes that can be observed in the history of madness in Tuscany during the eighteenth century are the result of a combination between the consolidation of a strong administration and the rhythms of private lives of Tuscan citizens.

The itineraries of this book

Itineraries and Languages of Madness in the Early Modern World is largely based on the records of interdiction procedures and the management of curatorships preserved in the archive of the Magistrato dei Pupilli. Although inquiries into mental capacity were part of the public provisions devised to respond to the challenges posed by madness in various European societies, this archive is a remarkable exception for it provides a long-term perspective that other European sources lack. Most of the studies that draw from this type of source have focused on the records left by the inquiries undertaken before it was decided that the person needed to be placed under guardianship.[42] This means that, although these studies focus on narratives that illuminate both the present of the reported mental condition and also its past, they are usually silent about what happened afterward. The records of the Magistrato dei Pupilli, on the contrary, do not stop once the interdiction was decreed but rather begin with it. We find not only the petition, its supporting testimonies, and the inquiries conducted by the authorities to decree the interdiction, but also a wide range of subsequent records that continue to shed light on many aspects of the life of the interdicted and their families. As a result, we are able to examine how madness was understood and experienced at different points of a person's life, sometimes throughout his or her entire adult life.

The voices recorded in this archive are varied, providing diverse perspectives and experiences from the point of view of various members of the family (with narratives many times handwritten by the signee and other times only signed by them), neighbors, medical practitioners, priests, and authorities, including the allegedly mentally afflicted. Two related issues require discussion here. One has to do with the legal script and the other with authorship. We know that during the early modern period, litigants knew how to use the system of justice and maneuver through its structure and that the judicial narratives were manufactured with specific aims. Litigants had to adapt their narratives to the legal formulas required in the judicial institution they turned to and to produce plausible stories. However, this does not transform these narratives into mere fictional artifacts.[43] Petitioners knew how much they were required to say and how they were supposed to say it, but beyond the formulas, they produced narratives that are unique and one of a kind. We have to take into account the extraordinary circumstances that led families to reveal mental afflictions to the authorities, which means that what appears in the records cannot be taken as ordinary experiences with madness. But it does illuminate how families resolved their conflicts; how they negotiated the boundaries of rational behavior, their attitudes to madness, and the language employed by litigants, authorities, and, on occasion, physicians, to identify and characterize mental disturbance.

The second issue just mentioned involves the question of authorship – that is, who composed the various documents submitted in judicial proceedings regarding madness. The voices recorded in the archive of the Magistrato dei Pupilli and, in particular, in its section of petitions (*suppliche*) were not always mediated by procurators, notaries, or clerks, something that can be understood by the comparison between the signature and the handwriting of the main text. These documents also offer reports on the authorities' investigations (and often interrogatories) regarding each case. Although many petitions and testimonies can be taken to be crafted by intermediaries (be they from the judicial administration, procurators, or by members of the family), the particular incidents they introduce and the variations given to the main story allows us to circumvent the issue regarding legal script and authorship.

This book examines the immensely rich archive of the Magistrato dei Pupilli placing interdiction procedures at the center of a network of institutions and agents that configured the itineraries of madness. Thus, interdiction procedures are examined together with the records of Santa Dorotea – namely, the procedures for admission and discharge of patients – and criminal proceedings of the Tuscan criminal court, the Otto di Guardia e Balìa, in which madness came under discussion to determine liability, devise possible arrangements regarding the destinies of the criminally insane, or rule for a mitigation of penalty. The study also explores documents from the office of the head of police and supervisor of criminal courts, the Auditore Fiscale, where families turned to seek help in curbing unruly or seemingly mentally unstable relatives. Additionally, it employs selected medical literature of the period, particularly published and unpublished Italian medical consultations. Although these sources do not provide the long-term view of the Magistrato dei Pupilli, when examined together they offer invaluable possibilities for the study of how notions, attitudes, and responses to madness were negotiated and how the destinations in the itineraries of madness were decided. Apparently composed in various different contexts, when examined as part of a network of measures, these sources disclose uncanny connections, completing the picture of the different ways in which madness was shaped, conceived, and managed in eighteenth-century Tuscany.

The timeframe chosen for this study is not only marked by the rhythms of the Magistrato dei Pupilli but it also reflects broader political and cultural changes. The study begins around 1700, to encompass the situation before 1718, when a reform of the statutes of the Pupilli determined the magistracy's exclusive prerogative over interdiction procedures, which produced a notable increase in the number of interdictions. During this period, the other spaces of madness remained mostly unaltered until 1750, when a law changed the procedure for admission to Santa Dorotea by making it open to any patient regardless of whether he or she could pay the required fee. As a result, the number of inmates increased significantly, augmenting the visibility of madness, which was already high as a result of the interdiction procedures. The mid-eighteenth century was in fact a landmark period for the changes that can be observed in the languages of madness, when the shift toward the vocabulary of emotional instability becomes more visible. The study ends in 1775, so as to include the decade following 1767, when a new reform granted Tuscan citizens free access to the services of the Magistrato dei Pupilli for those who previously could not pay the required fee, producing a radical increase in the number of interdictions issued from that time onward.

Itineraries and Languages of Madness in the Early Modern World is divided into six chapters. The first chapter is concerned with the foundations of the Magistrato dei Pupilli and the characteristics of interdiction procedures in Tuscany and provides a comparative perspective to place the Tuscan case in relation with other European inquiries into mental capacity. Chapters 2 and 3 examine prodigality and *demenza*, respectively. Explaining why petitioners resorted to interdiction, how they framed their denunciations, and how interdiction procedures served to introduce a mediator into family disputes, these chapters explore the extent to which perceptions of mental incapacity were inseparable from the experience of the family and the rhythms of its relationships. Chapter 4 delves into the itineraries of madness, expanding the view from interdiction procedures to the records of Santa Dorotea, proceedings of criminal justice where the defendant's mental state was under scrutiny, and private requests handled by the Auditore Fiscale. By examining the multiplicity of arrangements through which families and authorities could respond to the challenges posed by madness, it discusses the instrumental uses of the languages of madness and the presence of shared notions of what it meant to be mentally disturbed. Chapter 5 deals with the different agents who participated in the characterizations of madness recorded across the various Tuscan institutions that dealt with madness. It first explores the role of medical opinion in the legal assessment of mental incapacity and then examines the circulation of medical categories and the involvement of other agents such as priests, neighbors, and local authorities as expert witnesses; and ends with a discussion of the role of the Auditore Fiscale. Finally, chapter 6 examines the role ascribed to emotional disturbances as the defining indicators of the presence of mental affliction, casting light on the circulation of lay, medical, and legal languages of madness. The argument of the book builds incrementally chapter by chapter to form, by its end, a detailed portrait of madness in eighteenth-century Tuscany, its social construction, its languages, the itineraries through the institutions responsible for its treatment, and how Tuscan families dealt with its many challenges.

Notes

1 ASF, MPAP, *Memoriali*, F. 2301, no. 169(2), May 1745.
2 ASF, MPAP, *Campione di Deliberazioni, e Partiti*, F. 119, fol. 77, 4 January 1724/25; ASF, OGB, *Negozi dei Rettori*, F. 1729, Negozio 7067, no. 4, 3–8 March 1729; ASF, MPAP, *Memoriali*, F. 2300, no. 319, 2 August 1730; ASF, MS, *Atti e Scritture*, F. 1866, fol. 1529, 18 December 1724, F. 1912, fol. 6, 2 August 1730, and F. 2017, fol. 643, February 1740/41; ASF, MPAP, *Memoriali*, F. 2301, no. 110, February 1740/41; ASF, MS, *Suppliche*, F. 1188, fol. 871, August 1743; ASF, SD, F. 23, no. 3; ASF, MPAP, *Memoriali*, F. 2301, no. 192, August 1743; ASF, CR, *Fiscale*, F. 759, no. 11, June 1755; ASF, MPAP, *Memoriali*, F. 2303, no. 210, August 1754.
3 ASF, MPAP, *Memoriali*, F. 2301, no. 265, June 1747 and ASF, CR, *Fiscale*, F. 759, no. 11, report from Santa Maria Nuova.
4 ASF, CR, F. 755, no. 26, Report of the Auditore Fiscale to the Council of Regency, 29 June 1747.
5 ASF, MPAP, *Memoriali*, F. 2301, no. 265, June 1747.
6 These events are recounted in ASF, MPAP, *Memoriali*, F. 2303, no. 210, July–September 1754; and ASF, CR, F. 759, no. 11, June–July 1755.
7 ASF, MPAP, *Memoriali*, F. 2303, no. 210, July–August 1754.
8 ASF, MPAP, *Memoriali*, F. 2303, no. 210.

Introduction 17

9 Robert Allan Houston, *Madness and Society in Eighteenth-Century Scotland* (Oxford: Oxford University Press, 2000), 114–123; Lisa Roscioni, *Il governo della follia. Ospedali, medici e pazzi nell'età moderna* (Milan: Bruno Mondadori, 2003), 116–138 and *passim*; Jonathan Andrews and Andrew Scull, *Undertaker of the Mind: John Monro and Mad-Doctoring in Eighteenth-Century England* (Berkeley: University of California Press, 2001), xiv–xx, 145–148 and *passim*; Dana Rabin, *Identity, Crime, and Legal Responsibility in Eighteenth-Century England* (Basingstoke: Palgrave Macmillan, 2004), 2; Andrew Scull, *The Most Solitary of Afflictions: Madness and Society in Britain, 1700–1900* (New Haven and London: Yale University Press, 1993), 1–45; Joel Peter Eigen, *Witnessing Insanity: Madness and Mad-Doctors in the English Court* (New Haven and London: Yale University Press, 1995), 6–7; Akihito Suzuki, "The Household and the Care of Lunatics in Eighteenth-Century London," in *The Locus of Care: Families, Communities, Institutions, and the Provision of Welfare Since Antiquity*, ed. Peregrine Horden and Richard Smith (London and New York: Routledge, 1998), 153–175; Roy Porter, *Mind-Forg'd Manacles: A History of Madness in England from the Restoration to the Regency* (London: Penguin Books, 1990), 160–168; among many others.
10 Elizabeth W. Mellyn, *Mad Tuscans and Their Families: A History of Mental Disorder in Early Modern Italy* (Philadelphia: University of Pennsylvania Press, 2014), 9. Mellyn took issue with Graziella Magherini and Vittorio Biotti's Foucauldian view of increasing state control over the lives of the mentally disturbed in *L'isola delle Stinche e i percorsi della follia a Firenze nei secoli XIV-XVIII* (Florence: Ponte alle Grazie, 1992).
11 Magherini and Biotti, *L'isola delle Stinche*; Graziella Magherini and Vittorio Biotti, *"Un luogo della città per custodia de' pazzi." Santa Dorotea dei Pazzerelli di Firenze nelle delibere della sua congregazione (1642–1754)* (Florence: Le Lettere, 1997); Vittorio Biotti, *È matto e tristo, pazzo e fastidioso. I saperi sulla follia: magistrati, medici e inquisitori a Firenze e negli stati italiani del '600* (Florence: Nicomp L. E., 2002). Michel Foucault, *History of Madness* (London: Routledge, 2006).
12 Roscioni, *Il governo della follia*, 68.
13 Tracing the early development of a specialized medical knowledge, Lisa Roscioni has called for a more nuanced and flexible approach to the medicalization of madness, arguing that due to their therapeutic and not merely custodial aims, seventeenth- and eighteenth-centuries Italian mental institutions played a significant role as formative spaces for medical practitioners which came to be seminal to the "protoprofesionalization" of alienism. Lisa Roscioni, "Soin et/ou enfermement? Hôpitaux et folie sous l'Ancien Régime," *Genèses* 82 (2011): 32.
14 Roscioni, *Il governo della follia*, xviii.
15 Peter Bartlett and David Wright, eds., *Outside the Walls of the Asylum: The History of Care in the Community 1750–2000* (London: The Athlone Press, 1999), 4. Also Roscioni, *Il governo della follia*; Porter, *Mind-Forg'd Manacles*; Suzuki, "The Household and the Care of Lunatics"; and Akihito Suzuki, "Lunacy in Seventeenth- and Eighteenth-Century England: Analysis of Quarter Sessions Records, Part 1," *History of Psychiatry* 2 (1991): 437–456.
16 Seminal to this assertion were Roy Porter's studies and, in particular, *Mind-Forg'd Manacles*. For the case of Tuscany, see Mellyn, *Mad Tuscans*; and Roscioni, *Il governo della follia*.
17 Lisa Roscioni, "Un affare di famiglia. L'internamento manicomiale e la questione degli alimenti a Roma tra XVIII e XIX secolo," *Proposte e ricerche* 73 (2014): 95–108; Roscioni, *Il governo della follia*, 125; Angela Groppi, *Il welfare prima del welfare. Assistenza alla vecchiaia e solidarietà tra generazioni a Roma in*

età moderna (Roma: Viella, 2010), 9–18; and Peter Rushton, "Lunatics and Idiots: Mental Disorder, the Community, and the Poor Law in North-East England 1600–1800," *Medical History* 32, no. 1 (1988): 34–50.
18 Mellyn, *Mad Tuscans*, 24–39.
19 Houston, *Madness and Society*; Akihito Suzuki, *Madness at Home: The Psychiatrist, the Patient, and the Family in England, 1820–1860* (Berkeley: University of California Press, 2006); Mellyn, *Mad Tuscans*. See also Laurent Cartayrade, "Property, Prodigality, and Madness: A Study of Interdiction Records in Eighteenth-Century Paris" (PhD diss., University of Maryland, 1997); Thierry Nootens, *Fous, prodigues et ivrognes: Familles et déviance à Montréal au XIX siècle* (Montreal: McGill-Queen's University Press, 2007); Suzuki, *Madness at Home*; and María José Correa, *Historias de locura e incapacidad. Santiago y Valparaíso (1857–1900)* (Santiago: Acto Editores, 2013).
20 "Patrimonial rationality describes the belief held by families and governments that the prudent preservation, management, and devolution of patrimony were of supreme importance. It suggests that economic decisions could not be made outside the context of the family or independent of social concerns. Patrimonial rationality was an 'ethical habit', to borrow a phrase from Francis Fukuyama, implying the subordination of individual interest to that of one's lineage. But it was also a practical strategy for protecting the material interests of a lineage by using the courts to deactivate spendthrifts in the marketplace." Mellyn, *Mad Tuscans*, 103–104.
21 Houston, *Madness and Society*, 146; and Cartayrade, "Property, Prodigality," 174.
22 Mellyn, *Mad Tuscans*, 45–56.
23 For instance, scholars have noted that the differentiation between lunacy and idiocy or furiosity and idiocy were more subtle and flexible than what normative legal sources might lead us to believe. Houston, *Madness and Society*, 164–171; David Wright and Anne Digby, eds., *From Idiocy to Mental Deficiency* (London and New York: Routledge, 1996), particularly the articles written by Peter Rushton and Jonathan Andrews; and Suzuki, "Lunacy in Seventeenth- and Eighteenth-Century England." For the case of Tuscany, see Mellyn, *Mad Tuscans*; Roscioni, *Il governo della follia*; Magherini and Biotti, *L'isola delle Stinche*; and Biotti, *È matto e tristo*.
24 See Mellyn, *Mad Tuscans*; Roscioni, *Il governo della follia*; Houston, *Madness and Society*; Andrews and Scull, *Undertaker of the Mind*; H.C. Erik Midelfort, *A History of Madness in Sixteenth-Century Germany* (Stanford, CA: Stanford University Press, 1999); Porter, *Mind-Forg'd Manacles*; and Michael MacDonald, *Mystical Bedlam: Madness, Anxiety, and Healing in Seventeenth-Century England* (Cambridge: Cambridge University Press, 1981), among many others.
25 Mellyn, *Mad Tuscans*, 18; and Marco Boari, *Qui venit contra iura. Il furiosus nella criminalistica dei secoli XV e XVI* (Milan: Giuffrè, 1983).
26 Roscioni, *Il governo della follia*, 155–176.
27 Daniela Lombardi, *Matrimonio di antico regime* (Bologna: Il Mulino, 2001), 359–453; Roberto Bizzocchi, *Cicisbei. Morale privata e identità nazionale in Italia* (Roma and Bari: Laterza, 2008); Chiara La Rocca, *Tra moglie e marito. Matrimoni e separazioni a Livorno nel Settecento* (Bologna: Società editrice Il Molino, 2009).
28 Graziella Magherini and Vittorio Biotti, "Madness in Florence in 14th–18th Centuries: Judicial Inquiry and Medical Diagnosis, Care and Custody," *International Journal of Law and Psychiatry* 21, no. 4 (1998): 355–368; and Magherini and Biotti, *L'isola delle Stinche*.
29 On this issue, see Mellyn, *Mad Tuscans*, 128–192 and Houston, *Madness and Society*, 331–355; and Eigen, *Witnessing Insanity*, 134–136.

Introduction 19

30 Eigen, *Witnessing Insanity*, 28 and 95; and Houston, *Madness and Society*, 47–52. For a useful overview, see Michael Clark and Catherine Crawford, eds., *Legal Medicine in History* (Cambridge: Cambridge University Press, 1994).
31 Key to this assertion were the studies of MacDonald, *Mystical Bedlam*; and Porter, *Mind-Forg'd Manacles*.
32 Suzuki, "The Household," and Suzuki, "Lunacy in Seventeenth- and Eighteenth-Century England."
33 Houston, *Madness and Society*, 91.
34 Houston, *Madness and Society*, 119.
35 Fundamental to this discussion are the contributions of Martin Dinges and Mario Sbriccoli, who suggested the approaches of the uses of justice and of the interconnections between hegemonic justice and negotiated justice. See Marco Bellabarba, Gerd Schwerhoff, and Andrea Zorzi, eds., *Criminalità e giustizia in Germania e in Italia. Pratiche giudiziarie e linguaggi giuridici tra medioevo ed età moderna* (Bologna and Berlin: Il Mulino, 2001), particularly Martin Dinges, "Usi della giustizia come elemento di controllo sociale nella prima età moderna," 285–324; and Mario Sbriccoli, "Giustizia negoziata, giustizia egemonica. Riflessioni su una nuova fase degli studi di storia della giustizia criminale," 345–364. For an example on the uses of justice for resolving family affairs, see Julie Hardwick, *Family Business: Litigation and the Political Economies of Daily Life in Early Modern France* (Oxford and New York: Oxford University Press, 2009); and Daniela Lombardi, "Giustizia ecclesiastica e composizione dei conflitti matrimoniali (Firenze, secoli XVI-XVIII)," in *I tribunali del matrimonio (secoli XV-XVIII)*, ed. Silvana Seidel Menchi and Diego Quaglioni (Bologna: Il Mulino, 2006), 577–607.
36 Hernan Roodenburg, "Social Control Viewed from Below: New Perspectives," in *Social Control in Europe, vol. 1, 1500–1800*, ed. Herman Roodenburg and Pieter Spierenburg (Columbus, OH: Ohio State University Press, 2004), 145–158.
37 Arlette Farge and Michel Foucault, *Le désordre des familles: lettres de cachet des Archives de la Bastille au XVIIIe siècle* (Paris: Gallimard, Julliard, 1982); and Arlette Farge, "The Honor and Secrecy of Families," in *A History of Private Life*, vol. 3, ed. Roger Chartier (Cambridge, MA: Harvard University Press, 1989), 571–607.
38 Lombardi, *Matrimonio*; Bizzocchi, *Cicisbei*; and Isabel Morant Deusa and Mónica Bolufer Peruga, *Amor, matrimonio y familia* (Madrid: Editorial Síntesis, 1998).
39 For a comprehensive overview centered on matrimonial litigation, see Silvana Seidel Menchi, "I processi matrimoniali come fonte storica," in *Coniugi nemici. La separazione in Italia dal XII al XVIII secolo*, ed. Silvana Seidel Menchi and Diego Quaglioni (Bologna: Il Molino, 2000), 15–94. See also Lombardi, *Matrimonio*; La Rocca, *Tra moglie e marito*; Laura Gowing, *Domestic Dangers: Women, Words, and Sex in Early Modern London* (Oxford: Oxford University Press, 1996); Joanne Bailey, *Unquiet Lives: Marriage and Marriage Breakdown in England 1660–1800* (Cambridge: Cambridge University Press, 2003); and Lawrence Stone, *Road to Divorce: England 1530–1987* (Oxford: Oxford University Press, 1990), among many others.
40 On the negotiation between the state and families and the emergence of a welfare system, see Roscioni, "Un affare di famiglia;" Groppi, *Il welfare prima del welfare*; and Sandra Cavallo, "Family Obligations and Inequalities in Access to Care in Northern Italy, Seventeenth to Eighteenth Centuries," in *The Locus of Care: Families, Communities, Institutions, and the Provision of Welfare Since Antiquity*, ed. Peregrine Horden and Richard Smith (London and New York: Routledge, 1998), 90–110.

20 *Introduction*

41 Alessandra Contini, "Orientamenti recenti sul settecento Toscano," in *La Toscana in età moderna (secoli XVI-XVIII). Politica, istituzioni, società: studi recenti e prospettive di ricerca*, ed. Mario Ascheri and Alessandra Contini (Florence: Leo S. Olschki Editore, 2005), 91–127; R. Burr Litchfield, *Emergence of a Bureaucracy: The Florentine Patricians, 1530–1790* (Princeton, NJ: Princeton University Press, 1986); Marcello Verga, *Da "cittadini" a "nobili." Lotta politica e riforma delle istituzioni nella Toscana di Francesco Stefano* (Milan: Giuffrè, 1990); and Furio Diaz, *I Lorena in Toscana. La Reggenza* (Turin: UTET, 1988).
42 Houston, *Madness and Society*; Cartayrade, "Property, Prodigality," and Suzuki, *Madness at Home*.
43 Notable in this discussion is Natalie Zemon Davis, *Fiction in the Archives* (Stanford: Stanford University Press, 1987). See Seidel Menchi, "I processi matrimoniali"; La Rocca, *Tra moglie e marito*, 16–18; and Gowing, *Domestic Dangers*, 232–262. For the specific case of judicial records of madness, see Houston, *Madness and Society*, 42–43.

Bibliography introduction

Manuscripts

Archivio di Stato di Firenze (ASF)

- Consiglio di Reggenza (CR), F. 755, F. 759
- Magistrato dei Pupilli et Adulti del Principato (MPAP)

    - *Campione di Deliberazioni, e Partiti*, F. 119
    - *Memoriali e Negozi di Cancelleria*, F. 2300, F. 2301, F. 2303

- Magistrato Supremo (MS)

    - *Atti e Scritture*, F. 1866, F. 1912, F. 2017
    - *Suppliche*, F. 1188

- Otto di Guardia e Balìa (OGB)

    - *Negozi dei Rettori*, F. 1729

- Santa Dorotea (SD), F. 23

References

Andrews, Jonathan, and Andrew Scull. *Undertaker of the Mind: John Monro and Mad-Doctoring in Eighteenth-Century England*. Berkeley: University of California Press, 2001.
Bailey, Joanne. *Unquiet Lives: Marriage and Marriage Breakdown in England 1660–1800*. Cambridge: Cambridge University Press, 2003.
Bartlett, Peter, and David Wright, eds. *Outside the Walls of the Asylum: The History of Care in the Community 1750–2000*. London: The Athlone Press, 1999.
Bellabarba, Marco, Gerd Schwerhoff, and Andrea Zorzi, eds. *Criminalità e giustizia in Germania e in Italia. Pratiche giudiziarie e linguaggi giuridici tra medioevo ed età moderna*. Bologna and Berlin: Il Mulino, 2001.

Biotti, Vittorio. *È matto e tristo, pazzo e fastidioso. I saperi sulla follia: magistrati, medici e inquisitori a Firenze e negli stati italiani del '600*. Florence: Nicomp L. E., 2002.
Bizzocchi, Roberto. *Cicisbei. Morale privata e identità nazionale in Italia*. Rome and Bari: Laterza, 2008.
Boari, Marco. *Qui venit contra iura. Il* furiosus *nella criminalistica dei secoli XV e XVI*. Milan: Giuffrè, 1983.
Cartayrade, Laurent. "Property, Prodigality, and Madness: A Study of Interdiction Records in Eighteenth-Century Paris." PhD diss., University of Maryland, 1997.
Cavallo, Sandra. "Family Obligations and Inequalities in Access to Care in Northern Italy, Seventeenth to Eighteenth Centuries." In *The Locus of Care: Families, Communities, Institutions, and the Provision of Welfare Since Antiquity*, edited by Peregrine Horden and Richard Smith, 90–110. London and New York: Routledge, 1998.
Clark, Michael, and Catherine Crawford, eds. *Legal Medicine in History*. Cambridge: Cambridge University Press, 1994.
Contini, Alessandra. "Orientamenti recenti sul settecento Toscano." In *La Toscana in età moderna (secoli XVI-XVIII). Politica, istituzioni, società: studi recenti e prospettive di ricerca*, edited by Mario Ascheri and Alessandra Contini, 91–127. Florence: Leo S. Olschki Editore, 2005.
Correa, María José. *Historias de locura e incapacidad. Santiago y Valparaíso (1857–1900)*. Santiago: Acto Editores, 2013.
Diaz, Furio. *I Lorena in Toscana. La Reggenza*. Turin: UTET, 1988.
Eigen, Joel Peter. *Witnessing Insanity: Madness and Mad-Doctors in the English Court*. New Haven and London: Yale University Press, 1995.
Farge, Arlette. "The Honor and Secrecy of Families." In *A History of Private Life*, vol. 3, edited by Roger Chartier, 571–607. Cambridge, MA: Harvard University Press, 1989.
Farge, Arlette, and Michel Foucault. *Le Désordre des familles: lettres de cachet des Archives de la Bastille au XVIIIe siècle*. Paris: Gallimard, Julliard, 1982.
Galzigna, Mario, ed. *La follia, la norma, l'archivio: prospettive storiografiche e orientamenti archivistici*. Venice: Marsilio, 1984.
Gowing, Laura. *Domestic Dangers: Women, Words, and Sex in Early Modern London*. Oxford: Oxford University Press, 1996.
Groppi, Angela. *Il welfare prima del welfare. Assistenza alla vecchiaia e solidarietà tra generazioni a Roma in età moderna*. Rome: Viella, 2010.
Hardwick, Julie. *Family Business: Litigation and the Political Economies of Daily Life in Early Modern France*. Oxford and New York: Oxford University Press, 2009.
Houston, Robert Allan. *Madness and Society in Eighteenth-Century Scotland*. Oxford: Oxford University Press, 2000.
La Rocca, Chiara. *Tra moglie e marito. Matrimoni e separazioni a Livorno nel Settecento*. Bologna: Società editrice Il Molino, 2009.
Litchfield, R. Burr. *Emergence of a Bureaucracy: The Florentine Patricians, 1530–1790*. Princeton: Princeton University Press, 1986.
Lombardi, Daniela. "Giustizia ecclesiastica e composizione dei conflitti matrimoniali (Firenze, secoli XVI-XVIII)." In *I tribunali del matrimonio (secoli XV-XVIII)*, edited by Silvana Seidel Menchi and Diego Quaglioni, 577–607. Bologna: Il Mulino, 2006.

Lombardi, Daniela. *Matrimonio di antico regime*. Bologna: Il Mulino, 2001.

MacDonald, Michael. *Mystical Bedlam: Madness, Anxiety, and Healing in Seventeenth-Century England*. Cambridge: Cambridge University Press, 1981.

Magherini, Graziella, and Vittorio Biotti. *L'isola delle Stinche e i percorsi della follia a Firenze nei secoli XIV-XVIII*. Florence: Ponte alle Grazie, 1992.

Magherini, Graziella, and Vittorio Biotti. "Madness in Florence in 14th–18th Centuries: Judicial Inquiry and Medical Diagnosis, Care and Custody." *International Journal of Law and Psychiatry* 21, no. 4 (1998): 355–368.

Magherini, Graziella, and Vittorio Biotti. *"Un luogo della città per custodia de'pazzi". Santa Dorotea dei Pazzerelli di Firenze nelle delibere della sua congregazione (1642–1754)*. Florence: Le Lettere, 1997.

Mellyn, Elizabeth W. *Mad Tuscans and Their Families: A History of Mental Disorder in Early Modern Italy*. Philadelphia: University of Pennsylvania Press, 2014.

Midelfort, H.C. Erik. *A History of Madness in Sixteenth-Century Germany*. Stanford, CA: Stanford University Press, 1999.

Morant Deusa, Isabel, and Mónica Bolufer Peruga. *Amor, matrimonio y familia*. Madrid: Editorial Síntesis, 1998.

Nootens, Thierry. *Fous, prodigues et ivrognes: Familles et déviance à Montréal au XIX siècle*. Montreal: McGill-Queen's University Press, 2007.

Porter, Roy. *Mind-Forg'd Manacles: A History of Madness in England from the Restoration to the Regency*. London: Penguin Books, 1990.

Rabin, Dana. *Identity, Crime, and Legal Responsibility in Eighteenth-Century England*. Basingstoke: Palgrave Macmillan, 2004.

Roodenburg, Hernan. "Social Control Viewed from Below: New Perspectives." In *Social Control in Europe, vol. 1, 1500–1800*, edited by Herman Roodenburg and Pieter Spierenburg, 145–158. Columbus, OH: Ohio State University Press, 2004.

Roscioni, Lisa. *Il governo della follia. Ospedali, medici e pazzi nell'età moderna*. Milan: Bruno Mondadori, 2003.

Roscioni, Lisa. "Soin et/ou enfermement? Hôpitaux et folie sous l'Ancien Régime." *Genèses* 82 (2011): 31–51.

Roscioni, Lisa. "Un affare di famiglia. L'internamento manicomiale e la questione degli alimenti a Roma tra XVIII e XIX secolo." *Proposte e ricerche* 73 (2014): 95–108.

Rushton, Peter. "Lunatics and Idiots: Mental Disorder, the Community, and the Poor Law in North-East England 1600–1800." *Medical History* 32, no. 1 (1988): 34–50.

Scull, Andrew. *The Most Solitary of Afflictions: Madness and Society in Britain, 1700–1900*. New Haven and London: Yale University Press, 1993.

Stone, Lawrence. *Road to Divorce: England 1530–1987*. Oxford: Oxford University Press, 1990.

Suzuki, Akihito. "The Household and the Care of Lunatics in Eighteenth-Century London." In *The Locus of Care: Families, Communities, Institutions, and the Provision of Welfare Since Antiquity*, edited by Peregrine Horden and Richard Smith, 153–175. London and New York: Routledge, 1998.

Suzuki, Akihito. "Lunacy in Seventeenth- and Eighteenth-Century England: Analysis of Quarter Sessions Records: Part 1." *History of Psychiatry* 2 (1991): 437–456.

Suzuki, Akihito. *Madness at Home: The Psychiatrist, the Patient, and the Family in England, 1820–1860*. Berkeley: University of California Press, 2006.
Verga, Marcello. *Da "cittadini" a "nobili". Lotta politica e riforma delle istituzioni nella Toscana di Francesco Stefano*. Milan: Giuffrè, 1990.
Wright, David, and Anne Digby, eds. *From Idiocy to Mental Deficiency*. London and New York: Routledge, 1996.

1 Interdiction procedures

A context for public intervention in family life

In early modern Tuscany, interdiction procedures were under the jurisdiction of the Magistrato dei Pupilli et Adulti, the Tuscan Court of Wards in charge of guardianships and administering the patrimonies of orphans whose fathers had died intestate and of adults with physical or mental disabilities. By means of an interdiction sentence, people deemed mentally or physically impaired were deprived of their civil rights, which were transferred to a guardian (*curatore*) who would assume their protection, administer their patrimonies, and act in their name. The foundation and development of the Magistrato dei Pupilli is closely associated with the process of state building in Tuscany, starting with the configuration of the Florentine Republic, and going through its transformation into a Grand Duchy, the end of the Medici rule, the incorporation of Tuscany into the Hapsburg Empire and the Lorraine reforms, until its dissolution in 1808 during the Napoleonic period. Between reform and continuity, an institution like the Magistrato dei Pupilli provides a window onto the nuances of a pivotal period of Tuscan history, one that connects us with the particularities of local developments without losing the connections with the European scene and one that has received very little scholarly attention.[1]

This chapter discusses the involvement of the Magistrato dei Pupilli with mental incapacity. It first presents the institutional history of the magistracy to then examine the development of interdiction procedures, its legal framework, legal categories, and functioning. Finally, it explores the Tuscan interdiction procedures against other European judicial procedures devised to protect the patrimony and person of those deemed mentally impaired, presenting a European legal framework in which the Tuscan case can be inserted. Interdiction procedures, resorted to in order to solve familial conflicts as much as to control the economic consequences of mental incapacity, constituted a negotiated intervention of state administration into the private life of families.

The foundations of the Magistrato dei Pupilli and its involvement with mental incapacity

The Magistrato dei Pupilli was founded in 1393 by the Florentine Signoria to provide a governmental guardianship to families experiencing the devastating effects of the Black Death, originally devised as a voluntary alternative to familial guardianship.[2] The foundations of the Magistrato dei Pupilli circumscribed its area of involvement exclusively to underage wards, although scholars have claimed that already during this first stage the magistracy timidly managed the curatorship of mentally or physically impaired adults, despite the fact that its regulations made no direct reference to this capacity.[3] Adult guardianship (*curatela*) during this period was also available through the court of the Podestà (the highest authority involved in civil justice during the Republic). Provisions of the Magistrato dei Pupilli for mentally and physically incompetent adults were based on the 1415 statutes of the Comune di Firenze. These statutes stated that adults could be interdicted *per via ordinaria* following the request of a close relative, which had to be supported by the testimonies of two trustworthy witnesses.[4]

In 1473, a major reform of the statutes of the Pupilli established state guardianship as an obligatory task of the Florentine government, changing dramatically the purposes, functioning, and scope of the magistracy.[5] The reform entrusted the Magistrato dei Pupilli with the mandatory guardianship of orphans from Florence and its entire territory whose fathers had died intestate or without having assigned a tutor and with the administration of their patrimonies. As a result, the Pupilli officials were granted exclusive authority to administer and protect their wards' patrimonies and to appoint them suitable tutors, and they were also empowered to intervene in crucial matters affecting the personal destinies of the wards (from education to marriage).[6] The 1473 reform introduced for the first time a rubric with provisions for "the mad [*mentecapti*], dumb and deaf entrusted under the guardianship [*cura*] of the said Office," which declared that "those men or women who have passed the age of 18 years old and who are out of their natural senses [*fuori del naturale sentimento*]" could be entrusted to the authority of the Magistrato dei Pupilli, as was common practice with minors. The requisite measure was, though, that they were first declared by the officials of the Pupilli "to be mad [*mentecapti*] and out of their natural senses and that it has been agreed for them to be placed under the government of the said office."[7] Therefore, without clearly defining the procedure or the categories of adult incapacity that required guardianship, the statutes of 1473 opened the door for the state curatorship (*cura*) of adults with physical and mental disabilities, which would later be known as the interdiction procedure.

Further specifications concerning the categories accountable for the interdiction and guardianship of the mentally disabled appeared in 1565, when a new reform specified the involvement of the Magistrato dei Pupilli in adult curatorship. This statute reform restated that not only minors were entitled to the guardianship and protection of the Magistrato dei Pupilli, but also adults when they were found to be incapable of managing their affairs. The reform stated that the Pupilli officials could accept under their guardianship the dumb and deaf "of any age at the request of any individual without any other formality to be observed." They could also accept under their guardianship "the raving mad (*furiosi*), the fools (*mentecatti*) and demented (*dementi*), or prodigals (*prodighi*) and squanderers (*dilapidatori*) of their patrimony and wealth which are of public interest to preserve."[8]

This statute reform not only added more categories of adult incapacity that required state curatorship but also specified the procedure to ascertain the veracity of the denunciation and thus establish the need of the interdiction. The provisions operated under the principle that in the case of prodigals and the mentally disabled, abuses had to be prevented for "out of malice or any other cause someone could be called or reputed to be as such without being it." For this reason, the statutes established that in these cases, adults could only be submitted to the "curatorship and government" of the officials of the Pupilli after their prodigality or insanity had been previously confirmed by the Magistrato Supremo or following a direct commission from the Grand Duke.[9] In contrast, guardianship of the dumb and deaf could be established without any further confirmation besides the request of the relatives. In the end, it was stated that all incapacitated adults had to be "interdicted" from the administration of their patrimonies to preserve their properties and that the "interdiction" was to be publicized through announcements (*bandi*) placed in public places.[10]

In 1680, a new reform of the Pupilli statutes was issued to ensure the proper observance of the 1565 statutes. As the new law declared, "some of the things disposed in those Laws and reforms are neglected and not properly observed, and another part of them needs new additions, statements and provisions."[11] Particularly regarding the provisions for the mentally incompetent, the new dispositions made evident the jurisdictional overlap between the Magistrato dei Pupilli and the Magistrato Supremo produced by the reform of 1565.[12] These dispositions had stated that mental incapacity had to be confirmed by the Magistrato Supremo, which was a condition for the Pupilli to be able to assume the management of the guardianship. Moreover, the interdiction decree had to be issued by the Magistrato Supremo and only after that could the Pupilli assign a suitable guardian to administer the patrimony. The fact that the 1680 reforms needed to ratify that the Magistrato dei Pupilli was the institution with the prerogative over guardianship of adults, and thus over the administration of their patrimonies, suggests that the Magistrato Supremo had been trespassing into the Pupilli's territory. To counterbalance this situation, the new statutes emphasized that the requisite that subjected the Pupilli's power of intervention to the command of the Magistrato Supremo had "neither removed nor diminished" the faculties of the Pupilli over matters affecting the mentally incompetent. To guarantee the observance of the rules, the reform commanded that after the officials of the Magistrato Supremo had confirmed a person's incapacity, the guardianship was to be entrusted to the Magistrato dei Pupilli,

> save, nonetheless, for the cases where, given the circumstances of involvement, it would seem more convenient that the Magistrato Supremo itself appointed those curators, *attori*, or relatives that were considered necessary and opportune.[13]

As a result, the virtual disappearance of guardianships by reason of mental incompetence observed by Elizabeth Mellyn in the records of the Magistrato dei Pupilli during the seventeenth century is likely to be the result of the Supremo's involvement.[14] In this regard, Graziella Magherini and Vittorio Biotti have claimed that changes brought by this law entailed a significant reduction in the Pupilli's prerogative over the mentally incompetent, since it determined that in special circumstances, the officials of the Magistrato Supremo could directly designate the curator and supervise the guardianship without the intervention of the Pupilli.[15] However, the 1680 reform needs to be examined from a long-term perspective. On the one hand, it aimed to restrict the excessive involvement of the Supremo in the affairs of the mentally incompetent, not to augment it.[16] We must take into account the fact that the Supremo had been intervening in interdictions and adult guardianships since at least the 1565 reform, even though officially its involvement was supposed to be restricted to the ratification of mental incapacity. On the other hand, the evidence irrefutably shows that starting from the second decade of the eighteenth century, interdictions were predominantly managed by the Pupilli alone. Furthermore, if Elizabeth Mellyn has been able to find only 4 guardianships between 1387 and 1500 by reason of mental incapacity and 90 guardianships between 1500 and 1600 in the Pupilli records,[17] the numbers for the eighteenth century suggest a dramatic increase, exceeding 600 cases between 1700 and 1775.

This change was certainly not caused solely by the 1680 reform. The turning point can be found in the new regulations introduced in 1718, which significantly affected the involvement of the Magistrato dei Pupilli with adult curatorship. This new law stemmed from the observation that the dispositions made in 1565, and ratified in 1680, regarding the management of the interdiction and curatorship of adults manifesting mental or physical incompetence were not "accurately observed." As a result, the new regulation ratified once more the Pupilli's competence over the interdiction and guardianship of adults with mental or physical disabilities, only this time it clarified that this jurisdiction pertained exclusively to the Pupilli. The law declared that, henceforth, "the dumb and deaf, the raving mad (*furiosi*), the fools (*mentecatti*), the demented (*dementi*), prodigals (*prodighi*), squanderers (*dilapidatori*), or others to whom it may be convenient to interdict from the administration of their possessions and faculties" were "exclusively (*privativamente*)" under the jurisdiction of the Magistrato dei Pupilli. "No other tribunal or judge" could intervene in the affairs of the mentally or physically incompetent, and the involvement of the Magistrato Supremo was circumscribed to "declare, either by commission of His Royal Highness, or by their own decree if anyone is *furioso, mentecatto, demente, prodigo, dilapidatore*, or any other whom it might be convenient to interdict."[18] But, beyond the assessment of mental incapacity, the new regulation specified that they could not intervene any further. Immediately after a person was declared to be suffering from mental incapacity, the case had to be transferred to the Pupilli so that its officials could appoint an administrator or *attore*, supervise the administration of the ward's patrimony, and intervene in all the judicial procedures involving them.

The 1718 reform represented a milestone for the functioning of the Pupilli. After 1718, many cases that until then had been handled by the Magistrato Supremo now passed to "the protection and rule" of the Magistrato dei Pupilli, which explains the rising number of interdictions during the years following the reform (Figure 1.1).[19] Although, since 1565, adults with physical or mental disabilities "could" be submitted to the authority of the Pupilli, in fact only a minority of curatorships came under the supervision of the Pupilli before 1718. This can be explained not only as the effect of the Pupilli's lack of involvement, but also as an indicator that families before 1718 simply resorted less frequently to the mechanism than during the eighteenth century. From the perspective of the Pupilli officials, the requirement that mental incapacity had to be certified first by the Supremo hampered their power of intervention "to assist and oversee the interests" of the mentally incapacitated.[20] A further problem, according to the Pupilli officials, was the lack of clarity regarding the supervision of the curatorship after the defendant's incapacity had been confirmed by the Supremo or after the Grand

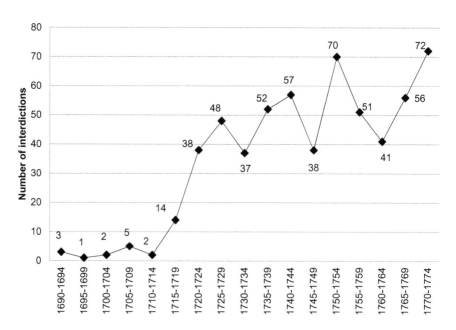

Figure 1.1 Number of interdiction procedures recorded in the Magistrato dei Pupilli between 1690 and 1774 in blocks of 5 years

Source: ASF, MPAP, *Memoriali e Negozi di Cancelleria*, F. 2299–F. 2310 and *Campione di Deliberazioni, e Partiti*, F. 112–F. 170.

Duke had ordered his or her interdiction, which allowed for the officials of the Supremo to assign a guardian (*curatore*) without turning the matter over to the hands of the Pupilli officials. When this occurred, the administration of the interdicted person's patrimony was often left unsupervised, and the lack of authority of some appointed guardians allowed the interdicted to continue managing their affairs in spite of the interdiction.[21]

The interdiction procedure during the eighteenth century

Inquiries into mental capacity in Tuscany were generally initiated through a petition by the defendant's next of kin to the Grand Duke, which was received and handled by the Consulta.[22] Every denunciation of mental incapacity had to be corroborated by the testimony of at least two witnesses "of good reputation," which generally came from family members or neighbors and only rarely involved medical opinion.[23] Alternatively, relatives could come directly in front of the Magistrato Supremo to initiate a cause of interdiction.[24] Once the petition or the initiated cause reached the central administration, an enquiry was conducted to investigate and assess the veracity of the denunciation (from beginning to end, the process could take between 2 and 3 months). Depending on the results of the enquiry, those deemed mentally incapacitated were interdicted by the Magistrato Supremo, officialized through an "interdiction decree" that publicly announced that the person had been deprived of his or her rights to administer their patrimony, take care of their affairs, and engage in any kind of legal contract. By means of the interdiction decree, the person was submitted to the "protection and rule" of the Magistrato dei Pupilli, which entitled its officials to appoint a guardian (*curatore*) or an agent (*attore*) to administer their property, act in their name and interests, and protect their person.

The basic point of an interdiction was to protect a person and his or her patrimony when they were found to be incapable (*inabile*, *incapace*, or *impotente* were the most common terms) of managing their own affairs. Thus, to declare a person incompetent, petitioners had to prove that he or she suffered from one of the kinds of incapacity defined by the Magistrato dei Pupilli as subject to an interdiction. The Pupilli statutes referred to the *furiosi, mentecatti, dementi, prodighi,* and *dilapidatori* as the categories of mental incapacity considered liable for interdiction and state guardianship. Of all these categories, interdiction procedures during the eighteenth century employed only two in practice: prodigality and *demenza* (Figure 1.2).[25] *Demenza* was the generic legal term employed in reference to all types of mental disturbance and encompassed the *mentecatto* and the *furioso*. Instead, prodigality – which in turn included *prodighi* (spendthrifts) and *dilapidatori* (dissipaters) – was a category that, at first glance, involved only inveterate reckless economic mismanagement, but which in fact enclosed a clear association with unreason.

30 *Interdiction procedures*

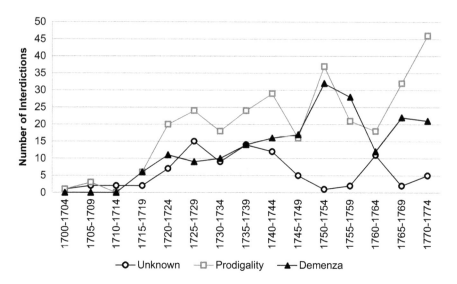

Figure 1.2 Distribution of the categories used in interdiction procedures between 1700 and 1774

Source: ASF, MPAP, *Memoriali e Negozi di Cancelleria*, F. 2299–F. 2310 and *Campione di Deliberazioni, e Partiti*, F. 112–F. 170.

Interdictions by reason of *demenza* are outnumbered by interdictions by reason of prodigality, although they show a relatively constant increase over the years studied. While prodigality and *demenza* were the most used categories, in some cases interdictions were decreed by reason of an unspecified lack of ability to manage one's financial and personal affairs. As can be observed in Figure 1.2, this third category was in use particularly during the first half of the century, while in the second half we can observe that the procedures tend to specify either prodigality or *demenza*. Toward 1770, however, this process somehow reversed itself, given that a new tendency for voluntary interdictions arose. In these voluntary requests, defendants argued for the "convenience" of the interdiction to safeguard their patrimonies on account of their "lack of experience" or their unawareness of the basic principles of financial management.[26]

The legal framework and the conflation between demenza *and prodigality*

The foundations for guardianship provisions for adults with physical and mental disability practiced in early modern Tuscany date back to Roman law. The principles of the Roman guardianship of minors (*tutela*) and curatorship of mentally or physically disabled adults (*cura*) were introduced and adapted with the revival of Roman law and the work of the glossators of *Justinian's Digest* in medieval Italy. Guardianship was originally designed as a judicial mechanism to administer the ward's property in the absence of the *paterfamilias* while his children attained full capacity to govern themselves, with the primary aim of protecting the interests of the family. Through the tutorship, the *patria potestas* was transferred to a tutor, who could be testamentary, statutory, or appointed by the state (*tutela testamentaria*, *legittima*, or *dativa*). The tutorship of minors lasted until puberty, while from that time until full majority, they were placed under the care of a curator.[27] In turn, the curatorship of adults was intended to provide protection to individuals who were unable to safeguard their interests but did not require full guardianship, following a procedure similar to the tutorship of minors.

For the purposes of this study, it is important to briefly define how the *cura prodigo* and the *cura furiosus* were conceived in Roman law, for this will allow us to understand to what extent they were transformed by medieval and early modern jurists, and how they came to be merged into one unique system of curatorship. The curatorships for prodigality and for insanity were conceived differently in Roman law, and so they entailed different consequences. While in the case of insanity the curator was entrusted with the custody of both the person and his or her patrimony, in the case of prodigals, the curator only had authority over the patrimony.[28] On the other hand, Roman law distinguished between the origins of the loss of civil capacity in the case of insanity and that of prodigality. The essential difference, if we follow Marco Boari, was that in the case of prodigals their lack of civil capacity was determined by the law, while in the case of the insane, their civil incapacity was a natural consequence of their condition. In other words, prodigality was a category created by the law to catalogue a self-inflicted condition, while insanity was a category that pre-existed the law, a "natural incapacity" that worked as "an objective extra juridical reality" that only had to be judicially "recognized."[29] The difference between natural and legal incapacity completely changed the terms of the curatorship and its conditions. Given that the mentally ill were considered incapacitated from the moment their insanity had been triggered, economic transactions carried out by a mentally disturbed person while attaining the state of insanity could be theoretically void. On the contrary, prodigals lost their capacity only after the law, by means of the interdiction, deprived them of their civil capacity. As a consequence, the interdiction made only future economic actions invalid, with no retroactive power. In both cases, nonetheless, the incapacity was understood as a temporary condition dependent upon the person's subsequent behavior, so the curatorship could be removed when their mental disturbance abated or when they demonstrated that they had reformed their behavior. The most important issue for us here is that in Roman law, interdictions were necessary only in the case of prodigality, for only a judge or a magistrate could deprive people of their civil rights. On the contrary, given that the mental incapacity of *furiosi* was thought to be natural, a legal interdiction was originally unnecessary. In both cases, their condition prevented them from selling their property or making any future transactions.

Elizabeth Mellyn has suggested that prodigality and mental incapacity were first implicitly associated during the Florentine Republic and came to be explicitly assimilated during the first century of the Medici Principate. The conflation between insanity and prodigality, Mellyn claims, served families so as "to regulate economic behavior in their household and to invalidate contracts made by reckless relatives," demonstrating a "pragmatic and instrumental use" of the legal mechanism of guardianship. The goal was not only to avoid future potentially disadvantageous contracts, but also to be able to declare past contracts void, for which prodigality had to be assimilated to insanity.[30] However, the eighteenth-century records suggest that interdiction sentences did not automatically entail the suspension of the payment of debts, much less the invalidation of past contracts, regardless of whether the interdiction had been decreed by reason of *demenza* or prodigality. If families wanted to institute legal actions against some creditor on the grounds that the debt had been contracted while the individual was mentally incompetent, it had to be done after the interdiction, through a different legal procedure. But, in general, financial agreements were not invalidated, and long-lasting litigation with creditors would follow the interdiction sentence in order to agree upon the terms of payment.

Another important change regarding Roman law tradition is that interdiction was a procedure used to legally declare mental incompetence so that a person could be assigned a curator. Adult curatorship was tied to interdiction already in the 1565 statutes of the Magistrato dei Pupilli.[31] Furthermore, interdiction was applied for both prodigality and insanity in its various forms (*furioso, mentecatto*, and *demente*), demonstrating that the legal framework made only one provision for all types of mental incapacity, irrespective of the type, level, and origin. The term "interdiction" seems to have been uncommon before the eighteenth century, according to existing studies.[32] During the sixteenth and seventeenth centuries, the most common term was *cura*. The magistrates decided whether defendants were in need of being "received under the *cura* and government" of the Pupilli or "required a curator."[33] By contrast, magistrates during the eighteenth century referred to their wards as the *interdetti* and the *sottoposti* (submitted), and, likewise, petitioners generally requested that their relatives be "interdicted" and "submitted to the authority and guardianship" of the Pupilli. This terminological change is also visible in the decrees issued by the Magistrato Supremo, where curator and *curatela* were replaced by the term interdiction, which survived with only a slight change in the Napoleonic Code.

Based on the fact that records of the previous centuries give no evidence for the use of the term interdiction, it can be concluded that the 1718 reform was responsible for this change. At the same time that it differentiated between the competences of the Magistrato Supremo and the Magistrato dei Pupilli regarding mental and physical incapacities, it created a new differentiation between interdiction and curatorship. The first, decreed by the Supremo, was the process by which a person was legally declared mentally incapacitated, thus creating the need for a curator to be assigned for his or her protection. The second started after the interdiction decree reached the offices of the Pupilli.

The consequences of an interdiction decree

As a consequence of an interdiction, the person was submitted to the protection and rule of the Magistrato dei Pupilli (*sottoposto a la cura e governo del Magistrato dei Pupilli*).[34] After the Magistrato Supremo issued the interdiction decree, the case passed to the offices of the Pupilli for the magistrates to manage all the details concerning the person's guardianship. The Magistrato dei Pupilli acted in its capacity of "universal curator," so technically the officials were the person's curators, while an *attore* (both administrator and agent) was designated to take care of the ward and legally represent him or her. Additionally, the *attore* was also entrusted with the administration of the ward's property. After the official assignment, the *attore* had to formally accept the task, provide a guarantor for his or her administration (*mallevadore*), and assume the obligation to give an annual account of the administration to the Pupilli.

No further regulations were introduced in the practice of interdiction sentences until 1767, when a new law was promulgated by the then recently arrived Peter Leopold of Habsburg-Lorraine, who among the many reforms he promulgated in the administration of the Grand Duchy, decided to modify some aspects of interdiction procedures. Two of these changes are relevant here. First, the reform eliminated the Magistrato dei Pupilli's capacity to act as "universal tutor and curator of all minors and adults of the Florentine dominium."[35] This meant that thereafter the officials of the Pupilli had to name an external curator or tutor, for they were no longer able to assume those responsibilities themselves. Although before the eighteenth century, the mentally disabled had been assigned external curators, the records of the eighteenth century demonstrate that the officials of the Pupilli almost invariably assumed the task, relegating the next of kin to the task of *attori*. The other important change regarding interdictions brought by the 1767 regulation was that it granted free access to the services of the magistracy to the "miserable and poor," provided their patrimonies did not exceed 500 *scudi*. As a result, for the first time those, whose patrimonies were not large enough to cover the costs of interdiction and guardianship, could also have an access to the service, causing a consequent increase in the numbers of interdiction petitions.

Special attention was paid to secure the *attore*'s trustworthiness and impartiality toward the interests of the interdicted. For this reason, wives and mothers were usually considered the preferred administrators. Given that they had no inheritance right over a male's property, it was believed that they had no personal interest in their husband's or son's patrimonies. Moreover, a proper administration was in the best interest of their children and themselves, securing their subsistence and future ability to recover their dowry.[36] On the other hand, agnates were usually regarded with suspicious eyes by the officials of the Pupilli, particularly when they were the direct inheritors of the ward's patrimony. But even maternal and matrimonial kinsmen who were not direct heirs were held to be too close and involved with the interdicted, thus increasing, instead of mitigating, the conflicts in the family. As a consequence, given that the Pupilli officials aimed to resolve existing family conflicts and avert the occurrence of future ones, males from either side of the family lines were often vetoed on the grounds that choosing them could generate further conflicts of interest. By contrast, when a patrimony was left in the hands of women, it was thought to create less disorder, even if it meant that temporarily the family structure was turned upside down, with women being given a role equivalent to that of a *paterfamilias*. When the administration was not given to women, it was generally entrusted to an external administrator, who charged for the service.

Guardianships generated a difficult relationship between the interdicted and their *attori*. As the interdicted were adults who had been abruptly deprived of their power over their affairs, they hardly ever accepted the new situation peacefully. The disorder their behavior and personality created for the household was not easily contained, and they often resisted the interdiction by having recourse to a wide range of strategies. For this reason, the records of interdiction procedures do not end with the issuing of the decree and the appointment of the guardian. This is not only because the Pupilli supervised the administration of the patrimony, but mostly because families continued to involve the officials of the Pupilli to resolve all kinds of conflicts and setbacks during the whole period in which the person was subject to the magistracy's authority.

Once a person was interdicted, every decision regarding their patrimony had to first be approved by the Pupilli. Some issues were even managed directly by the magistracy, like arrangements with creditors or the selling of goods and property at public auction to pay off debts. This meant time and money being spent, and it was not at all certain that the procedure would secure a favorable result. Similarly, in terms of the economic situation of the patrimony, the interdiction meant that the Magistrato dei Pupilli acted as an arbiter between the interests of the interdicted and their creditors in what was called the *giudizio universale di concorso dei creditori*. New conditions were set in this procedure to meet the creditors' interests within the interdicted's financial possibilities. But the debts certainly had to be paid, so interdiction could not be used as a mechanism to skip payment, only to delay it, when possible.

Every one of these actions entailed the payment of a fee to the magistracy, according to the tariffs specified in the 1565 statutes. In addition, the interdicted had to pay an annual fee to the officials of the Pupilli for their involvement to which the *attore*'s stipend had to be added, in the case that he was charging. For all these reasons, interdictions were an expensive matter entailing payments that created difficulties for families whose patrimonies were not large. Although some exceptions were made for small patrimonies, in general, the officials insisted that payment of the annual fee was mandatory. As a result, until 1767, interdiction was a mechanism available only to defendants whose patrimonies could afford the fees. However, this does not entail that only the high Tuscan aristocracy appears in the records of the Pupilli, for together with nobles and rich aristocrats in possession of various estates outside Florence and more than one residence in the city, interdictions also affected people whose possessions were limited to the residence where they lived or whose income was entirely dependent upon their "personal industry," from lawyers, surgeons, and merchants to cooks, coachmen, and shoemakers. After 1767, the procedure became available to every person in the Tuscan state, regardless of social or economic position.

The interdiction marked the suspension of a person's legal capacity, which resulted not only in being prohibited from administering his or her patrimony and engaging in economic activities, but also meant that the person could not stand trial, serve as a witness, or hold public office. As for the effects of the interdiction in other legal aspects of the interdicted's life, state officials were in much less agreement. Throughout the eighteenth century, it is possible to observe an unresolved debate over the capacity of the interdicted to choose their own lawyer or to make a legal will, although they could perfectly well marry. On some occasions, the authorities validated a person's capacity to make a will, provided that it respected the "good custom" (*buon costume*) and that his or her final dispositions were not against the law. But in many other cases, interdictions were requested precisely to prevent an unfavorable will.[37]

Contrary to what might be expected, confinement in Tuscany was not a part of interdiction and was, at any rate, never its consequence. The fact is that confinement was hardly ever requested in interdiction petitions, even when the described individual was troublesome and evidently difficult to handle. There are basically two reasons for this. First, incarceration and confinement in either of the existing Tuscan mental institutions (the *pazzeria* of Santa Maria Nuova and Santa Dorotea) was neither the preferred nor the easiest solution. Second, and more importantly, confinement followed a different legal course than interdiction, with no necessary connections between the two. While interdiction procedures were managed by the Magistrato dei Pupilli, confinement fell first under the competence of the administrative board of the hospital and then of the Auditore Fiscale – the officer who supervised criminal courts and was in charge of public order.[38] Thus, a person could be confined without ever being interdicted, and interdiction was not even considered a relevant antecedent for confinement, as we will see later on. Cases of people interdicted while being confined at Santa Dorotea or at Santa Maria Nuova can be found, but the majority of interdictions affected people who were kept at home.

By definition, interdiction was a temporary legal measure devised to last until it could be proved that the person had recovered his or her mental faculties. It could last from a couple of months to the whole life of the interdicted and could be declared as many times as was thought necessary. Interdictions could be partially or completely lifted, and this mainly depended, in addition to the development of the defendant's mental condition, on the family's support for the petition for removal. A partial lifting of the interdiction meant that the defendant was left under the direct supervision of an official of the Pupilli or another state officer, who had to approve every financial decision for it to be legally valid. Given that they were considered more secure, partial lifting was a common transitional stage between interdiction and the complete restoration of one's civil rights in Tuscany. If the interdiction was completely lifted, the person could resume complete powers of administration immediately.

Interdictions were used as a last resort by Tuscan families. They were a mechanism to turn to when previous measures to control, persuade, or force the person to change their attitude had proved useless. Petitioners often said that relatives, neighbors, or an influential person (prestigious neighbors, priests, and family friends) had tried to prevent the radical measure of turning to the Pupilli by a recourse to a series of unsuccessful arguments, such as illustrating the negative consequences the disorder caused in their families, to their patrimonies, or to their honor. In this sense, resorting to interdiction as a mechanism to cope with family conflict and deviant behavior demonstrates what historians have pointed out regarding early modern uses of justice. As happens with matrimonial disputes, economic disagreements, or the social responses to crime and assault, the disputants only resorted to the judicial system when every other measure to solve the conflict privately had failed, notwithstanding the countless efforts made by mediators.[39]

Interdiction procedures served a twofold purpose: on the one hand, they were intended to provide care and protection for the mentally incompetent against themselves or against others who could potentially take advantage of their weakness. On the other hand, it was a procedure aimed at securing the subsistence of the family patrimony on behalf of the interdicted's future heirs. In so doing, interdiction procedures served to negotiate with the people who was responsible for the mentally disturbed, which makes them an invaluable entry point to examine the articulation of a combined welfare provision for the mentally disabled with shared responsibilities between the families and the state. Interdiction was not only the act of depriving mentally disturbed persons of their civil rights; it also supposed the state's involvement in their protection. In fact, the Pupilli officials supervised the caring and feeding of these people and would generally defend their interests against ill-intentioned relatives. Therefore, interdictions provided the state's intervention as requested by the families, but this at the same time implied shared responsibilities.

By protecting the weak and incompetent members of society, the ducal administration was safeguarding the economic and moral welfare of the household. To fully grasp the significance of this, we have to bear in mind that preventing the economic collapse of a family meant preventing the need to procure different sources of maintenance for the affected family members. Furthermore, the economic subsistence of the family secured social reproduction and the preservation of Tuscany. The preservation of private patrimonies was beneficial for the state and was at the core of the foundation of the Magistrato dei Pupilli.

The importance of patrimony in early modern Tuscan society has been the subject of numerous studies. In a society based on trust and credit where families had learned "the precarious nature of fortunes," the difficulty of recovering from debts and the danger of mismanagement were written in stone.[40] The institution of interdiction, thus, builds upon this fear of mismanagement – it had in fact been tied to this concern since its appearance in Roman law. The hereditary system, the ethos of the aristocratic families, and, furthermore, the stability of Tuscan society as a whole were firmly based on the careful accumulation of familial wealth.[41] But by the eighteenth century, interdiction served a larger purpose than the conservation of family fortunes. Or, to put it in a better way, the subsistence of both middle-class and aristocratic families by the eighteenth century was centered on a complex conflation between patrimony preservation and compliance with moral normativity. The behavioral deviance disclosed in interdiction procedures thus went beyond purely economic concerns, to place the accent on the disorder of the family, and on conflicting views regarding proper behavior.

Abuses, strategies, and uses of interdiction procedures

In 1761, a petition for interdiction was sent by the underage son of a certain Rocco Giacchi, arguing that his father was stammering and "deprived of reason" (*privo di senno*) on account of the "fierce and frequent accidents of apoplexy and epilepsy" he suffered. The petition went on to say that due to his father's "impotence and inability," the son risked finding himself in "greater anguish," having nowhere that his father could stay and be cured and having no other relatives to "supervise" his conduct.[42] The interdiction, however, was not granted. The Pupilli officials claimed that the petition had been made only to avoid the payment of Rocco's debts. Furthermore, they arrived to the conclusion that it had been actually sent by the alleged demented himself and not by his son, who was absent from the Tuscan state at that time. The petition was thus considered to be a total fabrication by Rocco Giacchi, designed as a strategy to avoid payment of a debt to his father-in-law.

Financial mismanagement was mandatory in order to initiate an interdiction procedure. This did not, however, imply that every case of economic recklessness was liable for interdiction. Entrenched in a judicial system that conceived the protection of the family patrimony as a public responsibility, interdictions gave power to the state to intervene and thus prevent and

38 *Interdiction procedures*

control financial mismanagement but limited exclusively to cases where it was demonstrably caused by incapacity. Requests for someone's interdiction based solely on the argument that the patrimony was at risk of being lost or was "anguished" by debts, as it was said, were considered an abuse and were generally not granted. As the members of the Tuscan administration were well aware, "many times interdictions are decided when there is no vice of prodigality, grounded either in someone's inexperience in the management of his patrimony, or because he spends his resources on ends that are not laudable."[43] The assessment of mental incapacity was not determined by the presence of debts or excessive spending alone but much more by the behavior of the current holder of the patrimony and the reasons and circumstances surrounding the mismanagement. Why they had contracted debts, why their production had dropped, why they were selling household goods or liquidating assets, how was their daily performance, how were their relationships with other household members, and which of their actions indicated some kind of mental derangement were the issues under consideration.

The Tuscan ducal officers were particularly careful not to agree to petitions of interdiction that aimed at skipping or delaying payment of debts or to expose the abuses and machinations of greedy relatives. We cannot exclude the probability that families made an instrumental use of interdiction petitions, whether to take advantage of a weaker relative, to avoid or resolve financial difficulties, to accelerate an inheritance, to prevent an unfavorable will, or to produce a change in the balance of power relations in the household. Abuses did exist, and the system was constantly aware of that possibility. Petitions found to be abusive were not granted, but it sometimes happened that defendants made a petition shortly after the interdiction had been decreed or sometimes at the same time as their relatives turned to the Pupilli, claiming that the accusations were based on false grounds. If this was proven true, the interdiction was likely to be overturned and the defendant allowed to resume full civil rights.

Be that as it may, possible cases of ill-intentioned relatives requesting an interdiction only to accelerate the transfer of an inheritance or to take the patrimony from a weak family member do not constitute a relevant variable in the analysis of the perception and understanding of insanity. This is, first, because it was not the easiest or the fastest measure to take. A request for interdiction was expensive, presupposed hard and lengthy bureaucratic work, entailed constant payments, and entailed the intervention of the Pupilli in private family matters. For instance, the Pupilli officials did not necessarily side with petitioners to resolve residential conflicts, a situation frequently disclosed behind petitions for interdiction. Quite the contrary, the Pupilli officials largely privileged the unification of the household. Second, and perhaps more importantly, the probability of ill-intentioned requests does not interfere with the study of social perceptions of madness. We can explore how and when madness comes to the fore and the circulation of the languages and meanings of madness even when mental afflictions were instrumentally used to take advantage of a family member. Finally, ill-intentioned, greedy, or abusive motives should be taken as key elements in the articulation of interdiction narratives, but this does not necessarily imply that the denunciation of mental incapacity had been completely manufactured. As Robert Allan Houston puts it, even if becoming the subject of an inquiry into mental capacity "was partly, or perhaps mainly, a matter of contingencies and entitlements beyond the influence of the subject's behavior or words," it was in any case necessary that the person had previously displayed "symptoms which could be taken to indicate madness."[44]

Interdictions as a family matter

Although there were some interdiction procedures initiated by the Magistrato Supremo itself or by creditors, the great majority were initiated by petitions brought by family members. The state was at the service of the families through the Magistrato dei Pupilli, and families that could afford the procedure increasingly turned to the magistracy when seeking arbitration in the private conflicts arising from the presence of disordered members in the family. The Magistrato dei Pupilli was not only concerned with the economic subsistence of the Tuscan families, but could also act as a mediator in family conflicts caused by interdiction procedures.[45] In their capacity as universal guardians of the mentally disabled, the Pupilli officials were often called to resolve family tensions and to reconcile couples, siblings, or fathers and mothers with their sons and daughters. This placed the officials in the position, actively encouraged by the families themselves, whereby they could freely devise strategies to make household coexistence bearable, resorting to any possible means to pacify and normalize the chaotic environment that often accompanied the presence of the mentally disturbed in the household. These means ranged from admonishments to coercive measures, such as temporary incarceration, to try to put an end to their extravagances and often violent outbursts, combined with an attempt to provide the care and protection that the mentally disturbed deserved. The officials of the Pupilli could dissolve inconvenient marriages, force a fugitive prodigal husband to return home, or persuade a wife to endure a mad husband. They could act as guarantors of the proper obedience to the commands set by hierarchical gender roles and provide a negotiated response to the inconveniences caused by the mentally disturbed.

Public intervention in family affairs was a negotiated issue, settled from the beginning of the process of Florentine state formation. The logic behind the interference of the Magistrato dei Pupilli in family matters dates back to the construction of the Florentine Republic and the organization of the state as a "government of fathers."[46] Since its foundation, the magistracy had been an organ of the oligarchy's concern for the consolidation of family order and moral standards, and, during the Medici period, it continued to act as a space to resolve family conflicts, developing what Giulia Calvi has called a moral contract between the state and women. During the sixteenth century, the officials of the Pupilli positioned widows as privileged interlocutors, which demonstrates the magistracy's tendency to ascribe new value to the maternal line of the family structure. This meant that women's role in early modern Tuscany escaped from the image of segregation and exclusion previously assumed by scholars. Furthermore, precisely because women and their kin were excluded from the line of succession, they could play a predominant role as trustworthy guardians. Thus, their juridical and social role was inversely proportional to their participation in the hereditary system.[47]

The same model of negotiation and moral contract can be observed in eighteenth-century attitudes to mental disturbance, which also shows family strategies and dynamics that escaped the supposedly rigid patriarchal model. The cognatic structure of the family was empowered by the negotiation of alternatives offered by the Pupilli for dealing with mentally disturbed adults.[48] Although interdictions affected primarily men (only 28 women were interdicted between 1700 and 1775, compared to 583 men), this does not mean that the judicial space was dominated by men. On the contrary, women continued to be privileged interlocutors of the Pupilli during the eighteenth century, for we observe them as active agents in the negotiation of responses to control and handle their adult sons or husbands. Women, supported by their kin, learned to use in their favor their position as impartial actors derived from their exclusion from the hereditary line. In fact, of a total of 379 interdictions decreed between 1700 and 1775 in which the petitioner's blood relation was recorded, 222 (59%) were initiated after a supplication sent by a mother, a wife, or one of their kin (see Table 1.1). Of these, 198 were signed first by mothers, wives, sisters, or daughters. Women were not only active petitioners of interdiction procedures, but they were many times assigned to be administrators of their husbands' or sons' patrimonies and were the most recurrent interlocutors of the Pupilli in the discussions to determine living arrangements and possible strategies to solve the problems caused by mental disturbance.

It is of interest to point out that the number of female petitioners may not be representative of women's presence in the judicial arena. First, women hardly ever acted alone, and their signatures appear together with those of their relatives, generally their sons or kinsmen, but also of their brothers-in-law.[49] On the other hand, there are cases where women appear after their husband's or son's interdiction had been decreed, confessing that they never knew about the content of the petition and had been forced to sign it. Consequently, questions may be raised as to their actual agency behind these petitions.[50] Although we cannot rule out the possibility that their signature was included only because it was required that they agree with the legal action, it nonetheless highlights that their name played a significant role in the outcome of an interdiction procedure. Furthermore, women's voices take a leading part in subsequent proceedings regarding the management of the curatorship and its familial consequences. Second, precisely because we are not bound to a static image of the family conflicts surrounding the

Table 1.1 Distribution of interdiction petitioners according to their blood relation with the defendant, 1688–1775

Women and their family lines		Men and their family lines	
Wife	109	Brother	62
Mother	74	Son	51
Sister or daughter	15	Paternal uncle	22
Marriage kin	18	Nephew, cousin, grandson	15
Maternal kin	6	Father	7
Total	222	Total	157

interdiction procedure, we can also observe the crucial role played by women in the evolution and eventual resolution of the conflict and in how the deviant behavior was handled. The picture observed in Table 1.1 corresponds only to the initial interdiction petition, without taking into account the later actions carried out before the Pupilli following an interdiction decree, where women played a crucial role. The inquiries carried out following a petition for the interdiction to be lifted, usually sent by the interdicted himself, are also indicative of the role played by women. These inquiries took into particular consideration the opinion of women on the behavioral changes alleged by the interdicted. To secure the revocation of the interdiction, petitioners had to count on their mother's or wife's approval.

Inquiries into mental capacity in early modern Europe

Inquiries into mental capacity to determine a person's legal status and establish the necessary precautions to protect those deemed mentally incompetent and their patrimonies do not constitute a Tuscan exception. Called "interdictions" in places that followed the Roman law tradition such as France, Spain, and Italy, "commissions of lunacy" in England, and "brieves of idiotry and furiosity" in Scotland, these legal procedures shared common characteristics. They were devised to deprive people deemed mentally afflicted of their civil rights, leaving them under legal guardianship to protect them and their patrimonies. All of these procedures functioned as a legal mechanism to be activated at the families' request. This means that the understanding of mental incapacity that the historian may grasp from these sources changes the focus from the medical profession and governmental power to society and the family.[51]

Interdictions in France followed a pattern similar to that of Tuscany, both being profoundly entrenched in the Roman legal tradition.[52] However, although the two territories shared their legal frameworks, the societies in which these provisions were incorporated changed in practice the aims and application of the procedure, to the point that they followed different paths. As in Tuscany, interdiction in early modern France was employed as a legal procedure to deprive a person of his or her rights over his- or herself and their patrimony by reason either of prodigality or insanity. However, although in early modern France, prodigality (*prodigalité*) and insanity (*folie*) were both subjected to the same procedures, French legal practice never fully blurred the difference made by Roman law regarding the origins of the incompetence and its consequences. Preserving in this regard its Roman law roots, French law proscribed that the incapacity of prodigals was only partial and dependent upon the decision of a judge, while in the case of insanity, the incapacity was understood to be complete. In both cases, after the interdiction, the person was left under guardianship, although in the case of prodigals the curator protected only the person's patrimony, whereas in the case of the insane the guardian protected both the person and the patrimony.

Prodigality and insanity in France were conceived as two types of incapacity that produced the same consequence but whose origins were not equivalent. According to Laurent Cartayrade, what prodigals and the insane had in common was their irresponsibility, understood as an inability or unwillingness to abide by the rules of economic management, which only in the case of the insane was considered natural or accidental. A clear distinction was made between "the morally corrupt and guilty, and the sick and innocent," and in this division prodigality, which was regarded as a voluntary "moral depravity," was a lapse of the first group."[53] Therefore, although prodigality and insanity came under the same procedure in eighteenth-century France, they were kept as two distinct categories liable to interdiction, without any evolution of the conflation that can be observed in the Tuscan judicial practice. This difference highlights the divergence of the Tuscan procedure, which increasingly blurred the problem of the voluntariness of the prodigals' incapacity. Through a process that had started already during the sixteenth and seventeenth centuries, by the eighteenth century, prodigality was as pitied as insanity. As I will discuss further in chapter 2, the "vice" of prodigality was thought to give little choice to its victims. In fact, while interdiction for prodigality in France accounts for a minority of cases, in Tuscany it is by far the most commonly recorded cause of interdiction, which suggests that the moral condemnation suffered by prodigality in early modern France was not paralleled in Tuscany.

The French legal framework also allowed the option of the *conseil judiciaire*, which was a less invasive alternative than interdiction developed around the fifteenth century for the feeble-minded (*faibles d'esprit*). The judicial council functioned as a semi-interdiction process by which the individual was put under milder supervision to provide assistance in certain particular acts, which were determined on a case-by-case basis.[54] While interdictions were primarily requested by family members, councils were self-imposed and acquired increasing popularity during the eighteenth century. According to Cartayrade, the council experienced such success first, because it provided more flexibility than interdictions in terms of the categories liable to it, which in fact were applied at the judges' discretion; and second, because it could be tailored to particular circumstances, allowing for a personalized system to protect the patrimonies from economic mismanagement without the dishonorable mark that interdiction inevitably entailed.[55]

As we have seen, in Tuscany toward 1770, voluntary interdictions also started to become common, though the connotations and consequences of the procedure were equal to those of interdictions decreed by reason of prodigality or insanity. However, as in France, voluntary interdictions in Tuscany enjoyed greater flexibility and were carried out in a more personalized way. Taking into account that in these cases the measure was self-imposed, the authorities normally made compromises, giving some degree of autonomy to the interdicted. It could be argued that the categories of *demenza* and prodigality were already sufficiently flexible in Tuscany to allow for personalized variants. However, in terms of its consequences, all types of interdictions were subjected to the same rules, regardless of the category in which it was grounded. For this reason, to some extent the French council could be considered more akin to the Tuscan semi-revocation of the interdiction, the intermediate situation between interdiction, and its complete revocation that was usually preferred to a total lifting of the interdiction in the Grand Duchy. This comparison is useful despite the fact that in the latter case the measure was not self-imposed and was in fact quite resisted. This milder form of interdiction in Tuscany could last as long as the magistrates thought it to be necessary to secure the patrimony and in practice signified that every economic move made by the individual had to be pre-approved by an appointed ducal official in order to be valid.

Although, theoretically, interdictions were conceived as a temporary measure, only a small proportion of interdictions were revoked in France during the eighteenth century, and generally 1 to 10 years elapsed between the interdiction sentence and the first request for liberation (*mains-levées*). Meanwhile, revocations in Tuscany were common, suggesting that interdictions were much more flexible there than in France. In what appears to be an exclusively eighteenth-century feature, in Tuscany people could be interdicted up to five times in a lifetime, and the sentence could be overturned from just days to 20 years later, depending on the person and the circumstances surrounding each case.[56]

Another interesting difference between France and Tuscany is that in the former, requests for interdiction tend to decrease after the second half of the eighteenth century, while requests for voluntary council experienced a growing popularity. This suggests, according to Cartayrade, that voluntary council was preferred to a full interdiction, evidencing a movement opposite to what can be observed in Tuscany, where the numbers of interdictions tend to grow steadily throughout the century. To explain this, we have to take into account the fact that changes in interdiction procedures also respond to institutional changes (for instance, a change in the policies of the authorities in charge or a change in the procedure making it either easier or more difficult), which occur in parallel to social changes that might have influenced the rise or decline of families' decisions to initiate interdiction procedures. In this sense, Cartayrade takes the decline in interdiction procedures to be the effect of a change in the preferences of the families (and the allegedly incapable) toward the voluntary counsel, which was easier to obtain and entailed less troubles and dishonor. This accounts, he asserts, for an increasing reluctance of family members to resort to the authorities in favor of more private strategies to resolve their conflicts.[57] It is interesting to note here that the increase in the use of interdiction procedures in Tuscany can be taken to be the result of quite the opposite situation. It could in fact suggest that the concern for the consequences of irresponsible behavior increasingly called for a deeper public intervention in the private domain. This rise was further propelled by the effects of the 1767 regulation that made interdiction available to patrimonies that previously could not pay the fees charged by the Pupilli for its services.

A final difference concerns confinement. Toward the eighteenth century in France, petitioners often requested confinement along with the interdiction, and, similarly, interdiction sentences increasingly specified that the interdicted was to be confined in a specified institution. However, as Cartayrade warns us, interdiction did not mean automatic confinement. He argues that interdiction sentences explicitly stated that the guardian was entitled to confine his or her ward, which means that in the absence of such authorization, the guardian could not proceed with the internment.[58] This means that the primary aim of interdiction in France was the protection of the patrimony and the person, and not the person's confinement, for which a separate procedure existed as well (*lettres de cachet*). However, for our purposes, the fact remains that the causality of interdiction in eighteenth-century France was mostly attributed to insanity and that petitioners tended to request confinement with petitions for interdiction. The Napoleonic civil code ultimately finalized the differentiation between insanity and prodigality by establishing that only insanity was liable to interdiction, while prodigals and *faibles d'esprit* (feeble-minded) were subjected to the judicial council. In contrast, in Tuscany, interdiction and confinement of the mentally disturbed were kept as starkly different procedures, managed by completely different sections of the state bureaucracy, and only came to be associated with each other with the enactment of the Napoleonic Code.

Now, if we move to the British context, we can see that the aims and general characteristics of the legal procedure to deprive someone of his or her civil rights followed similar principles, although framed under a different legal tradition. However, if in the comparison between the French and the Tuscan scenarios it becomes clear that local variants were at play, the examination of the British context similarly suggests that the interpretation and practice of these procedures responded and adapted to local concerns. In other words, although inquiries into mental capacity were widely conceived as a mechanism to neutralize the negative economic consequences of madness, how these consequences were identified and interpreted was highly dependent upon the cultural values of the given society. As was the case in Tuscany, British inquiries into mental capacity were not connected to confinement. However, contrary to the French and Tuscan scenarios, neither the English nor the Scottish legal frameworks provided any measures for the consequences of prodigality. Although it was identified as a reprehensible vice, the category did not constitute legal reason to deprive someone of the right to administer his or her property.

The whole system regulating mental incapacity in English law was based on two categories – idiocy and lunacy. As defined by the influential English jurist William Blackstone, "an idiot, or natural fool, is one that hath had no understanding from his nativity; and therefore is by law presumed never likely to attain any."[59] In turn, the lunatic, or *non compos mentis*, was held to be "one who hath had understanding, but by disease, grief, or other accident hath lost the use of his reason."[60] English law considered that the protection and care of the mentally incapacitated and their estates was a royal prerogative. Therefore, since the thirteenth century, those deemed mentally afflicted were put under the guardianship of the Crown, first through the High Court of Chancery and then through the Court of Wards. After the latter was abolished in 1660, guardianship of lunatics and idiots came to be under the competence of the Court of Chancery.[61]

According to Michael MacDonald, the dissolution of the Court of Wards had markedly negative effects for the insane. The Court of Wards, he suggests, was not only concerned with administering the patrimony of landowners, as the Chancery was later reduced to doing, for although it was a much "hated institution," it also managed to protect the mentally ill. On the contrary, the Court of Chancery "exploited the insane as the Court of Wards had never done," being "notoriously corrupt, inefficient, and expensive."[62] The Chancery made the properties of the mentally incapacitated an open field for profit and corruption, bluntly disputed between judges, guardians, and lawyers. Furthermore, with the rising costs charged by the Court of Chancery for the guardianship of lunatics and idiots, the procedure became affordable only for the richer members of English society. However, further investigation into the records of the surviving eighteenth-century English inquiries into mental capacity should shed greater light on the subject, as a systematic study still needs to be done.

The legal procedure by which a petitioner could request the Lord Chancellor to inquire into the individual's state of mind was called commission of lunacy or of idiocy (commission *de idiota inquirendo* or *de lunatico inquirendo*). The investigation was directed not only to determine the defendant's state of mind, but also the date from which it could be established that he or she had become mentally incapacitated. This was fundamental, since commissions had retroactive implications and could be used to annul past contracts.[63] When the enquiry established that the defendant was indeed a lunatic or idiot, this person and his or her property were commissioned to the care of a suitable guardian, generally a next of kin, provided they were not the immediate heir. However, although incapacity by reason of lunacy and idiocy followed the same procedure, the legal consequences of the commission in each case were different. While the legal declaration of mental incapacity was irrevocable in the case of idiocy, the incapacity of lunatics was by definition understood to be temporary, and so they could regain their civil rights when their insanity abated. For this reason, according to Blackstone, very few individuals were declared to be natural idiots, for the deprivation of their rights would have been permanent.[64]

The Scottish legal framework provided a similar provision for the mentally incapacitated, also based on the dichotomy between idiocy and lunacy (called, in this case, furiosity). In Scotland, those deprived of reason were also put under curatorship, once a "brieve [writ or brief] of idiotry" or a "brieve of furiosity" had been requested from the Chancery.[65] As in the other cases examined here, brieves of idiocy and furiosity were requested by close relatives on the grounds that the person was incapable of administering his or her property and that this represented a threat to their financial well-being and that of their families. In order for a person to be declared mentally incapacitated, an inquiry was conducted by a judge to examine the capacities of the alleged insane, a procedure known as "cognition." People held to suffer from mental incapacity were put under the curatorship of a relative, generally the same one who had requested the brieve, and the person was deprived of her or his civil rights.

Cognitions not only established whether the defendant was mentally incapacitated, but they also indicated the exact time the incapacity had started. All deeds committed by the mentally afflicted since the onset of their condition could be nullified after cognition. The fact that both in England and in Scotland, the legal procedure that established someone's mental incapacity had retroactive power meant that not only economic contracts, but also legal contracts such as marriage could be nullified, a consequence that we do not observe in Tuscany, as we have seen. However, legal mental incapacity in Scotland did not entail a fixed array of consequences, as Robert Allan Houston has argued, for the law recognized different gradations and types of mental incapacity, which could be temporary or permanent and could affect the person in a myriad of ways. This means that cognition did not imply automatic invalidation of the acts committed by the insane, but only "threw them into doubt, and allowed their 'reduction' [overturn] at law."[66] Finally, in both the Scottish and English legal frameworks, inquiries into mental capacity were a separate procedure from confinement. To institutionalize or to imprison an insane relative served a whole different set of aims than cognitions or commissions of lunacy. Thus, they were regulated by a different set of rules, particularly because confinement was easier, less expensive, did not entail a court procedure, and was largely more discrete.

All of these inquiries into mental capacity had in common that they were aimed at protecting the patrimony and at the prevention or correction of economic mismanagement and were, consequently, used primarily by the privileged, affecting predominantly men. Rather than focusing on the specific label used, the evaluation of authorities and judges privileged how the families characterized the behavior, the reasons behind the denunciation, and the extent to which the behavior was believed to imperil the family. Thus, inquiries into mental capacity were chiefly concerned with the public and domestic consequences of madness, instead of being preoccupied with defining its nature, which explains why they were not really interested in determining clear diagnostic categories of madness. Their scope was to determine a person's level of responsibility and to negotiate "the balance between private and public provision" accordingly.[67] As Houston has put it, the broadness of the legal definition of insanity coming out of these procedures is explained precisely because of their focus on property.[68] Thus, the aim of the procedure shaped the definition of madness we find in these sources. The problem derived from this is that we are bound to a socially limited conception of what insanity amounted to, given that the perceptions of the non-privileged are not considered in the sample under scrutiny.

The connection between madness and property was at the core of the European inquiries into mental capacity. Families debated first and foremost the right to manage a person's financial affairs, placing control over property as the primary matter of concern. This highlights the extent to which European elite families conceived of patrimony as a collective rather than as a personal concern. Individual ownership was regarded as a temporary right, a sort of transfer from the family, which could be withdrawn the moment the person diverged from accepted behavior. Thus, individual disposal of one's patrimony was thought to be subject to family approval, and the disagreement over this issue was to a great extent responsible for requests to deprive a family member of his or her rights of administration on the grounds of mental incapacity. Hence, although inquiries into mental capacity do not only speak of patrimony, they do illuminate from a special point of view how patrimony was perceived, and the extent to which the disposal of patrimony was profoundly entrenched within the moral economy of the family.[69]

A brief examination of the British, French, and Tuscan civil procedures dealing with the consequences of mental incapacity largely demonstrates how the domestic environment shaped not only the ways in which the procedures were carried out, but also how madness was understood and the strategies devised to deal with it. In all the scenarios examined, mental incapacity was shaped primarily by the narratives of the families, with barely any intervention from medical testimonies. Civil and criminal courts seem to have been dominated by lay opinion on mental states, for, as Houston has put it, "'expert' medical testimony was neither sufficient nor necessary" in most of eighteenth-century Europe.[70] In Tuscany too, the identification of mental incapacity, until the eighteenth century at least, was a highly social matter, as will be discussed further in chapter 3. The alleged mad person had to be known to be mad by the whole community, which had to be ratified by the political authority of the place. If the officials of the Pupilli still had any doubts, the defendant was inspected by the officials themselves.

Scholars have pointed out that inquiries into mental capacity should be examined as a space provided by the legal framework to resolve private conflicts, which functioned as a legal measure that families could use at their own will. In all the European scenarios examined here, these procedures followed private initiatives which cannot be taken to be the product of a top-down disciplining strategy. As Nootens has stressed, in interdiction procedures, we find civil justice at the service of the families, something family members could turn to in order to solve conflicts identified and defined by them.[71] How mental incapacity was defined and which measures were to be taken to respond to it were the result of careful negotiations between families, authorities, and the defendants themselves.

Notes

1 See the discussion on the decadent image of Cosimo III's Tuscany in Elena Fasano Guarini, "Lo stato di Cosimo III. Dalle testimonianze contemporanee agli attuali orientamenti di ricerca. Note introduttive," in *La Toscana nell'età di Cosimo III*, ed. Franco Angiolini, Vieri Becagli, and Marcello Verga (Florence: Edifir-Edizioni Firenze, 1993), 113–136. For an overview of the historiography of the Tuscan eighteenth century, which was largely marked by the paradigm of enlightened late-eighteenth-century reforms, see Alessandra Contini, "Orientamenti recenti sul settecento Toscano," in *La Toscana in età moderna (Secoli XVI-XVIII). Politica, istituzioni, società: studi recenti e prospettive di ricerca*, ed. Mario Ascheri and Alessandra Contini (Florence: Leo S. Olschki Editore, 2005), 91–127. On the social and political changes brought by the Lorraines, see R. Burr Litchfield, *Emergence of a Bureaucracy: The Florentine Patricians, 1530–1790* (Princeton, NJ: Princeton University Press, 1986); Marcello Verga, *Da "cittadini" a "nobili." Lotta politica e riforma delle istituzioni nella Toscana di Francesco Stefano* (Milan: Giuffrè, 1990); and Furio Diaz, *I Lorena in Toscana. La Reggenza* (Turin: UTET, 1988).
2 Caroline M. Fisher, "The State as Surrogate Father: State Guardianship in Renaissance Florence. 1368–1532," (PhD diss., Brandeis University, 2003), 18–19.
3 Graziella Magherini and Vittorio Biotti, *L'isola delle Stinche e i percorsi della follia a Firenze nei secoli XIV-XVIII* (Florence: Ponte alle Grazie, 1992), 69.
4 This procedure was specified in rubric 118 of the second book of the Florentine statues; this provision was recalled by Marc'Antonio Savelli's famous compendium of the Tuscan legal practice. *Pratica universale* (Parma: Paolo Monti, 1717 [1st ed. 1665, seven editions until 1748]), 264, and was frequently cited in the interdiction procedures handled by the Magistrato dei Pupilli between 1728 and 1735.
5 The medieval statutes were compiled by Francesca Morandini in "Statuti e ordinamenti dell'Ufficio dei Pupilli et adulti nel periodo della Repubblica fiorentina (1388–1534)," *Archivio storico italiano* 113 (1955): 520–551, 114 (1956): 92–117, and 115 (1957): 87–104.
6 According to Caroline M. Fisher, state guardianship "was the most direct and comprehensive way in which the Florentine government intervened in the affairs of its subjects." Fisher, "The State as Surrogate Father," 4. For a thorough study on guardianships in Tuscany during the early modern period, see Giulia Calvi, *Il contratto morale. Madri e figli nella Toscana moderna* (Rome: Laterza, 1994).

7 Statute Reform of the Magistrato dei Pupilli, 1473, in Morandini, "Statuti e ordinamenti dell'Ufficio dei Pupilli," 113 (1955): 550.
8 ASF, MPAAP, F. 248, "Statuti et ordini della Corte et Magistrato delli Offittiali de' Pupilli et Adulti della Città di Fiorenza reformati et stabiliti per ordine di S.C.I. dal suo Mag. Cons. et Pratica Secreta sotto di 20 d'Agosto 1565," Rubric 2, fols. 4–4v.
9 Also known as the Tribunal of the Prince (*Tribunale del Principe*), the Magistrato Supremo was presided over by the Grand Duke's lieutenant (the *Luogotenente*) and his advisors (*Consiglieri*). Established as the highest civil court in Tuscany, its jurisdiction and competencies overlapped with many other magistracies, particularly the Ruota Civile and the Magistrato dei Pupilli. Among its official prerogatives, the Supremo was involved in the administration of justice, had jurisdiction, among other fields, over civil family disputes (mostly testamentary and related to patrimony), over judicial actions related to taxes and privileges, and over proceedings affecting the poor and incapacitated, in clear dispute with the Pupilli. See Giuseppe Pansini, "Il Magistrato Supremo e l'amministrazione della giustizia civile durante il Principato medico," *Studi senesi* 85 (1973): 283–315; Giuseppe Pansini, "La Ruota fiorentina nelle strutture giudiziarie del Granducato di Toscana sotto i Medici," in *La Formazione storica del diritto moderno in Europa*, vol. 2 (Florence: Leo S. Olschki Editore, 1977), 533–579.
10 ASF, MPAAP, F. 248, "Statuti et ordini," fols. 4v-5.
11 "Legge e Riforma del Magistrato e Ufizio de Pupilli, ed Adulti della città di Firenze, ottenuta nel Supremo Magistrato del di 19 Luglio 1680 ab Inc," in Lorenzo Cantini, *Legislazione Toscana*, vol. 19 (Florence: Stamp. Albizziniana da S. Maria in Campo, 1806), 156.
12 The overlap of the spheres of action between the Magistrato dei Pupilli and the Magistrato Supremo is not a coincidence nor an isolated event but a constitutional part of the jurisdictional overlap and juridical and institutional pluralism that characterized the Grand Duchy of Tuscany until the Lorraine reforms. Luca Mannori, *Il Sovrano Tutore: Pluralismo istituzionale e accentramento amministrativo nel principato dei Medici (secc. XVI-XVIII)* (Milan: Giuffrè, 1994).
13 "Legge e Riforma Del Magistrato e Ufizio de Pupilli," 160–161. These special cases in which the administration could fall under the direct oversight of the Magistrato Supremo referred in practice to the *Cavalieri* of the Order of Santo Stefano and other privileged men and women whose mental disorder was thought to be better protected if concealed under the wing of the Magistrato Supremo. A sample of interdictions and curatorships entirely managed by the Magistrato Supremo after 1680 can be found in the *Suppliche* of the Magistrato Supremo.
14 Elizabeth Mellyn, *Mad Tuscans and Their Families: A History of Mental Disorder in Early Modern Italy* (Philadelphia: University of Pennsylvania Press, 2014), 14.
15 Magherini and Biotti, *L'isola delle Stinche*, 75.
16 The evidence suggests that the decline of the Pupilli's involvement in the affairs of the mentally incompetent has more to do with the general overlap that characterized the Tuscan administration rather than with a deliberate reduction of the Pupilli's competences over mental incapacity. The fact that the Magistrato dei Pupilli's competence over the guardianship of incapacitated adults had to be ratified through a series of reforms during its whole period of existence needs to be interpreted in the light of the institutional disorder and lack of clear boundaries between the different public offices that characterized the Grand Duchy.
17 Mellyn, *Mad Tuscans*, 38.
18 "Bando. Circa l'Esecuzione de' Privilegi, e Statuti del Magistrato delli Signori Ufiziali de'Pupilli, ed Adulti della Città di Firenze, ottenuto nel Supremo Magistrato del di 28 Gennaio 1717 [1718]," ASF, MS, *Suppliche*, F. 1180, fol. 1311. The reform can also be consulted in ASF, Consulta poi Regia Consulta, Sezione I,

50 Interdiction procedures

Leggi, P. 14, Tomo XIV, fol. 145, and in Lorenzo Cantini, *Legislazione Toscana*, vol. 22, 253–254.
19 This can be observed in ASF, MPAP, *Campione di Deliberazioni e Partiti*, F. 112, year 1717, F. 113, year 1718, and F. 114, year 1719 and following, and also ASF, MPAP, *Memoriale e Informazioni*, F. 2299, corresponding to the years 1688–1722.
20 ASF, MPAP, *Memoriali e Informazioni*, F. 2299, no. 117, 8 January 1693/94.
21 For instance, see the Pupilli report on the interdiction of Gio. Batta Arrighi, in ASF, MPAP, *Memoriali e Informazioni*, F. 2299, no. 383, August 1718.
22 Although petitions were addressed directly to the Grand Duke, they were actually centralized in the Consulta, from where they were redirected to the competent magistracies. The Consulta was created at the beginning of the seventeenth century as a high court of appeals. According to Cecilia Nubola, petitions are to be inserted in the myth of sovereignty that sustained the Ancien Régime, which pictured the prince as "father, judge, legislator, and reference point of justice and of fairness, to whom subjects can turn." Thus, petitions were addressed directly to the sovereign although supplicants knew their requests were actually evaluated by state officials and magistrates. Cecilia Nubola, "Supplications between Politics and Justice: The Northern and Central Italian States in the Early Modern Age," *International Review of Social History* 26 (Supplement, 2001): 36–37. On the Consulta, Litchfield, *Emergence of a Bureaucracy*, 89.
23 Savelli, *Pratica universale*, 264.
24 In these cases, the *giustificazioni*, as the testimonies attesting petitions of interdiction were called, can be found in the series *Atti e Scritture* of the archive of the Magistrato Supremo, whereas in the case they were written supplications, they are filed in the section *Memoriali e Negozi* of the Magistrato dei Pupilli. The interdiction decree, the appointment of the curator, and all the following actions derived from an interdiction sentence are found in the Magistrato dei Pupilli.
25 Interdiction procedures on account of deafness and muteness not only are rare but also left scant evidence during the eighteenth century. Given that they pertain to a different set of conflicts, I do not take the few that exist into account in this study.
26 For instance, ASF, MPAP, *Memoriali*, F. 2307, no. 85, December 1767; F. 2308, no. 29, June 1770 and F. 2310, nos. 236, June 1775 and 266, July 1775.
27 For a general review of the guardianship of minors, see Carlo Calisse, *A History of Italian Law* (New York: Kelley, 1969), 598–602; and Enrico Besta, *La famiglia nella storia del diritto Italiano* (Milan: Giuffrè, 1962), 231–248. Among the most important changes raised by the glossators was the possibility of introducing a new order of desirable guardians, giving precedence to the cognate line, particularly the mother. For the Tuscan adjustments of Roman law principles, the backgrounds of the Magistrato dei Pupilli, and the development of the guardianship of minors, see Fisher, "The State as Surrogate Father," 16–27; and Calvi, *Il contratto morale*.
28 Magherini and Biotti, *L'isola delle Stinche*, 63.
29 Marco Boari, *Qui venit contra iura. Il furiosus nella criminalistica dei secoli XV e XVI* (Milan: Giuffré, 1983), 25. My translation. See also Besta, *La famiglia*, 249–251.
30 Mellyn, *Mad Tuscans*, 96–97.
31 ASF, MPAAP, F. 248, "Statuti et ordini della Corte et Magistrato delli Offittiali de' Pupilli," fol. 4v.
32 See Mellyn, *Mad Tuscans* and Magherini and Biotti, *L'isola delle Stinche*.
33 Mellyn, *Mad Tuscans*, 39 and 41.
34 An interdiction decree usually commanded ". . . sottoporsi il medesimo al detto Magistrato de Pupilli a tenore del disposto della riforma delli statuti di detto Magistrato de 20 Agosto 1565 e del Motuproprio di S.A.R. del di 5 febbraio

1717 nelle forme solite e consuete." From an interdiction decree of 1740, ASF, MPAP, *Memoriali*, F. 2301, no. 76.
35 "Legge per il Regolamento del Tribunale de' Pupilli del di 8 Giugno 1767," in Cantini, *Legislazione Toscana*, vol. 27, 356–372. For the heated debate caused by these unwelcome resolutions, see ASF, MPAP, *Memoriali*, F. 2307, nos. 24–27.
36 The appointment of a guardian for mentally afflicted adults was not so different from the policies regarding guardianship of underage wards, also largely entrusted to widows. See Calvi, *Il contratto morale* and Fisher, "The State as Surrogate Father."
37 The magistrates of the Supremo and the Pupilli engaged in several discussions regarding these topics, involving also the Consiglio di Reggenza. Overall, the criterion was decided case-by-case, so that the particular circumstances of each testator and his or her family could be taken into account, together with their particular mental condition. For example, see ASF, MPAP, *Memoriali*, F. 2302, no. 115, July 1749 or ASF, CR, *Fiscale*, F. 756, no. 42, 1750.
38 The overarching competences of the Auditore Fiscale are examined in Chapter 4.
39 Ottavia Niccoli, *Perdonare. Idee, pratiche, rituali in Italia tra Cinque e Seicento* (Rome: Laterza, 2007); Chiara La Rocca, *Tra moglie e marito. Matrimoni e separazioni a Livorno nel Settecento* (Bologna: Società editrice Il Molino, 2009); and Marco Bellabarba, Gerd Schwerhoff, and Andrea Zorzi, eds., *Criminalità e giustizia in Germania e in Italia. Pratiche giudiziarie e linguaggi giuridici tra medioevo ed età moderna* (Bologna and Berlin: Il Mulino, 2001), especially Martin Dinges, "Usi della giustizia come elemento di controllo sociale nella prima età moderna," 284–324; and Mario Sbriccoli, "Giustizia negoziata, giustizia egemonica. Riflessioni su una nuova fase degli studi di storia della giustizia criminale," 345–364.
40 Thomas Kuehn, *Heirs, Kin and Creditors in Renaissance Florence* (Cambridge: Cambridge University Press, 2008), 5. Patrimony was not only at the base of Tuscan society, but also at the same time the object of flexible interpretation and strategies, as Thomas Kuehn's study of inheritance shows. He examines property starting from the repudiation of inheritance to demonstrate the complex ways in which Florentine families interpreted legal structures in service of their aims.
41 See, for instance, the line of argument developed by Jean Boutier in "Una nobiltà urbana in età moderna. Aspetti della morfologia sociale della nobiltà fiorentina," *Dimensioni e problemi della Ricerca storica* 2 (1993): 141–159, or "Les noblesses du grand-duché (XVe-XIXe siècle)," in *Florence et la Toscane XIVe-XIXe siècles. Les dynamiques d'un État italien*, ed. Jean Boutier, Sandro Landi, and Olivier Rouchon (Rennes: Presses Universitaires de Rennes, 2004), 265–285.
42 ASF, MPAP, *Memoriali*, F. 2305, no. 127, February 1761.
43 Pronouncement of the members of the Consulta regarding a controversy aroused over the validity of a testament made by an interdicted prodigal. ASF, CR, *Fiscale*, F. 756, no. 42, August 1750.
44 Robert Allan Houston, *Madness and Society in Eighteenth-Century Scotland* (Oxford: Oxford University Press, 2000), 173. Scholars working on legal records long ago warned us about the manufactured truth produced by judicial proceedings, disclosing "plausible stories" or "legal truths." Narratives were manufactured according to how much petitioners were willing to disclose. However, the fact that narratives had to be plausible should not lead us to assume they were entirely manufactured. The literature here is vast. See Natalie Zemon Davis, *Fiction in the Archives* (Stanford: Stanford University Press, 1987); Laura Gowing, *Domestic Dangers: Women, Words, and Sex in Early Modern London* (Oxford: Oxford University Press, 1996); Carlo Ginzburg, "El inquisidor como antropólogo," in *El hilo y las huellas. Lo verdadero, lo falso y lo ficticio* (México: Fondo de Cultura Económica, 2010), 395–411. On the plausibility of the narratives of mental incapacity in particular, see Houston, *Madness and Society*, 42–45.

52 Interdiction procedures

45 The other magistracy concerned with civil litigations was the Magistrato Supremo, whose concerns often overlapped with those of the Pupilli. A similar logic regarding private family conflicts being disclosed for state arbitration has been pointed out by Giovanna Benadusi, "La madre e il Granduca. Stato e famiglia nelle suppliche al Magistrato Supremo (Firenze, XVII secolo)," in *Famiglie e Poteri in Italia tra medioevo ed età moderna*, ed. Anna Bellavitis and Isabelle Chabot (Rome: École Française de Rome, 2009), 397–415.
46 Isabelle Chabot, "Le gouvernement des pères: l'État florentin et la famille (XIVe-XVe siècles)," in *Florence et la Toscane XIVe-XIXe siècles. Les dynamiques d'un État italien*, ed. Jean Boutier, Sandro Landi, and Olivier Rouchon (Rennes: Presses Universitaires de Rennes, 2004), 241–262.
47 Calvi, *Il contratto morale*, 28–29.
48 The capacity of women to negotiate in the legal arena, notwithstanding the legal constraints posed by the patriarchal system, has been recognized in different areas of the early modern Tuscan legal system, particularly regarding matrimonial disputes. On the legal restrictions against women, see Thomas Kuehn, *Law, Family and Women: Toward a Legal Anthropology of Renaissance Italy* (Chicago and London: The University of Chicago Press, 1991). See also Daniela Lombardi, *Matrimonio di antico regime* (Bologna: Il Mulino, 2001), particularly 12–13 for her critique of Kuehn's approach. Historians have stressed the fact that an overwhelming majority of the matrimonial disputes in early modern Europe derived from petitions sent by women. The capacity of women to negotiate and their flexible maneuvering around legal situations, which they managed to shift in their favor, have been thoroughly explored in matrimonial litigation. These records show women in a position far from the common image that depicted them as weak, passive, helpless, or victimized by men. See, among many others, La Rocca, *Tra moglie e marito*; Elisabetta Picchietti, "'L'oratrice umilissima devotamente l'espone'. Le suppliche matrimoniali," in *Scritture di donne. La memoria restituita*, ed. Marina Caffiero and Manola Ida Venzo (Rome: Viella, 2007), 313–325; Silvana Seidel Menchi and Diego Quaglioni, eds., *Coniugi nemici. La separazione in Italia dal XII al XVIII secolo* (Bologna: Il Molino, 2000).
49 Matrimonial kinsmen were usually part of the interdiction procedure at some point to back up the denunciation made either by women or by men of the agnatic line. Other times, a brother- or father-in-law was preferred as administrator instead of a son or a brother, whose interests as direct inheritors of the patrimony made them suspicious in the eyes of the Magistrato dei Pupilli officials. Matrimonial kinsmen were also part of the living arrangements made by the Pupilli officials in their efforts to settle the disorders produced by prodigals and the demented. This highlights the importance of the horizontal family, manifested through the involvement of brothers, who were particularly active in the protection of their married sisters. Sandra Cavallo, "L'importanza della 'famiglia orizzontale' nella storia della famiglia italiana," in *Generazioni. Legami di parentela tra passato e presente*, ed. Ida Fazio and Daniela Lombardi (Rome: Viella, 2006), 69–92.
50 On the problem of assessing authorship in petitions, particularly when they were signed by women, see Bianca Premo, "Before the Law: Women's Petitions in the Eighteenth-Century Spanish Empire," *Comparative Studies in Society and History* 53, no. 2 (2011): 261–289.
51 For the early modern period, see Houston, *Madness and Society*; Laurent Cartayrade, "Property, Prodigality, and Madness: A Study of Interdiction Records in Eighteenth-Century Paris," (PhD diss., University of Maryland, 1997); Mellyn, *Mad Tuscans*. For the nineteenth century, Thierry Nootens, *Fous, prodigues et ivrognes: Familles et déviance à Montréal au XIX siècle* (Montreal: McGill-Queen's University Press, 2007); Akihito Suzuki, *Madness at Home: The*

Psychiatrist, the Patient, and the Family in England, 1820–1860 (Berkeley: University of California Press, 2006); and Maria José Correa, "Lay People, Medical Experts and Mental Disorders. The Medicalization of Insanity through the Incapacitation of the Mentally Ill, 1830–1925," (PhD diss., University College London, 2012).

52 For the practice of interdiction in France, I draw upon Cartayrade, "Property, Prodigality, and Madness," and Thierry Nootens, "Fous, prodigues et faibles d'esprit: l'interdiction et le conseil judiciaire dans le tribunal de première instance d'Angers 1820–1835, 1880–1883," *Déviance et société* 24, no. 1 (2000): 47–67.
53 Cartayrade, "Property, Prodigality, and Madness," 70 and 72. Cartayrade explains the use of interdiction for the insane individual also as a practical solution to the difficulty of assessing the exact time from when legal actions were considered invalid, which coincided with the moment the alleged insanity had started. From then on, the incapacity of those deemed insane also started legally with the interdiction decree, avoiding long suits over the need to revoke a past contract supposedly made in a state of insanity.
54 Nootens, "Fous, prodigues et faibles d'esprit," 49.
55 Cartayrade, "Property, Prodigality, and Madness," 62.
56 This flexibility and recurrence of interdiction procedures seems not to be applicable to the previous centuries, if we follow Mellyn's findings. Mellyn, *Mad Tuscans*, 24–57.
57 Cartayrade, "Property, Prodigality, and Madness," 93.
58 Cartayrade, "Property, Prodigality, and Madness," 65.
59 William Blackstone, *Commentaries on the Laws of England*, Book 1 (Oxford: Clarendon Press, 1765), 292.
60 Blackstone, *Commentaries*, 294.
61 On the medieval inquiries into mental capacity, see Richard Neugebauer, "Mental Handicap in Medieval and Early Modern England: Criteria, Measurement and Care," in *From Idiocy to Mental Deficiency*, ed. David Wright and Anne Digby (London and New York: Routledge, 1996), 22–43.
62 Michael MacDonald, "Lunatics and the State in Georgian England," *Social History of Medicine* 2, no. 2 (1989): 302. MacDonald's assertion was a direct criticism to the benevolent diagnostic given by historians such as Roy Porter. The latter had claimed that the British early modern state's intervention in the life and affairs of the mad "hardly show the state in an aggressively interventionist mood, attempting to police or exploit the subnormal." Roy Porter, *Mind-Forg'd Manacles: A History of Madness in England from the Restoration to the Regency* (London: Penguin Books, 1990), 113.
63 Suzuki, *Madness at Home*, 19.
64 Blackstone, *Commentaries*, 293–295.
65 Scottish inquiries into mental capacity have been thoroughly examined by Houston in *Madness and Society*.
66 Houston, *Madness and Society*, 62.
67 Peter Rushton, "Idiocy, the Family and the Community in Early Modern North-East England," in *From Idiocy to Mental Deficiency*, ed. David Wright and Anne Digby (London and New York: Routledge, 1996), 57.
68 Houston, *Madness and Society*, 24.
69 For instance, Akihito Suzuki examined the issue by suggesting that physicians conceived of their intervention in commissions of lunacy in similar terms, presenting themselves as "guardians of family property." Suzuki, *Madness at Home*, 66–71.
70 Robert Allan Houston, "Courts, Doctors, and Insanity Defences in 18th and Early 19th Century Scotland," *International Journal of Law and Psychiatry* 26, no. 4 (2003): 343.
71 Nootens, "Fous, prodigues et faibles d'esprit," 48.

Bibliography chapter 1

Manuscripts

Archivio di Stato di Firenze (ASF)
- Consiglio di Reggenza (CR)
  - *Fiscale*, F. 754–762.
- Consulta poi Regia Consulta, Sezione I, Leggi, P. 14, Tomo XIV
- Magistrato dei Pupilli et Adulti avanti il Principato (MPAAP), F. 248
- Magistrato dei Pupilli et Adulti del Principato (MPAP)
  - *Campione di Deliberazioni e Partiti*, F. 108–F. 166
  - *Atti e Sentenze*, F. 1144–F. 1362
  - *Suppliche e informazioni: Memoriali e Negozi di Cancelleria*, F. 2299–F. 2318
  - *Filza Lettere e Responsive*, F. 2480–F. 2519
- Magistrato Supremo (MS)
  - *Suppliche*, F. 1179–F. 1188
  - *Atti e Scritture*, F. 1845–F. 2103

Printed sources

Blackstone, William. *Commentaries on the Laws of England*. Book. 1. Oxford: Clarendon Press, 1765.

Cantini, Lorenzo. *Legislazione Toscana*, vols. 19, 22 and 27. Florence: Stamp. Albizziniana da S. Maria in Campo, 1806.

Savelli, Marc'Antonio. *Pratica universale del Dottor Marc'Antonio Savelli Auditore della Rota Criminale di Firenze*. Parma: Paolo Monti, 1717 [1° ed. 1665].

References

Bellabarba, Marco, Gerd Schwerhoff, and Andrea Zorzi, eds. *Criminalità e giustizia in Germania e in Italia. Pratiche giudiziarie e linguaggi giuridici tra medioevo ed età moderna*. Bologna and Berlin: Il Mulino, 2001.

Benadusi, Giovanna. "La madre e il Granduca. Stato e famiglia nelle suppliche al Magistrato Supremo (Firenze, XVII secolo)." In *Famiglie e Poteri in Italia tra medioevo ed età moderna*, edited by Anna Bellavitis and Isabelle Chabot, 397–415. Rome: École Française de Rome, 2009.

Besta, Enrico. *La famiglia nella storia del diritto Italiano*. Milan: Giuffrè, 1962.

Boari, Marco. *Qui venit contra iura. Il furiosus nella criminalistica dei secoli XV e XVI*. Milan: Giuffrè, 1983.

Boutier, Jean. "Les noblesses du grand-duché (XVe-XIXe siècle)." In *Florence et la Toscane XIVe-XIXe siècles. Les dynamiques d'un État italien*, edited by Jean Boutier, Sandro Landi, and Olivier Rouchon, 265–285. Rennes: Presses Universitaires de Rennes, 2004.

Boutier, Jean. "Una nobiltà urbana in età moderna. Aspetti della morfologia sociale della nobiltà fiorentina." *Dimensioni e problemi della ricerca storica* 2 (1993): 141–159.

Calisse, Carlo. *A History of Italian Law*. New York: Kelley, 1969.

Calvi, Giulia. *Il contratto morale. Madri e figli nella Toscana moderna*. Rome: Laterza, 1994.

Cartayrade, Laurent. "Property, Prodigality, and Madness: A Study of Interdiction Records in Eighteenth-Century Paris." PhD diss., University of Maryland, 1997.

Cavallo, Sandra. "L'importanza della 'famiglia orizzontale' nella storia della famiglia italiana." In *Generazioni. Legami di parentela tra passato e presente*, edited by Ida Fazio and Daniela Lombardi, 69–92. Rome: Viella, 2006.

Chabot, Isabelle. "Le gouvernement des pères: l'État florentin et la famille (XIVe-XVe siècles)." In *Florence et la Toscane XIVe-XIXe siècles. Les dynamiques d'un État italien*, edited by Jean Boutier, Sandro Landi, and Olivier Rouchon, 241–262. Rennes: Presses Universitaires de Rennes, 2004.

Contini, Alessandra. "Orientamenti recenti sul settecento Toscano." In *La Toscana in età moderna (Secoli XVI-XVIII). Politica, istituzioni, società: studi recenti e prospettive di ricerca*, edited by Mario Ascheri and Alessandra Contini, 91–127. Florence: Leo S. Olschki Editore, 2005.

Correa Gómez, María José. "Lay People, Medical Experts and Mental Disorders: The Medicalization of Insanity through the Incapacitation of the Mentally Ill, 1830–1925." PhD diss., University College London, 2012.

Davis, Natalie Zemon. *Fiction in the Archives*. Stanford: Stanford University Press, 1987.

Diaz, Furio. *I Lorena in Toscana. La Reggenza*. Turin: UTET, 1988.

Fasano Guarini, Elena. "Lo stato di Cosimo III. Dalle testimonianze contemporanee agli attuali orientamenti di ricerca. Note introduttive." In *La Toscana nell'età di Cosimo III*, edited by Franco Angiolini, Vieri Becagli, and Marcello Verga, 113–136. Florence: Edifir-Edizioni Firenze, 1993.

Fisher, Caroline M. "The State as Surrogate Father: State Guardianship in Renaissance Florence, 1368–1532." PhD diss., Brandeis University, 2003.

Ginzburg, Carlo. "El inquisidor como antropólogo." In *El hilo y las huellas. Lo verdadero, lo falso y lo ficticio*, 395–411. México: Fondo de Cultura Económica, 2010.

Gowing, Laura. *Domestic Dangers: Women, Words, and Sex in Early Modern London*. Oxford: Oxford University Press, 1996.

Houston, Robert Allan. "Courts, Doctors, and Insanity Defences in 18th and Early 19th Century Scotland." *International Journal of Law and Psychiatry* 26, no. 4 (2003): 339–354.

Houston, Robert Allan. *Madness and Society in Eighteenth-Century Scotland*. Oxford: Oxford University Press, 2000.

Kuehn, Thomas. *Heirs, Kin and Creditors in Renaissance Florence*. Cambridge: Cambridge University Press, 2008.

Kuehn, Thomas. *Law, Family and Women: Toward a Legal Anthropology of Renaissance Italy*. Chicago and London: The University of Chicago Press, 1991.

La Rocca, Chiara. *Tra moglie e marito. Matrimoni e separazioni a Livorno nel Settecento*. Bologna: Società editrice Il Molino, 2009.

Litchfield, R. Burr. *Emergence of a Bureaucracy: The Florentine Patricians, 1530–1790*. Princeton: Princeton University Press, 1986.

Lombardi, Daniela. *Matrimonio di antico regime*. Bologna: Il Mulino, 2001.
MacDonald, Michael. "Lunatics and the State in Georgian England." *Social History of Medicine* 2, no. 2 (1989): 299–313.
Magherini, Graziella, and Vittorio Biotti. *L'isola delle Stinche e i percorsi della follia a Firenze nei secoli XIV-XVIII*. Florence: Ponte alle Grazie, 1992.
Mannori, Luca. *Il Sovrano Tutore: Pluralismo istituzionale e accentramento amministrativo nel principato dei Medici (secc. XVI-XVIII)*. Milan: Giuffrè, 1994.
Mellyn, Elizabeth W. *Mad Tuscans and Their Families: A History of Mental Disorder in Early Modern Italy*. Philadelphia: University of Pennsylvania Press, 2014.
Morandini, Francesca. "Statuti e ordinamenti dell'Ufficio dei Pupilli et adulti nel periodo della Repubblica fiorentina (1388–1534)." *Archivio storico italiano* 113 (1955): 520–551, 114 (1956): 92–117, and 115 (1957): 87–104.
Neugebauer, Richard. "Mental Handicap in Medieval and Early Modern England: Criteria, Measurement and Care." In *From Idiocy to Mental Deficiency*, edited by David Wright and Anne Digby, 22–43. London and New York: Routledge, 1996.
Niccoli, Ottavia. *Perdonare. Idee, pratiche, rituali in Italia tra Cinque e Seicento*. Rome: Laterza, 2007.
Nootens, Thierry. "Fous, prodigues et faibles d'esprit: l'interdiction et le conseil judiciaire dans le tribunal de première instance d'Angers 1820–1835, 1880–1883." *Déviance et société* 24, no. 1 (2000): 47–67.
Nootens, Thierry. *Fous, prodigues et ivrognes: Familles et déviance à Montréal au XIX siècle*. Montreal: McGill-Queen's University Press, 2007.
Nubola, Cecilia. "Supplications between Politics and Justice: The Northern and Central Italian States in the Early Modern Age." *International Review of Social History* 26 (Supplement, 2001): 35–56.
Pansini, Giuseppe. "Il Magistrato Supremo e l'amministrazione della giustizia civile durante il Principato mediceo." *Studi senesi* 85 (1973): 283–315.
Pansini, Giuseppe. "La Ruota fiorentina nelle strutture giudiziarie del Granducato di Toscana sotto i Medici." In *La Formazione storica del diritto moderno in Europa*, vol. 2, 533–579. Florence: Leo S. Olschki Editore, 1977.
Picchietti, Elisabetta. "'L'oratrice umilissima devotamente l'espone'. Le suppliche matrimoniali." In *Scritture di donne. La memoria restituita*, edited by Marina Caffiero and Manola Ida Venzo, 313–325. Rome: Viella, 2007.
Porter, Roy. *Mind-Forg'd Manacles: A History of Madness in England from the Restoration to the Regency*. London: Penguin Books, 1990.
Premo, Bianca. "Before the Law: Women's Petitions in the Eighteenth-Century Spanish Empire." *Comparative Studies in Society and History* 53, no. 2 (2011): 261–289.
Rushton, Peter. "Idiocy, the Family and the Community in Early Modern North-East England." In *From Idiocy to Mental Deficiency*, edited by David Wright and Anne Digby, 44–64. London and New York: Routledge, 1996.
Seidel Menchi, Silvana, and Diego Quaglioni, eds. *Coniugi nemici. La separazione in Italia dal XII al XVIII secolo*. Bologna: Il Molino, 2000.
Suzuki, Akihito. *Madness at Home: The Psychiatrist, the Patient, and the Family in England, 1820–1860*. Berkeley: University of California Press, 2006.
Verga, Marcello. *Da "cittadini" a "nobili". Lotta politica e riforma delle istituzioni nella Toscana di Francesco Stefano*. Milan: Giuffrè, 1990.

2 Mad spendthrift men
Prodigality as a category of mental incapacity

Petitioning for an interdiction was not the easiest or the fastest solution to control a spendthrift. Interdiction was dishonorable to the family when the reprehensible practices and licentious living of the man were made public by the magistracy. Further, it entailed more money being spent, as families had to pay the annual fee charged by the Pupilli and the income of the administrator in the case he was not a family member – an option usually taken to avoid further conflicts in the family. Also, every action that was made through the Pupilli had to be paid for, and interdictions usually presupposed the inventory of the spendthrift's goods, selling part of them, or renting others in order to pay the accumulated debts incurred by the defendant. So, from neither the economic nor the social point of view was it the easiest solution. Furthermore, an interdiction entailed a series of relational conflicts inside the family, which were many times not solved during the curatorship. Yet, despite the difficulties an interdiction would cause in family life, it was nonetheless used to control disorderly members of the family and, in particular, prodigality.

The 1718 reform of the statutes of the Magistrato dei Pupilli listed five types of possible incapacities that could result in an interdiction sentence of which the most commonly used was prodigality. Although the Pupilli statues listed *prodighi* and *dilapidatori* as two different categories, in practice interdiction by reason of prodigality conflated both; that is, the individual was interdicted because he was a prodigal and also a squanderer (*dilapidatore*) of the patrimony. Bearing in mind that interdictions could be decreed by reason of prodigality, insanity (*demenza*) or physical impairment, the question is why were the majority of these persons accused of being prodigals instead of being demented? The answer lies first in how prodigality was understood and represented, second in the qualitative differences of having a relative interdicted as prodigal rather than as demented, and third in the strategies undertaken by families in their quest to handle their difficult members.

Prodigality was a condition that was not exclusively ascribed to youth. In fact, contrary to what the popular image of the prodigal son might lead us to think, prodigals were not only young sons who acted recklessly by contravening basic social norms and then repented. On the contrary, interdiction records reveal that men throughout their life, from youths to the elderly, could be defined as prodigals, a feature that differentiates Tuscany from France, for instance, where prodigals were mostly young sons.[1] Furthermore, the most typical characteristic of a young prodigal was that he lacked a paternal figure and was the direct holder of the family patrimony. In this sense, the concept had more to do with the juridical notion of prodigality, as developed in Roman law than with the Christian parable.

As explained in the first chapter, interdiction was originally designed for prodigality in Roman law, devised as a mechanism to control economic mismanagement by reckless squanderers of family fortunes. While the incapacity of the insane was thought to be natural (and so they were assigned a curator), what established the prodigal's legal incapacity was the interdiction decree. During the early modern period, the interdiction of prodigals also occurred in France, but not in England or Scotland, for example, where the law only provided guardianship for the insane. The transformation of the Roman tradition to respond to the early modern needs of France resulted in the equivalence between interdiction and legal incapacity; that is, prodigals and the insane were treated through the same juridical procedure.[2] Similarly, in Tuscany, prodigality and insanity (*demenza*) came to be conflated within the institutionalization of the Magistrato dei Pupilli, reaching complete legal equivalence in the eighteenth century.[3] Legally, the instrument and its consequences may have been the same, but nevertheless, qualitatively it was different to have a family member interdicted as demented than to have them interdicted as prodigal. Although judicial characterizations of prodigality closely resemble descriptions given in interdictions by reason of *demenza*, an interdiction on the grounds of the former allowed the family to avoid an open ascription of mental illness, which probably accounts for the higher numbers of interdictions for prodigality.

In the eighteenth century, the conception of prodigality was still based on what Elizabeth Mellyn has called "patrimonial rationality;" that is, the shared belief "that the prudent preservation, management, and devolution of patrimony were of supreme importance."[4] Nevertheless, new concerns had been raised over the forms of enlightened sociability, with clear condemnations not only of excessive expenditure, grandeur, and the pursuit of pleasures, but also of moral depravity.[5] In these new concerns, the family was placed at the center of attention, particularly considerations of how a person was supposed to act according to his or her age, gender, and family role. Descriptions of prodigal behavior evidence a clash of conceptions about propriety and accepted patterns of expenditure, how social position was to be shown, how relations between sexes were supposed to be enacted, how fathers had to behave with their sons, husbands with their wives, and firstborns with their mothers. Defining prodigality entailed, together with considerations of financial responsibility, a redefinition of decorum and honor, measured against how men controlled their tempers, managed their emotions, and behaved in the domestic space.

Prodigality was considered a seriously damaging disorder, which had the power of impairing a person's rational faculties. Applied only to men, it was seen as a distortion of the ideal of the *paterfamilias*, since it damaged their ability to provide for the economic and moral needs of the family. Their squandering of resources, open defiance of family hierarchies, and disrespect for behavioral codes were seen as a serious diminution of the masculine ideal. Prodigality had different connotations according to age and social role, but all of the interdicted had powers of administration over the family patrimony (even 18-year-olds who had recently inherited) and in most cases were interdicted at the request of a close relative – a mother, a wife, an elder son, or a brother. Actions typical of a prodigal included excessive spending, reckless behavior, extravagant actions, indiscriminate selling of household goods to finance their pleasures, gambling, and frequent drunkenness, all marked by manifestations of unrestrained passions, recognized in their uncontrollable characters, changeable tempers, and frequent violent eruptions. All these indicators fitted under the umbrella of the "vice of prodigality," a disorder considered severe enough to have the affected person declared mentally incapable of managing his affairs, interdicted, and submitted to the authority of the Magistrato dei Pupilli.

Prodigality was characterized differently according to age, and we can identify three typologies: young and mostly unmarried men, middle-aged married men, and elderly widowers. Age and gender are at the core of the characterizations of prodigality, entailing a profound reflection regarding proper behavior according to the different family roles through the stages of male life. In this evaluation, the individual's behavior, reactions, and, most of all, psychological disposition were taken as indicators of their mental capacity. Prodigality was understood as a category of incapacity that, on the surface, related only to economic mismanagement but which involved assessments that pointed to an underlying disordered mind and disturbed disposition, to the extent of blending with the categories of madness (*demente, mentecatto, furioso*). The study of prodigality sheds light on the characterization of mental incapacity, broadening the picture of what was defined as madness. In the process of petitioning for the interdiction of a prodigal, families reshaped legal and medical knowledge of madness into a socially meaningful language. Mental incapacity was defined through and by social experience, disclosing a new concern for the mental and emotional worlds that tended to explain disordered behaviors as a mental dysfunction.

Adolescents and young prodigals: indiscipline, irreverence, and pleasures

When they applied to young men, interdiction petitions by reason of prodigality generally specified how old they were, and the disorder was distinctly constructed in relation to their tender age. Thus, the study of young prodigals sheds light on the understanding of youth as a separate period of life.[6]

Although also tied to cultural representations and social role, the beginning of a male adult life was strongly marked by the legal framework. While the Magistrato dei Pupilli established majority at 18 years, orphans would be under supervision of the Pupilli until 25, and interdiction procedures ascribed the category of youth to men until they were about 28 to 30 years old. Legally speaking, the history of prodigals started at the age of 18 in early modern Tuscany because, in order to be interdicted, the individual had to have gained the right to administer his patrimony (whether by receiving an inheritance or, in the case of orphans, because they had come of age). Practically speaking, however, the career of prodigals often started before they acquired the right to administer their patrimonies.

The case of young spendthrifts is also marked by the fact that they were usually unmarried firstborn sons, and most of the time their fathers had passed away and they had been under the legal guardianship of their mothers or under the care of another close relative. As a consequence, they were usually denounced by their mothers, followed by their tutors and agnate uncles. In this respect, young prodigals are to be examined in the context of the legal powers given to women by the Tuscan patrilineal system in so far as their cases were, in many instances, managed by their mothers, who would usually be appointed administrators of the patrimony after the interdiction.[7] This means that young prodigals were under their mothers' power, who would be able to intervene in their lives and youthful actions by means of the powers granted to them by the interdiction. The fact that mothers were the recurring petitioners in the interdiction of young spendthrifts is significant. Most had been appointed legal guardians (by their deceased husbands or by the Pupilli), which meant that petitioning for the interdiction of their son would not be the first time they came into contact with the Pupilli. They, therefore, had a practical knowledge of the judicial system that wives, for example, did not necessarily possess. They knew the mechanisms of the institution; they were familiar with the language that had to be employed; and they knew, finally, how to manage the system to accomplish what they intended.

Timing in the identification of young prodigality was crucial. When cases of young spendthrifts were disclosed to the authorities, mothers commonly supported their petition with the claim that the sons had shown a "bad inclination" toward dissipation from adolescence.[8] Proof of this tendency was often provided by special clauses in the father's will, who had stated that his elder son was not to obtain full administration of the patrimony until he was 22 (and sometimes older) or even completely denying him the right to inherit. Elders saw young prodigals as a direct threat to the family (both economically and morally speaking), because of the early onset of a behavioral disorder that was widely known and feared in Tuscan society.

Prodigality of the young men was characterized by their tendency to spend excessively to satisfy their pleasures and passions (from clothing to alcohol, women, and gambling), which led them to compulsively sell all kinds of items in order to cover their expenses. For the same purpose, they were said to engage in illegal transactions, take on debts, and commit fraud. These actions were generally accompanied by being openly confrontational toward their mothers' authority and family hierarchies and the possession of an unruly character and an uncertain temper, manifested through abrupt changes of mood and an uneasy disposition.[9] Petitioners usually argued that, in the absence of a strong paternal figure, the young man who manifested the signs of prodigality would be lost in the perils posed by uncontrolled passions if he were not controlled with the help of the Pupilli in due time. But, in fact, the career of the young prodigal often proved that, notwithstanding the interdiction and the Pupilli's intervention and although the officials of the Pupilli had the support of the police forces to make spendthrifts yield to their mother's authority, they would continue to have uncontrollable characters, committing all sorts of extravagancies and excesses. As a result, some of them remained interdicted for life, others were interdicted for a short period, and others were interdicted at various points during their lives, in which case we have the opportunity of following their careers of prodigality through their entire lifecycles, and to observe how it changed according to their age and family role. Prodigality had particular connotations when affecting young men, but it was not exclusive to youth nor did it end with it.

The young prodigal had a disorder the roots of which were to be found in adolescence, but which came to light with the inheritance of his patrimony, whether because he had turned 18 (if he had been fatherless before he came of age) or because his father had recently died. The fact that they had recently come of age or that they were in their early twenties was relevant insofar as it defined both the kind of dangers they posed to the family and determined the way their disorder manifested itself. The case of Alcino Contucci from Montepulciano, interdicted just before he turned 18, seems particularly illustrative. His disorder had started after the death of his father, when he was 14 years old, in the form of continuous escapades from the different places he had been sent for his education (seminars and schools), open disrespect for the authority of his mother and tutors, disregard for his rank, and a clear tendency to squander family monies.[10] When his mother and uncles succeeded in bringing him back home (he had escaped to Naples to enroll as a soldier), he went as far as to steal from his mother and announce that when he turned 18, he would abandon her for good, threatening to divide the patrimony and dissipate the portion belonging to him.

Youth was regarded as a particularly problematic period and a crucial one for a man.[11] The importance of youth was enhanced by the circumstances in which a young spendthrift found himself: most of them had faced the experience of changing from a subordinate position to being their own masters and having the family patrimony at their disposal. In a prodigal, youth appeared as a force difficult to resist driving toward a complete loss of control. However, a young man defined as prodigal was not necessarily thought to be experiencing a crisis of youth or having a temporary derangement. In this sense, prodigality was not only seen as the effect of a wild stage or a difficult

62 *Mad spendthrift men*

phase. Interdiction was a powerful weapon to control difficult young men, but the notion of difficulty must be extended so as to include the perception of a disorder that went beyond the framework of deliberate recklessness.

Interdiction of young spendthrifts acted as a preventive measure that had a twofold purpose: to avoid economic ruin and to control or restrain the individual, saving him from a future of moral ruin. In this regard, early detection of the tendency to the vice of prodigality was considered particularly important. The seed that was planted in youth would be difficult to extirpate later. If a young boy under 18 years of age was corrupt, this represented a strong clue as to how he would behave in the future, "his present life being a strong indication and argument of his future life."[12] The very fact that they had developed the tendency toward prodigality in adolescence was used to maintain that they were unlikely to change and that it was in their nature to be vicious, uncontrollable, passionate, and therefore disturbed. Or, as a state official said in the case of the 26-year-old Simeone Carlo Beroardi, his "vice of prodigality, and natural instinct to squander and dissipate" were so deeply entrenched, that it had not been possible "to remove it, or eradicate it from his soul [*animo*]."[13] But, generally, they were not necessarily considered doomed to prodigality, the proof being that the interdiction could be and was lifted as soon as they could prove they were capable of managing their affairs. Youth could be framed as a conditioning factor that increased tendencies to prodigality, but it was commonly supposed that with time and, most of all, marriage, they would be able to resume control over their mental faculties.

The incapacity of young men aged from around 18 to their early twenties was also presented by their relatives in terms of inexperience, who argued that given their "immature age," they were not yet prepared to act as property holders.[14] This situation was rendered more grave by the fact that, together with the administration of the family patrimony, they had inherited the duty of providing for their mothers' and siblings' wellbeing, a completely new role which, given their reprehensible background, was not considered appropriate for them to perform. Above all, they were presented as lacking the necessary prudence for proper economic behavior, not only because of their youth, but also because of their unruliness, their characters, and their opprobrious tendencies. That they were of "such a fresh age" (*età così fresca*) made them both prone to diversions and passions and weak and inexperienced in economic management.[15] Their mothers or tutors denounced them as being subject to useless distractions, behaving imprudently and lacking the necessary character and talent to manage their affairs. But they were also thought to "lack experience of the world" (*senza esperienza di mondo*), which prevented them from being aware of the risks of living a life of pleasure and dissipation.[16] For all these reasons, "youth" could be used as the determining factor to argue in support of an interdiction petition, as happened in the case of the 20-year-old Vincenzio Fossi, whose relatives declared that "because of his youth, and imprudent conduct, we think it is convenient that his administration be interdicted."[17] However, although youth was thought to play such a crucial role in the development of prodigality, young men were not interdicted at a higher proportion than middle-aged or old men.

Young men denounced as prodigals to the Pupilli were also described by their families as frivolous pursuers of social prestige, devoted to superfluous diversions, and consumed by their desire to appear as independent gentlemen who treated themselves splendidly (*trattarsi splendidamente*).[18] This was particularly true in the cases of impoverished noble families, as young men made desperate attempts to maintain their status. Such was the case of the 26-year-old Simeon Carlo Beroardi, who indulged his "natural instinct to squander" in an effort to live in grandeur, an instinct in other cases framed as "the passion that dominates him."[19] Noble of birth, Simeon Carlo became an orphan at 20 and taking advantage of his position as the only direct heir, he went to Florence to have the time of his life and dissipate all his inheritance on carriages, servants, showy clothing, feasts, and socializing (*conversazioni geniali*). He refused to leave Florence to confine himself in Castiglion Fiorentino, as the officials of the Pupilli fruitlessly ordered, controlled as he was by his vices. He devoted himself to idleness, maintained a close friendship with a married woman and, due to his quarrelsome character, was more than once challenged to duels.[20]

As in the case of Simeon Carlo Beroardi, petitioners recognized the disorder of prodigality in these men's indiscipline and irreverence and in their open disrespect for legal rules and behavioral norms. They were bent on living above their means or trying to appear as if they were of a higher rank than they actually were. Often laden with debts, these young men would leave the city to avoid paying their creditors or even to avoid direct commands of the officials of the Pupilli. In a feature that we will also encounter with regard to middle-aged and old prodigals, their disorder spoke of conflicting expectations of life, their gender roles, and their masculinity.[21] If middle-aged prodigals breached the accepted codes of behavior with their disregard for their role as *paterfamilias*, young men did it with their obstinate preference for idleness, grandeur, and debauchery. They refused to work or study (depending on the case and their social rank), preferring instead to completely dedicate their time to the satisfaction of their passions and appetites, recklessly pursuing the excesses of the new enlightened sociability. In this respect, compared to middle-aged and old-age prodigality, the aristocratic ethos is central in the evaluation of young prodigals' behavior, particularly their breaches of propriety in their excessive spending, and their interpretation of the identity, prerogatives, and duties of their rank.

Perceptions of prodigal behavior should be thus interpreted as entrenched in changing notions of masculinity and marked by the eighteenth-century clash between different conceptions of it among different generations.[22] In this sense, the conflicts between other family members and young spendthrifts shed light on a debate about masculinity, normativity, and expected moral and economic behavior, particularly visible in the opposing poles of spending and saving, where the former was accompanied by following a career of drinking, dueling, and leisurely pursuits and the latter by the more rational, polite, and self-controlled model of behavior. The boundaries between a social life *à la mode* and the carrier of a prodigal doomed to interdiction were hard to define, and it mostly depended on generational conceptions of social life and decorous and desirable levels of spending, which were increasingly contrasting.[23]

One excellent example of this is the growing fear that arose in Georgian England against profligacy. Nicola Phillips has examined the memoirs of a father who recorded the descent of his profligate son into financial ruin, delinquency, and moral depravation, which she takes as a case study in order to examine intergenerational conflicts and clashing conceptions of social status, gentlemanly behavior, masculinity, and financial values.[24] The father of the profligate son was at first desperate and then firmly condemnatory of his son's behavior, until he eventually decided to observe and keep written records of his son's depravity. Although Phillips only touches upon the connection between moral depravity and insanity, the profligate son of her study posed challenges to society that his contemporaries often took to be a sign of "some form of insanity."[25] This case and the life of the Tuscan prodigal bear an interesting resemblance. Profligacy generated a similar condemnation than in Tuscany, only that in the latter's case the prodigal's disruption of social norms and family duties was liable for interdiction, an alternative not available in England. Furthermore, in Tuscany, this line of behavior was many times openly taken to be an indicator of mental disturbance.

Refusal to work and persistent or obstinate idleness are a characteristic of all three different ages of prodigality, but in young men it was presented as particularly troublesome because they had no direct paternal authority.[26] In fact, the absence of a paternal figure was identified as one of the causes that could lead to the manifestation of prodigality. Tutors would often complain to the Magistrato dei Pupilli about their pupil's disobedience during adolescence, when they refused to go to school or obey any of their commands, constantly escaping, and taking refuge with their mothers when they were not the legal guardians. This behavior would escalate with their coming of age, when their disrespect for authority and family hierarchies was increasingly characterized by a life completely dedicated to vices and passions, gambling, and squandering. One such case was Giuseppe Maria Fede, an 18-year-old who,

> seduced by bad company, has abandoned his studies, and has devoted himself to pleasures and conversations, and has in such a way shaken off his subjection to the tutor, that he does not come back home if not after midnight, to rest few hours in his bed, and return the next morning to the usual career completely opposed to good custom, and to the education he received.[27]

Interdiction in such cases came as a valuable (and external) resource to restrain an otherwise uncontrollable, intractable young man, over whom the tutor and mother had lost all possibility of re-establishing their authority. Interdictions were used as a last resort, once all other possible resources to control the young man had been exhausted. Sending an interdiction petition meant that a state of urgency had been reached, when the prodigal had trespassed the accepted limits of tolerance, putting himself and the patrimony at eminent risk. Every available family strategy had been put to work before turning to the Pupilli, as is evidenced by the fact that interdiction petitions were generally supported by the extended family. For instance, mothers were supported by their kin or by paternal relatives of the defendant, who had previously tried, unsuccessfully, to influence the behavior of the individual. A similar feature appears when petitions were sent by elder brothers, uncles, or even young wives, all of whom appear strongly backed by the rest of the family. Particularly in the case of young prodigals, both family lines tended to be united by the aim of controlling them, suggesting an agreement that is less present in cases concerning older prodigals or in the case of interdictions by reason of *demenza*, in all of which conflicting views and contesting positions about defendants are much more visible.

However, interdiction was not always successful in governing an individual, and sometimes it would not even achieve the purpose of reducing his spending. The family conflict would not necessarily be resolved with the interdiction, and problematic situations would follow, sometimes during the whole life of the interdicted. The case of Count Giovacchino Ceuli from Pisa is particularly interesting here because, although his age was not given, he appears repeatedly in the records of the Magistrato dei Pupilli, giving us a long-term view of his character; the evolution of his disorder; and the reactions of his relatives, his surrounding community, and the state officials. He was interdicted in August of 1749 when his creditors petitioned the Pupilli describing him as a prodigal consumed by a passion for gambling. He reappears again in 1752, now married with a small child, having left Pisa, and still ruled by his passions. On this occasion, he was depicted by his wife Anna Maria Lorenzani as a violent man, capable of doing anything in order to obtain more money to satisfy his passions. She feared him and denounced his continuing insults and mistreatments to the magistracy. She had been unsuccessful in trying to straighten her husband out and even petitioned to be allowed to live separate from him, so that she and their child could be safe from his disruptive character.[28] According to the local authority's report, the mistreatments she suffered were driven by Giovacchino's constant need for money and her refusal to give it to him. His unruly and increasingly violent character led to his incarceration in 1757, this time on the initiative of the officials of the Pupilli themselves.[29] Eight years after the interdiction, he had become a man completely ruled by his passions, manifesting increasingly dangerous outbursts of rage, performing "criminal and arbitrary acts" that were mostly fraud, and a willingness to fight with whoever opposed his intentions, be it a creditor or a state official.

Giovacchino Ceuli was perceived as uncontrollable, unreasonable, and unmanageable, and his disruptiveness did not seem to change with age.

Articulated upon narratives that from diverse perspectives, through different voices, and at various times concurred in their negative assessment, the case shows that the disorder behind the prodigal often went beyond a mere life crisis that would yield with adulthood. His behavioral disorder and disturbed disposition accompanied him and tortured his relatives for over 15 years. Although his interdiction was lifted in 1758 after a promise on his part to mend his ways, he still appears in the records until at least 1764, as continuing his profligate ways.

At the same time, this case shows that the conflicts and tensions surrounding a prodigal were not necessarily solved by the interdiction, regardless of his age. After the interdiction, all the signs of unruly character, and especially the outbursts of fury, and the overwhelming passions that were said to govern those individuals were generally redirected toward the person who had been appointed the new administrator of their patrimonies. In the case of young prodigals, this task was often given to the mother, which could cause the conflict to flare up, instead of reducing it. All their anger was aimed at the person who denied them the use of their resources, with increasing irritation when it was not possible to demand from the "obstinate administrator [in this case the mother] who had never wanted to obey his command, neither through letters, nor through begging."[30]

In the power games between family members, mothers and wives could sometimes be in opposing positions, as the interdicted son would use his wife as means of diminishing the mother's power. The issue of the administration of the patrimony was at the very core of the conflict both before and also after the interdiction. Giovacchino Ceuli chose between his mother and his wife as to which would have control over him, deciding ultimately for the latter. In general, wives played an instrumental role in the attempts to govern unruly prodigals both before and after the interdiction. Wives appear as influential agents that could convince their husbands to return home and reassume their duties as *paterfamilias*, in a last resort to bring them to their senses. When Giovacchino Ceuli fled Pisa for the city of Massa, where he continued his disorderly life "gambling and spending needlessly," his wife Anna Maria Lorenzani also went there, "advised by relatives in order to induce her husband to return to Pisa and to conduct himself prudently."[31] Wives could be valuable in trying to reclaim a prodigal, but success was not guaranteed and deeper conflicts could arise from their intervention as in this case. Ana Maria's attempts to correct her husband ended violently and unsuccessfully, as she herself informed the Pupilli. But 7 years later, Giovacchino petitioned for his wife to be appointed as administrator instead of his mother, whom he said he could not trust, and with his wife as administrator, "at least the supplicant would be sure of everything, and quiet in soul and body."[32]

Overall, the young prodigal's disorder was constructed in terms of a lack of control, indicated by his unrestrained ways of living (*sregolato modo di vivere*),[33] his unruly character, and by the fact that he lived his life completely at the mercy of all kinds of pleasures and vices. All this would engender what was called improper and/or extravagant behavior, and these were all characteristics that were identified as the symptoms of an "irregular head" (*capo irregolare*).[34] These men were disqualified from administering their patrimony and managing their own affairs because of their irrational behavior, being ruled by their passions and appetites. They were thought to be gentlemen lost in their passions (*gentiluomo perduto*),[35] were they drinking, gambling, women, or *crapule* – the vice of eating and drinking excessively. Their youth was also declared responsible for their frivolous desires and particularly for their weakness or their easily influenced nature. They were presented as having a temper that was too complaisant and easy, which made them prone to the influence of friends of *bel tempo*.[36] The pernicious influence of these kinds of friends was thought to act as a seductive force pushing them toward taverns, gambling, and other vices. And those vices were precisely the sign needed to declare a man mentally unable to manage his affairs, for they indicated that other forces, different from will and rationality, controlled him.

Thus the young spendthrift proved his incapacity to administer his patrimony particularly through this lack of rationality. This was demonstrated by his dissipation, his pursuit of pleasure, and his unwise conduct. But it was also proved by his emotional behavior, constant disruptions, and uncontained rage. Prodigality, thus, also presupposed emotional disturbances, making the man prone to *furiosi trasporti* (furious agitations or perturbations of the soul) or making the man prone, in general, to violent outbursts of anger.[37]

Young prodigals were prisoners of vices that were thought to overshadow their capacity for discernment. It was on account of this that they acted unwisely and irrationally, as if their minds were not functioning properly. It was thought that a man who spent so much time in taverns in the company of married women, caring only for vanities and pleasures, had lost his senses. In fact, when a prodigal was declared "cured" from his vicious inclinations, it was because he had started to demonstrate better discernment and a wiser conduct. For instance, Elena Poletti argued that her son should be freed from interdiction: "because those vicious inclinations for which she made recourse to interdict him from the administration have ceased in him, and because he is bound to a better discernment and wiser conduct."[38]

The adult prodigal: vicious and passionate heads of family

Another group that can be identified among the prodigals is that of middle-aged heads of family, whose precise age was usually not recorded, but which can be roughly established as being between their thirties and fifties. Constituting the majority of the interdicted by reason of prodigality, these men have in common that they were usually married and had young offspring and that their disorder was strongly connected to their breaching of their role as *paterfamilias*. Petitions, most of them signed by their wives, characterized them as husbands and fathers who had openly abandoned their

68 *Mad spendthrift men*

duties. As in the cases of young prodigals, women generally petitioned with the support of kinsmen of either line of the family, although it could also happen that wives made an alliance with their mothers-in-law, together requesting the interdiction.

The notion of natural incapacity is of particular importance in the case of middle-aged prodigals, as if it was natural for them to squander just because they lacked the (mental) capacity to act differently. A middle-aged prodigal's dissipation stemmed from the "lack of capacity [*mancanza di capacità*] to administer his patrimony and regulate his affairs," as was said regarding a prodigal in 1767.[39] It is precisely because this *mancanza di capacità* was implicated that there is nothing to suggest that prodigality was deemed a voluntary disorder while only madness was considered an involuntary condition.[40] There are cases when prodigal actions were deemed to be the effect of deliberate recklessness and where vices and passions were judged as tendencies that could have been controlled if they had a stronger willpower. But in any case, the disorder was presented in terms of an inherent tendency, natural incapacity, or innate instability – all of which occurred regardless of the intentions of the affected individual.

Descriptions of the middle-aged prodigal include the same symptoms that we found in young prodigals: dissipation, a propensity to take on needless and capricious debts, irregular or illegal economic practices, dissoluteness, and debauchery. They were also described as extravagant and disturbed, of unruly and violent character, emotionally unstable, and governed by their passions and vices. The difference between constructions of young and middle-aged prodigals lies in how these signs were attached to a setting contingent upon their position in the family. On the one hand, their breaching of behavioral codes was gauged against what was expected for a good head of family. But on the other, their disorder posed a set of problems which differed from the ones posed by young or old prodigals.

The aggravating factor in the case of middle-aged prodigality was their open disregard toward their role as *paterfamilias* and their responsibility toward their wife and children. In this category, the nuclear family is invariably mentioned when petitioners tried to illustrate the negative effects of the disordered behavior. The father's desire to escape from them or the actual abandonment of wife and children commonly appear in descriptions given by women and their male kin. Wives accuse their husbands of incurring all kinds of unnecessary debts; dissipating the patrimony in all sorts of vices and diversions; and then abandoning wife, children, and debts. Consequently, the abandonment of their duties as active heads of the family comes as the first symptom of the middle-aged prodigal disorder to both prove the negative consequences of a prodigal career and illustrate the gravity of the disorder itself. This is important, because in eighteenth-century Tuscany it could be proven that debts had been contracted for justified reasons, in which case, the man responsible would not be interdicted. Although, in this case, he would not have escaped, and he would not have been described as vicious.

Most of all, a man incurring in justified debts would not have failed in his gender duties.

The most obvious particularity of these men's prodigality can be framed in terms of their having wife and young children that they were responsible for, which in the case of young prodigals was not yet on the horizon and in the case of elder prodigals had ceased to be. Thus the offense of the middle-aged prodigal was aggravated by the fact that, through his dissipation, he was denying his wife and children the necessary resources for living. The disorder of the prodigal *paterfamilias*, namely that he was neglecting (or that he had "always" neglected) his role as head of the family, had its roots in a mental faculty that did not work properly. For instance, the prodigal Ranieri Fares, interdicted in June 1765, was described in the testimonies as a father of 10 children who wasted all his income on useless things and who had "never thought about giving a good education to his family, or about their necessary maintenance, having gambled all the money he had earned."[41]

Interdiction procedures show the extent to which the model of a good head of family was defined by their behaviors in both the private or domestic sphere as well as in the public world.[42] The private behavior could affect the reputation of a man and his family, particularly if he did not perform his duties as father and husband with an adequate measure of rationality, self-control, and economic management. Similarly, idleness, a refusal to work, conduct their business, or supervise the good functioning of their possessions were also taken as measure of an internal and domestic disorder and figure in many complaints. Quite at odds with what was expected for the ideal head of family, prodigals persisted in giving priority to the fulfillment of their passions and caprices over their duties, an aberration that forced their relatives to request interdiction.

Their prodigal actions and behavior put not only the family reputation at risk, but also the economic resources for its subsistence. The interdiction of a middle-aged prodigal, especially when he had a wife and young children, often reflected the desire of his next of kin to avoid the responsibility (which, in the absence of the father, would fall to them) of feeding and maintaining the abandoned family. For instance, Francesco Guastalli was denounced as a squanderer by his brothers because, in addition to his prodigal behavior, he had abandoned his family, with great "disadvantage and disaster for his family." They tried to convince him to come back and reassume his duties, even promising that they would pay all his debts if he would abandon his vices, but "his pertinacity in wanting to live only according to his own caprice" forced them to turn to the magistracy, requesting the interdiction.[43] As this case shows, when men could not be convinced by words to leave their pleasures and caprices, or to come back home and guarantee a proper life for their wife and children, they would have to be forced by the Magistrato dei Pupilli. If their behavior could not be changed by such a corrective measure, at least the patrimony would be secured for their wives' and children's maintenance. Here lies another interesting difference compared to young and elderly prodigality, where the petitioners' major concern was the inheritance.

Denunciations of prodigality were not only centered on reckless economic mismanagement. The behavior typical of a spendthrift also comprised other behavioral irregularities, including some that would lead to petitioning for the interdiction of an insane person. As in the case of young prodigals, violent behavior was also a recurring image in the description of the middle-age spendthrift, with the difference that in the cases of the former the anger was directed against creditors and occasionally against the mother, and in the public sphere, anger was vented in street brawls. In the case of heads of family, on the contrary, anger was usually directed against the wife. In the context of shaping notions of mental incapacity, descriptions of violent reactions of prodigals are particularly interesting given the recurring reference to their perturbed emotional states. Because they were known to be ungovernable, of high temper, and subject to unrestrained passions, they were also feared. Besides the evident similarity with declared cases of madness, the violent outbursts of prodigals were often the reason for the magistracy's intervention. With this behavior, they showed not only disregard for their duties but also a lack of the self-control that was deemed so important in a good, rational head of family. Men should never lose their tempers in the grip of uncontrolled passions, for a man enslaved by his passions was a man who had lost his rational capacities.[44] An uncontrolled body was connected to an uncontrolled mind, which in turn signified irrationality. In this context, their lack of control over their mental and emotional state was used by the families as arguments to justify an interdiction. In addition, allegations of vice, especially with regard to drinking and gambling, were crucial.

If drinking and gambling were sometimes a part of the young prodigal's disorder, in the case of the middle-aged they often appear as the defining factor of the disorder. Heavy gambling and a tendency to drunkenness were strong grounds for a petition for interdiction. This is particularly the case in the narratives of middle-aged prodigality, many of which characterized the defendants' altered states of mind due to inebriation and an uncontrollable desire to gamble. These two so-called "vices" were identified both as the paradigmatic symptoms of the middle-aged prodigal and its causal factors. Rather than being reckless pursuers of splendor and pleasures, undisciplined, violently disobedient, and disrespectful of social hierarchies, as young prodigals were said to be, the middle-aged were primarily described by their relatives as consumed by alcohol and gambling; lost in the effects of such vices; and, because of this, irrational, violent, and unable to control themselves.

Alcohol and, perhaps to a lesser degree, gambling were thought to seriously compromise the mental faculties, producing mental incapacity. Scholars have suggested that patterns of alcohol consumption changed in eighteenth-century Europe, producing a shift in the cultures of alcohol. As there was an increase in the amount consumed, alcohol and the private and social conflicts associated with it acquired new visibility as one of the century's public concerns.[45] This went hand in hand with changes in the representations of drunkenness, particularly regarding the damaging effects it had on mental faculties.[46] In the course of the century, it became clear that excessive drinking could not only produce physical damage, but could also cause insanity, destroying the reason and neutralizing will.[47] The eighteenth-century period in Tuscany witnessed the proliferation of a series of measures to regulate gambling and public spaces devoted to alcohol consumption (*bettolle, cantine*), demonstrating the new public concern generated by these "vices."[48]

The most negative consequence of excessive alcohol consumption was believed to be the effects it produced in the mental faculties of the drinker. Alcohol was deemed able to obscure rationality and will, making the person "stupid in mind."[49] In fact, the Italian term used was *ebrio*, which meant "to have one's mind disturbed and the intellect altered by inebriation." *Ebbrezza*, in turn, was defined as the obfuscation of the mind caused by excessive alcohol consumption.[50] Similarly, to get drunk (*imbriacare*) was to ingest "so much wine, that the vapors and spirits ascend to the brain, obfuscating the intellect."[51] Attesting to the ubiquity of these understandings of the effects of alcohol, the expressions used in interdiction petitions were that the drunkard had "almost lost the use of reason."[52] Petitioners identified drunkenness as a causal factor of madness that made the individual mentally deranged and incapable of governing himself, and this was said to be the main causality of their squandering behavior. The very fact that the individual was continuously under the effect of alcohol and controlled by the desire to gamble was thought to demonstrate that there was no possibility of a future change in his behavior. Drunkenness, in particular, was seen as proof that it was not a temporary crisis or a difficult phase in their lives. Besides, given the effects these vices exerted on the defendants' minds, they were seen as helpless victims to the seductions of ill-intentioned friends, who could deceive them and profit from their weakness and alleged stupidity.[53] Furthermore, petitioners argued that because the mental capacities of a drunkard were compromised, he could not be held responsible for managing his life and affairs.

In the reprobation of excessive alcohol consumption, we also find a strong disapproval of taverns as places of homosociability. Rather than focused on the violence commonly associated with taverns in criminal records, interdiction petitions centered their condemnation on the type of men that could be found drinking in them, usually characterized as coming from a lower rank than the defendant. Honor and respectability were at risk to those frequenting these places, which had such a power over men that they could even become their homes (there are frequent reports of drunk prodigals who were said to actually live in the taverns). They were also places associated with a licentious life and the presence of women of ill repute, where men would forget their honor and basic duties.

Drinking also made the task of the administrator difficult, as the interdicted would demand money to support his vice, and the cases prove that often it was easier to have the prodigal drinking at the tavern than at home making violent outbursts because alcohol was denied to him. The administrators were in fact accused of wasting resources vital to the daily living of the family through their "conceding to the desires, and irregular conduct of the submitted [the interdicted], giving him the indulgence of living in drunkenness, and of being constantly in taverns."[54] The domestic difficulties aroused by drinking, gambling, and debauchery were aggravated by the emotional component of the prodigal's disorder. They were thought to be emotionally unstable, which was expressed with references to an unruly character, uncontrolled temper, or, more commonly, extravagant humor. This instability often resulted in violent reactions, stemming from their need to satisfy their vices. The vicious prodigal, especially one consumed by the need for alcohol and gambling, was greatly feared by his wife, who would often seek refuge from her husband's outbursts of rage in her parents' home.

Some interdiction procedures, in addition to mentioning the dissipation of the patrimony, violent reactions, drinking, gambling, and an immoderate way of living, report the presence of a mistress and the consequent disrespect and mistreatment of the wife. Prodigality was understood as a category of mental incapacity that encompassed a recklessness and lack of control that affected not only economic behavior, but also morality. It was not only that they took on innumerable debts and unprofitable contracts and compulsively sold goods to finance their vices, but also that they were involved, repeatedly, with different women. This was generally not presented as a single adulterous relationship, or a unique affection for the wrong woman, but rather a tendency to strike up one relationship after another.

In many of these cases, the wife's petition centered exclusively around the defendant's economic misbehavior, while it was only in the extended and detailed accounts in the testimonies collected by the magistracy's informers that other misbehaviors emerged. For instance, in June of 1759, Agata Sammicheli, supported by her elder son, petitioned for the interdiction of Giovanni Sammicheli, her husband. In her description of her husband's behavior, she confined herself to describing his economic mismanagement, and it was only in the testimonies where his dissipation was connected with dishonorable behavior and violent actions against his wife. From Giovanni's place of origin, the magistracy was informed that Giovanni regularly frequented a lower-class woman's house "where he ordinarily spends most of the day eating, drinking, and having a good time (*bel tempo*) causing public scandal, this being one of the main reasons why he mistreats his wife both in words and in actions."[55] On account of these evidences, he was interdicted and submitted to the authority of the Pupilli.

Some months later, Giovanni Sammicheli petitioned to be released from his interdiction, claiming that the supplication made by his wife and elder son was false and arguing that they had plotted against him.[56] Strikingly, an official disavowal by his son and wife of their initial accusations supported Giovanni's petition. The case is illustrative because their retraction elicited skepticism from the Pupilli officials, and a series of interrogatories followed in order to make sure that Giovanni had not forced them to withdraw their complaint. This case is also remarkable because the strategy followed to petition for the release was a retraction and not a declaration of amendment, a path commonly taken in petitions for the interdiction to be removed. Be that as it may, Giovanni Sammicheli was indeed freed from the interdiction.

The act of denouncing a husband for prodigality must have been a difficult thing for a woman to do in the eighteenth century. Women were often worried that their husbands would react violently to their denunciation, as evidenced by the case of a wife who asked the Pupilli officials that they act as soon as possible because her husband's "extravagant humor" made her fear she was in danger.[57] Women's petitions do indicate their fear, but this does not mean that their vulnerability was translated into weakness. Interdiction procedures tend to show women as active agents in the process of shaping notions of legal incapacity, protected by their sons or by their kinsmen. In the theatre of legal proceedings related to prodigality, it was common for the interdicted to denounce family plots against them, and sometimes this must have been the case. Nonetheless, when the interdiction was requested for motives other than the protection of the patrimony and the family, we usually have a petition for the interdiction to be lifted following shortly after the initial sentence.

A wife's involvement in an interdiction procedure was not reduced to the act of denouncing her husband as squanderer; they also pleaded in his favor with the intention of demonstrating his improvement, his "honorable" behavior, sane state of mind, and economic abilities when they requested the interdiction be revoked. In most of these latter cases, women adduced the perils suffered by the family during the head of the family's submission to the Pupilli, the high expenses resulting from this situation, and the advantages that a restoration of the original hierarchical order would offer to the family. In many cases, the patrimony's administration was assigned to the wife, and this distortion of the traditional family structure was increased by the fact that women also became the de facto heads of family. In these cases, new conflicts followed the initial ones. The disempowerment of the head of the family imperiled the reputation and social position of the family and could also affect its economic future. It also seriously affected family life, for the interdicted seldom reacted passively to their disempowerment. All these facts indicate that petitioning for interdiction was not the easiest solution for controlling an unruly husband or for resolving a marital conflict. The interdiction of their husbands did not necessarily resolve women's conflicts.

Elderly prodigals: the liberties and restrictions of old age

The prodigal disorder affecting the elderly was primarily defined by age, with petitions generally presenting the defendant as being of an "advanced" or "decrepit" age. Their prodigality was attributed either to the natural decline of age or to the effect of some sort of seizure or "accident" as the petitions generally called it. But in both cases, the physical and mental effects of aging, identified as the central cause of their prodigality, played a crucial role. Historians have discussed the difficulty of determining the time that different societies defined as marking the onset of old age in the past. The marks of the change between adulthood and elderliness depended on cultural perceptions, legal precepts, and administrative regulations, but it has been established that the onset of old age in Early Modern Europe was held to occur in the sixties and seventies for men, and in the fifties for women, depending on the sources and their purposes.[58] In the case of eighteenth-century Tuscany, interdiction procedures defined men as of advanced or decrepit age when they were between their late sixties and their early eighties.[59]

As in the other two categories of prodigality, the disorder of old prodigals was identified primarily by their wrong economic decisions, excessive expenditure and growing debts, but with the difference that their squandering was said to be caused by the physical and mental consequences of their "decrepit" age. Their incapacity could range from physical impediments to mental derangement, which were identified as responsible for their capricious and extravagant actions, their vicious and licentious life, and their uncontrolled passions. The degree to which petitioners considered the defendant's decaying mental faculties to be the cause varied, for other factors were also held to play a role, such as the presence of the so-called natural tendency to squander. Notwithstanding the importance attributed by petitioners to their advanced age, descriptions of old-age prodigality often included expressions such as "he has always been a man of diversions" (*uomo di bel'tempo*).[60]

While young prodigals were usually denounced by their mothers or uncles and middle-aged prodigals by their wives, elderly prodigals were usually interdicted after a petition sent by their eldest son. That means that in the case of the elderly, their interdiction has to do with how old age was perceived by the younger members of the family, in particular, by those closest kin who had to confront the family and social problems produced by old age. The fact that old age was identified as a distinct and particularly problematic stage in life is confirmed by the fact that the interdiction petitions specifically defined these men as being of an advanced or decrepit age, many times stating their precise age. This suggests that their age was considered an important factor to be taken into account in order to understand their prodigality, measure its consequences, and design the possible solutions that the Pupilli's intervention could offer.

Bearing witness to the visibility of this age group, interdictions open a window onto the social responses to the challenges posed by the elderly, making them another entry point into what Angela Groppi has called "welfare before welfare." The care of the elderly, she argues, was considered a shared responsibility in early modern Europe, and the responses to old age resulted from a connection between private assistance and public intervention, both in the so-called "nuclear" families of the north of Europe and in the "extended" families of the south.[61] Focusing on eighteenth-century Rome, Groppi has suggested that the problem of the elderly was tackled through a carefully negotiated partnership between state policies and family strategies. The care of the elderly was considered a family responsibility, and the legal system promoted and imposed a rigid observance of this social duty.[62] Old people were admitted into institutional facilities only when their decrepitude could be proven and when the family could pay for them or in cases where their total abandonment by or lack of relatives was certain. At the core of Groppi's analysis lies the assertion that the care of the elderly in eighteenth-century Rome was the result of negotiated and constructed values of solidarity.[63] Judging from interdiction procedures, the situation of the elderly in eighteenth-century Tuscany posed challenges similar to those described by Groppi. The cases in which the officials of the Pupilli had to legally force a male son to pay for the maintenance of an elder parent are indeed significant. In this regard, the interdiction of an old father was a complicated matter, because the pleading son had to take responsibility for the care of the father, if he could manage to prove that the latter had reached a state of incapacity.

The elderly prodigals posed different problems than their younger counterparts, particularly when they were described as having a natural tendency to squander or had always been known to be extravagant and odd. In these latter cases, the extravagances, aggressive behavior, and dishonorable conduct of the denounced old man had been a permanent presence in the life of the family, but for some reason his misbehavior had become unbearable. This in part explains why squandering alone did not prompt families to request interdiction nor did the decision rest solely on economic concerns. This issue is discussed further in chapter 3, but is worth noting here that the moment for petitioning the interdiction of an old father had more to do with the exacerbation of his misbehavior, his lack of respect for the family honor, the aggravation of his mental derangement, the flaring up of family conflicts, or a change in the power balance of the family group.

Another difference that can be found in the perception of prodigality in the case of the elderly, compared to that of young or middle-aged defendants, has to do with the consequences of their squandering, which in the case of older prodigals was judged differently. The main concern of their kin when petitioning for an interdiction was no longer the maintenance and education of a young family, but, rather the inheritance, and in particular, the right of the eldest son to inherit an intact patrimony. But, again, it was not merely an economic concern. It is true that petitions contained a series of accusations that pointed to the defendants' lack of respect toward social norms, to their unreasonable economic behavior, and, above all, to the future of the inheritance. Nonetheless, the records of the Magistrato dei Pupilli also reveal that denouncing an old father as a prodigal was often used as a mechanism to resolve the conflicts caused by cohabitation with old parents, which could be even harder when adult sons and daughters had to cope with "powerful" fathers.

It is well known that power relations and shifting balances marked the relationships of the early modern family. Accusations against old squanderers often disclose these kinds of conflicts marked by a negative view, on the part of petitioners, of what it meant to be old. Their advanced age made the fathers useless and extremely problematic in the eyes of their closest kin. On the fathers' side, because the interdiction of an old father was an act of disempowerment, they usually did not remain passive in the face of an interdiction. A number of testimonies submitted by the old prodigals themselves reveal the abuses they had had to suffer. They expressed a feeling of being humiliated by their relatives, treated as if they were foolish, childish, and deprived of reason. In response to these accusations, they highlighted their strong will and clear awareness of the situation, expressing a distinct desire to be liberated from their son's or heir's control and often denouncing some sort of plot against them.

The petitions submitted to the Pupilli suggest that old parents could become a burden to their families, a constant inconvenience not only because they had to be taken care of, but also because their problematic and improper behavior compromised the family's honor and the transmission of the patrimony. At an age where most of them had married sons and daughters, they demonstrated an unrestrained desire for freedom to be liberated from their social and economic responsibilities, their paternal role, and their duties as husband, if they were still married. According to their relatives, their old age made them incapable of controlling themselves and behaving properly. They had lost their capacity of discernment and indeed their reason and were therefore intractable. The disturbed state of mind affecting the old prodigal prevented him from making rational decisions, whether because – due to this weakness – he was seduced into dissipation and extravagant actions or because his so-called "decrepit age" made him "impotent" in mind.

Old-age prodigality could also be aggravated by excessive alcohol consumption, which was often mentioned as being instrumental in the disorder. First, it was considered a dishonor to have an old father known to be a drunk and a habitué of taverns and other public places where alcohol was consumed. Second, the natural mental decay that developed with age was thought to be aggravated by the "abuse he makes of wine, to the point of being always in such a continual drunkenness, that it provokes in him a complete alienation of mind."[64] This "alienation of mind" caused by drunkenness, affecting the 85-year-old Giovan Battista Vinattieri, was held accountable for his intention to squander all his income with his young fiancée. Thus, it not only led him to attempt the complete dissipation of his patrimony but also moved him to choose a wife of a lower social rank, a decision considered completely contrary to good decorum and honor.

In fact, remarriage (most times with a younger women of a lower social rank) was another cause that could induce a son to petition for his old father's interdiction. Late remarriage was identified by petitioners as an endless source of family conflicts, and it was even used as confirmation of an old man's altered state of mind. For instance, they were said to spend all their income with the new wife, neglecting the rights of their sons and daughters.

As Gerardo del Ponte, an allegedly vicious prodigal who wanted to remarry, spend his remaining patrimony on his pleasures and denied a dowry and maintenance to his daughters and sons (aged between 17 and 21).[65] When they had offspring with the new wife, the conflicts increased, as in the case of the 77-year-old Girolamo Cocci, a man married for the third time who, according to the sons of his previous marriage, dissipated what they identified as *their* patrimony on his new and constantly growing new family.[66]

They could even be accused of dissipating their patrimony pursuing the love of the young lady without even marrying her. For example, Giuseppe Caiozzi at the age of 77 conceived an affection (*invaghitosi*) for a younger woman of inferior rank, whom he managed to marry to another man to avoid any suspicious rumors regarding their own romance, afterwards inviting the married couple to live with him. According to his daughter, who petitioned for the interdiction, the newlyweds were taking advantage of him and dissipating his patrimony, and Caiozzi was completely enraptured by the woman, which proved his state of mental incapacity.[67] It was certainly regarded as "extravagant" (either as an extravagant behavior or due to extravagant humor) to wish to remarry at such an old age. The disorder and offence in these cases was living with people of an inferior social rank, feeding them, financing their distractions and diversions, and thus seriously disrupting the codes of honor and the loyalty commanded by blood. Driven by their new infatuation, they would forget the blood ties that attached them to their sons and daughters and to their family name.[68] A father who mistreated his sons and daughters and who denied them what was "necessary for their living" to instead spend it in the satisfaction of his desires was a man of "extravagant humor."[69]

From this point of view, the old prodigal's disorder was characterized by his lack of respect for the codes and norms appropriate to his gender and social rank. Old prodigals were usually said to follow their inclinations freely, showing a total disdain toward their relatives and family name. They were represented as being disrespectful of family hierarchies, disregarding the rights of the firstborn son, whether disinheriting him or discrediting him in front of the rest of the household.[70] A petition to submit an old prodigal to the Pupilli's arbitration was, therefore, an act of disempowerment of the head of the family and was one of the strategies that sons could use to undermine patriarchal authority.[71]

To illustrate the reprobation that the old prodigal's actions generated in his relatives, petitions often made reference to the character of the defendant, stressing particularly his inquietude, from his irritability and extravagant humor to his low spirits or oppressed spirits (*spirito abbattuto*). Petitioners shaped their accounts of old-age prodigality mostly based on the recognition of emotional disturbances, much more so than in petitions regarding younger prodigals. This suggests that the emotional disturbance recognized in the old prodigal was thought to be a sign of insanity more than in the other two types of prodigality.[72] The actions, gestures, manner of speaking, and emotional state of the old prodigal fit the expected pattern of madness. But, as in the cases of the young and middle-aged, they were interdicted on the grounds of prodigality, not of *demenza*.

It has to be said that interdiction procedures affecting old prodigals present narratives very similar to those appearing in cases of declared madness. But, in spite of the fact that most of the interdicted old men were more or less explicitly declared to be mentally disturbed, they were commonly categorized and interdicted as prodigals, and not as *dementi*. On account of this, the question here is why their families had tried to interdict them only at the end of their lives, if they had always been prodigals. The interdiction of Piero Bencivenni of "advanced age" is illustrative for this issue.[73] The supplication, made by his younger brother, alleged not only strictly economic misbehavior but also moral flaws, emotional instability, and mental dysfunction. The closing argument probably says more than the opening ones: the petitioner was 29 years old and, being Piero's younger brother, had hopes of inheriting his patrimony soon, and he was "fairly" worried that by that time it would be reduced to nothing. Consequently, the question remains: was the argument of supposed insanity and emotional instability presented as a means to accelerate the inheritance, or was it included because the man's behavior had become worse and he was unbearable to live with? The repetitive and vague testimonies included in this particular petition shed no light on the matter.

***

Here is where the problem of what determined the use of one category over the other (prodigality or *demenza*) in the interdiction proceedings comes to the forefront. It is perfectly reasonable to assume that for social and cultural reasons and particularly because interdiction in itself was dishonorable to the family, Tuscans preferred to declare that their deviant kin was prodigal rather than mad, which would entail labeling them under the category of *demenza*. A considerable number of petitions simply described the deviant actions of the defendant without using any label. In some of these cases, the behavior motivating the denouncement would only later be explicitly ascribed to madness, as in the case of Lorenzo Baldinotti, whom we met at the beginning of this book. The records of the Magistrato dei Pupilli also show that the label of prodigal was often interchangeable with the label of *demente*. A person could be interdicted for prodigality and afterwards, when lifting the interdiction, the officials of the Pupilli could say it had been originally issued by reason of *demenza*.[74] Or, someone could be labeled as prodigal even if he had been committed to the Tuscan mental hospital, Santa Dorotea.[75] This is not to imply that prodigality was only a category that allowed petitioners to disguise insanity. Instead, interdiction records suggest that prodigality was a category that included within it the notion of insanity.

As we saw in the first chapter, the practical conflation in which prodigality and *demenza* found themselves was not clear in traditional jurisprudence, but the interdiction records generally show that there was no practical reason to differentiate prodigality from insanity. Prodigal behavior in itself was held to result from a kind of mental disturbance. Being a prodigal was thought to entail irrationality, and a prodigal's reprehensible behavior "seems to arrive up to madness [*demenza*]."[76] Whether because of their excessive drinking, their irregular behavior, extravagant humor, and unrestrained passions, they all were thought to have lost control over their mental faculties. Petitioners attributed the actions of a prodigal to a perturbed and irrational state of mind. In so doing, the language they used to describe and explain prodigality speaks of a lay knowledge about mental disturbances entrenched in the particularities of social life. Eighteenth-century Tuscans were at ease in explaining their relative's behavior in terms of mental dysfunction and emotional imbalance and in identifying a lack of rationality as the key factor responsible for such a disorder.

Notes

1 Laurent Cartayrade, "Property, Prodigality, and Madness: A Study of Interdiction Records in Eighteenth-Century Paris," (PhD diss., University of Maryland, 1997), 308–310.
2 Cartayrade, "Property, Prodigality, and Madness," 60.
3 Elizabeth W. Mellyn, *Mad Tuscans and Their Families: A History of Mental Disorder in Early Modern Italy* (Philadelphia: University of Pennsylvania Press, 2014), 97.
4 Mellyn, *Mad Tuscans*, 103.
5 On the new concerns over enlightened sociability in Italy, see Roberto Bizzocchi, *Cicisbei. Morale privata e identità nazionale in Italia* (Rome and Bari: Laterza, 2008), 21–34 and 82–159.
6 Historians have tended to identify the time of the end of youth between 28 and 30 years old. Stages of life were determined not only by biological age, but also by cultural and legal considerations. Regarding adolescence and youth, see Ilaria Taddei, *Fanciulli e Giovani: Crescere a Firenze nel Rinascimento* (Florence: Leo S. Olschki Editore, 2001), 13–63; Richard Trexler, *Public Life in Renaissance Florence* (New York: Academic Press, 1980), 387–388; and J.A. Sharpe, "Disruption in the Well-Ordered Household: Age, Authority, and Possessed Young People," in *The Experience of Authority in Early Modern England*, ed. Paul Griffiths, Adam Fox, and Steve Hindle (Basingstoke: Palgrave Macmillan, 1996), 187–212.
7 The Florentine patrilineal system and its influence on the family structure, marriage alliances, and the role of women have been of major concern for historians of Renaissance and early modern Tuscany. See Giulia Calvi, *Il contratto morale. Madri e figli nella Toscana moderna* (Rome: Laterza, 1994); Isabelle Chabot, "Le gouvernement des pères: l'État florentin et la famille (XIVe-XVe siècles)," in *Florence et la Toscane XIVe-XIXe siècles. Les dynamiques d'un État italien*, ed. Jean Boutier, Sandro Landi, and Olivier Rouchon (Rennes: Presses Universitaires de Rennes, 2004), 241–262; Thomas Kuehn, *Law, Family and Women: Toward a Legal Anthropology of Renaissance Italy* (Chicago and London: The University of Chicago Press, 1991); among others.
8 ASF, MPAP, *Memoriali*, F. 2302, no. 286, September 1751.
9 From this point of view, the career of the Florentine prodigal seems no different from that of the English one, although, as shown by Nicola Phillips, parents did

80 *Mad spendthrift men*

not have the resource of interdiction to control them. See Nicola Phillips, *The Profligate Son: Or, a True Story of Family Conflict, Fashionable Vice, and Financial Ruin in Regency England* (Oxford: Oxford University Press, 2013).
10 ASF, MPAP, *Memoriali*, F. 2306, no. 65, December 1763.
11 See, for example, Sharpe, "Disruption in the Well-Ordered Household," and Trexler, *Public Life*, 387–399. The depths of the intergenerational conflicts of the eighteenth century, especially those associated with conflicting notions of masculinity, have been examined by Phillips, *The Profligate Son*.
12 ASF, MPAP, *Memoriali*, F. 2306, no. 77, February 1764.
13 ASF, MPAP, *Memoriali*, F. 2303, no. 189, June 1754.
14 ASF, MPAP, *Memoriali*, F. 2301, no. 166, November 1742.
15 ASF, MPAP, *Memoriali*, F. 2307, no. 77, September 1767.
16 ASF, MPAP, *Memoriali*, F. 2304, no. 53, August 1756.
17 ASF, MPAP, *Memoriali*, F. 2304, no. 104, June 1753.
18 ASF, MPAP, *Memoriali*, F. 2303, no. 26, March 1752.
19 ASF, MPAP, *Memoriali*, F. 2303, no. 189, June 1754 and ASF, MPAP, *Memoriali*, F. 2303, no. 49, August 1752, respectively.
20 In the absence of close relatives, the interdiction was petitioned in 1952 by his creditors. Two years later, his behavior still created a great concern for the authorities. ASF, MPAP, *Memoriali*, F. 2303, no. 22, February 1752, no. 26, March 1752 and no. 189, June 1754.
21 The discussion on the conflicting expectations with regard to gender roles in family disputes is vast. See, for instance, Linda A. Pollock, "Rethinking Patriarchy and the Family in Seventeenth-Century England," *Journal of Family History* 23, no. 1 (1998): 3–27; Suzanne Desan and Jeffrey Merrick, eds., *Family, Gender, and Law in Early Modern France* (Pennsylvania: The Pennsylvania State University Press, 2009); Alexander Cowan, *Marriage, Manners and Mobility in Early Modern Venice* (Aldershot: Ashgate, 2007); and Silvana Seidel Menchi and Diego Quaglioni, eds., *Coniugi nemici. La separazione in Italia dal XII al XVIII secolo* (Bologna: Il Molino, 2000).
22 Nicola Phillips, "Parenting the Profligate Son: Masculinity, Gentility and Juvenile Delinquency in England, 1791–1814," *Gender & History* 22, no. 1 (2010): 92–108; Henry French and Mark Rothery, "'Upon Your Entry into the World': Masculine Values and the Threshold of Adulthood among Landed Elites in England 1680–1800," *Social History* 33, no. 4 (2008): 402–422; and Michèle Cohen, "'Manners' Make the Man: Politeness, Chivalry, and the Construction of Masculinity, 1750–1830," *Journal of British Studies* 44, no. 2 (2005): 312–329.
23 On this, see Bizzocchi, *Cicisbei*, 64–66 and 94–96.
24 Phillips, *The Profligate Son*.
25 Phillips, *The Profligate Son*, 148, and also 50 and 62–63.
26 As discussed before, the majority of the cases presented before the Pupilli regarding young men correspond to individuals whose fathers had died and who were under the care either of their mothers or uncles. Of a total of 611 interdictions decreed between 1700 and 1775, I have found only five cases where the petitions for interdiction were signed by fathers.
27 ASF, MPAP, *Memoriali*, F. 2304, no. 53, August 1756.
28 Letter of Anna Maria Lorenzani, 16 May 1750, in ASF, MPAP, *Memoriali*, F. 2303, no. 31.
29 ASF, MPAP, *Memoriali*, F. 2304, no. 133, 23 August 1757.
30 ASF, MPAP, *Memoriali*, F. 2306, no. 109, July 1764.
31 ASF, MPAP, *Memoriali*, F. 2303, no. 31, 29 August 1757.
32 ASF, MPAP, *Memoriali*, F. 2306, no. 109, July 1764.
33 ASF, MPAP, *Memoriali*, F. 2302, no. 21, March 1747/48.
34 ASF, MPAP, *Memoriali*, F. 2303, no. 52, September 1752.

35 ASF, MPAP, *Memoriali*, F. 2302, no. 128, 12 August 1749.
36 The prodigality of Paolo del Rosso, nearly 20 years old, was explained in terms of his young age and his "complaisant and easy" temper. ASF, MPAP, *Memoriali*, F. 2303, no. 30, April 1752.
37 ASF, MPAP, *Memoriali*, F. 2304, no. 133, August 1757 and ASF, MPAP, Memoriali, F. 2303, no. 231, December 1754.
38 ASF, MPAP, *Memoriali*, F. 2306, no. 223, October 1765.
39 ASF, MPAP, *Memoriali*, F. 2307, no. 13, April 1767.
40 In contrast, interdiction procedures in eighteenth-century France made a distinction between financial irresponsibility derived from prodigality and that caused by madness, the first being voluntary and the second involuntary. Cartayrade, "Property, Prodigality, and Madness," 72.
41 ASF, MPAP, *Memoriali*, F. 2306, no. 170, June 1765.
42 It holds, thus, a close resemblance to what has been asserted by Leonore Davidoff and Catherine Hall regarding the ideal of domesticity of the middle class in late eighteenth-century England. See Leonore Davidoff and Catherine Hall, *Family Fortunes: Men and Women of the English Middle Class 1780–1850* (London: Hutchinson, 1987), 31–34, 149–180.
43 ASF, MPAP, *Memoriali*, F. 2307, no. 45, August 1767.
44 Elizabeth Foyster, "Male Honour, Social Control and Wife Beating in Late Stuart England," *Transactions of the Royal Historical Society* Sixth Series, 6 (1996): 215–224.
45 A. Lynn Martin, *Alcohol, Violence, and Disorder in Traditional Europe* (Kirksville, MO: Truman State University Press, 2009). For a more complete background on the cultures of alcohol before the eighteenth century, see Beat Kümin, *Drinking Matters: Public Houses and Social Exchange in Early Modern Central Europe* (Basingstoke and New York: Palgrave Macmillan, 2007); Beat Kümin and B. Ann Tlusty, eds., *The World of the Tavern: Public Houses in Early Modern Europe* (Aldershot: Ashgate, 2002); B. Ann Tlusty, *Bacchus and Civic Order: The Culture of Drink in Early Modern Germany* (Charlottesville and London: University Press of Virginia, 2001).
46 Dana Rabin, "Drunkenness and Responsibility for Crime in the Eighteenth Century," *Journal of British Studies* 44 (2005): 457–477.
47 Roy Porter, *Mind-Forg'd Manacles: A History of Madness in England from the Restoration to the Regency* (London: Penguin Books, 1990), 201; and Tlusty, *Bacchus and Civic Order*, 58.
48 See Lorenzo Cantini, *Legislazione Toscana*, vols. 20–27 (Florence: Stamp. Albizziniana da S. Maria in Campo, 1806), for instance, vol. 22, 154 and 203; vol. 23, 16, 187, 369, and vol. 26, 106, 158, 345. On the legislation regarding gambling, see also Andrea Addobbati, "I guastafeste. La legge toscana sul gioco del 1773," *Quaderni storici* 95, no. 2 (1997): 495–538, and, for the previous centuries, John K. Brackett, *Criminal Justice and Crime in Late Renaissance Florence 1536–1609* (Cambridge: Cambridge University Press, 1992), 116–117.
49 ASF, MPAP, *Memoriali*, F. 2304, no. 26, May 1756.
50 "Ebbro, Ebrio: Che ha la mente turbata, e lo intelletto alterato dall'ebbrezza," and "Ebbrezza: Offuscamento dello intelletto, cagionato da soperchio ber vino, o da simile cagione." *Vocabolario degli accademici della Crusca* (Florence: Appresso Domenico Maria Manni, 1729–1738), s.v. "ebbro, ebrio" and s.v. "ebbrezza," www.lessicografia.it/Controller?lemma=ebbro and www.lessicografia.it/Controller?lemma=ebbrezza, accessed August 8, 2020.
51 "Divenir briaco, che vale Bere tanto vino, che i fummi, e gli spiriti salgano al cervello, e offuschino lo 'ntelletto," *Vocabolario*, s.v. "imbriacare," www.lessicografia.it/Controller?lemma=imbriacare, accessed August 8, 2020.
52 ASF, MPAP, *Memoriali*, F. 2304, no. 115, July 1757.

Mad spendthrift men

53 For example, it could be said that "there is no shortage of people who profit from his weakness, leaving him bereft of money with gambling [*giuoco*] and with disadvantageous contracts." ASF, MPAP, *Memoriali*, F. 2303, no. 27, February 1752.
54 ASF, MPAP, *Memoriali*, F. 2304, no. 12, case initiated in September 1755.
55 ASF, MPAP, *Memoriali*, F. 2305, no. 14, September 1759.
56 ASF, MPAP, *Memoriali*, F. 2305, no. 53, February 1760 and ASF, MPAP, *Filza Lettere e Responsive*, F. 2522, 29 February 1760.
57 ASF, MPAP, *Memoriali*, F. 2306, no. 265, April 1766.
58 Paul Johnson, "Historical Readings of Old Age and Ageing," *Old Age from Antiquity to Post-Modernity*, ed. Paul Johnson and Pat Thane (London and New York: Routledge, 1998), 3–4. For instance, the beginning of old age in eighteenth-century Rome was signaled by the incapacity of the individual to take care of him or herself, which was connected to the possibilities of their relatives to assume their care. Angela Groppi, *Il welfare prima del welfare. Assistenza alla vecchiaia e solidarietà tra generazioni a Roma in età moderna* (Rome: Viella, 2010), 71–79. Biological and cultural conceptions and representations of old age have been the subject of numerous studies. See, for instance, Elizabeth Sears, *The Ages of Man: Medieval Interpretations of the Life Cycle* (Princeton, NJ: Princeton University Press, 1986); and Pat Thane, ed., *The Long History of Old Age* (London: Thames & Hudson, 2005).
59 On the visibility of old age, see Susannah Ottaway, *The Decline of Life: Old Age in Eighteenth-Century England* (Cambridge: Cambridge University Press, 2004); Groppi, *Il welfare prima del welfare*; Albrecht Classen, ed., *Old Age in the Middle Ages and the Renaissance: Interdisciplinary Approaches to a Neglected Topic* (Berlin: De Gruyter, 2007); Thane, *The Long History*; and Lynn Botelho and Pat Thane, eds., *Women and Ageing in British Society since 1500* (Harlow: Longman, 2001).
60 ASF, MPAP, *Memoriali*, F. 2304, no. 31, January 1756.
61 Groppi, *Il welfare prima del welfare*, 13.
62 Angela Groppi, "Assistenza alla vecchiaia e solidarietà tra generazioni in età moderna," in *Generazioni. Legami di parentela tra passato e presente*, ed. Ida Fazio and Daniela Lombardi (Rome: Viella, 2006), 51–68.
63 Groppi has stressed that early modern records suggest that intergenerational relationships were not natural but constructed by the judicial system and social practices through a negotiation between the public and institutional level and the private, familiar level. The elderly emerged as a socially meaningful group along with the emergence of public policies of assistance. Groppi, *Il welfare prima del welfare*, 9.
64 ASF, MPAP, *Memoriali*, F. 2304, no. 156, February 1758.
65 ASF, MPAP, *Memoriali*, F. 2304, no. 57, September 1756.
66 ASF, MPAP, *Memoriali*, F. 2304, no. 59, October 1756.
67 See, for example, ASF, MPAP, *Memoriali*, F. 2307, no. 46, August 1767.
68 Patricia Crawford has examined the influence of blood and kinship in the experience of fatherhood. Blood, she contends, is a key notion to take into account in the study of the early modern family. Patricia Crawford, *Blood, Bodies and Families in Early Modern England* (Harlow: Longman, 2004).
69 ASF, MPAP, *Memoriali*, F. 2304, no. 158, January 1758.
70 ASF, MPAP, *Memoriali*, F. 2300, no. 249 and 274.
71 The issue has been discussed by Linda Pollock starting from a family litigation in seventeenth-century England. Pollock, "Rethinking Patriarchy."
72 I have elaborated on this in Mariana Labarca, "The Emotional Disturbances of Old Age: On the Articulation of Old-Age Mental Incapacity in Eighteenth-Century Tuscany," *Historical Reflections/Reflexions Historiques* 41, no. 2 (2015): 19–36.

73 ASF, MPAP, *Memoriali*, F. 2307, no. 19, May 1767.
74 This was the case, for instance, of Giuseppe Rossi, ASF, MPAP, *Memoriali*, F. 2300, no. 195, August 1726, ASF, MPAP, *Campione*, F. 121, September 1726, f. 50; and ASF, MPAP, *Memoriali*, F. 2300, no. 288, August 1729.
75 As Cosimo Casacci, whom despite having been committed to Santa Dorotea, was referred to only as prodigal and accused to be of imperfect behavior by his wife when she petitioned for the lifting of his interdiction. ASF, MPAP, *Memoriali*, F. 2300, no. 14, October 1723. The order to send him to Santa Dorotea appears in ASF, MPAP, *Campione*, F. 118, April 1723, f. 5.
76 ASF, MPAP, *Memoriali*, F. 2303, no. 72, February 1753.

Bibliography chapter 2

Manuscripts

Archivio di Stato di Firenze (ASF)

- Magistrato dei Pupilli et Adulti Avanti il Principato (MPAAP), F. 248
- Magistrato dei Pupilli et Adulti del Principato (MPAP)
  - *Campione di Deliberazioni e Partiti*, F. 108–F. 166
  - *Atti e Sentenze*, F. 1144–F. 1362
  - *Suppliche e informazioni: Memoriali e Negozi di Cancelleria*, F. 2299–F. 2318
  - *Filza Lettere e Responsive*, F. 2480–F. 2519
- Magistrato Supremo (MS)
  - *Suppliche*, F. 1179–F. 1188
  - *Atti e Scritture*, F. 1845–F. 2103

Printed sources

Cantini, Lorenzo. *Legislazione Toscana*, vols. 20–27. Florence: Stamp. Albizziniana da S. Maria in Campo, 1806.

Vocabolario degli accademici della Crusca, 6 vols. Florence: Appresso Domenico Maria Manni, 1729–1738. DOI:10.23833/BD/LESSICOGRAFIA, www.lessicografia.it/index.jsp. Accessed August 8, 2020.

References

Addobbati, Andrea. "I guastafeste. La legge toscana sul gioco del 1773." *Quaderni storici* 95, no. 2 (1997): 495–538.

Bizzocchi, Roberto. *Cicisbei. Morale privata e identità nazionale in Italia*. Rome and Bari: Laterza, 2008.

Botelho, Lynn, and Pat Thane, eds. *Women and Ageing in British Society since 1500*. Harlow: Longman, 2001.

Brackett, John K. *Criminal Justice and Crime in Late Renaissance Florence 1536–1609*. Cambridge: Cambridge University Press, 1992.

Calvi, Giulia. *Il contratto morale. Madri e figli nella Toscana moderna*. Rome: Laterza, 1994.
Cartayrade, Laurent. "Property, Prodigality, and Madness: A Study of Interdiction Records in Eighteenth-Century Paris." PhD diss., University of Maryland, 1997.
Chabot, Isabelle. "Le gouvernement des pères: l'État florentin et la famille (XIVe-XVe siècles)." In *Florence et la Toscane XIVe-XIXe siècles. Les dynamiques d'un État italien*, edited by Jean Boutier, Sandro Landi, and Olivier Rouchon, 241–262. Rennes: Presses Universitaires de Rennes, 2004.
Classen, Albrecht, ed. *Old Age in the Middle Ages and the Renaissance: Interdisciplinary Approaches to a Neglected Topic*. Berlin: De Gruyter, 2007.
Cohen, Michèle. "'Manners' Make the Man: Politeness, Chivalry, and the Construction of Masculinity, 1750–1830." *Journal of British Studies* 44, no. 2 (2005): 312–329.
Crawford, Patricia. *Blood, Bodies and Families in Early Modern England*. Harlow: Longman, 2004.
Davidoff, Leonore, and Catherine Hall. *Family Fortunes: Men and Women of the English Middle Class, 1780–1850*. London: Hutchinson, 1987.
Desan, Suzanne, and Jeffrey Merrick, eds. *Family, Gender, and Law in Early Modern France*. Pennsylvania: The Pennsylvania State University Press, 2009.
Foyster, Elizabeth. "Male Honour, Social Control and Wife Beating in Late Stuart England." *Transactions of the Royal Historical Society* Sixth Series, 6 (1996): 215–224.
French, Henry, and Mark Rothery. "'Upon Your Entry into the World': Masculine Values and the Threshold of Adulthood among Landed Elites in England 1680–1800." *Social History* 33, no. 4 (2008): 402–422.
Groppi, Angela. "Assistenza alla vecchiaia e solidarietà tra generazioni in età moderna." In *Generazioni. Legami di parentela tra passato e presente*, edited by Ida Fazio and Daniela Lombardi, 51–68. Rome: Viella, 2006.
Groppi, Angela. *Il welfare prima del welfare. Assistenza alla vecchiaia e solidarietà tra generazioni a Roma in età moderna*. Rome: Viella, 2010.
Johnson, Paul. "Historical Readings of Old Age and Ageing." In *Old Age from Antiquity to Post-Modernity*, edited by Paul Johnson and Pat Thane, 1–18. London and New York: Routledge, 1998.
Kuehn, Thomas. *Law, Family and Women: Toward a Legal Anthropology of Renaissance Italy*. Chicago and London: The University of Chicago Press, 1991.
Kümin, Beat. *Drinking Matters: Public Houses and Social Exchange in Early Modern Central Europe*. Basingstoke and New York: Palgrave Macmillan, 2007.
Kümin, Beat, and B. Ann Tlusty, eds. *The World of the Tavern: Public Houses in Early Modern Europe*. Aldershot: Ashgate, 2002.
Labarca, Mariana. "The Emotional Disturbances of Old Age: On the Articulation of Old-Age Mental Incapacity in Eighteenth-Century Tuscany." *Historical Reflections/Réflexions Historiques* 41, no. 2 (2015): 19–36.
Martin, A. Lynn. *Alcohol, Violence, and Disorder in Traditional Europe*. Kirksville, MO: Truman State University Press, 2009.
Mellyn, Elizabeth W. *Mad Tuscans and Their Families: A History of Mental Disorder in Early Modern Italy*. Philadelphia: University of Pennsylvania Press, 2014.
Ottaway, Susannah. *The Decline of Life: Old Age in Eighteenth-Century England*. Cambridge: Cambridge University Press, 2004.
Phillips, Nicola. "Parenting the Profligate Son: Masculinity, Gentility and Juvenile Delinquency in England, 1791–1814." *Gender & History* 22, no. 1 (2010): 92–108.

Phillips, Nicola. *The Profligate Son: Or, a True Story of Family Conflict, Fashionable Vice, and Financial Ruin in Regency England.* Oxford: Oxford University Press, 2013.

Porter, Roy. *Mind-Forg'd Manacles: A History of Madness in England from the Restoration to the Regency.* London: Penguin Books, 1990.

Rabin, Dana. "Drunkenness and Responsibility for Crime in the Eighteenth Century." *Journal of British Studies* 44 (2005): 457–477.

Sears, Elizabeth. *The Ages of Man: Medieval Interpretations of the Life Cycle.* Princeton, NJ: Princeton University Press, 1986.

Seidel Menchi, Silvana, and Diego Quaglioni, eds. *Coniugi nemici. La separazione in Italia dal XII al XVIII secolo.* Bologna: Il Molino, 2000.

Sharpe, J.A. "Disruption in the Well-Ordered Household: Age, Authority, and Possessed Young People." In *The Experience of Authority in Early Modern England*, edited by Paul Griffiths, Adam Fox, and Steve Hindle, 187–212. Basingstoke: Palgrave Macmillan, 1996.

Taddei, Ilaria. *Fanciulli e Giovani: Crescere a Firenze nel Rinascimento.* Florence: Leo S. Olschki Editore, 2001.

Thane, Pat, ed. *The Long History of Old Age.* London: Thames & Hudson, 2005.

Tlusty, B. Ann. *Bacchus and Civic Order: The Culture of Drink in Early Modern Germany.* Charlottesville and London: University of Virginia Press, 2001.

Trexler, Richard. *Public Life in Renaissance Florence.* New York: Academic Press, 1980.

3 Beyond financial mismanagement
Interdictions by reason of *demenza*

In 1749, a petition reached the Tuscan grand ducal administration requesting the interdiction of the 90-year-old Antonio Forenzani from San Gimignano. The petition declared that Antonio, "due to his decrepit age or because he frequently falls into frenzy, as he has fallen many other times in the past, puts his house and family under great disturbance and confusion." The numerous testimonies said that he was a "fantastical and disquiet man" subject to a "continual uneasiness [*inquietudine*]" which drove him to madness, that he mistreated his wife and sons every day, declaring he would be happy to see them in a state of misery in the streets, and that he disturbed the peace and had the whole neighborhood under great disquiet and scandal. As in many other cases, the timeline of his mental condition was unclear. One of the testimonies explained that he had been in a state of mental derangement for 18 months and after that he had "many more times fallen back into the same frenzies." Another one declared that he had been mad many times before, but that this had worsened because of his decrepit age and his unwillingness to change.[1]

The case of Antonio Forenzani is in many ways representative of eighteenth-century interdiction procedures by reason of *demenza*, the overarching medico-legal category comprising all labels of mental incapacity except for prodigality. Elaborated with a language that combined well-established medico-legal categories such as frenzy with culturally meaningful notions such as uneasiness (*inquietudine*) and providing a characterization that privileged behavioral signs over physiological explanations, the narratives that make up Antonio's case are full of details regarding his behavior toward his closest relatives and his tormented familial environment. As in many other interdiction procedures, Antonio's behavior put his patrimony at risk, but above all, his frenzies put him in open opposition to his wife and two sons. Requesting the interdiction was a call for help as much as it was a measure to protect the patrimony, a request by his relatives for the intervention of state officials in their private discords.

The Tuscan grand ducal system provided different remedies according to the types of madness and the particular needs of the families, each one with its different procedure. Each step in the itinerary entailed the employment of a particular set of categories to identify mental disturbance, but all of them were mechanisms that families could use to cope with madness. This chapter takes us through interdiction procedures by reason of *demenza*, while other provisions are examined in the next chapter. I first discuss the profiles of defendants and petitioners according to their ages and genders, an issue which is crucial to understand not only how mental incapacity was represented but also how families reacted to it. I then describe the procedures, examining the uses and meanings of the legal category of *demenza*, and exploring the nuanced representations it encompassed. Finally, I discuss the backdrop of the disclosure of mental derangement. The central argument is that the reasons propelling families to turn to the ducal administration were profoundly connected with the domestic circumstances involving mental disturbance and the rhythms of family life. The dynamics of family relationships and the domestic atmosphere surrounding each case tainted the connotations and legal consequences attached to the category of *demenza*, how it was understood and argued, and the choice of its defining indicators. During the eighteenth century, interdiction procedures were more than a mechanism to neutralize financial mismanagement. They were employed to control dissipation and protect the family patrimony and also served to introduce a mediator in the frictions between members of a family, providing the opportunity to recompose family order and mend broken relationships.

Interdiction procedures tend to center on events that demonstrate how and why the individual imperiled family life. Asserting which type of *demenza* the defendants suffered with generally mattered less than establishing how it affected their relatives, for this determined what was to be done in each case. Thus, notions of madness were profoundly intertwined with how it disrupted the normal functioning of the family and how the allegedly mentally incapable person related to his or her parents, siblings, spouse, and children. The records of the Magistrato dei Pupilli unequivocally demonstrate that family conflicts were not only of private importance, but were also held to have a direct impact on social life, thus entering into the sphere of public concern. The involvement of patrimony in the private disputes that were described to the Pupilli officials only heightened this incursion of the private into the public arena. Through its involvement with the protection of the Tuscan patrimonies, the Magistrato dei Pupilli provided a space where families could turn to in order to vent and solve their conflicts by means of an interdiction procedure.

Defendants and petitioners: age, gender, and family roles

In interdictions by reason of *demenza*, gender and the position occupied by the defendant in the family structure were key factors that shaped how mental incapacity was described to the authorities, for they conditioned the impact that the denounced mental disturbance exerted on the family. The defendant's domestic circumstances played a crucial role, such as marital status, whether they had children or not, who they lived with, and who took care of them. A clear pattern regarding age and marital status differentiates male from female *demenza*, in close relation to their position in the family structure and to the circumstances that led families to request an interdiction.

Except for the case of the elderly, age was not at the center of the narrative in interdiction procedures by reason of *demenza* affecting men. Elderly men, by contrast, formed a distinct category of mental incapacity which posed particular challenges to families, disclosing a characteristic set of disputes, typically involving bitter disagreements between fathers and sons, as will be shown later on in this chapter. But when they were not said to be old, age mattered less than distinguishing whether they were bachelors, married, or widowers, each being a status which configured different residential patterns. In the case of bachelors, descriptions tend to focus on their relationships with their mothers, siblings, and uncles. Descriptions of married men also focus on their behavior in the private sphere, but with special attention to their relations with their wives and sons. Finally, the behavior of older men was contextualized in their relationships with their sons, with the particularity that the female voice is not as present as in the cases of younger defendants, for the petitions were submitted mostly by men.

Eighteenth-century inquiries into mental capacity affected mostly men from the upper ranks in different parts of Europe. However, marital status seems to have exerted a different influence in Tuscany, compared to other locations. Contrary to what has been shown in the countries of France, England, and Scotland, interdiction procedures in Tuscany largely affected married men. In Scotland and France, the single status of a mentally afflicted man was a decisive factor that moved families to resort to public assistance for his supervision and care. Historians have attributed the appearance of madness in the public records to failures of the domestic sphere, reading it as a clear result of a breakdown in the family structure and, particularly, as the effect of a domestic space crippled by the absence of a female figure. Conversely, being married has been singled out as a factor that allowed those deemed mentally incompetent to continue their lives under the vigilance and care of their spouses.[2]

However, as Akihito Suzuki has suggested in the case of England, the appearance of mental affliction in the records responds above all to the failure of the domestic sphere, that is to say, to a problem larger than bachelorhood or widowhood in and of itself.[3] The Tuscan interdiction procedures support this assertion, for the appearance of single men in the records, whether widowers or bachelors, seems not to be determined by their marital status, but rather by other factors disturbing the family order, such as the squandering of the patrimony, changes in the family's balance of power, enmities and complicated relationships, economic constraints, and illness.

In Tuscany, men were interdicted not because they lacked family support or family networks or because women were absent, but quite the contrary.

Interdicted men came from well constituted but troubled families. In the case of bachelors, they lived either with their mothers or their brothers, and most of them married after they were interdicted.[4] In the case of married men, their wives wished to counteract the consequences of their squandering at the same time they sought the intervention of the magistrates in their dysfunctional marriages – not to dissolve them, but to recompose them. Given that most defendants were married men, interdiction accounts in Tuscany are concentrated to a large extent on how defendants conducted their relations with their nuclear families, particularly with women. In this sense, interdictions had more to do with the intention to safeguard the composition of the family rather than being the outcome of a dismembered family.

The case of interdiction of women is different, for it affected mostly women who had been left alone and, more precisely, who lacked a male figure to protect and take care of them. They were usually unmarried, and characterizations of their *demenza* and its consequences were contingent upon their age. In this sense, female mental incapacity sheds light on how the cultural concerns over the specific stages of a woman's life were strongly connected with their role and position of a daughter, wife, mother, or widow in the family.[5] The descriptions of women who were interdicted and submitted to the authority of the Pupilli highlighted their relationships with men or, rather, highlighted the absence of men from their lives. Contrary to what happens in the case of men, women were interdicted when they no longer had a position in the traditional family structure, and they were mostly women with no close relatives willing to undertake their custody.

Mental incapacity in women usually appears in the records when some external factor had placed them outside the range of male authority: the death of their father, their refusal to marry, their abandonment by their husband, or widowhood. They were usually not young, although in some cases we know they must have been under the age of 50 (when they are said to have small children). In most cases, they were widows or spinsters (a condition almost requisite in order for them to be in a position to squander) and largely characterized as being of advanced age. Petitioners based their argument on these women's unskilled financial management, representing their access to patrimony as an anomaly that should have never occurred. As they were largely solitary women, fewer details were given regarding their relationships with other members of the family.

The petitioners' identity was very much connected with the defendants' marital status and family role. Most generally, petitions for the interdiction of a man on the grounds of *demenza* were sent by wives, brothers, mothers, sons, daughters, and uncles, in this order. Mothers took a prominent role when the defendant was unmarried, whereas, when the defendant was married, the petition was made by his wife or brothers, depending on the family circumstances. Elderly men were usually interdicted by their sons, as a large majority of them were widowers. When the petitioners were women, they were generally supported by kinsmen from both sides of the family lines. In

90 *Beyond financial mismanagement*

some cases, the petition was made by a member of the marriage family, such as a husband denouncing the disorders caused by his brother's wife or a concerned father whose daughter was married to a mentally disturbed man. In the case of interdicted women, as they were mostly unmarried, the petitioners were generally male comprising their sons, brothers, and sometimes nephews, again, depending on the composition of the family group.

Quantitative study of the identities of petitioners is hindered by the fact that we do not always have access to the written petitions. Furthermore, signatures and the order in which they appear do not necessarily reveal who had had the idea to request the interdiction or who was leading the process. Later proceedings, be it further enquiries carried out by the officers of the Pupilli or subsequent supplications sent by women regarding their sons' or husbands' behavior, suggest that women exerted a prevalent role in the domestic handling of madness. Although women usually signed collective petitions together with their sons or their brothers-in-law (for example), on many occasions it is they who continue the dialogue with the Magistrato dei Pupilli. In fact, women were the nexus between the magistracy and the interdicted, even when the administration of the patrimony was assigned to a third party. As wives were the family members who most frequently requested the mediation of the Pupilli after the interdiction was decreed, we get to know more details regarding the behavior and relationships of married men than of bachelors or the elderly.

Meanings and judicial uses of *demenza*

In order to know what petitioners were arguing and how they were shaping their accounts, we have to delve first into the meanings and uses of *demenza*, the generic medico-legal category employed to designate any mental condition that affected one's rational faculties and normal functioning, subsuming all other labels.[6] The statutes of the Magistrato dei Pupilli provided five categories of mental incapacity that were liable to interdiction. These included the *furiosi* (furious or raving mad), the *mentecatti* (fools or idiots), the *dementi* (demented), the *prodighi* (prodigals), and *dilapidatori* (dissipaters).[7] However, although the statutes listed five types of mental incapacity, interdiction procedures in practice rested heavily on only two categories, prodigality and *demenza*.

Between 1700 and 1775, of a total of 611 interdictions, 320 defendants were labeled as prodigals, 201 as demented, and 90 were left with no classification (see Table 3.1). In terms of gender, only 28 out of 611 interdictions affected women, and they were mostly labeled demented. However, there are some caveats to bear in mind when examining the uses and meanings of one label versus another. First, the terms prodigality and *demenza* were employed interchangeably, as if they referred to two aspects of the same kind of incapacity. As a result, interdictions by reason of *demenza* are many times hidden behind cases that initially appeared to relate only to prodigality.

Table 3.1 Categories of mental incapacity used in interdiction procedures between 1700 and 1775

Category	N	%
Prodigality	320	52.3 %
Demenza	201	33 %
Unspecified incapacity	90	14.7 %
Total	611	100 %

Note: The category of *demenza* considers cases that at some point employed either *demente* or any other term by which the behavior was explicitly attributed to mental illness or intellectual impairment. In many of these cases the category of prodigality was also employed, but was coupled with a series of other terms specifying that the economic mismanagement was caused by mental affliction. In other cases, the category of *demenza*, or the different labels it encompassed, was introduced after the interdiction was decreed, whether during the period the person was under curatorship, or in the proceedings for the revocation of the interdiction. Cases of "unspecified incapacity" correspond to proceedings that do not specify a category, which for the most part relate to interdictions for which only the decrees have survived.

Source: ASF, MPAP, *Memoriali e Negozi di Cancelleria*, F. 2299 – F. 2310 and ASF, MPAP, *Campione di Deliberazioni, e Partiti*, F. 112 – F. 170.

Second, prodigality was at the very base of interdiction procedures, since in order for a person to be interdicted, there had to be an economic mismanagement of some kind. Reckless spending, excessive and growing debts, the selling of household goods, emotional instability and debauchery, the defining features of prodigality, were characteristics shared by most of the defendants, regardless the category used to label them. Thus, it could be argued that a larger number of families perceived the defendant as mentally afflicted than is reflected in the number of procedures that employed the category of *demenza*, for only by attributing the disorder to prodigality could they secure an interdiction decree. It also could be argued that classification responded more to the interests and intentions of litigants than to the characteristics of the behavior denounced to the authorities. However, this does not prevent us from examining the uses and meanings of the category, regardless of whether the categorization related to an "actual" disease or was merely useful to greedy or abusive relatives.[8]

To have a relative declared mentally incapacitated entailed that something that was better off concealed would be made public. The higher numbers of interdictions by reason of prodigality speak of a society that found less shame in the label of prodigality than that of *demenza*. Even if prodigality was not free of social stigma in early modern Tuscany, it was certainly less disgraceful than *demenza*, and the financial prospects of a family, although affected temporarily, seems to have been less disrupted if a member was interdicted for prodigality. Evidently this depends on the kind of prodigality manifested by the person, but, in general, marriage proposals or financial contracts seem hardly to have been affected. That prodigality was generally less stigmatized is proven by the rising number of voluntary interdictions observed toward 1770, which were precisely formulated around the defendants' constitutional tendency toward financial mismanagement. Furthermore, prodigality could be taken to be the result of the demands of eighteenth-century sociability rather than the outcome of mental impairment and thus could be understood as a sign of the times.

Accompanying *demente*, the categories most commonly used were *melenso* and *mentecatto* and slightly less frequently, *stupido* and *stolido*. These terms worked as alternative descriptors of *demenza* and were employed mostly in combination. According to contemporary definitions, a *mentecatto* was somebody "mentally ill, stupid [*sciocco*] and mad [*pazzo*]."[9] While the term *mentecatto* seems to have covered a broader range of mental afflictions, from stupidity to outright madness, the other three concepts appear exclusively related to a loss or diminution of intellectual faculties. *Melenso* was "*sciocco*, imbecile [*scimunito*], foolish [*balordo*]," and *sciocco* was "someone who lacks wisdom and prudence."[10] In turn, *stupido* and *stolido*, as the other synonyms used to define *melenso*, all point to different variants of intellectual disability or an absence of reasoning faculties.[11] In general, people labeled with those terms were described as lacking capacity and intellect (*privo di capacità e intelletto*);[12] as bereft of sense, reason, or judgement (*privo di senno, privo di ragione, privo affatto di cognizione*);[13] as weak of mind (*debole di mente*);[14] as weak and stupid of wit (*debole e stupido ingegno*, or *capo debole*);[15] as empty of talent (*scemo di talento*);[16] or as imbecile in mind or spirit (*imbecille di mente* or *imbecille di spirito*).[17]

Thus, as can be observed, the Tuscan eighteenth-century legal categories were largely conservative, corresponding for the most part to Italian translations of Latin terms introduced when the official language of the Tuscan courts of law was changed into the vernacular at the beginning of the sixteenth century.[18] But, while in the previous centuries, *furioso, mentecatto, matto*, among others, were used indistinctly but with no overarching category, by the eighteenth century, the legal category of *demente* had come to predominate.

If we were to limit our interpretation only to the set of categories that were employed, we would think that people interdicted in early modern Tuscany as *demente* suffered almost exclusively from intellectual disability. However, the labels *mentecatto, melenso, imbecille,* or *stolido* simply indicated that the person was in a mental state that obstructed his or her normal functioning and, thus, was in need of being interdicted. Almost any kind of madness could fit under this general lack of reason. Someone could be classified as *melenso* and at the same time be said to manifest signs of *frenesia* or be subjected to a manic furor (*furore maniaco*). On many occasions, terms that seem strikingly contradictory at first sight could easily coexist as descriptors for one and the same person. For instance, Orazio Penci was interdicted in August 1752 after a petition signed by his mother and three sisters declared that he dissipated his patrimony "on account of his *demenza*." Their petition was supported by a testimony signed by a priest and some "respectable" neighbors, which said that for the past weeks, Orazio Penci "does not find himself healthy of mind, and it can be said he is demented," a state which caused him to dissipate his patrimony to the extent that the maintenance of his mother and sister was at serious risk. Among the signatories of the testimony was a physician who stated that Orazio Penci suffered from frenzy (*frenesia*), which made him completely lose the use of reason. On these grounds, the report of the authorities concluded that Penci was currently *melenso* and *debole di mente* but made no reference to the said frenzy.[19]

While Penci's relatives and acquaintances described him in terms that highlighted his level of intellectual disability, the physician pointed toward a more violent condition, introducing a term that neither the petitioners in their testimonies nor the authorities wanted to employ. Interestingly enough, the conclusion of the magistrates repeated the lay language, not the medical one. For the purposes of interdiction procedures, Penci's mental incapacity was exhibited by his irrational insistence in squandering and his neglect of his primary social role – providing for the economic subsistence of his mother and sisters.

Scholarship on the history of madness has provided suggestive studies on the extent to which legal categories of mental incapacity overlapped and were used interchangeably, producing a conflation of categories which, however, by no means implies that early modern judicial practice made no space for different gradations. As Peter Rushton has written regarding the categories of lunacy and idiocy in the English legal framework, the theoretically stark differentiation of categories was much less determinate in practice and can be taken to be the product of a "careful legalistic vagueness."[20] Similar to what has been found regarding the uses of the legal categories of fatuous, furious, and idiotic in eighteenth-century Scotland, the legal categories of madness in Tuscany were flexible and apparently simple but were employed to describe a wide range of behaviors.[21]

Representations of mental incapacity

Petitions commonly began by declaring that the defendant, because of his or her madness, was dissipating the patrimony (*stante la sua demenza, va dilapidando*).[22] The first and foremost sign of *demenza* was prodigality in close connection with how Tuscan society valued patrimony and how patrimony defined the elite. In fact, as seen in previous chapters, from its foundation the Magistrato dei Pupilli had been bound to the social and political aspiration to preserve the patrimonies and wealth of families, which was considered a service of public utility. Like prodigals, the *dementi* were deemed mentally incapacitated because they had been proven to be unable to manage their affairs, take care of their family, and perform their duties as *paterfamilias*. They were usually said to sign disadvantageous contracts, not out of ambition or reckless spending, but out of pure incapacity, a clear evidence, according to one contemporary Florentine, of the individual's alteration of mind.[23] For only a disturbed state of mind could account for his inability to understand that he was selling property below its market value. In other cases, they were described as stubbornly contracting loans and signing illicit contracts that they would afterwards not acknowledge any responsibility for, behaving arbitrarily and demonstrating no concern for the consequences of their actions. In the end, they were also described as being easily tricked into unfavorable financial actions or contradicting the basic rules of the patrilineal transmission of patrimony by their intent to donate their portion of it to an unknown third party.[24]

Women were perceived as incapable of respecting the limits of their position as temporary property holders. The few women who were interdicted, however, were hardly ever defined as prodigals, because prodigality was an intrinsically masculine category. But women were also thought to be perfectly capable of squandering and even to be the cause of their husband's prodigality. The new characteristics of eighteenth-century sociability, with its increasing expenses, resulted in women spending above their means, even when they were not the direct holders of the assets. In aristocratic circles, in particular, within the context of the new relationships that have been studied by Roberto Bizzocchi, women were often at the center of criticism for their excessive expenditures and loose morality.[25] As was the case with men, in order to interdict a woman, it had to be proven that their patrimonies were at risk, and in many cases this was ascribed to the excessive spending brought by the new forms of sociability.[26]

Mental incapacity was measured against behavioral norms that were embedded in cultural and religious precepts that had been at the core of the formation of the Tuscan society, which were reinforced by the post-Tridentine church and later grounded the family order that both enlightenment authors and the justice system tried to enforce.[27] The failure to control one's wife was presented as a major indicator of mental incapacity, as was the failure to perform as *paterfamilias*, to behave as a respectable mother or aunt, to oversee the education of one's children, or to respect social hierarchies. Immersed in the defense of what Elizabeth Mellyn has called "patrimonial rationality," mental incapacity supposed the inability to situate oneself in a given context, to perform the expected activities, to differentiate beneficial from harmful, and to comply with basic social norms, which had been at the core of inquiries into mental capacity in Tuscany since the Pupilli's involvement with adult guardianship.[28]

Extravagance, uneasiness, and instability

Financial irresponsibility was at the core of how madness was understood in Tuscany, but it was not per se a sign of mental derangement. Thus, squandering and/or the risk of bankruptcy were only the starting points for much more detailed arguments to prove why dissipation was caused by or was the symptom of mental disturbance. Petitions and testimonies dedicated most of their ink to descriptions of irrational and extravagant actions to illustrate why the defendant deserved the label of *demente*, *mentecatto*, or *melenso*. In their effort to demonstrate that the alleged mental disturbance justified an interdiction, petitioners provided a list of the defendant's record of irrational acts, introducing behavioral keys such as acting strangely or extravagantly, showing emotional instability, and suffering violent outbursts, together with changes in their usual domestic behavior, in the ways they treated people, and in the ways they behaved at the public sphere.

Antonio Corsi was interdicted in August 1754 because he had turned "frenetic and weak of mind," giving "evident signs and demonstrations of his unhealthy mind," as the officials of the Pupilli stated.[29] The interdiction petition was signed by Antonio's sister, who claimed that he "has started to give clear signs not only of his incapacity to manage his affairs in the way that any good head of family does, but furthermore, that he is of an unsound mind." The first sign of insanity she recorded was Antonio's sudden refusal to fulfill his duties at the *Tribunale della Mercanzia* (the commercial court), where he was employed as assistant of the court records' keeper. "I have many times advised him and begged him to come back to his working post," attested an official from the tribunal, but he had not been able to succeed, and Antonio prolonged his absence without giving any justification. He simply would not assume any responsibility for the abandonment of his post, even if some of his unattended tasks needed prompt attention. This, in the eyes of his sister, witnesses, and authorities demonstrated his detachment from the social world (and consequently, his insanity).[30]

Afterwards, he unexpectedly dismissed his own servants to live in complete isolation, manifesting no interest in supervising his affairs or administering his patrimony. The main concern of Antonio's sister was his refusal to participate in social life, whereby he had begun to "give evident signs of not being right in mind," according to the testimonies. Through a testimony his sister later sent to the Pupilli, we know that Antonio not only longed for solitude, but also insisted on confining himself in his residence with bladed weapons and firearms, refusing to see anybody. His sister explained that he also carried weapons wherever he went, which, apart from being illegal, demonstrated to her eyes that he was a source of particular risk to society on account of his well-known mental disturbance.

A clear example of the proximity of terms like *frenetico* and *debole di mente* (weak of mind), Antonio Corsi's behavior was depicted as violent and extravagant. He would not only live alone in his villa with weapons with which he might eventually harm himself, but also when he did leave home, he carried them with him. To demonstrate the danger he posed to public life, one witness recorded that Antonio passed every day in front of his shop "making a thousand gestures at people" which showed that he was mad (*pazzo*). Once the witness even saw him approach and threaten to attack a soldier who was speaking with a barber, for no reason. The soldier had been on the verge of responding to the provocation with his sword, but his companion prevented him by saying that Antonio was a *pazzo* and so could not defend himself. The soldier, according to the witness, later said that there was no point in killing a madman. In the eyes of the witness and his two victims, Antonio's provocation was nothing but the mad actions of an insane person, given its utter absurdity and stark disregard for the rules of civility.

Behind the apparent vagueness and simplicity of legal categories, we find nuanced characterizations of what was deemed mentally disturbed behavior. Tuscan accounts of mental incapacity reveal the existence of shared cultural assumptions regarding what mental affliction was and what were its manifestations.[31] The story of Antonio Corsi shares many characteristics with descriptions of insane behavior that can be found in other areas of early modern Europe in documents from civil and criminal courts, in asylum records, and in medical literature.[32] He refused to work, insisted on isolating himself, and engaged in pointless street brawls, all actions that were thought to denote a lack of reason. While his sister and officers of the Magistrato Supremo talked about his "manifest signs and demonstrations of his unsound mind," witnesses used the label *pazzo* and the officials of the Pupilli concluded that he had become *frenetico e debole di mente*. No medical testimony was added, and no further attempt was made to categorize Antonio Corsi's insanity.

Interdiction accounts favored descriptions of mad behavior as indicators of altered mental states over physiological explanations. The identification of signs entailed an examination of how and why a person behaved as he or she did, rather than a listing of medical symptoms. Madness was indisputably taken to be a sickness caused by an injured brain, but medical categories and a medical diagnosis were not necessary for the purpose of securing an interdiction sentence. Given that no specialized knowledge was required to denounce a relative of mental incapacity, the characterizations could instead focus on individual perceptions, particular events, and the emotional atmosphere surrounding each individual.

Well-known characteristics of madness such as a refusal to work; neglect of healthy habits such as a regular diet, sleep, and exercise; unrestrained indulgence in pleasures; sexual misconduct; and acting and behaving extravagantly are also present in interdiction records. We find indicators such as having extravagant, fluctuating, and peculiar ideas and being unable to choose one or too fixed in another. As was said regarding a *demente* in 1760, an insane person could be recognized "both by the volubility of his determinations [*sentimenti*], and by the extravagance of his behavior, by his way of speaking and by the fixation in his resolutions ... unreasonable to the extent of not being able to persuade or move him to do what is convenient."[33] These representations are accompanied by expressions to describe disturbed states of mind, such as "extravagant brain," "extravagant ideas," "altered fantasy," "distorted and improper ideas and maxims," and "mental fixations."[34] All of these were presented as signs of a disordered disposition, which encompassed a wide spectrum of psychological states, from a tendency to furious fits and excessive irascibility to melancholic fixations. They were said to be of an "uneasy spirit" (*spirito inquieto*) or "uneasy nature" (*naturale inquieto*), be of "such an irregular character that nobody is able to deal with him," or be subject to "alterations of spirit."[35]

Drunkenness is another feature frequently cited as a part of the disordered disposition that was both cause and symptom of *demenza*.[36] We saw that frequent inebriation was part of the behavioral disorders recognized in prodigality, but in the case of *demenza* it was singled out as a straightforward sign of a deranged mind. The effects that petitioners and witnesses attributed to excessive alcohol consumption were loss of control and damage in the person's intellectual faculties in a vicious circle where cause and effect were inextricably intermingled. One had "lost the use of reason" because "he is always drunk," another was "out of himself [*fuori di se*] by reason of his immoderate use of wine," and a third one was "stupid [*stolido*]" and "manifestly insane" from the same cause.[37] The fact that drunkenness was self-inflicted made no difference in the argument for interdiction. If anything, it corroborated the defendant's mental incapacity and the behavioral disorder affecting its victim.

Mental incapacity and the body

The foundations of a legal assessment of madness relied on the principle that madness could be recognized through its outward signs.[38] As it was an internal phenomenon which could not be directly observed, it was thought that the only way to know what was happening in the mind was through bodily signs. Gestures, behaviors, demeanor, external appearance, the way a person spoke, walked, and related and reacted to others were its verifiable signs. The typical line of argument in testimonies to demonstrate the insanity of a defendant was that witnesses had "heard and seen him say and commit continual and diverse absurdities and acts of a real mad person."[39] Because speech was thought to be particularly revealing of a person's state of mind, testimonies commenting on this were crucial. For "although [a defendant] at a first meeting might seem to speak judiciously, when one continues to converse with him it becomes clear that his mind is not where it should be [*non sta a dovere*]."[40] In fact, the Pupilli officials often contrasted denunciations with face-to-face assessments of defendants, summoning them to court if they were able to move by themselves or otherwise sending an examiner.

However, descriptions of facial expressions and gestures are not easily found in the Tuscan interdiction procedures of the eighteenth century. The same is true of accounts of nudity and indecent appearance, which is at odds with what studies have shown for the previous centuries in Tuscany and in other parts of Europe.[41] The Tuscan interdiction accounts present alternative models to the stereotype of the raving mad running naked or unconventionally dressed, whose frantic and frenetic behavior threatened social order. The eighteenth-century interdicted evidently were a threat to social order, but only 1 of the 611 interdictions that make up this study include a description of a naked woman wandering mad.[42] There are abundant references to indecency, but these are mostly related to behavior, not appearance.

98 *Beyond financial mismanagement*

Furthermore, interdiction accounts do speak of clothing but usually in reference to excessive acquisition of them, not to their absence. If anything, the Tuscan interdicted were overdressed, in some cases clothed above their economic means and in others leaving the rest of the household deprived of decent clothing to wear.

Rather than reading the Tuscan accounts as an exception to the more common early modern European cultural notions of madness, the difference can be understood as the result of the special characteristics of the interdiction records under examination here. Petitioners and witnesses were extremely selective in their characterizations and their lexicon, accommodating their descriptions to each institutional space they turned to, as will be discussed in the following chapters. For the purpose of securing an interdiction, instead of giving descriptions of physical symptoms, it was more effective to delve into the defendants' financial performance and illustrate their alleged mental derangement through descriptions of their characters and behavior toward other members of the family.

That said, interdiction accounts do show that mental and physical impairment were strongly connected in early modern culture. We have to bear in mind that being deaf or mute was listed among the debilities that could justify interdiction, according to the Pupilli statutes.[43] Further, deafness, blindness, and reduced mobility were also included as physical symptoms that indicated the presence of madness, together with speech disorders. In interdiction procedures, the fact that a defendant's mental incapacity was accompanied by some level of physical impairment served to illustrate the extent to which the person's normal functioning was obstructed, not necessarily because physical, sensorial, and mental impairment were equated, but mostly because they were seen as leading to the same consequences.[44]

Old-age mental incapacity

The case of old-age mental incapacity deserves further examination, both because a more precise cause, and thus starting point, was identified, and because these aged people constitute a group of defendants with distinctive characteristics. In Tuscany, the elderly were particularly liable to interdiction, both by reason of prodigality and of *demenza*, making old age a new source of conflict in family relationships that was not so visible in similar sources from previous centuries.[45] The potentially damaging effects of old age on one's mental faculties were commonly mentioned in interdiction procedures. While in many cases the date of onset of mental incapacity was not specified, when affecting the elderly the condition was presented with an identifiable origin. Configuring a distinct typology of mental illness, old age mental incapacity was presented as a natural consequence of ageing that signaled a descent into decrepitude, diminishing mental faculties, affecting daily performance, and ultimately leading to the loss of the ability to manage one's own affairs.[46] The image frequently conveyed in petitions was that of a mind which had turned childish (*rimbambito*) or had begun the irrevocable path toward *melensaggine* (understood in this case as intellectual disability) and *imbecillità di mente* (literally, imbecility of mind). Old-age mental incapacity often appeared combined with other symptoms such as past illnesses or, more commonly, apoplectic strokes or epileptic seizures. Apoplexy and epilepsy, though also present in cases of younger defendants, are most visible in the case of the elderly. The presence of apoplexy served particularly well to argue that the person had reached a stage of mental and physical decay, leaving him or her bereft of reason and partially or totally immobilized.[47] Epilepsy was similarly mentioned as a mark of decrepitude, as in the case of a woman whose "corporal indispositions" had been aggravated by more "accidents" – in this case, epileptic seizures – which rendered her "mentally obfuscated, and absent of memory."[48]

The connection between mental and physical impairment is best illustrated by the signs of old-age mental incapacity, which frequently included the inability to elaborate a coherent discourse, to use the right words to express themselves, and to follow a conversation. Difficulties of speech were in these cases accompanied by defective vision, difficulties of hearing, and problems of mobility, all of which were singled out as proofs that the defendants' minds were deteriorating. Physical impediments such as the inability to see, speak, and move served, in this context, not only to support the assertion of mental decrepitude, but even more to emphasize the need for the interdiction. The critical consequences of the elderly's reprehensible financial conduct, with their inappropriate decisions, their indiscriminate selling of goods below their market value, and their total opposition to any well-intended advice assumed more convincing tones when combined with a "decrepit age," "bodily indispositions," and problems of speech, which on the whole demonstrated their being a "man stupefied and bereft of reason [*uomo stordito, e privo de ragione*]."[49]

Interdiction petitions affecting the elderly began by stating that the defendant was of a "decrepit age," as if it was the decisive fact that was supported by all other arguments: petitioners declared an elderly relative incapable of managing their affairs "due to her age and the damage she caused."[50] However, whether they had actually become demented was debatable, and so petitioners were expected to provide evidence beyond the mention of their advanced age. As expressed by a Pupilli official in 1728, advanced age by itself was not enough to determine that someone had become foolish or childish (*rimbambitto*), for they could perfectly well be of "a sturdy nature and sound mind" all the same.[51] For this reason, the interdiction procedures involving the elderly often involved controversy regarding the assessment of their state of mind, with heated debates among the authorities, the elderly, and their families. Indeed, the elderly were the age group that most eagerly contested interdictions, sending numerous petitions for their revocation and refuting the accounts of their relatives.

Even if a person had been declared to be mentally unfit to manage his or her affairs on account of decrepitude, an interdiction was not necessarily an irrevocable measure. In fact, it is not rare to find that they were interdicted for an alleged decrepitude said to have cost them their senses to the point of turning childish or foolish, but would later be reinstated to their civil capacities because, as in the case of an 80-year-old man, "for some time now he has demonstrated a wiser behavior in the management of his interests and a better attention to his household and family."[52]

As discussed in the previous chapter, interdiction procedures affecting the elderly were entangled with discussions about what it meant to grow old, what were the defining signs of mental decay, and how old age affected the family structure and balance of powers. For this reason, these procedures illuminate the shaping of a pathologized conception of decrepitude, presenting it as a negotiation between families, authorities, and the elderly. As such, decrepitude was thought to put a considerable strain on family life, forcing its members to deal with issues ranging from patrimonial mismanagement to care provisions and emotional distress. Interdiction procedures attest to the profound suffering generated by ageing, something that can be perceived not only in testimonies given by the elderly, but also in those given by people around them. This suffering was the root of the intergenerational conflicts generated in relation to old age when the person had reached a state of dependency, which necessitated the intervention of public institutions and at the same time gave the elderly the possibility to participate and fight for their independence.[53]

Physical and sensorial impairments were supposed to hinder people's normal functioning, constraining their capacity to manage their own affairs and conduct their own business, making them the potential victims of fraud and manipulation. This meant not only that they could easily be defrauded, but also that they were not self-sufficient. For instance, Michele Frulli, around 60 years old, according to his brothers "was and has always been *demente*, and incapable of managing his own affairs, and has always lived deprived of sight, and under the custody and care of the supplicants."[54] The argument that he "has always been demented" was combined here with that of his physical impairment, which emphasized that the man was dependent upon the care of others and could not perform his duties as head of the family. Given that he had been able to exert his rights to administer his patrimony until then, the employment of the formula of "has always been" raises questions about why families resorted to interdiction at any given time.

The domestic circumstances of madness: to repair the disorder of the families

Interdictions were marked by the iniquities of an inheritance system that favored exclusively the elder son, but there were other iniquities as well which go some distance to explain why families at a certain point decided, first, to disclose mental affliction to the ducal administration and, then, do so through a petition for interdiction. The mere need to control the financial consequences of mental disturbance does not completely explain resorting to this drastic solution. This is even more clear if we bear in mind that a wide range of provisions to address the consequences of madness existed in the eighteenth century. While other institutional remedies such as confinement and recourse to criminal courts and to the office of the Auditore Fiscale are examined later on, we need to address here the circumstances that explain why families decided to resort to interdiction among the available options.

In some cases, the reasons for requesting the interdiction are openly stated, for example, in the case of 65-year-old Cosimo Cambelloti, who was interdicted after his son argued that his madness had overcome the family's limits because he had been incarcerated, his assets impounded, and his patrimony risked total ruin.[55] However, the reasons explaining why families resorted to interdiction are not always disclosed. In this scenario, how families described the context of mental incapacity and the circumstances surrounding the behavior give interesting clues as to what moved them to resort to an interdiction procedure at a particular time.

Time frames

There are several factors behind the decision to initiate an interdiction procedure by reason of *demenza* worth taking into account, which relate to what Robert Allan Houston has called the "contingencies" which determined the disclosure of madness.[56] A crucial issue to take into account is the time elapsed between the first identification of the mental condition and its disclosure. Although it is possible to find mental afflictions that were said to be of recent manifestation that were soon revealed to the authorities, the majority of interdictions relate to cases in which defendants were said always to have been mentally disturbed or to cases in which the more-or-less defined onset of the derangement is said to have occurred many years before the petition was made.

In most cases, petitioners only said that for some time the person had shown signs of mental disturbance, or simply said that the person was mentally incapable of managing his or her affairs, regardless of whether they had been so since birth or whether the affliction was more recent. For instance, a declaration that a defendant "is, due to his bad fortune, of a weak head, and almost *mentecatto*" could suffice.[57] In other cases, petitioners simply stated that the person had "fallen" into *demenza* (or any other of its subsidiary categories), or "had fallen into many and diverse indispositions, [which] reduced him to unsound mind," without disclosing the nature of those indispositions.[58]

Attributing madness to a specific cause or giving a precise date for its commencement introduced the problem of duration into the assessment of mental incapacity. Compared to other European legal frameworks, Tuscan judicial practice did not differentiate between those said to suffer an inborn condition and those who had developed their mental affliction later in life, and the onset was many times not described. By contrast, the English and

Scottish legal systems required litigants to specify a precise date on which the condition had started, for only from that time on could contracts and economic transactions be declared void.[59] In the case of Tuscany, contracts were not automatically invalidated, and legal administrators (*attori*) had to litigate contracts one by one if they wanted to abrogate them. For this reason, a vague starting point was preferable. For instance, a man was said to have turned "*melenso* and *debole di mente* because of a series of illnesses." In a slightly differing explanation, a priest had testified in this case saying that he had "always thought of him as a man of little judgment and reprehensible conduct."[60] In most cases, little information was given as to the nature of the illness, except for mentions of epileptic seizures and apoplectic strokes, which are among the most cited when petitioners decided to specify a cause. However, even in these cases, either a precise date for the event was not given, or no immediate connection can be found between the first stroke and the decision to request the interdiction. Claims that an illness or an accident was the cause of mental impairment could easily coexist with a declaration that the defendant had "always" been demented, which transferred the discussion from when the defendant had started to give the first signs and the probable causes of mental impairment, both highly debatable, to its effects, which could be ratified by witnesses and confirmed with facts.

Even if in the case of the elderly, the state of *demenza* had a clearer starting point, the time elapsed between its manifestation and the decision to request interdiction were not necessarily connected. This chapter began with the case of Antonio Forenzani, who had been in a state of madness for 18 months, and after that he had "many more times fallen back into the same frenzies."[61] Similarly, Giuseppe Sgrilli was interdicted at 80 years after he had been confined in the *pazzeria* of Santa Maria Nuova for 16 years. He had been discharged in 1745, but the interdiction was petitioned by his second-born-son after 11 years. As was usual in these cases, his son declared he was requesting the interdiction "not only because of his advanced age and because he suffers in the rational part [*parte razionale*]," but also because "given his natural inclination he has always been prone to dissipate and destroy his own patrimony."[62] So, why turn to the Pupilli now and not 18 months before, as in the case of Antonio Forenzani, or 27 years before, as in the case of Giuseppe Sgrilli? By themselves, neither the first appearance of mental derangement nor the passage into a state of decrepitude was a reason enough to request interdiction. Something else needed to happen, related to the rhythms of property transmission, but not reduced to them.

Petitions could also be conditioned by concerns over inheritance, particularly by the fear that the allegedly mentally incapable could make an unlawful testamentary disposition. This happened in the cases both of old fathers who threatened to dispossess their sons and of women, in whose case the line of inheritance was undetermined. Consequently, in interdiction requests involving old women, we can observe a recurring concern for the future of their inheritance, presenting advanced age as a factor that put women at the risk of being victims of insidious comments regarding how they would dispose of their patrimonies. In these cases, the ultimate goal of petitioners was to prevent the allegedly mentally ill from making any undesirable transfer of property or making a testament contrary to the petitioners' interests, a concern that can be observed both in male and female petitioners.[63]

Another set of concerns motivating interdiction petitions relates to men who had recently come into their inheritance, be it because the defendant had come of age or because the death of a relative had given them access to the family's patrimony. Coming into one's inheritance evidently sparked the request for an interdiction, although in these cases mental affliction could have been present long before a defendant gained control of the inheritance.[64] However, the fact that cases involving men and women who had recently inherited do not exceed cases relating to people who had long before gained power to administer their patrimonies suggests that coming into one's inheritance was not the only factor, nor the decisive one, which explained a recourse to interdiction. Similarly, the Pupilli officers generally appointed third-party administrators to the patrimony when wives or mothers could not assume the task, so interdictions did not grant rights of administration to prospective legal inheritors. Interdiction was meant to secure the property for future inheritors and offered no immediate access to the property, and so even if petitioning for an interdiction could be motivated by the intention to seize someone's patrimony, the question of why people resorted to the measure at a particular time is not fully elucidated by taking into account possible cases of ill-intentioned relatives.[65]

Squandering alone is an equally unsatisfactory factor for explaining why families resorted to interdiction procedures at a particular time. Interdiction narratives generally present squandering as a behavioral tendency that had long been a part of the defendant's personality. It is true that in many cases, the dissipation is said to have reached a point of risking bankruptcy for the family. However, as in the case of concerns over inheritance, we should take the squandering only as a window into other less obvious factors related to patrimony and financial behavior, but not reduced to them.

Rhythms of family life

The timing of interdiction petitions appears to be closely connected to the rhythms of family life; among these, we find changes in the family which affected the distribution of power, such as deaths and marriages. The interdiction could be part of a testamentary disposition, as happened with defendants whose fathers or brothers had established they were not to be left unattended in the administration of their patrimonies.[66] Defendants may have been under the care of a curator who had recently died, or they may have been under the care of their next of kin until, for some reason, they were left unattended. For instance, Gaetano Migliorini, who had "always been considered demented," was interdicted after his daughter-in-law sent a petition arguing he needed a curator now that his wife, who had taken care of his patrimony and affairs until then, had died.[67] Recent marriages were also destabilizing factors, as they introduced new members to the family group, either because a parent had married (or intended to marry) against the advice of their progeny, or because it was one of the latter who had married against the will of their elders. Disputes regarding the distribution of the patrimony between the old and the new family in the cases of remarriage and bitter discords between aged fathers and their sons on account of the latter's wives were many times singled out as causes of the family breakdown, leading to interdiction.[68]

Among the circumstances that generated petitions regarding mental incapacity, living arrangements and the composition of the household take a leading part. The case of Francesca Paoli del Feo illustrates how living arrangements marked the timing of interdiction petitions. She was first interdicted because she had allegedly become stupid and *melensa* following the absence of her husband and "the many misfortunes and maladies she had suffered" and 4 years later a second time because she had "relapsed into her prodigality."[69] According to her appointed administrator, with her husband's disappearance she had been left "without the guidance of any relative who could supervise the administration of her resources," which she had dissipated to the point of reducing her "to wandering the streets, almost naked."[70] Her behavior was described as violent and insufferable, and her next of kin refused to cohabit with her, a situation that resurfaced 10 years after the second interdiction, when she was once again denounced to the authorities for dressing indecently, being permanently drunk, and tormenting her daughter near the monastery to which she was promised as a nun. Francesca was confined in the Conservatory of the Malmaritate, an institution for women of ill repute, for she was found not to be mad (*pazza*) enough as to be committed to Santa Dorotea, but neither was she sufficiently "wise" to be left "free in the streets."[71]

We also find defendants who refused to live with their relatives or household members who had been forced to flee from the house to escape the defendant's frenzies.[72] The difficulty of sharing the same roof with the mentally afflicted was a common source of complaints to the magistrates. Petitioners confided their troubles to the magistrates, describing the recurrent mistreatments "of facts and words" their fathers or husbands exerted on them, in the hope that the interdiction would induce these men to change. For example, Isabella Salvatori added to the declaration that her husband had given "many signs of not being entirely on himself, and of being inclined to prodigality and madness," an account of the continual mistreatments she and her four children suffered from him.[73] In some cases, the petition intended to restore damaged relationships in order to make cohabitation bearable, but in others, the solution was a change in the residential arrangements. Wives, for instance, requested permission to be allowed to live separately from their husbands, arguing that their behavioral disorders and disquieting characters made cohabitation unbearable, petitions that were weighed carefully by the magistrates in order to combine respect for the sacrament of matrimony with the family's harmony and integrity.[74]

Relatives could also request the transfer of the defendant to a different residence, some suggesting that they be put to lodge with a particular person, others requesting them to be sent to a different family residence, as happened in the case of Lorenzo Baldinotti, whom we met at the beginning of this book. His "extravagant brain" and "furious nature" made him a burden to both his wife and his brothers, who categorically refused to share their roofs with him.[75] In many of these cases, the authorities had to negotiate different measures with the family to handle the persistent misdeeds of defendants, which in turn produced an itinerancy from one place to another, given the recurrent unwillingness of the different family members to live with them, or the refusal of third persons to continue lodging them.

Concerns regarding who was to be held responsible for the custody and care of the mentally afflicted pervade interdiction petitions. Since women interdicted and placed under the guardianship of the Pupilli generally lived alone, the problem of their care and maintenance was at the very center of the petition for interdiction. For instance, the 55-year-old Maria Maddalena Scardigli was interdicted after a petition sent by her cognate nephews, who declared that their spinster aunt possessed a small house from which "out of her *demenza* and madness [she] has dissipated all the furniture it had," proving she could not manage her affairs.[76] Stressing the fact that she was alone and, as such, was in desperate need of protection and help, they added that she could not earn her living and had reduced herself to poverty. The petitioners sought to prevent Maria Maddalena from completely dissipating what was left of her resources, so that they would not be forced to provide for her living. Cases such as this one, where petitioners sought to avoid the eventuality of being legally forced to maintain old women, are frequent, whether it was sons who refused to assume their care or other members of the family in the case they were spinsters.

Interdictions as a mechanism to solve family disputes

The records suggest that a major motivation behind interdiction petitions was the need to seek the intervention of the officers of the Pupilli to resolve family disputes related to patrimony, to the interaction with the mentally disturbed, and to the upheavals of familial relationships. Interdiction procedures tackled two main issues: they addressed the problem of financial mismanagement at the same time they introduced a mediating party into family discords. In this sense, patrimony mismanagement generated an opportunity to vent frictions between husbands and wives, fathers and sons, wives and brothers-in-law, and so on, which made the Magistrato dei Pupilli an institution that acted to provide public intervention in private life at the request of the families.

Interdictions functioned as a mechanism to solve the disorders of the families that put social order at risk.[77] This could explain why family members at some point in the life of a person deemed mentally afflicted "since always" decided to petition for an interdiction. In fact, restoration of the family order is by far the most frequent reason given by petitioners to explain why they were initiating the procedure; petitioners requested the authorities to intervene as soon as possible in order to "oppose," "impede," or "repair" the disorders caused by deviant behavior (*per ovviare, per riparare, per provvedere*, or *per impedire ulteriori disordini*). Mentally disturbed individuals were generally depicted as troublesome and ungovernable members of the family who refused to abide to social norms. Economic mismanagement worked thus as a pretext through which resolution to aggravated family conflicts could be channeled.

Interdictions were often the way out of the intensification of a family conflict that stemmed from a change in the balance of powers. They can be read as part of the renewed familial conflicts that during the eighteenth century demonstrated that second-born sons (*cadetti*) and women from the aristocracy were discontented with the traditional hierarchies of the patriarchal family.[78] These conflicts, which can be observed in litigations that placed the problem of unequal marriages at the center of the conflict with increasing frequency, constitute a different side of the same problem. Intergenerational conflicts, marital disputes, and tensions between siblings were also vented through interdiction procedures. We see fathers who refused to hand over their position as heads of family to their elder sons, sons and daughters who wished to impose their authority over their parents; second-born sons who disputed the management of the family patrimony and demanded their right to decide on their marriages and life courses; and women who were not willing to live submissively under the authority of men.

In these disputes, as might be expected in the records of a magistracy in charge of the Tuscan patrimonies, patrimony played a leading role. Patrimonial disputes tainted family relationships, producing harsh disagreements and profoundly altering domestic arrangements, something most visible in interdiction procedures. Concerns about inheritance frequently disclose bitter family disputes, particularly tensions between first-born sons and old fathers, and frictions between siblings. These disputes, in fact, continue to appear in the records after the interdiction had been decreed. The active opposition of an old man to renouncing to his patrimony in favor of his sons and his reluctance to share a roof with them were many times combined with disputes between sons of different matrimonies over their inheritance.[79] For instance, the 80-year-old Giuseppe Sgrilli, cited before, had been interdicted at the request of his first-born son 11 years after he had been discharged from the *pazzeria* of Santa Maria Nuova. The petition, as we saw, could not have been motivated by the onset and development of his mental condition but responded more to the dynamics of the relations between Giuseppe and his two sons. The petitioner's line of argument was to combine the declaration that Giuseppe, on account of his illness, had always been inclined to dissipate his patrimony, with accusations against his second-born brother, whom allegedly refused to find any useful occupation, dedicating his time exclusively to gambling and entertainments. As many other similar cases suggest, Giuseppe's elder son was in opposition not only to his father, but also particularly to his brother, from whom he intended to protect the patrimony he was entitled by law to inherit. That animosity must have subsided, however, as 5 years later Giuseppe Sgrilli, now 85 years old, had his interdiction lifted with the expressed consent of both of his sons.[80]

Interdiction procedures describe the extravagant actions of the allegedly mentally incapable in the specific context of the composition of each household. The domestic circumstances of women, mostly spinsters, were many times left concealed, but the domestic behavior of men, who represent the majority of interdiction procedures, was placed at the center of attention. Descriptions of men said to be demented, compared with those demonstrating prodigality, focused less on their debauchery and excessive expenditure and more on their behavior toward other family members, particularly on their inability to maintain good relationships with them, which was presented as a sign of their altered states of mind. There is the case of Filippo Gori, 84 years old, who was said to be unable to govern his sons properly because of his decrepitude and weakness of mind,[81] and Pier Antonio Piccioli, 88 years old, who notwithstanding his "mind" was almost "faded away," stubbornly insisted on "doing everything in his own way" (*voler far tutto di sua testa*) without listening to anyone.[82] In the end, 46-year-old Gaetano Damiani was denounced for being not *sui compos*, "defective in his hearing, speaking and brain" and "incapable of reason," on account of which, acting as a "furious man," he refused to recognize the authority of his elder brother, pretended to be "the owner of everything and that he commands," and threatened the lives of his mother and uncle, both in their late 80s.[83]

The conflicts disclosed to the Magistrato dei Pupilli relate not only to disputes between men, but also involve women. We have seen how wives were the most frequent petitioners, together with mothers. Conflicts between mother and son and between spouses were often behind requests of wives and mothers, requiring a decision that, as argued for the case of prodigals, was not an easy one to make. A request for interdiction from a wife was a step in a series of strategies taken to mitigate the strains of sharing a roof with a man whose extravagancies were taken to be the result of a mental illness and to secure the integrity of the husband's patrimony for the sake of their children.[84] Interdiction could help women restrain their husbands while providing them a mediator in their quarrels, which in fact did not end with an interdiction decree.

Conflicts between spouses were never isolated, taking place in a larger familial context where family branches often clashed. For instance, we can find references to the "bitterness" between mothers and daughters-in-law in relation to the administration of an interdicted man's patrimony, which entailed changes in the curator from one woman to another as discords unfolded.[85] Another important source of conflict is related to enmities

108 *Beyond financial mismanagement*

between a wife and her husband's relatives. For instance, Giovan Battista Becciani from Mugello, married and the father of four children, was interdicted by request of "his closest relatives," most probably from the Becciani line. The petitioners declared that both Giovan Battista and his wife were incapable of administering the patrimony, the former because he was *mentecatto* and the latter because she lacked the necessary economy. Furthermore, they claimed the main problem was his wife who, by being prone to splendor and excessive spending, "makes her family suffer greatly." The accusation was that as the couple lived separately, she consumed her husband's resources in socializing with other people, leaving nothing for him. As the local authorities reported, Giovan Battista was "so imbecile and of unsound mind" that nobody believed him capable of managing his affairs, because he completely lacked the necessary economy and prudence.[86]

The petition's core argument was that Giovan Battista needed someone to assist him in the management of his affairs and to protect the patrimony from his wife's excessive spending, whereas no information was given regarding the duration of his state of incapacity. Thus, the justification of the petition was not so much the defendant's behavior and state of mind but rather the concerns of Giovan Battista's relatives about his wife. In fact, all the consulted parties agreed that his wife could not be the administrator, arguing that if she were, she would most certainly squander the patrimony to the direct detriment of her children. Therefore, the petition for interdiction aimed more to distance Giovan Battista's allegedly squandering wife from the patrimony than to deprive him of his rights of administration. In the case of the Becciani family, the same line of argument was employed by this allegedly squandering woman nearly 20 years later, when she petitioned for his elder son, Antonio Becciani, to be interdicted, raising similar accusations against her daughter-in-law.[87]

Interdiction records suggest that the Magistrato dei Pupilli was more than an institution where patrimony could be protected. Families could disclose their animosities to its officials and confide their worries, and they could discuss with them the best way out of the conflict for as long as the interdiction lasted. As petitions continue to appear after the interdiction was decreed and during proceedings for the interdiction to be lifted, we learn how and to what extent family conflicts could be resolved, both because the interdiction changed the balance of powers and because the magistrates exerted a soothing effect on relationships, seeking always the best ways to achieve family harmony. They were strongly concerned with smoothing discords, for instance, appeasing the "hatred" between an interdicted and his male kin by changing the curator to one chosen by the former, or even allowing for a change of residence so that they would not be forced to live together, all with the intention of soothing the bitterness and thus impeding "tragic events" from happening.[88] They intervened when sons attempted to disempower their fathers by carefully pondering each side of the story and trying to come up with the best solution to end the quarrels. Their intervention could entail that interdictions were decreed and lifted many times, as in the case of Giovan Battista Vinattieri, who actively protested the four interdictions decreed against him between 1733 and 1764, during which time the family made their bitter disagreements public and negotiated various ways out of them.[89] The officials had to carefully maintain an equilibrium between the different forces that governed a family, interceding now on behalf of one and then on behalf of another. They could grant a petition for the interdiction to be lifted from an old father who declared he could not continue "suffering" the mistreatments by a son who intended to command his house and afterwards rule for its reinstatement when the son requested it again, arguing his father intended to disinherit him "under the impetus of scorn and ire."[90]

The interdicted usually argued in their defense that the petition was part of a plot against them, the product of new alliances among their relatives. Although the decision to turn to the authorities for their intervention not necessarily had the desired outcome always, interdiction procedures were an arena open for negotiation, and authorities often supported the voice of the weak members of the family. For instance, 86-year-old Michele Fabbroni was considered by the authorities as still capable of managing his affairs. In fact, the magistrates sided with the father, who had depicted "a constant discord between father and sons" in a violent atmosphere illustrated through the accusation that one of his sons had even dared beat him while he slept, which forced him to flee from the residence they all shared.[91]

The extent to which interdiction procedures were employed as a mechanism to solve family conflicts is best shown by petitions for the interdiction to be lifted and the reasons given by authorities to grant it or not. The cases of interdictions that were revoked on the grounds that harmony had returned to the family are particularly illustrative. For example, an old man interdicted based on the declaration that "he has become almost demented" and that "he seems to have become furious [*furioso*] because he often insults atrociously his said sons and their respective wives" had his interdiction lifted only 1 month afterwards.[92] The explanation given by the Pupilli officials was that the interdiction had only been requested "due to some disputes [*dissapori*] that involved the said petitioners," which had now been resolved.[93] On some occasions, details of the family conflict behind the interdiction were not revealed and neither were the terms of reconciliation. But interdictions in which the whole household, including those who had initially requested the interdiction, signed in approval for its lifting months later point to a reconciliation between the parties. They could manifest their agreement by arguing the interdicted was now showing signs of good behavior, or they could retract what they had initially declared, but in any case, the conflicts that had motivated the request for interdiction had abated.[94]

Contrary to what might be expected, interdictions were not only revoked once defendants could prove they had regained their mental faculties or had emerged from derangement. In fact, most times this was very hard to prove, except for the cases in which the disorder had been said to be episodic. As interdiction procedures were much more about the familial dimension of mental incapacity than about the precise characteristics of the alleged mental disorder, petitions for the interdiction to be lifted usually centered around the defendant's change in attitude with regard to their financial behavior and in relation to the way in which they related to their family members.

Acquiring familiarity with interdiction procedures

Hereditary mental incapacity and recurrent episodes of mental derangement provide privileged insight into how families dealt with madness and how they gave shape to the narrative they presented to the authorities. Establishing that the alleged mental derangement was hereditary, a well-established notion by the eighteenth century, served as proof "that the vice is in the blood," giving enough grounds to grant an interdiction or refuse a petition for its revocation.[95] But the presence of hereditary mental incapacity or episodic madness in the history of the family also entailed that relatives requested interdiction several times, be it repeatedly for a same individual or for different members of the same family. Not only do we find cases of people subject to recurrent episodes of madness that alternated with lucid intervals which allowed them to periodically come out of curatorship, as in the case of Lorenzo Baldinotti, but we also encounter mental disorders transmitted from generation to generation, such as from Lorenzo Baldinotti to his son Antonio who was said to have inherited "a spirit and character similar to that of his father, whose extreme extravagance was notorious."[96] It is also possible to find families requesting the interdiction of different family members without it being taken to be a hereditary condition, as is the case with the Panfi family. Pier Francesco Panfi was interdicted in 1732 following a petition claiming that he was absentminded in his advanced age, sent by his daughter Maria Maddalena Panfi with the support of her husband. In 1743, Maria Maddalena Panfi was herself interdicted when her two sons and their guardians said she suffered from epilepsy, which left her with "mind obfuscation and deprived of memory."[97]

What the records suggest is that recourse to the authorities to request interdiction, the subsequent interventions of the Pupilli officials in relation to the curatorship, and the various requests made by family members for them to intervene in ongoing disputes resulted in a familiarity with the procedure and the languages of madness that could explain the repetition of family names. For instance, the Vinattieri family was at different times in communication with the Magistrato dei Pupilli on account of the alleged mental incapacity of two of its members. Giovan Battista Vinattieri was interdicted four times between 1733 and 1764. During this period, the language employed to describe his condition experienced a curious evolution, starting with prodigality, passing through apoplexy, extravagance, and decrepitude, to end in mental alienation caused by drunkenness. Through a series of petitions made by Giovan Battista in a persistent effort to revoke his interdictions, the Pupilli officials negotiated with his relatives and with Giovan Battista himself for different arrangements to settle their ongoing disputes. Years of continual litigation probably gave his daughter the necessary tools to secure an interdiction decree against her husband in 1751 on account of prodigality.[98]

When insanity was recurrent in the family history, its members were more aware of the requirements and functioning of interdiction procedures, knowing precisely what to say and how to say it. Recurring contact with the judicial structure resulted in a clear sophistication of the arguments, strategies, and vocabularies employed by petitioners. Women appear here as the most active agents, empowered by the position the Pupilli had for centuries ascribed to them, and pulling the strings of family life. For instance, according to Elisabetta Montanti, her son Anton Gaetano Diacceti had seriously imperiled the family patrimony with his misbehavior, "disquieting the entire household" with his unsound mind.[99] Suggesting that she had sought help before, she explained in her petition that it was already known to the Pupilli that Anton Gaetano had a "weak mind and uneasy spirit" (*debolezza di mente ed inquieto spirito*). Moreover, his father had been interdicted as demented, as Anton Gaetano would be after his mother's request. The petition was backed up by testimonies that described Anton Gaetano's irrational and extravagant behavior and his open defiance of social hierarchies and of the basic norms of conduct.

We find in this case the usual flexibility of terms. His mother spoke of his uneasy spirit and his weakness of mind, while testimonies characterized him as "stupid of brain" (*scemo di cervello*) and "without judgment" (*senza giudizio*). Witnesses also said that he unsettled his neighbors and prevented them from sleeping, making annoying noises during his continual wanderings, rattling doors, and performing other "impertinences." Recognizing no authority but himself, he slept most of the day and acted extravagantly at night. He had been banished from his lodging for his annoying habits and was in desperate need, according to the testimonies, of being placed under the authority of somebody who would control him. As we have seen, irrationality was recognized in men who were unable to abide by social hierarchies, which was aggravated in those cases, such as the present one, where there was no paternal authority to contain and direct them. According to the testimonies, Anton Gaetano needed to have somebody who would intimidate him, because only then he would stop harassing and mistreating his parents.

From the magistracy's report, we know that mother and son had been in conflict since Anton Gaetano had come of age, when his desire to be appointed administrator of his father's patrimony, which was under the guardianship of Elisabetta Montanti, made him take all kinds of actions against his mother, including legal actions and accusing her of squandering the Diacceti patrimony. The officials of the Pupilli stated the necessity of providing protection for the "anguished" mother against her son's harassments so as to prevent any further vexation.

The case of Anton Gaetano Diacceti shows us a woman, Elisabetta Montanti, who had learned to deal with madness years before, at least since her husband's interdiction in 1718 (i.e., 38 years earlier).[100] The fact that she had been appointed legal guardian of her husband and had administered the patrimony ever since means that she had learned to navigate the judicial measures offered by the Magistrato dei Pupilli long ago. She managed to control her son because she knew how to argue the case in legal terms. Although Anton Gaetano tried to reverse the interdiction sentence, the officials of the Pupilli, with the consent of the Magistrato Supremo, sided with the mother, ruling in her favor.[101] Never during the suit was it necessary for the Pupilli to rely on a medical opinion to assess Anton Gaetano's mental disturbance.

Interdictions and gender

Given the Tuscan patriarchal system of inheritance and property possession, interdiction procedures were, by default, a legal mechanism destined to control the consequences of male mental deviance. The numbers in the records of the Magistrato dei Pupilli are telling: only 28 out of 611 interdictions decreed between 1700 and 1775 affected women. The marginal presence of female insanity in interdiction records is partly amended when we turn to medical documentation. In particular, the examination of the admission records of Santa Dorotea shows that between 1647 and 1750, women represented a minority of the patients admitted to the hospital, but numbers tended to even out during the second half of the century.[102] However, the aforementioned female visibility in Santa Dorotea is not necessarily representative, particularly when we take into account that only the raving mad (*pazzi furiosi*) were admitted to the institution. This means that only those men and women considered a serious danger either to themselves or to the society were deemed liable for committal.

The fact that Tuscan society recorded male madness with such an overwhelming predominance when compared with its female counterpart is in itself a clear sign of the gendered categorization of madness. The ways in which madness made its appearance in eighteenth-century Tuscany suggest at least two things in this regard: first, that the concerns generated by madness were predominantly related to the consequences of male mental disturbance; and second, that female insanity continued to be largely concealed in the domestic sphere. As interdiction procedures were bound to the existence of a property over which the individual had ownership rights, there was simply no need to interdict most women in Tuscany. So long as they were excluded from the inheritance system (beyond their dowry), irrational and irresponsible actions committed by women did not have the same damaging economic effects as those perpetrated by men. In fact, for the most part, women had no patrimony of their own to squander. As a result, female mental disturbances came to the surface only in extraordinary cases, for example, those of widows with administrative power over their family patrimony, usually at the end of their lives; and suicidal and scandalous women of various ages, whose families could not control them or whose families were absent and who ended up in Santa Dorotea.

The fact that female insanity is underrepresented in the Tuscan records, a characteristic that has also been identified in other European contexts, strongly contradicts earlier contentions developed by some scholars regarding the feminization of madness during the eighteenth century.[103] Elaine Showalter, in an influential study published in 1987, claimed that madness toward the end of the eighteenth century had come to be seen as "one of the wrongs of woman," portraying an "essential feminine nature unveiling itself before scientific male rationality."[104] As insanity was enthroned as "the female malady," the madwoman became "the prototype of the confined lunatic" and "a cultural icon."[105] Since the appearance of Showalter's study, scholars have searched for the origins of the construction of madness as a feminine disturbance. This endeavor produced studies on the gendered meanings of lovesickness, the political uses of female melancholy, and the feminine origins of depression.[106] Allan Ingram and Michelle Faubert, for instance, have claimed that madness was regarded as a condition that enhanced feminine characteristics.[107] Madmen, from this point of view, were thought to have lost their masculine attributes, falling into a feminization of their character, being sensibilized by emotions, and weakened by their passions.

Interdiction procedures call into question the assessment made by these studies regarding the process of the "feminization" of madness. In eighteenth-century Tuscany, interdiction procedures were used by the families to control the damage caused by men who were acting against the basic paradigms of their social roles. These records suggest that men's insanity elicited more concern in Tuscan society than women's, producing characterizations that focused almost exclusively on masculine contexts. Men deemed mentally incapacitated failed to act with rationality, economy, and propriety, manifesting their total incapacity to control themselves. The overwhelming number of men interdicted during the eighteenth century who were described as manifesting a wide range of emotional disturbances suggests that psychological suffering was not considered an exclusive prerogative of women. Furthermore, men's instability, extravagances, and recklessness were not considered by Tuscan families as a sign of effeminacy. To be overwhelmed by one's passions was identified as a symptom of both male and female mental disturbance.

There is a key issue to examine regarding the representation of women in interdiction records. The few women interdicted and submitted to the Magistrato dei Pupilli were generally under no direct masculine authority, and, consequently, they were presented as defenseless against deception. This defenseless state was deemed particularly harmful because they were in a position to squander, being the direct holders of the family patrimony. They are said to have been under the direction or supervision of a man (if they were widows or spinsters who had long been the direct holders of a patrimony, this could be a brother or a son) whose recent death had left them defenseless and totally vulnerable to the possibility of people taking advantage of them. This was the case of Lisabetta Miralda Gaci, interdicted in 1730 because of her "poor conduct, judgment and stability."[108] Until then, she had been under the supervision of her brother, who was a priest, but because he had recently passed away, Lisabetta was unsupervised. According to the petitioners, who happened to be her future inheritors, since she completely lacked the capacity to manage her affairs, she could be the victim of fraud by the people surrounding her.

Whereas women denounced for mental incapacity were thought to need the assistance of a man to behave properly and manage their economic affairs, in the case of men, it was usually the opposite: they needed the supervision of a woman. Compared to kinsmen, who were thought to introduce more disturbances into the domestic disorders caused by the interdicted when they were appointed administrators, women were thought to exert a soothing effect. Precisely because women were by nature and law shielded from the dangers posed by patrimony mismanagement, they were positioned as the interim heads of family and entrusted with the responsibility of reintroducing the lost rationality to the household. Both their male kin and the authorities considered them the most appropriate palliative to the disorder caused by male insanity. Furthermore, the possibility that men could re-emerge from their disordered state of mind was very much based on women's feminine capacities to improve the situation.

Women repeatedly appear playing a pivotal role as disciplining agents in the family. Their petitions to interdict their husbands or sons, for instance, frequently recalled their previous efforts to restrain and correct them.[109] We can thus consider that petitioning for an interdiction was a mechanism to empower women so that they could complete a task they had already been executing before the intervention of the authorities. Furthermore, it is interesting to note that their intervention was not necessarily received negatively by the affected men. We have, for instance, the case of Marco Barni, who petitioned for his interdiction to be revoked arguing that "given that now he has a spouse and children, he is now released [*spogliato*] from all those passions that before moved him to spend unnecessarily."[110] Similarly, men many times explicitly requested that their wives be appointed administrators, either because this was perceived to be a way to avoid incurring the payments that would be necessary if an external person were entrusted with the task, or because they did not trust other members of the family. This was the case of Andrea Patriarchi who, distrusting his mother, explicitly asked for the woman he had married, after he had been interdicted, to be appointed administrator of his patrimony.[111] Hidden discords were usually behind these kinds of requests, for in this case the disagreement was not only between Andrea and his mother, but probably most of all between wife and mother-in-law, for it was his wife who filed the petition for the change in the administration. In turn, when the interdicted petitioned for the revocation of the interdiction, it was frequently the support of a mother's or wife's voice that moved the authorities in their favor.

Thus, interdicted women were portrayed in the opposite spectrum of the numerous women who were appointed administrators of their sons' or husbands' patrimonies. In this sense, there is a clear contrast between the rational and independent role played by women as guardians of their children and husbands and the secondary and weak position they were said to hold when they were the object of interdiction. On the other hand, women were many times the object of the domestic consequences of madness, and so they were recurrent petitioners during the period their sons, husbands, or fathers were under the curatorship of the Pupilli. They were protected by the magistrates, and they were granted permission to live separated from their husbands on account of their husbands' known follies, but they were not necessarily in a weak position. The solution to family disorder and to patrimonial mismanagement was placed in the hands of women, namely the mothers, wives, or widows who were seen to have the power to produce the desired change in men. Alternatively, if men's mental condition was seen as irreparable, women were the best option to reduce the damage it caused. Only in the cases of elderly men does the role of the female members of the family seem to have been less decisive, for although wives and daughters frequently took the leading role, on many other occasions it was transferred to the first-born son.

The role assumed in Tuscany by the female members of the family as the privileged interlocutors with the authorities, on the one hand, and as primary performers of the role of curbing and caring for incapacitated adults, on the other, seems to be a peculiarity of the Tuscan context.[112] That women were becoming active participants in the administration of justice in a wide range of jurisdictions between the seventeenth and eighteenth centuries is well known.[113] However, studies on the early modern inquiries into mental capacity are silent regarding the role assumed by women once the judicial procedure was over, that is, during the guardianship of the mentally incapable. This can be partly explained by their primary focus on the procedures and not on the guardianship. Historians such as Robert Allan Houston and Laurent Cartayrade have been mostly concerned with how inquiries into mental capacity were carried out, the representations and meanings of madness revealed in the procedures, and the general patterns of insane behavior that can be drawn from them.[114] But both historians seem to lack the possibility offered by the Tuscan records of tracing what happened after the interdiction had been decreed. In fact, the Tuscan interdiction records allow us to follow the cases from the initial petition until the revocation of the interdiction sentence (which could cover from several days to the whole life of the defendant). This advantage not only allows us to achieve a more thorough understanding of madness, but it also sheds light on the crucial role played by the female members of the family in the experience of and responses to mental incapacity.

***

The language of mental incapacity developed in the eighteenth-century records of the Magistrato dei Pupilli was a cultural translation of the juridical language that had been used in civil trials for centuries. Legal knowledge had been appropriated, matured, and reformulated, incorporating the new concerns of the eighteenth century. Overall, categories of mental incapacity did not change compared to the previous centuries, except for a preference for the term *demente*, which came to encompass all the other categories of mental incapacity except for prodigality. The openness and vagueness of legal categories enabled petitioners and witnesses to focus their descriptions on the behavior of the defendant by using their own terminology, giving space for a cultural negotiation over the indicators of insanity, and the possible mechanisms to minimize its domestic and social consequences.

Perceptions of mental incapacity in eighteenth-century Tuscany appear inseparable from the experience of the family and the rhythms of its relationships. For this reason, while interdiction procedures provide very little information about medical categories, they are generous in the information they give about the family. Through them, and with the excuse of describing a mentally disturbed relative, interdiction narratives ultimately define the Tuscan families in all their complexity. Through the interdiction procedures, we witness a family structure that escapes the rigid patriarchal model, presenting interconnected relations between maternal and paternal kin, shared and negotiated responsibilities, clashing personalities with conflicting agencies, all placed in the legal arena of the Magistrato dei Pupilli seeking public arbitration. Furthermore, the way out of the disorder produced by mental incapacity, predominantly male, was the appointment of women as interim heads of family. The cure for the social consequences of madness was, thus, not only to secure the patrimony from the madman's financial mismanagement, but also, ultimately, to place him under the custody of a woman.

Interdiction procedures show that Tuscan litigants knew how to shape their narratives. But this familiarity with the languages of madness was part of a wider structure, stemming out of the particular itinerary followed by the allegedly mad and their families through the different remedies offered by the ducal administration. Families could request the interdiction of somebody more than once, and they could request it for different individuals of the same family. Families could resort to different measures contemporaneously or subsequently. An individual could be admitted to Santa Dorotea or Santa Maria Nuova without him or her being interdicted, and an interdicted could be sent to a hospital before, during, or after the interdiction, for which families had to move through a different legal path. The appearance of the same individual in different stages of the itineraries of madness shows a family group well acquainted with what it meant to be mad; how madness had to be represented in civil courts, criminal courts, and in medical environments; and what remedies were available to cope with its consequences. To fully grasp the shaping of notions of madness and the circulation of its languages, we now need to open our view to include the walls of Santa Dorotea, the judicial arena of criminal courts, and the activities of the Auditore Fiscale in his capacity as head of police and supervisor of the criminal courts.

Notes

1 ASF, MPAP, *Memoriali*, F. 2302, no. 73, November 1748–January 1749.
2 Robert Allan Houston, *Madness and Society in Eighteenth-Century Scotland* (Oxford: Oxford University Press, 2000), 144–151; and Laurent Cartayrade, "Property, Prodigality, and Madness: A Study of Interdiction Records in Eighteenth-Century Paris," (PhD diss., University of Maryland, 1997), 174–186.
3 Akihito Suzuki, "The Household and the Care of Lunatics in Eighteenth-Century London," in *The Locus of Care: Families, Communities, Institutions, and the Provision of Welfare Since Antiquity*, ed. Peregrine Horden and Richard Smith (London and New York: Routledge, 1998), 156.
4 This is also a difference compared to Scotland, where people who had been legally declared to be mentally incapable (and cognosed) could not marry. Houston, *Madness and Society*, 147.
5 The stages of a woman's life were usually conceived in accordance with their relationships with men. Silvana Seidel Menchi, "The Girl and the Hourglass: Periodization of Women's Lives in Western Preindustrial Societies," in *Time, Space and Women's Lives*, ed. Anne Jacobson Schutte, Thomas Kuehn, and Silvana Seidel Menchi (Kirksville, MO: Truman State University Press, 2001), 41–74; Renée Baernstein, "'Sposa, figlia, sorella e vecchia matre'. Invecchiare donna in età moderna, tra demografia e cultura," *Storia delle donne* 2 (2006): 213–230.
6 Paolo Zacchia, *Quaestionum medico-legalium tomi tres* (Nuremberg: Sumptibus Joannis Georgii Lochneri, 1726), Book II, Title I, 112–159.
7 ASF, MPAAP, F. 248, "Statuti et ordini della Corte et Magistrato delli Offittiali de' Pupilli," Rubric 2, fols. 4–4v; and "Bando. Circa l'Esecuzione de' Privilegi, e Statuti del Magistrato delli Signori Ufiziali de' Pupilli." ASF, MS, *Suppliche*, F. 1180, fols. 1307–1311 and fols. 1332–1333.
8 The possibilities and limitations of notions of madness as a socially constructed or as a natural phenomenon have been rigorously discussed by scholars. For an overview, see W.F. Bynum, Roy Porter, and Michael Shepherd, eds., *The Anatomy of Madness*, vol. 2, "Introduction" (London and New York: Routledge, 2004), 1–16; and Houston, *Madness and Society*, 19–27, among many others.
9 *Vocabolario degli accademici della Crusca* (Florence: Appresso Domenico Maria Manni, 1729–1738), s.v. "mentecatto," www.lessicografia.it/Controller?lemma=MENTECATTO, accessed August 8, 2020.
10 *Vocabolario*, s.v. "milenso/melenso," www.lessicografia.it/Controller?lemma=MILENSO, accessed August 8, 2020.
11 *Vocabolario*, s.v. "stupido" and s.v. "stolido," www.lessicografia.it/Controller?lemma=STUPIDO, and www.lessicografia.it/Controller?lemma=STOLIDO, accessed August 8, 2020.

12 ASF, MPAP, *Memoriali*, F. 2303, no. 256, March 1753.
13 ASF, MPAP, *Memoriali*, F. 2304, no. 60, September 1756; ASF, MPAP, *Memoriali*, F. 2305, no. 127, February 1761; ASF, MS, *Atti*, 1867, January 1724/25, f. 661; ASF, MPAP, *Memoriali*, F. 2305, no. 150, August 1761.
14 ASF, MPAP, *Memoriali*, F. 2304, no. 31, June 1756.
15 ASF, MPAP, *Memoriali*, F. 2304, no. 2, November 1755; ASF, MPAP, *Memoriali*, 2309, no. 147, August 1773.
16 ASF, MPAP, *Memoriali*, F. 2307, no. 191, November 1768.
17 ASF, MPAP, *Memoriali*, F. 2307, no. 96, January 1768; ASF, MPAP, *Memoriali*, F. 2307, no. 106, March 1768.
18 Elizabeth Mellyn, *Mad Tuscans and Their Families: A History of Mental Disorder in Early Modern Italy* (Philadelphia: University of Pennsylvania Press, 2014), 129. For early modern medico-legal taxonomies of mental illnesses before 1700, see, for instance, Rita Mazza, "La malattia mentale nella medicina del cinquecento: Tassonomia e casi clinici," in *Follia, psichiatria e società*, ed. Alberto De Bernardi (Milan: Franco Angeli, 1982), 304–316; Carlo Colombero, "Un contributo alla formazione della nozione di malattia mentale: le 'Questioni medico-legali' di Paolo Zacchia," in *Follia, psichiatria e società. Istituzioni manicomiali, scienza psichiatrica e classi sociali nell'Italia moderna e contemporanea*, ed. Alberto De Bernardi (Milan: Franco Angeli, 1982), 317–329; and Alessandro Dini, ed., *Il medico e la follia. Cinquanta casi di malattia mentale della letteratura medica italiana del Seicento* (Florence: Le Lettere, 1997).
19 ASF, MPAP, *Memoriali*, F. 2303, no. 50, August 1752. Orazio Penci's interdiction was revoked in July 1754, when a priest's testimony certified that he had recovered his soundness of mind. See ASF, MPAP, *Memoriali*, F. 2303, no. 195, July 1754.
20 Peter Rushton, "Idiocy, the Family and the Community in Early Modern North-East England," in *From Idiocy to Mental Deficiency*, ed. David Wright and Anne Digby (London and New York: Routledge, 1996), 49. However, Jonathan Andrews has drawn attention to the problematic consequences of exaggerating the deliberate vagueness and flexibility of early modern categories of madness and mental disability: see Jonathan Andrews, "Identifying and Providing for the Mentally Disabled," in *From Idiocy to Mental Deficiency*, 66. On the meanings of lunacy and idiocy, their contexts, implications, and provisions, see Wright and Digby, *From Idiocy to Mental Deficiency*; and Akihito Suzuki, "Lunacy in Seventeenth- and Eighteenth-Century England: Analysis of Quarter Sessions Records: Part 1" *History of Psychiatry* 2 (1991): 437–456.
21 Houston, *Madness and Society*, 164–171. On the overlapping of categories in Tuscany prior to the eighteenth century, Mellyn, *Mad Tuscans*, 18.
22 ASF, MPAP, *Memoriali*, F. 2303, no. 50, August 1752.
23 ASF, MPAP, *Memoriali*, F. 2306, no. 176 and no. 247, July and May 1765.
24 This is what Elizabeth Mellyn has called "patrimonial rationality." Mellyn, *Mad Tuscans*, 103–104.
25 Roberto Bizzocchi, *Cicisbei. Morale privata e identità nazionale in Italia* (Rome and Bari: Laterza, 2008).
26 For instance, ASF, MPAP, *Memoriali*, F. 2300, no. 440, April 1734 and no. 482, April 1735.
27 Elisa Novi Chavarria, "Ideologia e comportamenti familiari nei predicatori italiani fra Cinque e Settecento. Tematiche e modelli," *Rivista Storica Italiana* 100, no. 3 (1988): 679–723 and Isabel Morant and Mónica Bolufer, *Amor, Matrimonio y Familia* (Madrid: Editorial Síntesis, 1998), 55–141.
28 Mellyn, *Mad Tuscans*, 10 and 103–104.
29 ASF, MPAP, *Memoriali*, F. 2304, no. 194, August 1758.

30 He refused to give back the keys of the cupboards where money to be paid to third parties was kept, even after he was legally ordered to do so. His stubborn refusal was identified as another sign of insanity.
31 Similarly, Jonathan Andrews and Andrew Scull in their study on the case book of the English mad-doctor John Monro speak of "the existence of relatively broadly shared and nonconflictual cultural assumptions that served as the basis for negotiating agreements about the nature and causality of patient's afflictions and the meaning of their speech and behavior." Jonathan Andrews and Andrew Scull, *Customers and Patrons of the Mad-Trade: The Management of Lunacy in Eighteenth-Century London* (Berkeley: University of California Press, 2003), 57.
32 Mellyn, *Mad Tuscans*, 113–148 and *passim*; Lisa Roscioni, *Il governo della follia. Ospedali, medici e pazzi nell'età moderna* (Milan: Bruno Mondadori, 2003), 155–176 and *passim*; Houston, *Madness and Society*, 173–236; Andrews and Scull, *Customers and Patrons*, 58–81; Joel Peter Eigen, *Witnessing Insanity: Madness and Mad-Doctors in the English Court* (New Haven and London: Yale University Press, 1995), 82–107; Roy Porter, *Mind-Forg'd Manacles: A History of Madness in England from the Restoration to the Regency* (London: Penguin Books, 1990), 33–109; and Michael MacDonald, *Mystical Bedlam: Madness, Anxiety, and Healing in Seventeenth-Century England* (Cambridge: Cambridge University Press, 1981), 112–172 among others.
33 ASF, MPAP, *Memoriali*, F. 2304, no. 60, September 1756.
34 ASF, MPAP, *Memoriali*, F. 2303, no. 210, August 1754; ASF, MPAP, *Memoriali*, F. 2310, no. 237, March 1775; ASF, MPAP, *Memoriali*, F. 2303, no. 62, December 1752; and ASF, MPAP, *Memoriali*, F. 2303, no. 245, February 1755, respectively.
35 ASF, MPAP, *Memoriali*, F. 2310, no. 237, June 1775; ASF, MPAP, *Memoriali*, F. 2307, no. 19, May 1767; and ASF, CR, *Fiscale*, F. 758, no. 60 June 1755 and ASF, MPAP, *Memoriali*, F. 2308, no. 47, August 1770, respectively.
36 The conflation between cause and symptom pervades early modern conceptions of disease. Andrew Wear, *Knowledge & Practice in English Medicine, 1550–1680* (Cambridge: Cambridge University Press, 2000), 120.
37 ASF, MPAP, *Memoriali*, F. 2304, no. 115, April 1757; ASF, MPAP, *Memoriali*, F. 2303, no. 249, March 1755; and ASF, MPAP, *Memoriali*, F. 2302, no. 243, March 1751.
38 Fabio Stok, "Modelli e tradizione antica nella psicopatologia di Zacchia," in *Paolo Zacchia. Alle origini della medicina legale 1584–1659*, ed. Alessandro Pastore and Giovanni Rossi (Milan: Franco Angeli, 2008), 74–90; Colombero, "Un contributo alla formazione," 317–329; Houston, *Madness and Society*, 176–182; and Porter, *Mind-Forg'd Manacles*, 35.
39 ASF, MPAP, *Memoriali*, F. 2305, no. 2, July 1759.
40 ASF, MPAP, *Memoriali*, F. 2300, no. 311, June 1730.
41 Among the outward signs of madness, the naked madman or madwoman running amok through the streets is a well-known cultural stereotype. Nudity generally occupies a space in the studies of madness, and it has been singled out as a valuable key to grasp the meanings of early modern mental derangement. For instance, historians working with inquiries into mental capacity have argued, on the one hand, that external appearance was a determinant clue in early modern societies for indicating social status, which placed nudity as symbol of poverty and as a source of shame and lack of decorum. On the other hand, historians have also read the disdain and rejection of the nudity and filthiness of the mad body by using the interpretative codes provided by the framework of the civilizing process and the growing importance of hygiene and manners. Houston, *Madness and Society*, 173–183; Cartayrade, "Property, Prodigality, and Madness," 417–425; and the cases examined in Mellyn, *Mad*

Tuscans, 95 and *passim*. See also Roscioni, *Il governo della follia*, 163–168; Graziella Magherini and Vittorio Biotti, *L'isola delle Stinche e i percorsi della follia a Firenze nei secoli XIV-XVIII* (Florence: Ponte alle Grazie, 1992), 32, 39 and 117; MacDonald, *Mystical Bedlam*, 129–132; Monica Calabritto, "'Furor' melanconico tra teoria e pratica legale," *Studi storici* 51, no. 1 (2010): 113–137; and Jonathan Andrews, "The (Un)dress of the Mad Poor in England, c.1650–1850," Part 1 and Part 1. *History of Psychiatry* 18, no. 1 and 18, no. 2 (2007): 5–24 and 131–156, among many others.

42 Francesca Paoli del Feo, interdicted twice, was said to have dissipated her patrimony to the point of "reducing herself to wandering through the streets almost naked." ASF, MPAP, *Memoriali*, F. 2303, no. 264, December 1754.

43 Procedures based on deafness or muteness were, in general, decided with little contention. Almost no evidence was given by the petitioners as if the physical condition itself was proof enough.

44 However, as Mellyn warns us, "The mad may have suffered from some kind of physical impairment, but the physically impaired were not necessarily considered mad." Mellyn, *Mad Tuscans*, 19.

45 Judging from Mellyn's study, it seems that old age did not generate the same anxieties in Tuscany before the eighteenth century. Mellyn, *Mad Tuscans*.

46 Although studies have stressed that early modern societies did not equate old age with senility or a state of dependency, what this senility or decrepitude amounted to, how it was experienced, and what measures were taken to cope with it remain an open field of study. See Daniel Schäfer, "'That Senescence Itself Is an Illness': A Transitional Medical Concept of Age and Ageing in the Eighteenth Century," *Medical History* 46, no. 4 (2002): 525–548; Susannah Ottaway, *The Decline of Life: Old Age in Eighteenth-Century England* (Cambridge: Cambridge University Press, 2004), 26–44; German Berrios and Roy Porter, "Dementia," in *A History of Clinical Psychiatry*, ed. German Berrios and Roy Porter (London: The Athlone Press, 1995), 34–62; Susannah Ottaway, "Medicine and Old Age," in *The Oxford Handbook of the History of Medicine*, ed. Mark Jackson (Oxford: Oxford University Press, 2011), 338–354; and David G. Troyansky, *Old Age in the Old Regime* (Ithaca, NY: Cornell University Press, 1989), 109–124. I have examined further the emotional dimensions of old-age mental incapacity in "The Emotional Disturbances of Old Age: On the Articulation of Old-Age Mental Incapacity in Eighteenth-Century Tuscany," *Historical Reflections/Reflexions Historiques* 41, no. 2 (2015): 19–36; and "Cuando la mente se oscurece y el cuerpo se debilita. El dolor de la ancianidad en el Gran Ducado de Toscana, siglo XVIII," in *Homo Dolens. Cartografías del dolor: sentidos, experiencias, registros*, ed. Rafael Gaune and Claudio Rolle (Santiago: FCE, 2018), 293–314.

47 See, for instance, the interdictions of Marc. Antonio Baldelli, said to be "of a most advanced age," and the 75-year-old Salomone Calò. ASF, MPAP, *Memoriali*, F. 2303, no. 3, October 1751 and ASF, MPAP, *Memoriali*, F. 2303, no. 8, December 1751.

48 ASF, MPAP, *Memoriali*, F. 2301, no. 201, September 1743.
49 ASF, MPAP, *Memoriali*, F. 2306, no. 245, March 1766.
50 ASF, MPAP, *Memoriali*, F. 2300, no. 440, April 1734.
51 ASF, MPAP, *Memoriali*, F. 2300, no. 249, July 1728.
52 ASF, MPAP, *Memoriali*, F. 2303, no. 120, July 1753 and no. 240, January 1755.
53 Labarca, "Cuando la mente se oscurece," 296–297. On the negotiations between families and authorities over the intervention of public institutions in the care of the elderly and the interplay between "imposed" solidarity and affective bonds, see Angela Groppi, *Il welfare prima del welfare. Assistenza alla*

vecchiaia e solidarietà tra generazioni a Roma in età moderna (Roma: Viella, 2010), 117–229.
54 ASF, MPAP, *Memoriali*, F. 2304, no. 2, July 1759.
55 ASF, MPAP, *Memoriali*, F. 2307, no. 147, June 1768.
56 Houston, *Madness and Society*, 91–107.
57 ASF, MPAP, *Memoriali*, F. 2304, no. 31, June 1756.
58 ASF, MPAP, *Memoriali*, F. 2302, no. 270, July 1751.
59 Houston, *Madness and Society*, 127; and Akihito Suzuki, *Madness at Home: The Psychiatrist, the Patient, and the Family in England, 1820–1860* (Berkeley: University of California Press, 2006), 19.
60 ASF, MPAP, *Memoriali*, F. 2304, no. 85, March 1757.
61 ASF, MPAP, *Memoriali*, F. 2302, no. 73, November 1748–January 1749.
62 ASF, MPAP, *Memoriali*, F. 2304, no. 68, December 1756.
63 This line of argument was raised by the daughters of Maria Eleonora Faraoni. ASF, MPAP, *Memoriali*, F. 2302, no. 209, August 1750.
64 Interdiction of Ipolito Francesco Gaetano Giuducci, ASF, MS, *Atti e Scritture*, F. 1867, fols. 638–661, January 1735/25.
65 For a discussion of the problem of abuses behind the disclosure of madness, see Houston, *Madness and Society*, 93–97.
66 For instance, Gio. Francesco Miniati's brother left a testamentary disposition indicating that his wife was to be appointed curator of his brother so that he would be cared for and served "with the same love as if he was her son, father or brother." ASF, MPAP, *Memoriali*, F. 2307, no. 75, July 1767.
67 ASF, MPAP, *Memoriali*, F. 2307, no. 2, March 1767.
68 For instance, see the interdiction of Girolamo Cocci and his request for the interdiction to be lifted in ASF, MPAP, *Memoriali*, F. 2304, no. 59 and no. 70, October 1756; and Niccolò Boldrini's petition for his interdiction to be revoked, ASF, MPAP, *Memoriali*, F. 2304, no. 105, May 1757.
69 ASF, MPAP, *Memoriali*, F. 2303, no. 13, December 1751; no. 196, July 1754; and no. 264, January 1755. Francesca Paoli del Feo is one of the few defendants whose physical appearance was described in the interdiction records.
70 ASF, MPAP, *Memoriali*, F. 2303, no. 264, December 1754.
71 ASF, CR, *Fiscale*, F. 762, no. 2, August 1765.
72 Interdiction of Marco Antonio Barli and of Gaetano Damiani. ASF, MPAP, *Memoriali*, F. 2304, no. 12, and February 1752 and F. 2303, no. 62, December 1752, respectively.
73 Interdiction of Carlo Antonio Porcellotti, ASF, MPAP, *Memoriali*, F. 2307, no. 189, May 1768.
74 While Margherita Bizzochi received a favorable response for her request that her demented husband Lorenzo Maestrini not be allowed to come near her home, Francesca Arcangioli was forced to resume cohabitation with her husband Giuseppe Rossi on the grounds that she had married him already knowing he was demented, so she could not raise it as a reason for separation. ASF, MPAP, *Memoriali*, F. 2300, no. 492, November 1735 and ASF, MPAP, *Memoriali*, F. 2300, no. 288, October 1729.
75 ASF, MPAP, *Memoriali*, F. 2301, no. 265, June 1747.
76 ASF, MPAP, *Memoriali*, F. 2302, no. 129, July 1749.
77 It is tempting to associate this Tuscan practice with French mechanisms for dealing with the *désordre des familles*. Nonetheless, we have to take into account that interdictions are not really equivalent to the French *lettres de cachet*. Unlike the latter, interdictions were generally not the resort of executive power and they had nothing to do with confinement. Further, interdictions were exclusively concerned with mental incapacity defined (even if broadly) according to pre-established categories. Nonetheless, interdictions and *lettres*

de cachet are similar insofar as they both entailed that private matters were made public so that the state, through its police or judicial administration, could mediate, solve, or at least hinder family disorder. Arlette Farge and Michel Foucault, *Le Désordre des familles: lettres de cachet des Archives de la Bastille au XVIIIe siècle* (Paris: Gallimard, Julliard, 1982).
78 Daniela Lombardi, *Matrimonio di antico regime* (Bologna: Il Mulino, 2001), 386–391.
79 This is what later petitions sent by the sons of the interdicted Filippo Catani show. ASF, MPAP, *Memoriali*, F. 2300, no. 249, July 1728.
80 ASF, MPAP, *Memoriali*, F. 2304, no. 68, December 1756 and F. 2305, no. 155, July 1761.
81 ASF, MPAP, *Memoriali*, F. 2304, no. 114, July 1757.
82 ASF, MPAP, *Memoriali*, F. 2302, no. 161, 1750.
83 ASF, MPAP, *Memoriali*, F. 2303, no. 62, December 1752.
84 For instance, the request of Maria Rosa Altoviti to be appointed administrator of her husband's patrimony was only one of the many times she turned to the grand ducal administration in her long struggle with Franco del Sera's widely acknowledged madness. ASF, MPAP, *Memoriali*, F. 2307, no. 47, August 1770. A more complete picture of this case appears in other requests made by Maria Rosa directly to the Auditore Fiscale, for instance, in ASF, CR, *Fiscale*, F. 755, no. 10 and F. 758, no. 60. On this case, see also Chapter 4.
85 As was the case with relation to Orazio Pennetti, which was debated in a series of petitions sent by his mother and daughter-in-law. ASF, MPAP, *Memoriali*, F. 2303, no. 179 and no. 197, May 1754.
86 ASF, MPAP, *Memoriali*, F. 2301, no. 285, June 1747.
87 ASF, MPAP, *Memoriali*, F. 2306, no. 120, August 1764; ASF, MPAP, *Memoriali*, F. 2308, no. 79, January 1771; and ASF, MPAP, *Memoriali*, F. 2309, no. 280, October 1773. This case is examined further in Chapter 6.
88 Petition of Lorenzo Galli for his interdiction to be lifted, ASF, MPAP, *Memoriali*, F. 2300, no. 235, January 1727/28; petition of Giuseppe Buonamici for his administrator to be changed, ASF, MPAP, *Memoriali*, F. 2302, no. 93, April 1749; and petition of Marc'Antonio Barli for the removal of his brother from the *attoria*, ASF, MPAP, *Memoriali*, F. 2303, no. 169, April 1754.
89 ASF, MPAP, *Memoriali*, F. 2300, no. 425, September 1733; ASF, MPAP, *Memoriali*, F. 2301, no. 99, October 1740; ASF, MPAP, *Memoriali*, F. 2301, no. 137, October 1741; ASF, MPAP, *Memoriali*, F. 2301, no. 164, September 1742, ASF, MPAP, *Memoriali*, F. 2301, no. 204, November 1743; ASF, MPAP, *Memoriali*, F. 2301, no. 121(2°), May 1744; ASF, MPAP, *Memoriali*, F. 2301, no. 132(2°), July 1744; ASF, MPAP, *Memoriali*, F. 2304, no. 156, February 1758; ASF, MPAP, *Memoriali*, F. 2304, no. 168; ASF, MPAP, *Memoriali*, F. 2304, no. 210, July 1758; ASF, MPAP, *Memoriali*, F. 2304, no. 239, March 1759; ASF, MPAP, *Memoriali*, F. 2305, no. 55, April 1760; and ASF, MPAP, *Memoriali*, F. 2306, no. 76, February 1764.
90 Petition of Carlo Felici for his interdiction to be lifted, ASF, MPAP, *Memoriali*, F. 2301, no. 163, August 1742; and petition of his son for a second interdiction, F. 2301, no. 218, April–May 1744.
91 ASF, MS, *Suppliche*, F. 1209, January 1762, fols. 78–79.
92 Interdiction of Giovanni Magherini. ASF, MPAP, *Memoriali*, F. 2301, no. 215(2°), May 1746.
93 Petition sent by Giovanni Magherini together with his sons for his interdiction to be lifted. ASF, MPAP, *Memoriali*, F. 2301, no. 226, July 1746.
94 Petition of Gio Franco Natucci for his interdiction to be lifted. ASF, MPAP, *Memoriali*, F. 2303, no. 144, September 1753.

Beyond financial mismanagement 123

95 Argument given by the officials of the Magistrato Supremo for not granting the petition made by Gaetano Migliorini for his interdiction to be lifted. ASF, MPAP, *Memoriali*, F. 2307, no. 22, June 1767.
96 This is how his father's curator, Marco Guerrini, described him when he requested his imprisonment 1 year before he managed to secure his interdiction. ASF, CR, *Fiscale*, F. 759, no. 11, February 1759; and ASF, MPAP, *Memoriali*, F. 2307, no. 169, September 1768, respectively. See also the next chapter for a further discussion.
97 ASF, MPAP, *Memoriali*, F. 2300, no. 380, May 1732; and F. 2301, no. 201, September 1743, respectively.
98 ASF, MPAP, *Memoriali*, F. 2305, no. 55, March 1760. The interdictions can be found in ASF, MPAP, *Memoriali*, F. 2300, no. 425, September 1733; ASF, MPAP, *Memoriali*, F. 2301, no. 99, October 1740; ASF, MPAP, *Memoriali*, F. 2302, no. 287, September 1751; ASF, MPAP, *Memoriali*, F. 2304, no. 156, February 1758; and ASF, MPAP, *Memoriali*, F. 2306, no. 76, February 1764.
99 ASF, MPAP, *Memoriali*, F. 2304, no. 32, June 1756.
100 ASF, MPAP, *Campione*, F. 112, fol. 51v.
101 For Anton Gaetano Diacceti's petition to reverse the interdiction sentence, see ASF, MPAP, *Memoriali*, F. 2304, no. 42, July 1756.
102 Roscioni, *Il governo della follia*, 124.
103 The fact that women are underrepresented in the eighteenth-century records of madness led Houston to assert that female confinement constitutes a myth, particularly the idea that "men used asylums to get rid of unwanted wives." Robert Allan Houston, "Madness and Gender in the Long Eighteenth Century," *Social History* 27, no. 3 (2002): 314–115. Women are equally underrepresented in inquiries into mental capacity in Scotland: see Houston, *Madness and Society*, 124.
104 Elaine Showalter, *The Female Malady: Women, Madness, and English Culture, 1830–1980* (New York: Penguin Books, 1987), 3.
105 Showalter, *The Female Malady*, 8.
106 Among others, see Jane E. Kromm, "The Feminization of Madness in Visual Representation," *Feminist Studies* 20, no. 3 (1994): 507–535; Juliana Schiesari, *The Gendering of Melancholia: Feminism, Psychoanalysis, and the Symbolics of the Loss in Renaissance Literature* (Ithaca and London: Cornell University Press, 1992); Magdalena S. Sánchez, "Melancholy and Female Illness: Habsburg Women and Politics at the Court of Philip III," *Journal of Women's History* 8, no. 2 (1996): 81–102; Angela Groppi, "La malinconia di Lucrezia Barberini d'Este," in *I linguaggi del potere nell'età barocca, vol. 2. Donne e sfera pubblica*, ed. Francesca Cantù (Rome: Viella, 2009), 197–227; George Rousseau, "Depression's Forgotten Genealogy: Notes towards a History of Depression," *History of Psychiatry* 11 (2000): 71–106.
107 Allan Ingram and Michelle Faubert, *Cultural Constructions of Madness in Eighteenth Century Writing* (Basingstoke: Palgrave Macmillan, 2005), 136–169.
108 ASF, MPAP, *Memoriali*, F. 2300, no. 329, November 1730.
109 Isabella Corbini, wife of the interdicted Cammillo Moresi. ASF, MS, *Suppliche*, F. 1208, fol. 337, April 1761.
110 ASF, MPAP, *Memoriali*, F. 2305, no. 92, September 1760.
111 ASF, MPAP, *Memoriali*, F. 2306, no. 109, July 1764.
112 It is important to recall here that, since its early beginnings, the Magistrato dei Pupilli tended to give guardianship and patrimony administration to widows; so having women with administrative power over the family inheritance was not a novelty or a rarity in the eighteenth century. As Giulia Calvi has argued, women in this context appear not as the weak member of the household but rather as a powerful agent legitimized by the state through what she has called the moral contract between state and widows. Giulia Calvi, *Il contratto morale. Madri e figli nella Toscana moderna* (Rome: Laterza, 1994), 16–18 and 25–29.

113 Chiara La Rocca, *Tra moglie e marito. Matrimoni e separazioni a Livorno nel Settecento* (Bologna: Società editrice Il Molino, 2009); Silvana Seidel Menchi and Diego Quaglioni, eds., *Coniugi nemici. La separazione in Italia dal XII al XVIII secolo* (Bologna: Il Molino, 2000); and Laura Gowing, *Domestic Dangers: Women, Words, and Sex in Early Modern London* (Oxford: Oxford University Press, 1996), among many others.

114 Houston, *Madness and Society*; and Cartayrade, "Property, Prodigality, and Madness."

Bibliography chapter 3

Manuscripts

Archivio di Stato di Firenze (ASF)

- Consiglio di Reggenza (CR), *Fiscale*, F. 754–762
- Magistrato dei Pupilli ed Adulti Avanti il Principato (MPAAP), F. 248
- Magistrato dei Pupilli et Adulti del Principato (MPAP)

  - *Campione di Deliberazioni e Partiti*, F. 108–F. 166
  - *Atti e Sentenze*, F. 1144–F. 1362
  - *Suppliche e informazioni: Memoriali e Negozi di Cancelleria*, F. 2299–F. 2318
  - *Filza Lettere e Responsive*, F. 2480–F. 2519

- Magistrato Supremo (MS)

  - *Suppliche*, F. 1179–F. 1188
  - *Atti e Scritture*, F. 1845–F. 2103

Printed sources

Vocabolario degli accademici della Crusca, 6 vols. Florence: Appresso Domenico Maria Manni, 1729–1738. DOI:10.23833/BD/LESSICOGRAFIA, www.lessicografia.it/index.jsp. Accessed August 8, 2020.

Zacchia, Paolo. *Quaestionum medico-legalium tomi tres*. Nuremberg: Sumptibus Joannis Georgii Lochneri, 1726.

References

Andrews, Jonathan. "Identifying and Providing for the Mentally Disabled." In *From Idiocy to Mental Deficiency*, edited by David Wright and Anne Digby, 65–92. London and New York: Routledge, 1996.

Andrews, Jonathan. "The (Un)dress of the Mad Poor in England, c.1650–1850," Part 1 and Part 2. *History of Psychiatry* 18, no. 1 and 18, no. 2 (2007): 5–24 and 131–156.

Andrews, Jonathan, and Andrew Scull. *Customers and Patrons of the Mad-Trade: The Management of Lunacy in Eighteenth-Century London*. Berkeley: University of California Press, 2003.

Baernstein, Renée. "'Sposa, figlia, sorella e vecchia matre'. Invecchiare donna in età moderna, tra demografia e cultura." *Storia delle donne* 2 (2006): 213–230.
Berrios, German, and Roy Porter. "Dementia." In *A History of Clinical Psychiatry*, edited by German Berrios and Roy Porter, 34–62. London: The Athlone Press, 1995.
Bizzocchi, Roberto. *Cicisbei. Morale privata e identità nazionale in Italia*. Rome and Bari: Laterza, 2008.
Bynum, W.F., Roy Porter, and Michael Shepherd, eds. *The Anatomy of Madness*, vol. 2. London and New York: Routledge, 2004.
Calabritto, Monica. "'Furor' melanconico tra teoria e pratica legale." *Studi storici* 51, no. 1 (2010): 113–137.
Calvi, Giulia. *Il contratto morale. Madri e figli nella Toscana moderna*. Rome: Laterza, 1994.
Cartayrade, Laurent. "Property, Prodigality, and Madness: A Study of Interdiction Records in Eighteenth-Century Paris." PhD diss., University of Maryland, 1997.
Chavarria, Elisa Novi. "Ideologia e comportamenti familiari nei predicatori italiani fra Cinque e Settecento. Tematiche e modelli." *Rivista Storica Italiana* 100, no. 3 (1988): 679–723.
Colombero, Carlo. "Un contributo alla formazione della nozione di malattia mentale: le 'Questioni medico-legali' di Paolo Zacchia." In *Follia, psichiatria e società. Istituzioni manicomiali, scienza psichiatrica e classi sociali nell'Italia moderna e contemporanea*, edited by Alberto De Bernardi, 317–329. Milan: Franco Angeli, 1982.
Dini, Alessandro, ed. *Il medico e la follia. Cinquanta casi di malattia mentale della letteratura medica italiana del Seicento*. Florence: Le Lettere, 1997.
Eigen, Joel Peter. *Witnessing Insanity: Madness and Mad-Doctors in the English Court*. New Haven and London: Yale University Press, 1995.
Farge, Arlette, and Michel Foucault. *Le Désordre des familles: lettres de cachet des Archives de la Bastille au XVIIIe siècle*. Paris: Gallimard, Julliard, 1982.
Gowing, Laura. *Domestic Dangers: Women, Words, and Sex in Early Modern London*. Oxford: Oxford University Press, 1996.
Groppi, Angela. *Il welfare prima del welfare. Assistenza alla vecchiaia e solidarietà tra generazioni a Roma in età moderna*. Roma: Viella, 2010.
Groppi, Angela. "La malinconia di Lucrezia Barberini d'Este." In *I linguaggi del potere nell'età barocca, vol. 2. Donne e sfera pubblica*, edited by Francesca Cantù, 197–227. Rome: Viella, 2009.
Houston, Robert Allan. "Madness and Gender in the Long Eighteenth Century." *Social History* 27, no. 3 (2002): 314–115.
Houston, Robert Allan. *Madness and Society in Eighteenth-Century Scotland*. Oxford: Oxford University Press, 2000.
Ingram, Allan, and Michelle Faubert. *Cultural Constructions of Madness in Eighteenth Century Writing*. Basingstoke: Palgrave Macmillan, 2005.
Kromm, Jane E. "The Feminization of Madness in Visual Representation." *Feminist Studies* 20, no. 3 (1994): 507–535.
Labarca, Mariana. "Cuando la mente se oscurece y el cuerpo se debilita. El dolor de la ancianidad en el Gran Ducado de Toscana, siglo XVIII." In *Homo Dolens. Cartografías del dolor: sentidos, experiencias, registros*, edited by Rafael Gaune and Claudio Rolle, 293–314. Santiago: Fondo de Cultura Económica, 2018.
Labarca, Mariana. "The Emotional Disturbances of Old Age: On the Articulation of Old-Age Mental Incapacity in Eighteenth-Century Tuscany." *Historical Reflections/Reflexions Historiques* 41, no. 2 (2015): 19–36.

La Rocca, Chiara. *Tra moglie e marito. Matrimoni e separazioni a Livorno nel Settecento*. Bologna: Società editrice Il Molino, 2009.
Lombardi, Daniela. *Matrimonio di antico regime*. Bologna: Il Mulino, 2001.
Lombardi, Daniela. *Povertà maschile, povertà femminile. L'Ospedale dei Mendicanti nella Firenze dei Medici*. Bologna: Il Mulino, 1988.
MacDonald, Michael. *Mystical Bedlam: Madness, Anxiety, and Healing in Seventeenth-Century England*. Cambridge: Cambridge University Press, 1981.
Magherini, Graziella, and Vittorio Biotti. *L'isola delle Stinche e i percorsi della follia a Firenze nei secoli XIV-XVIII*. Florence: Ponte alle Grazie, 1992.
Mazza, Rita. "La malattia mentale nella medicina del cinquecento: Tassonomia e casi clinici." In *Follia, psichiatria e società*, edited by Alberto De Bernardi, 304–316. Milan: Franco Angeli, 1982.
Mellyn, Elizabeth W. *Mad Tuscans and Their Families: A History of Mental Disorder in Early Modern Italy*. Philadelphia: University of Pennsylvania Press, 2014.
Morant Deusa, Isabel, and Mónica Bolufer Peruga. *Amor, matrimonio y familia*. Madrid: Editorial Síntesis, 1998.
Ottaway, Susannah. *The Decline of Life: Old Age in Eighteenth-Century England*. Cambridge: Cambridge University Press, 2004.
Ottaway, Susannah. "Medicine and Old Age." In *The Oxford Handbook of the History of Medicine*, edited by Mark Jackson, 338–354. Oxford: Oxford University Press, 2011.
Porter, Roy. *Mind-Forg'd Manacles: A History of Madness in England from the Restoration to the Regency*. London: Penguin Books, 1990.
Roscioni, Lisa. *Il governo della follia. Ospedali, medici e pazzi nell'età moderna*. Milan: Bruno Mondadori, 2003.
Rousseau, George. "Depression's Forgotten Genealogy: Notes towards a History of Depression." *History of Psychiatry* 11 (2000): 71–106.
Rushton, Peter. "Idiocy, the Family and the Community in Early Modern North-East England." In *From Idiocy to Mental Deficiency*, edited by David Wright and Anne Digby, 44–64. London and New York: Routledge, 1996.
Sánchez, Magdalena S. "Melancholy and Female Illness: Habsburg Women and Politics at the Court of Philip III." *Journal of Women's History* 8, no. 2 (1996): 81–102.
Schäfer, Daniel. "'That Senescence Itself Is an Illness': A Transitional Medical Concept of Age and Ageing in the Eighteenth Century." *Medical History* 46, no. 4 (2002): 525–548.
Schiesari, Juliana. *The Gendering of Melancholia: Feminism, Psychoanalysis, and the Symbolics of the Loss in Renaissance Literature*. Ithaca and London: Cornell University Press, 1992.
Seidel Menchi, Silvana. "The Girl and the Hourglass: Periodization of Women's Lives in Western Preindustrial Societies." In *Time, Space and Women's Lives*, edited by Anne Jacobson Schutte, Thomas Kuehn, and Silvana Seidel Menchi, 41–74. Kirksville, MO: Truman State University Press, 2001.
Seidel Menchi, Silvana, and Diego Quaglioni, eds. *Coniugi nemici. La separazione in Italia dal XII al XVIII secolo*. Bologna: Il Molino, 2000.
Showalter, Elaine. *The Female Malady: Women, Madness, and English Culture, 1830–1980*. New York: Penguin Books, 1987.
Stok, Fabio. "Modelli e tradizione antica nella psicopatologia di Zacchia." In *Paolo Zacchia. Alle origini della medicina legale 1584–1659*, edited by Alessandro Pastore and Giovanni Rossi, 74–90. Milan: Franco Angeli, 2008.

Suzuki, Akihito. "The Household and the Care of Lunatics in Eighteenth-Century London." In *The Locus of Care: Families, Communities, Institutions, and the Provision of Welfare Since Antiquity*, edited by Peregrine Horden and Richard Smith, 153–175. London and New York: Routledge, 1998.

Suzuki, Akihito. "Lunacy in Seventeenth- and Eighteenth-Century England: Analysis of Quarter Sessions Records: Part 1." *History of Psychiatry* 2 (1991): 437–456.

Suzuki, Akihito. *Madness at Home: The Psychiatrist, the Patient, and the Family in England, 1820–1860*. Berkeley: University of California Press, 2006.

Thane, Pat, ed. *The Long History of Old Age*. London: Thames & Hudson, 2005.

Troyansky, David G. *Old Age in the Old Regime*. Ithaca, NY: Cornell University Press, 1989.

Wear, Andrew. *Knowledge & Practice in English Medicine, 1550–1680*. Cambridge: Cambridge University Press, 2000.

Wright, David, and Anne Digby, eds. *From Idiocy to Mental Deficiency*. London and New York: Routledge, 1996.

4 Spaces and itineraries of madness

Lorenzo Maestrini, a wealthy Florentine who had been Cancelliere of Empoli, was interdicted in 1730 and then committed to Santa Dorotea because he had fallen into madness (*caduto in pazzia*), on account of which he was deemed "capable of taking the resolutions of a *mentecatto*," such as to commit suicide or kill his wife.[1] The "insufferable frenzies" (*frenesie insoffribili*) that recurrently overcame Lorenzo Maestrini forced his wife and daughter to request his committal to Santa Dorotea several times, but as he was each time discharged after a short period of time, they had to resort to other measures to prevent his return home.[2] He was kept under the custody of various people, never lasting long in one place. Under close supervision of the Auditore Fiscale, he was also imprisoned several times.[3] But neither his family nor the authorities could find a permanent remedy for the strains caused by his behavior.

Lorenzo Maestrini's episodes of madness alternated with periods of lucidity, and these variations, together with his conflictive relationship with his closest relatives, determined his itinerary through the different spaces of madness. In 1735, he was once again discharged from Santa Dorotea during a period of lucidity, but he shortly after relapsed into "greater madnesses" (*maggiori pazzie*). The solution, this time, was to keep him under close custody in a fortress. The Auditore Fiscale voiced the assessment, shared by Lorenzo's close relatives and the Pupilli officials, that his liberty could simply not be granted, not even during the intervals of sanity that he enjoyed. The Fiscale believed that liberty to move around freely and socialize could be particularly harmful for Lorenzo's madness, for "too much discourse is precisely what can be prejudicial to him." Motivated by this concern, the Auditore Fiscale had turned to the "preventive remedy" of depriving him once more of his liberty, albeit unsuccessfully, as he ran away shortly after.[4] The Auditore Fiscale reported to the Pupilli that Lorenzo repeatedly contravened his authority and that it was not possible "to have him steadily in one place," for either he would be ejected from the places he was kept due to his "continual frenzy," wretched behavior, and the abuse he dealt out on any person near him, or he would escape from them with great scandal.[5] In November 1735, the Pupilli declared that there was no other solution left but to confine him to a fortress again, given that even the *pazzeria* of Santa

Maria Nuova had declined to receive him. He appears in the records again in 1739, when his relatives initiated a long suit for his inheritance. He died in 1736.[6]

As shown by this case, during the eighteenth century, Tuscan families could resort to various remedies to deal with the difficulties posed by madness. In their battle to govern, curb, contain, and cure their mentally disturbed relatives, families took different courses of action depending on their aims and needs, sometimes experimenting with various of them, other times holding to one. Scholars have convincingly argued that the mechanisms employed to control or deal with madness in early modern Europe were eminently temporary and flexible and were activated following careful negotiations between families and authorities.[7] The case of Lorenzo Maestrini invites us to pay close attention to the connections between one arrangement or space of appearance and another, to examine the forces behind the configuration of the itineraries of madness, and to explore its meanings and languages.

This chapter expands the focus from interdiction procedures to other spaces and mechanisms where madness makes an appearance in the eighteenth-century Tuscan records. The itinerary takes us through Santa Dorotea to criminal justice and insanity pleas and finally to the special private matters handled by the Auditore Fiscale. The primary concern is to examine the multiplicity of arrangements through which families, society, and authorities could respond to the challenges posed by madness. The itinerary sheds light on the instrumental use of the languages of madness, the presence of shared notions of what it meant to be mentally disturbed, and a social awareness of its implications. The increasing concern for madness that we have seen in interdiction procedures can also be traced in other institutional scenarios. Madness could also appear in criminal procedures and in hospitals destined for the custody and cure of the mentally ill. It could also be the object of official reprimands or of executive measures like imprisonment or conscription to serve on a ship's crew. These measures are to be interpreted as a combined effort to control the public and private effects of madness in which authorities and families worked hand in hand.

Mapping the itineraries of madness discloses a web of possible destinies and available courses of action to cope with mental disturbances. Tracing the itineraries of those labeled as mentally disturbed allows us to significantly enrich our understanding of how madness was perceived, conceptualized, and handled. Madness could assume the form of mental incapacity, justifying interdiction, or assume the form of raving madness (*pazzia furiosa*) that justified confinement. It could be used to argue for exemption from punishment in a criminal procedure or as grounds for judgment in an intergenerational or matrimonial dispute disclosed to the authorities in special petitions submitted to the Auditore Fiscale. Madness could thus assume manifold forms, and the same person could be depicted differently according to the context in which his or her mental disorder was disclosed. The identification and evaluation of disordered behaviors that were singled out as evidence of mental derangement were deeply rooted in the context in which the behavior developed and the institutional space in which it was disclosed. Why the behavior was denounced, why it received public attention, and where determined the signs listed to support the accusation. Civil law, we saw in the previous chapters, conditioned characterizations of mental incapacity to fit the parameters set by interdiction procedures. The same happens with the admission procedure to Santa Dorotea, criminal law, and the special requests handled by the Auditore Fiscale.

Santa Dorotea and the *pazzeria* of Santa Maria Nuova

As we saw in the case of Lorenzo Maestrini, during the eighteenth century, the mentally afflicted could be sent either to the *pazzeria* of Santa Maria Nuova or to Santa Dorotea, the two Tuscan medical institutions for the custody and care of the mentally afflicted. Founded in Florence in 1643, the Pia Casa di Santa Dorotea dei Pazzerelli opened its doors in 1647. Admissions were managed by the administrative board of the institution, composed of a group of "distinguished" lay Florentines, and were contingent upon the ability of the patient's family to pay the maintenance fee. For this reason, and particularly in response to the problem of the insane kept at the Stinche prison, a special ward for the insane (the *pazzeria*) was opened in the general Tuscan hospital of Santa Maria Nuova in 1688.[8] The space destined for the mentally ill in Santa Maria Nuova was thus created to receive patients who could not pay the fees of Santa Dorotea, although there is evidence that wealthy patients were also among its inmates from time to time. As we have seen, the records of the Magistrato dei Pupilli attest that Santa Maria Nuova was as common a destination as Santa Dorotea for the mentally incompetent whose patrimonies had been interdicted and who had been put under the curatorship of a relative until 1750.

The criteria for admission to Santa Dorotea between 1647 and 1750 were fairly vague. Medical certification of the alleged madness was not required, and little clarification was made regarding the notion and degree of *pazzia* that merited confinement.[9] Closer to jurisprudential than to medical notions of madness, patients were admitted because they were *mentecatti*, *matterelli*, *matti*, *pazzi*, or *furiosi*, terms that were used as equivalents. Even if admission during this period was decided by the administrative board of Santa Dorotea, the institution provided medical treatment for those who "could be brought back to a sound intellect," relying on a resident surgeon and the weekly visit of a physician.[10] Although admission was a bureaucratic procedure, based on lay definitions of insanity and dependent upon the families' ability to pay, the institution since its foundation aimed to provide a cure and not only to confine, as Lisa Roscioni has convincingly argued.[11] To give an idea about the limited extent of the institutionalization of the mentally ill during this early period, between 1682 and 1714, Santa Dorotea held an average of 12 patients per year and 15 between 1715 and 1750.[12] Although the first decades of the eighteenth century witnessed an increasing number of requests for committal, confinement was a solution of last resort.

The middle of the eighteenth century proved to be a turning point in the history of the institutionalization of the insane in Tuscany. In 1750, the *pazzeria* of Santa Maria Nuova was closed, and the Pia Casa di Santa Dorotea was transformed into a new, bigger institution, acquiring the status of grand ducal hospital "for the cure of all the diseases comprised in mania and the custody of those which are incurable." The aim of the reform was "to redress the many inconveniences innocently caused to the public by the furious mad [who are] abandoned and wander through the public streets."[13] The reform established that only people whose madness was certified by medical opinion could be admitted, preferably by a physician, and in his absence by a surgeon. In the end, the ordinance stated that from that point forward, patients could be received at public expense, to be paid by Santa Maria Nuova and other charitable institutions if the person was from Florence, or by the community of origin if they were from elsewhere in the grand ducal territory. As a consequence, between 1751 and 1788, around half of the patients were admitted at public expense, and only a quarter of the total patients were Florentine. Between 1647 and 1750, there were 429 admissions to Santa Dorotea, but between 1751 and 1788, the number rose to 2411.[14]

The admission procedure was a matter of intense discussion between 1740 and 1760. Of particular concern were not only the mechanisms to certify madness, but also the strategies for resolving the problem of financing the entry of those patients who could not pay. The provisions of 1750 aimed to provide a solution for the problem of the vagrant and poor mad who could not afford the fees of Santa Dorotea but who nonetheless generated severe problems for public life. Dangerousness and "disturbance" of "public quietness and honesty" were major criteria for committal, particularly when caused by the "wandering" and "abandoned" mad.[15] The dispositions adopted in 1750 were the corollary of a long discussion between state officials regarding responsibility for the problem of the mentally ill. Particularly during the first 3 decades of the eighteenth century, Santa Dorotea and the *pazzeria* of Santa Maria Nuova captured the attention of the ducal administration. The key issue under discussion was under whose competence the custody and cure of the mentally disturbed came, especially of those who could not pay Santa Dorotea. It was not only a financial problem but also a discussion that concerned ideological standpoints on public involvement in the provision of assistance and the balance between charity, social, and family responsibility.

For instance, in April 1722, the Auditore Fiscale, in his capacity as head of police and public order, ordered the banishment from Florence of a certain Maria Laura Maioli, known to be "half mad [*mezza pazzarella*] with a very mordacious tongue, impertinent and temerarious." A native of Pisa, Maria Laura had been caught wandering in the streets of Florence and imprisoned, while an order was sent to her only relative, a paternal uncle, which gave him a term of 8 days to send for his niece and personally assume or provide for her custody. The uncle, "a poor and miserable painter," was finally exempted from his "duty" as the closest family member to assume her custody, given his "extreme poverty" and his "just motives for not desiring her proximity."[16]

Cases in which family members were either not alive or unable to assume responsibility for a mad relative put the Tuscan administrative structure under considerable strain. Close evaluation had to be made of the economic and familial circumstances that surrounded the patient to come up with the most suitable solution, carefully balancing private and public interests. As an example of how restrictions on admission to Santa Dorotea and the absence of family networks placed the authorities in a difficult position, Maria Laura was not sent to the *pazzeria* of Santa Maria Nuova nor left at the Stinche because she was not deemed to have the kind of madness that justified confinement at the expense of the state. Instead, she was banished from Florence. The recognition of poverty did not automatically secure admission to Santa Dorotea, and the problem of what to do with the insane who lacked family support, had no means of living, and did not qualify to be committed continued to be present.

The authorities in charge of assessing the petitions for confinement after 1750 were the Auditore Fiscale for the Florentine inhabitants and the magistracy of the Nove Conservatori del Dominio for the inhabitants of the rest of the dominion.[17] The investigation conducted by the Auditore Fiscale and the Nove Conservatori del Dominio comprised the collection of at least one medical testimony regarding the mental condition of the patient and the testimony of priests and neighbors confirming his or her level of dangerousness. Upon confirmation of madness, they had to rigorously investigate the economic situation of the person to determine if he or she deserved to be admitted at public expense (*pubbliche spese*). In the end, every admission had to be ratified by royal command (*real rescritto*).[18] Thus, although the admission procedure continued to be an administrative one, categorized as a police matter and under the direct control of the state, the new requirement stipulated by the reforms of 1750 was that of medical certification.

The admission procedures generated particular concerns regarding the kind and degree of madness that qualified for committal, given the high costs of interment at public expense. The 1750 reform had stated the government's intention to provide for abandoned *furiosi* who caused a serious disruption to public life. But cases during the first decade following the reform demonstrated that the degrees of mental affliction had to be further specified in order to avoid "abuses." Particularly in the case of patients admitted at public expense, dangerousness was to be the primary criterion. The admission procedure gradually came to equate madness (*pazzia*) with raving madness (*pazzia furiosa*), excluding its harmless forms – the *melensi* and *mentecatti* – that were so common in interdiction procedures. And, thus, a criterion for determining discharge from Santa Dorotea was that the patients were only *melensi* who "have not given any manifest sign of madness" during their time at the hospital and consequently that the administrators considered them unable "to disturb either the public quietness or the public honesty."[19]

Discussions regarding why the *melensi* or *mentecatti* did not need to be committed, while the *pazzi furiosi* were, extended to other considerations besides the amount of danger they created for society. The administration of Santa Dorotea approached the problem from a practical perspective, considering that the admission of the passive and harmless mad used up the available beds and public funds, when their fee was not privately paid. The target was focused, therefore, on guaranteeing a place for the raving mad, as can be seen in the regular discharges of non-paying patients as soon as they stopped showing signs of dangerousness.[20] But the matter generated divergent views. The politico-practical differentiation between *melenso* and *pazzo furioso* concealed a larger problem affecting not only private life, but also social life which had not been tackled by the reform of 1750. The perception of some state officials and family members was that on occasion, non-violent types of madness also required special measures, be it custody, personal care, or medical treatment – measures that families were not always able or willing to take. As shown by the case of Maria Laura Maioli, homecare was at times unfeasible and economically impossible. Pauperization, household composition, and even the absence of available relatives conspired to make public the life of the mentally afflicted. Attesting to the problems stemming from the practical division between *pazzia furiosa* and the non-violent types of madness, we find the case of an abandoned 14-year-old *melensa* from the community of Greve who was sent to Santa Dorotea in 1769 after being caught wandering in the streets. Although the medical and civil authorities were well aware that her type of madness did not fit the parameters of *pazzia furiosa*, she was left in the hospital for about a year while the authorities endeavored to find a long-term solution to her situation.[21]

Wealthier families had more resources, but like poorer families they also turned to the authorities seeking for help with their mentally ill relatives. All types of families turned to the Grand Duke, requesting to obtain the *grazia* of having a person committed to the hospital even if they did not fit the pattern of the *pazzo furioso*. The quest of families to find a remedy for the challenges posed by a mentally disturbed relative is vividly illustrated in the case of Lorenzo Baldinotti, presented at the beginning of this book. He had been deranged for most of his life – his first appearance in the records was in 1725 – was interdicted four times and confined both in Santa Maria Nuova and in Santa Dorotea several times, and was a recurring problem for his relatives. Over the years, he was portrayed as a mad person whose mental derangement made him unruly, scandalous, dissolute and utterly extravagant. And yet, when his relatives requested his committal once again in 1755, the petition was not granted, regardless of the fact that it was to be an interment entirely paid for by the patient. The physician of Santa Dorotea determined that Lorenzo was not "in a state of furious *demenza*," arguing that "notwithstanding his prattling [*garrulo*], fervid [*focoso*] and disordered discourse, he is not capable of returning to his furious acts." As such, he was "far from the need of being detained in the Hospital of S. Dorotea."[22] Strikingly, only a year before his brother had described him as "of an extravagant, furious and uneasy nature, and sick in his mind" to the officials of the Magistrato dei Pupilli.[23]

The problem of how to ensure that only *pazzi furiosi* were admitted to Santa Dorotea was first tackled with the appointment of Antonio Lulli as the permanent physician of the hospital in 1756.[24] Together with curing patients, he was entrusted with the special commission of assessing whether prospective or current patients were qualified to be housed in the hospital. Attesting to the growing conflict aroused by the typification of the kind of madness that was eligible for committal, in 1757, the hospital administrators requested that the Consulta appoint two physicians to certify that the requests for admission indeed referred to people who were either maniac or raving mad (*pazzo furioso*, or *maniaco*) to avoid what were called "abuses" by their families. The physicians elected were Giovanni Targioni Tozzetti[25] and Lodovico Scutellari,[26] chosen for their experience as *medici fiscali*. The scope of this new addition to the admission procedure was to ensure that those who were allegedly *pazzi furiosi* were visited by more than one physician to verify the basis of the requests for committal. These visits had to be repeated, as the *provveditore* Niccolò Martelli wrote, "in order to assert, if they really are in a state [that requires for them] to be guarded and cured in the hospital destined for the maniacs, and not attacked by some accidental delirium, or by other illness."[27] The problem, as the *provveditore* Niccolò Martelli informed the Auditore Fiscale, was that families sometimes petitioned for the committal of patients who were only foolish (*melensi*) instead of insane (*pazzi*), or who had become stupid from a stroke. Although the appointment of Targioni Tozzetti and Scutellari officially established that a medical certification of madness was compulsory before admission, in 1759 a *biglietto* from the Council of Regency still warned about the "easiness" by which relatives could request and obtain the admission of a relative.[28] To counteract this situation, the Council indicated that after patients were admitted, they were to be further examined by physicians who had not been involved in the initial assessment to corroborate the diagnosis and that patients should be visited once a month by an external physician.

A medical certification of madness did not secure admission to Santa Dorotea, particularly for the poor and abandoned mad. The case of a poor prisoner whose madness became an "intolerable annoyance" to her fellow inmates at the Stinche is illustrative of the problem of interment at public expense. It was in March 1759 when a petition from some female prisoners at the Stinche requested the transfer of a certain Lucrezia Gambassi to Santa Dorotea because she was "in a demented state," of the kind that "disturbs the [other] prisoners night and day with howls."[29] A medical note had been included, signed by Antonio Lulli and Giovanni Targioni Tozzetti, establishing that the woman was indeed demented and, as such, was found "worthy of being confined [*riserrata*] and cured in the Conservatory of Santa Dorotea."[30] Even the Auditore Fiscale Domenico Brichieri Colombi expressed his agreement, writing that the Stinche was not "a proper place for the custody of the mad [*pazzarelli*]."[31]

The problem was, however, that the woman was from the Tuscan locality of Montevarchi, and thus her admission to Santa Dorotea, if decided, was to be at the expense of her local community, which was under the jurisdiction of the Magistrato dei Nove. Never during the proceedings was her pauperism put into doubt – only the seriousness of her mental condition. Apparently ruling with the intention of reducing public expenditure, the head official of the Nove considered Lucrezia Gambassi to be suffering a madness that was not of the "furious kind," given that it consisted only in howling. As such, he continued, she did not fall into the category of *pazzia furiosa* liable for committal in Santa Dorotea at public expense. She posed no serious threat to public quietness and public honesty, and so they were not willing to pay for her confinement.

The line of argument used in this case is revealing: administrative criteria were pitted against medical knowledge, and the victory went to the former. Any welfare provision for the mentally ill poor was dependent upon the availability of resources, an availability that in this case had more to do with the administrative issues of the Tuscan dominion in its relation with Florence than with a systematic policy regarding the problem of madness. Since Lucrezia had already been convicted and was serving time in the Stinche at public expense (i.e., covered by the central administration), it is understandable that the officials of the Nove made their best effort to avoid transferring that burden to the provinces. In fact, they could resolve the matter easily on this occasion precisely because she was already in custody in a public institution, was under the category of a convicted criminal who had become mad, and was not a furious abandoned vagrant.

The category of the *pazzo furioso* was not a medical one, in the sense that it related first to the public consequences of mad behavior, and was only secondarily intended to constitute a medical diagnosis of a disease. The languages of madness had to adapt to each institutional space, and in eighteenth-century Tuscany, the admission procedure to the mental hospital, even if it required medical certification, contained much more of the legal and political languages of criminal and civil procedures than the language of medical literature. For most of the century, physicians moved between the legal and medical worlds, adapting their language to the requirements of each space. However, this did not entail that they did not put forward their own agendas. Medical considerations regarding the most suitable environment for the mentally ill to achieve the best custodial and therapeutic results were not dictated only by the legal and governmental commands issued by the *motuproprio*. This is proved by the fact that Giovanni Targioni Tozzetti, who had been involved with criminal procedures for at least a decade, recommended Lucrezia Gambassi's committal to Santa Dorotea even though he also acknowledged that she was not a *pazza furiosa*. The omission of this category in his testimony (he had only declared she was *demente*) should not be taken as a fortuitous lapse but as the conscious choice of a man long familiar with judicial procedures and administrative concerns. He could have said *melensa* or *mentecatta* (categories that we know were contentious in the discussion about the admission procedure to Santa Dorotea), but he chose the legal but more comprehensive term, *demente*.[32]

Although Lucrezia Gambassi's mental condition had been corroborated by the two physicians specifically appointed for certifying madness and suitability for committal, her transfer to the hospital was not permitted. Medical knowledge, political concerns, legal requirements, and familial preferences were in continual negotiation in an ebb and flow that marked the foundation of welfare provisions. The dynamics of this negotiation are better grasped when we expand the scale of analysis into the itineraries of madness to examine how families and authorities resorted to more than one mechanism in their joint quest to address the problems of madness, accommodating languages and interests in a careful, but unstable, balance.

Criminal insanity and the assessment of diminished liability

As we have seen, both interdiction procedures and committal to a mental hospital were connected with the administration of justice. The mentally disturbed roamed not only through the court of the Magistrato dei Pupilli and the walls of Santa Dorotea, but also ended up in front of the Otto di Guardia e Balìa, Tuscany's central criminal court, which supervised all the other criminal courts of the territory. Criminal prosecution in grand ducal Tuscany aimed at establishing liability, which was contingent upon providing evidence of criminal intent and motivation for committing the crime.[33] However, as Roman law had established, the very nature of madness supposed that the mentally afflicted lacked criminal intent and motivation for they were taken to be devoid of judgement, intention, and will. Following this classical principle, the Tuscan legal framework placed the criminally insane under the "exception of innocence" (*eccezione d'innocenza*) which released them from punishment.[34]

Diminished responsibility by reason of madness could be established in two ways in early modern Tuscany: during trial or alternatively through a *supplica* submitted after conviction and once the sentence had been pronounced. According to the famous summary of Tuscan legal practice compiled by Marc'Antonio Savelli, the criminally insane could plead insanity through a procurator or a relative even if they were contumacious. As Savelli warned his readers, this could turn in their favor, because if they were not found to be mad after all, they could continue without being punished.[35]

As in other parts of Europe, insanity pleas entered during trial are difficult to find in the eighteenth-century records of the Otto di Guardia, which is particularly striking compared to the high rate of interdiction decrees issued during the same period.[36] Their scarcity is explained in part because, by definition, an insanity defense required that the accused plead that he or she was guilty but not responsible by reason of mental incapacity, which was hazardous and entailed the mastering of basic legal principles or, alternatively, receiving legal advice. It was safer either to attend the trial alleging innocence in the expectation that the evidence would exculpate them or be inconclusive or remain contumacious to the Otto's instruction to appear in court. The other explanation for the scarcity of insanity pleas is connected with the characteristics of the archive of the Otto di Guardia itself. In particular, its massive size, combined with its frequent lacunae, make it difficult to conduct a thorough search.[37] In the end, it is possible that exemption from legal liability by reason of insanity was determined through informal pre-trial resolutions that left no trace.

To a certain extent, insanity pleas could be better argued after trial, once the accused had been convicted and the sentence pronounced, using the instrument of the *supplica*. Supplications to obtain a *grazia* from the Grand Duke in the form of a mitigated sentence or a full pardon were the only available mechanism to appeal a sentence. Supplications constituted a legal course of action in which personal and more emotional experiences, so necessary to sustain an insanity plea, could be received with more sympathy, contributing to a more favorable response. Accordingly, many insanity pleas in the eighteenth-century records come to light in the form of petitions sent after conviction.

In terms of legal practice, the conviction and sentencing of criminals found to be mentally afflicted rested entirely on the judges' power of *arbitrio*, which gave them liberty to decide without following the statutory law.[38] Exemption from statutory penalty was not understood as automatically liberating the criminally insane from all kinds of punishment but only as the possibility of diminishing the penalty at the judge's discretion. Recourse to arbitrary penalties gave the Tuscan legal system the necessary flexibility to deal with criminal insanity, adjusting each penalty according to the varying levels of responsibility that could be found in the different forms of madness.

Exemption from punishment by reason of madness generated a complicated dilemma for the practice of law, particularly regarding the identification of the different kinds and levels of madness, the assessment of how each kind affected the person's legal responsibility, and the decision of what to do, as a result, with the criminally insane. As we can see in Marc'Antonio Savelli's *Pratica universale*, legal theory was still largely based on the principles stated in the famous work of Paolo Zacchia, who had established different levels of legal responsibility according to the various categories of madness. Referencing Zacchia's work, Savelli recalled that there were different kinds of "madness, *furore* and dementia," which were differentiated according to the origins and gradations of mental disturbance.[39] Whereas Savelli used the categories of *pazzia, furore,* and *demenza* as equivalent, Zacchia in his *Quaestiones medico legales* had proposed the use of *demenza* as a generic term comprising all kinds of mental afflictions.[40] Focusing on the various signs and manifestations of madness, he classified them according to the degrees to which the rational faculties were compromised: *fatuitas* (with diminished mental faculties), *delirium* (altered mental faculties), and *mania* (where mental faculties were completely lost). After classifying the kinds of *demenza*, Zacchia thoroughly examined the different signs of madness (codified not only in specific behaviors but also in physical signs) so that judges could carefully assess the level of mental impairment they were faced with and establish a penalty in accordance with the degree of responsibility it entailed.[41]

As shown in the previous chapter, the Tuscan interdiction procedures were largely built upon the category of *demenza* as the generic term for legal mental incapacity. In criminal records, on the contrary, it is difficult to find a pattern in the use of categories of insanity. The evidence examined suggests that insanity pleas during the eighteenth century employed mostly simple, non-specialized categories, and that there was very little recourse to medical opinion. The lexicon is generally confined to the basic legal language, such as *demente* and *mentecatto,* or terms denoting intellectual impairment, such as *melenso, stolido,* and *scemo*. These denominations are usually accompanied by descriptions such as "suffering in the brain" (*patire nel cervello*), "without brain" (*senza cervello*), "diminished in the brain" (*scema di cervello*), "imbecile and of unsound mind" (*imbecille e di mente non sana*), "without perfect cognition" (*non era in perfetta cognizione*), "devoid of wit and cognition" (*privo di senno e cognizione*), or "simplicity and foolishness" (*semplicità e sciocchezza*).[42] However, what largely prevails is the recurrent use of the less specialized *pazzia* or even undefined unsoundness of mind. The legal category of *demente,* so vital for assessing mental incapacity in interdiction procedures, is here even further diluted into a plain denomination of *pazzo* or *matto*. Medico-legal categories such as lucid intervals, melancholy, or frenzy (*frenesia*) can be found in some records that are particularly generous in their descriptions, but they nonetheless correspond to concepts that had been largely present in the medico-legal language introduced by Renaissance jurists.[43] What prevails, then, is the employment of simple categories of madness with cursory descriptions, differing from the complex nuances presented in Zacchia's *Quaestiones medico-legales* or in early modern Italian *Consilia*.[44] Even if the influential work of Zacchia had organized and categorized a series of possible variants for *demenza* with their corresponding legal implications, the criminal proceedings of the eighteenth century had diluted its employment to routine quotations of the author with no further disquisition.

Institutional eighteenth-century records consistently demonstrate that the use of specialized language was highly dependent on the requirements of each procedural space in which madness was disclosed. Interdiction procedures show that the term employed was not what mattered for assessing mental incapacity but rather the events and circumstances surrounding the alleged insanity. To determine if a person (and their patrimony) needed the interdiction, state officials were mostly concerned with the context and much less with the categories used or the ascribed causes. Likewise, criminal insanity was also assessed by close examination of the events surrounding the crime, with particular attention to the biography of the accused and his or her behavior before and after the crime was perpetrated.

Criminal procedures for suspected suicide are particularly useful for examining the principles used to assert soundness of mind and liability. In these cases, defensive efforts were directed to rebut the suspicion of madness, which required a different line of argument. Instead of proving an absence of wrongful intent on account of a lack of discernment, the defense had to demonstrate that although the suspects had dangerously injured themselves, it had been fortuitous or accidental and not "out of desperation." The context surrounding the events was the key element used to complete the puzzle, together with expert medical opinion on the self-inflicted wounds. It could happen that testimonies identified a motive to commit suicide, declaring that the injury had been committed "out of desperation because he was litigating with his brother Carlo because of their paternal inheritance," or that after a serious fall suffered some months before, the accused had given signs that he was "of imperfect soundness of mind (*non perfetta sanità di mente*)."[45] However, even when certified by expert medical opinion, physical evidence could be judged inconclusive. In these two cases, the charges were dropped based on the argument that the injuries had not been lethal, and that the evidence was not enough to show that the injury had been self-inflicted.

Two elements were carefully assessed by the judges: the physical evidence and the mental state of the injured prior to the alleged attempted suicide. The first consideration was in the purview of medical experts, while the second was largely based on hearsay testimonies. Although in the cases cited before, the self-injurers were acquitted in the end, the testimonies gathered regarding their state of mind are nonetheless interesting. A clear connection was made between desperation or unmanageable emotional turmoil and suicide, on the one hand, and between mental impairment and suicide, on the other.

Another case of attempted suicide, this time with fatal consequences, gives further insight into the logic employed to assess the state of mind in which the man found himself before and as he committed his desperate action. The case was discussed in an extrajudicial inquiry developed by the Auditore Fiscale to ascertain if murder could be ruled out in a reported case of suicide. The information was that a *fratello converso* serving in the Jesuit college of San Giovannino had jumped off a terrace, "oppressed by a furor of madness" (*soppresso da furore di pazzia*). The inquiry revealed that the *fratello* had a known tendency to suffer similar episodes of madness and in fact had been "oppressed by a similar furor" in the past, on account of which he had been sent to Rome where he had managed to heal and had been consequently sent to serve in the college in Florence. The Auditore Fiscale was informed:

> that he had not given other signs of mental confusion [*sconcerto di mente*], but that a few days before the accident occurred he had demonstrated melancholy, and that the same morning, while he was doing his service in the cell of father Niccolai, all of a sudden he threw himself at his feet, asking for forgiveness for all his faults, and that this [behavior] had confirmed the suspicion of some new perturbation.

The members of the congregation were so aware of the possible consequences of this new melancholy and perturbation that, just before the fatal accident occurred, they had arranged for his transfer to a place where he could be held in custody. Consequently, according to the Auditore Fiscale, there was no need for a further inquiry into the "unfortunate accident," given that it was evident that "he had exposed himself to the danger in which he died oppressed by a fit of frenzy [*assalto di frenesia*]."[46] That he acted motivated by the mental confusion caused by melancholy was therefore proven by his biography and previous behavior. It was clear to the legally trained Auditore Fiscale that responsibility for the crime could only be assigned to the poor *converso* and that his perturbed state of mind had led him to the fatal end. Moreover, the situation was so clear to the authorities that it was decided not to follow regular criminal proceedings.

The differentiation between actions which denoted awareness of one's doings and those which were the product of a deranged mind was highly dependent not only on the context and events surrounding the crimes, but also on the behavior of the defendant during trial. It was vital to assess whether they understood the consequences of their actions, whether they remembered them, whether they felt any remorse, and how they explained what had happened. Here the supervision exerted by the Otto di Guardia over local criminal courts could result in a harsher sentence for someone whose insanity defense had at first been considered plausible.[47] This was the case for Santa Venturini, tried for infanticide in 1730, who pleaded innocent claiming that she had not been aware of her pregnancy and that she had suffered a natural abortion. To uphold her innocence, she argued that her actions were the result of her "simplicity and foolishness" (*semplicità e stolidezza*), which made her behave "like a mad person without a brain" (*come una pazzerella, e senza cervello*). She had let herself be deflowered only due to her simplicity and naivety (*dabbenaggine*), she explained to the authorities. Nonetheless, her simplicity and foolishness could not be proven according to the Otto officials, and, quite the contrary, her depositions were deemed to demonstrate that she possessed sufficient intelligence to have realized she was pregnant and understood the consequence of her actions – particularly since she had confessed her crime several times during the proceedings, although afterwards she had retracted her confession.

Thus, her actions were held "to come from malice and not from simplicity," causing her to be sentenced to 7 years at the Stinche (the Florentine prison) instead of the 2 years of exile from the Tuscan state originally proposed by the regional court.[48]

The crucial point in an insanity defense was to demonstrate that the accused was indeed devoid of will and intention. According to the legal principles, absence of will and intention implied lack of malice and premeditation, which were the fundamental grounds to determine liability. For this reason, criminals resorting to the insanity defense strived to convince the judges that they lacked malice and that the crime, particularly if it were murder, had been the result of an accident or the effect of their diminished grasp of reality. At the base of insanity defenses, therefore, was the argument that there was no motive for the crime. Nothing could have predicted it and nothing in the previous behavior of the accused, except from the fact that they were deemed mad, anticipated the crime.

The case of Natale Righini from Firenzuola, tried in 1730 for attempted parricide, illustrates how insanity defenses were considered by Tuscan criminal justice. Although witnesses argued on his behalf – including Righini's father and brother, who stated that he was *matto* – the judges questioned the level of mental disturbance he suffered from and, particularly, the legal consequences that derived from it. The facts surrounding the crime were that Righini was a young man who refused to work and insisted on wandering about in complete idleness, as did many other disorderly young men of the time. He had shot his father when the latter was reproving him for his refusal to stay at home and work as he was supposed to. Although the officials of the Otto di Guardia in Florence conceded that a motive for the crime could not be identified, given the father had been only "lovingly" reprimanding his son when the so-called *matto* had pulled the trigger, Righini's alleged *demenza* (*se sia o non sia veramente demente*) needed further proof. Four new witnesses were examined regarding his mental condition, about whom we are given no information. The inquiry revealed, according to the Florentine officials, that he

> is not mad [*pazzo*] but only slightly diminished of the brain [*scemo di cervello*], which is not in a degree that deprives him the cognition of what he does, since both before and after the crime under inquiry, he managed his affairs [*fare i fatti suoi*] as any man.[49]

The magistrates, therefore, considered him to be an ordinary man who gave motive neither to be laughed at nor to be admired. They conceded, nonetheless, that "maybe" he occasionally manifested some "inconsistences in his speech" and sometimes walked decidedly toward a certain destination only to suddenly change his course for no reason, "which gave motive to those watching him to call him *pazzo*." However, the fact that after the crime he fled from the paternal residence stood against him, for it was taken

142 Spaces and itineraries of madness

to reveal his awareness of the significance of his actions. Consequently, on account of the evidence gathered, the magistrates considered that "such a foolishness" (*melensaggine*), which showed that he was only partially estranged from reason, could "excuse him" to a certain extent but not completely. As a consequence, although he was spared the death sentence, he was sentenced to the arbitrary penalty (*pena arbitraria*) of 10 years in the galleys plus a fine for illegal possession of weapons.[50]

The assessment of liability, motivation, and criminal intent considered not only mental impairment and madness as exculpatory, but also other circumstances such as drunkenness and justified angry reactions. Crimes committed while heavily inebriated or seriously influenced by a strong and justified rage were considered attenuating circumstances and thus deserving a lenient sentence, provided the accused had appeared before court. If the accused were contumacious, on the contrary, any attenuating circumstance was insufficient argument against the presumption of guilt derived from being a fugitive.

Drunkenness constituted a common line of defense in criminal prosecution and in petitions for a reduction of sentence, demonstrating the new concern aroused by the effects of inebriation we saw in the records of the Magistrato dei Pupilli.[51] Drunkenness appears particularly connected to crimes of violence and assault committed by men, but it surpasses violent crimes to become a sort of immanent presence in male criminal behavior generally. Although it is possible to find inebriated women involved in criminal acts, it was mostly tied to prostitution and to raving madness.[52] Alleging drunkenness at the moment of the crime served both to demonstrate that the crime had been unintentional and to diminish liability. Crimes committed while "altered by wine" (*alterato dal vino*) or while "not being in a perfect cognition" (*non era in perfetta cognizione*) by reason of drunkenness could be taken to deserve mitigated sentences, provided this state could be corroborated and had been so evident as to give recognizable signs.[53] Supplicants would explain that their crime had been committed while they were "overheated with wine" (*riscaldati dal vino*), "drunk and out of himself," "not in a rational state," or so "drunk" that he "staggered due to the wine he had consumed."[54] Additionally, it helped the cause if the accused could prove that the crime had been unpremeditated and fortuitous, so that motive and wrongful intent could be set aside.

The frequent presence of this argument both in the criminal proceedings and in supplications for reduction of sentences suggests that the effects of alcohol and the instrumental use of the plea of drunkenness were known throughout all segments of society. However, pleas of drunkenness evidently did not always result in a lenient sentence. Precisely because of its popularity and association with male criminality, judges were particularly cautious in examining the level of inebriation, a delicate matter to prove. Additionally, diminished responsibility by reason of inebriation produced a moral dilemma for the authorities, only enlarged by its permeation throughout all social levels. In this sense, the need to pass exemplary and deterrent sentences was a particular concern regarding drunkenness, for it was too easy to allege total intoxication at the moment a crime had been committed and thus escape punishment. For this reason, pleas of drunkenness in Tuscany resulted in mitigated sentences which in the case of homicide or theft served to commute from the death penalty or a lifetime sentence in the galleys to *confino* (relegation in a specific area within the Tuscan sate) for life. For less serious crimes, such as brawls with no injuries, arbitrary penalties were less severe and could even result in no penalty, provided the accused could present a peace settlement with the injured parties.

Drunkenness fell under the category of exculpatory circumstances because the temporary mental obfuscation caused by inebriation was held to produce a total loss of control. If a drunkard had no control over himself when committing the crime, he could not be held responsible for it; he could not have avoided it, had not planned it, and was not conscious when committing it. Provided the person had not planned the crime before getting drunk, once inebriated it was not anymore in his ability to avoid it, and, furthermore, he had not been conscious of his actions while committing it. The same argument applied to other temporary derangements, such as strong passions, similarly believed to have the power of obfuscating the person's mental faculties. However, as Savelli warned his readers, to escape from ordinary penalty, the crime must have been committed under "just rage, anger, or pain caused by offences, provocation or other just causes."[55] To be given a lighter punishment, the offender needed to prove both that his or her rage had been justified and that it had been such as to temporarily obfuscate his or her judgement.

The degree to which the legal foundations of insanity pleas permeated Tuscan society is hard to assess. When mental incapacity was argued during the trial, the records give only glimpses into the characteristics of the alleged mental disturbance, and we often have no way of knowing how the defense was conducted or by whom. Moreover, it has to be taken into account that eighteenth-century records of the crimes judged by the Otto di Guardia for the most part present just summaries of the proceedings. For this reason, the language of madness that we can access is even more circumscribed and mediated than that examined in interdiction procedures. Some clues are given regarding the judges' reasoning, but usually there are no records of the interrogatories. Against this scenario, supplications provide a valuable counterpart, as their records tend to incorporate a wider variety of voices, although authorship is anyways a controversial matter.[56]

Studies on criminal justice in medieval and early modern Europe have argued that there was a widespread knowledge of legal matters and the judicial structure, which enabled people to make use of defensive strategies and make an instrumental use of the justice system.[57] Centuries of appropriation and maturation of legal principles and judicial mechanisms explain the elite's wide use of interdiction procedures in the eighteenth century. The case of criminal insanity is less clear. Records of the Otto di Guardia suggest that there was a widespread social awareness regarding the implications of madness for legal responsibility. Petitioners usually alleged that they were or that the accused was *mentecatto*, *pazzo*, unable to understand what they were doing, unable to act with premeditation. The basic principle was that their intellectual impairment and altered mental state prevented them from commanding their actions or understanding their surroundings. However, I am more cautious regarding the social permeation of more specialized legal concepts, such as lack of malice, impunity, or notions about the different gradations of criminal intent and diminished accountability derived from madness. The appearance of these notions can be interpreted, we can safely assume, as the sign of the involvement of legal advice. At a social, non-specialized level, there was a well-established awareness of the effects of pleading insanity, but the arguments and resources of knowledge to do it varied greatly according to wealth and education.

When judges considered that there was enough evidence to establish that the accused was not liable for his or her actions by reason of madness, the legal proceedings were likely to be abbreviated and end with a lighter penalty than that usually imposed for the given crime. It could even happen that the "mania" suffered by the accused prevented the criminal court from initiating normal criminal proceedings, forcing the central government to come up with an alternative solution.[58] In any case, criminal insanity not only posed the problem of how to identify madness and determine liability, but also created the dilemma of what to do with the criminally insane, where to send them, and who would be held responsible for their subsequent behavior, as Elizabeth Mellyn has convincingly argued.[59]

Criminal responsibility was a highly delicate matter, not only because it was bound up with the contextual nature of insanity but also because it posed the difficulty of coming up with a sentence that was both fair and exemplary.[60] The preferred path for dealing with criminal insanity was remission through grace, which left intact the deterrent effect without contradicting the principle of impunity by reason of madness. When dealing with insanity pleas, Tuscan judges tended to favor the strategy of giving mitigated sentences that could be further remitted through a supplication rather than resorting to open acquittal.[61]

The criminally insane were usually spared the death sentence and the galleys but not necessarily prison. Criminal insanity, although not deserving punishment, needed confinement both for security reasons and for exemplary purposes. However, imprisonment generally was not for life, given the financial constraints it inevitably carried. Even when criminals were sentenced to prison for life, they were likely to be able to supplicate for their release years later or be eligible for a ducal pardon. As the Auditore Fiscale explained to the Council of Regency in 1747, it was advisable for the Grand Duke to demonstrate his mercy every once in a while by giving general pardons to criminals who had been imprisoned in the Stinche for a long time and whose crimes, preferably of a minor nature, had been expiated through the "vexations of imprisonment" (*gravità della prigionia*).[62] At the same time that a pardon demonstrated the Duke's compassion and pity, it served to relieve the fiscal burden of maintaining those prisoners whose families could not finance their imprisonment. Some restrictions applied to the potential beneficiaries of the pardon, among them mad prisoners who lacked family networks that could care for them. Thus, liberation or confinement of the criminally mad was tied to their family or social situation. If they had nobody to take care of them, they could not be left alone to wander the streets.

Madness as a police matter: special requests *per porre freno a detti disordini*

Responses to madness were the result of a concerted effort by family members, society and authorities, and could take many forms according to the alternatives offered by the grand ducal system. A valuable source for examining madness in a different context than the one provided by interdictions, Santa Dorotea, and criminal prosecution are the cases handled by the office of the Auditore Fiscale, which involved many special requests and summary measures affecting people openly labeled as mad or with features closely resembling madness.[63]

The Auditore Fiscale supervised criminal sentences, participated in the Consulta and the Council of State, was in charge of public order, and as head of police administered the admission procedure to Santa Dorotea.[64] His executive power also allowed him to order other forms of confinement that lay outside of ordinary legal proceedings. But his sphere of maneuver was not limited to confinement, for the Auditore Fiscale came to have a key role in handling delicate and special matters regarding the insane. The evidence suggests that the Auditori Fiscali wielded a wide array of corrective and persuasive mechanisms in their efforts to curb deviant behaviors without having to resort to confinement. Counting on their legal training, they could artfully combine legal reasoning with police strategies and medical arguments. Following the tradition of negotiated public intervention in private life, these special requests were directly handled by the Auditore Fiscale, who acted under the attentive inspection of the members of the Council of Regency and the Consulta.[65]

In terms of social profile, these cases were not restricted to the aristocracy nor to Florence. They involve not only wealthy and privileged people who wished to avoid the dishonor of using the ordinary legal channels, but also families from various social backgrounds who sought the authorities' direct intervention as a desperate solution. Last, we find police matters involving individuals from the poorer classes, many times abandoned by society and their families, who in their marginality had become a matter of police and public concern. These records illuminate the forging of notions of madness and the range of measures and reactions taken to address its family and social consequences from a broader perspective, including a wider social spectrum, and presenting a more balanced picture in terms of gender. Seeking "to restrain the said disorders" (*porre freno a detti disordini*), the parties involved gathered to define and classify problematic behaviors, discuss whether they were the consequence of a voluntary or involuntary act, if this meant it could be held to be an illness, and finally negotiate possible remedies.[66] Recourse to the intervention of the Auditore Fiscale was, overall, a step in the itineraries followed by families in their effort to cope with what they saw as signs of mental disturbance.

In their descriptions of behaviors held to indicate mental disturbance, family members crafted accounts that were designed in accordance to the result they were expecting to achieve. Madness was shaped with gestures and actions that were carefully selected to prove that one was a prodigal or demented and in need of interdiction. Alternatively, mental derangement could be molded to prove that a person was a criminally insane *pazza* or *matto*, hence not accountable for her or his actions and thus deserving of a mitigated penalty. It could also be cast with the necessary features of *pazzia furiosa* in order to secure admission to a mental institution. But madness was also identified in behaviors that would not lead to any of these legal outcomes. Interdiction, criminal insanity, and confinement capture the moments in which madness was enclosed within specific categories that conditioned its characterization. The special cases dealt with by the Auditore Fiscale, in contrast, involve situations and behaviors that had not (yet) been assigned legal categories. Some involve behaviors and mental states that, if aggravated, could eventually lead to interdiction, conviction, or confinement. Others concern behaviors characterized by the terms and notions that we have been examining, but which for one reason or another were dealt with by resorting to the Auditore Fiscale.

The eighteenth century witnessed the appearance of new forms of sociability and conflicting views about gender roles, relationships, affections, and rationality. Enlightened sociability had brought new conceptions of social relations and affective bonds between the sexes. These new perspectives produced virulent intergenerational conflicts and introduced a new component to matrimonial litigation.[67] The changes in family models, the rising conflicts of co-habitation, the appearance of new expectations and conflicting conceptions of gender roles, parenting and matrimony are issues that come to the fore in the debates surrounding what it meant to be mentally ill. In this regard, the settings of the problematic behaviors appearing in the files of the Auditore Fiscale bear close resemblance to the characterizations of the mentally disturbed recorded in interdiction procedures and criminal records.

The configuration of prodigality and *demenza*, as discussed before, suggests that family roles and gender identities were under public renewed scrutiny during the century. Interdictions, regardless of the category classifying the denunciation, served as a mechanism to debate proper parenthood, the relationship between father and son, or the expected behavior of a spouse, all framed under the overarching discussion of patrimony administration and economic mismanagement. These discussions are also reflected in the special requests handled by the Auditore Fiscale directly or via the Otto di Guardia. Families from all social backgrounds resorted to the authorities for help in controlling unruly and disordered relatives. At the request of families, state officials, judges, and public institutions played a decisive role in enforcing respect for traditional family hierarchies and gender roles. Social disciplining appears here as a joint effort of families and authorities to re-establish a rational, productive, and emotionally regulated family model, a model which – judging from the rising numbers of interdiction petitions, requests for admission to a mental hospital or a prison, and petitions for the arbitration of ever-growing family conflicts – was anything but settled.

Disobedience and violent behaviors

During the eighteenth century, the identification of deviant behavior was part of a battle against disobedience, unruliness (*indocilità*), and defiance against established behavioral norms.[68] In fact, many of the cases filed in the office of the Auditore Fiscale relate to parental requests to incarcerate or, more frequently, embark by force disobedient young men to serve in a ship's crew, labeled *discoli*.[69] In general terms, a *discolo* was a disobedient young man aged between 14 and his early twenties, who refused to work or study, was frequently violent, and lived a life of debauchery. Accusations ranged from "impertinences and disrespect for their parents"[70] to different degrees of unreasonable and often violent reactions against household members up to and including death threats.[71] With many of the characteristics of juvenile prodigals, a *discolo* was sometimes a less wealthy version of the prodigal and other times his forerunner. Three major differences can be found: *discoli* came from varied social origins, they were mostly denounced by their fathers, and their disorder was to a greater extent connected with criminality.[72] This is also due to the requirements of the institution in which they were denounced. The Magistrato dei Pupilli posed different requirements and called for a different language than used by the Auditore Fiscale and the Otto di Guardia, which were much more focused on criminal behavior.

As prodigals, *discoli* were the object of widespread moral condemnation for their disruptive breaches of social norms, their unruly characters, their obstinate idleness, and strong refusal to work. In other respects, they can be seen as a sort of criminal counterpart of the prodigal, so long as their cases were handled as a police matter, either before the Otto di Guardia or directly through the office of the Auditore Fiscale. Because a *discolo*'s behavior was part of the prehistory of the prodigal, the narratives of these unruly and dissolute young men illuminate the initial steps of what could develop into prodigal behavior, presenting tendencies that could eventually lead to criminal activities, strongly marked by the association between moral degradation and mental derangement.

148 Spaces and itineraries of madness

A *discolo* was a dissipater par excellence, but they were not necessarily subject to interdiction. Some of them were denounced before the age of 18 and were interdicted afterwards when they came of age or when they eventually inherited. But the great majority of *discoli* do not appear in the records of the Magistrato dei Pupilli. Mostly, a *discolo* was a second-born son with no inheritance rights or a firstborn with a patrimony that was not considerable enough to justify (and finance) interdiction. Given that in the majority of the cases, the *discoli* were not direct holders of a family patrimony, their greatest offence against property was committed through domestic stealing. They were usually described as compulsive stealers of all sorts of household goods, which they would afterwards sell in order to finance their debauchery. As, for example one who "took away from his own home a great quantity of furniture, clothes, silver, jewelry, money, grain, oil, and other things," for which he "forced doors, cupboards, trunks and other places where the goods were."[73] The degree of compulsiveness ascribed to their behavior varies from case to case, but largely they resemble descriptions of the interdicted for prodigality or *demenza*.[74] They were described as if a driving force compelled them to steal and afterwards sell the goods to finance their vices, which was thought to denote both viciousness and a lack of will power. The inability to control one's impulses and the tendency to be overcome by irrational needs were indicative, as explained before, of the absence of reasoning faculties.

In accordance with the preventive nature of the measures taken by the Auditore Fiscale, many of these accusations were supported by the argument that, because "he fears neither God nor men, if he were to continue living every day in the taverns without any expected revenue and without earnings, it can be justly feared that in little time he will precipitate into some mistake that will cause serious dishonor to the whole family."[75] Unruliness and persistent economic and sexual debauchery were widely feared by eighteenth-century European societies, for they had been identified as a clear path toward degeneration and criminality.[76] Even during early youth an uncontrolled *discolo* could expose himself to irreversible damage, such as a 13-year-old boy found hanged in the cellar's house by his mother after weeks of disobedience, disrespectful behavior, and refusal to engage in any productive activity. The inquiry conducted by the Auditore Fiscale to determine if his death had been self-inflicted demonstrated that the boy fit the usual parameters of a *discolo*, with his "nature predominantly impertinent and riotous [*discolo*]," his refusal to work, his running away from home, states of confusion, and disturbed disposition.[77]

Prodigals and *discoli* shared the same vice and committed the same offence against property and family hierarchies. A *discolo*, nonetheless, was closer to criminality than his counterpart, with the main indicator of deviance being displaced from dissipation to unruliness and incorrigibility. Parents requesting that their son "be embarked in any ship" that would go far away from Tuscany to serve as crew member presented this element of criminality as a justification for this desperate measure.[78] The Auditore Fiscale would order their conscription to serve on a ship's crew only when it could be established that they were "reduced to the most extreme degree of incorrigibility."[79] As these features were part of the judicial script required to justify the involvement of the Auditore Fiscale, the interest in examining them here lies not in the descriptions of unruliness and violent reactions per se but in the extent to which these reactions were taken to be signs of a disturbed mind.

Although the primary purpose of these petitions was to convince the authorities of the seriousness of the case, at the same time they reveal profound reflections about what it meant to be sane and which were the signs indicating that the line had been crossed. In some cases, allusions to a disordered mind are reduced to timid hints in the midst of descriptions of dissoluteness, disobedience, and proto-criminal activities. In other cases, the mental state of a *discolo* comes to the fore through marginal but straightforward comments. In the end, there are also cases in which a disturbed mental state is placed at the very foundation of the accusation, being identified as the main cause of the disorder.

The notion of incorrigibility and its association with madness is best elucidated by the ways in which supplicants described the excessive violence of *discoli*. They often combined domestic theft with attempts on the lives of their close relatives in rampages that closely resembled the furious fits of those labeled as *dementi* or *pazzi furiosi*. Zanobi Bini, for instance, although he had been "kindly admonished [*ammonito amorevolmente*]" on various occasions by his parents for his uncontrolled stealing and unruly behavior, had "revolted against them by attempting to kill them and had mistreated them in deeds and words."[80] His attacks had been so fierce that his parents had been forced to escape and leave the house to save themselves. For several years, they had tried to curb him by requesting his imprisonment for some months or enrolling him in the ducal army but to no avail. Given that he had lately made an attempt against the life of his mother, they were petitioning again, this time requesting that he be conscripted as a crew member in any ship that would be willing to take him.

We have to bear in mind that exacerbated violence did not necessarily mean that the perpetrator was mentally disturbed. For instance, accusations of life-threatening domestic violence were a cause of *separatio thori* (separation of bed and board) argued before the ecclesiastical courts of the period without any need to ascribe it to madness, and life-threatening violence in criminal courts was not necessarily identified as a sign of mental derangement.[81] But the clue here lies in the fact that events leading to Zanobi Bini's forced embarkation, as in many other cases, were substantially similar to those recounted by families to explain why they were forced to request interdiction or petition for confinement in Santa Dorotea.

When we examine how petitions of committal to Santa Dorotea framed deranged violence, we can better grasp what made violence, or violent reactions, an indicator of madness, and even more clearly, how these same indicators could be shaped and labeled with different terms according to the institution in which the complaint was made. A wife, for instance, petitioned for her husband's committal to Santa Dorotea arguing that he had ceased to be a "good and diligent" head of family, neglecting his duties and becoming a "disordered [man] and a dissipater, no different than a maniac and mad man."[82] The family had tried to curb his disorder through imprisonment, but that had proved to be insufficient, for even if at first he gave some "signs of correction and of being liberated from his fixations and madness," he resumed his past mad behavior shortly after his release. Given that he made an attempt against the life of his wife and children, he was again imprisoned while the petition for his committal was being processed.

While this man's disordered and violent behavior was medically categorized as *pazzia furiosa*, Zanobi Bini had only been labeled as *discolo*. Both behaviors were similarly framed, and the assessments of their consequences were alike, the *discolo* being a younger version of the married *pazzo furioso*, in this case. There are evidently many circumstances that explain why a violent individual was labeled as *discolo, prodigal, demente*, or *pazzo furioso*. But a crucial issue is that the institution where the complaint was lodged profoundly shaped the language employed. Dissipation and disordered or uncontrolled behavior combined with escalating violence against family members or against themselves were undoubtedly perceived as the effects of a deranged mind.

The fact that families had tried several strategies to induce a *discolo* to change his behavior without any result is always highlighted in the narratives, so as to give a clear sign that the disorder was inveterate and unaffected by any reprimand or corrective measure. The issue is significant here for it is the key that connects incorrigibility with madness. The accusations brought against *discoli*, at first sight connecting them purely to matters of police and social discipline, suggest the presence of notions of madness at a social level, particularly the evaluation of the recklessness or the violence shown by *discoli*. The key to the connection with madness can be found in the frequency of their violent outbursts, who their victims were, and what the circumstances were.[83] In particular, the fact that they repeatedly gave vent to their anger against their parents was considered a revealing detail. It was deemed distorted and abnormal to try to kill one's own mother, even more so if the episode was part of a pattern.

Requests for the forced embarkation of a *discolo* had no need to employ the legal labels of madness that were required in criminal prosecution or in civil litigation. However, whereas legal categories were unnecessary, the descriptors and expressions appear strikingly similar to those used in judicial procedures. The *discoli* were characterized using terms that were often employed in interdiction procedures or in other characterizations of the mentally disturbed to describe altered states of mind, which can be observed in expressions such as "extravagant brain" (*cervello stravagante*)[84] or references to their disturbed or troubled humor (*umore troppo torbido*)[85] or their being of a "difficult, disturbed and uneasy disposition" (*animo difficile, torbido e inquieto*).⁸⁶ A young man could begin his career as a *discolo* in his early youth, be alternatively incarcerated, exiled and incarcerated again for decades, and in the process be described in a way that over the years increasingly resembled accounts of madmen.⁸⁷ Some of them ended up interdicted in the Pupilli, some continued to appear in the office of the Auditore Fiscale, and others disappeared from the records after they were forced to live in Tuscany serving on a ship's crew, but overall the language employed to describe them suggests that the connection with insanity was frequently made, though not always verbalized.

Licentious behavior

The languages of madness also appear in denunciations of libertinage, dissolute tendencies, and adulterous relationships. Examination of these cases suggests that sexual misconduct could be understood as caused by a disturbed mind, recognized in behaviors that are strikingly similar to the indicators of madness recorded in interdiction accounts, the proceedings of criminal justice, and hospital records. For instance, denunciations of disordered men mingled references to idleness, vices, debauchery, and libertine tendencies with considerations on the individual's mental capacities. This connection can be found in interdiction accounts as well as in the characterizations of young men falling into the category of *discoli* or of disordered middle-aged married men.

In accounts of the improper or adulterous affairs of these men, women, usually of a lower social status, were represented as the instigators of the vices of weak men who fell into their schemes and diverted them from the path of obedience, labor, and virtue. The vision of the female power of seduction, which had pervaded religious writings against premarital relations and, particularly, against unequal marriages between elite men and low-born women since the late seventeenth century, acquires interesting meanings in relation to notions of masculinity and the mental state expected of a man.⁸⁸ An important element of the cases handled by the Auditore Fiscale resides in the way male weakness was portrayed, and how it was used as evidence of poor rational faculties. Rather than pointing toward the traditional view of the malice and seductive arts of women, the narratives highlighted these men's lack of rational powers to respond to female schemes. Shedding light on the extent to which these cases were associated with mental incapacity, the recurrence of this behavior, and in particular, the fact that the individual had engaged in this conduct for several years could be presented as grounds for arguing later that a man needed to be interdicted.

For instance, Domenico Rigi was first denounced when he intended to marry a servant, again when he eloped with another woman taking away valuable household goods, and a last time when he was involved in a shooting by reason of his promise of marriage to a third woman.⁸⁹ The idea that love in the form of a strong passion could dangerously obscure men's mental faculties can also be observed in the "moral rigor" that characterized

152 *Spaces and itineraries of madness*

the eighteenth-century religious understanding of the dangers of love.[90] But suggestions regarding altered or weakened mental faculties caused by passionate affection and heightened by the schemes of women served here, interestingly, to diminish the man's responsibility for his wrongdoings.

The common provision against these kinds of disorders was to ensure the woman's banishment from the surroundings of the helpless man, so that he could return to the good path. Either because of their "fickleness" (*leggerezze*) or their excessive "volubility," they let themselves be "persuaded" by these women into committing actions that were detrimental to them, as was said regarding Bindo Maria Peruzzi, who eloped with a woman while involved in matrimonial negotiations with another and was interdicted 10 years later.[91] What was only hinted at in some cases was openly expressed in others, such as when a father explicitly referred to his son's "weakness" and "little and no judgement" (*poco e niuno giudizio*) to explain his involvement with three different women and his engagement in two promises of marriage. The same weakness and little judgement was adduced by his family to interdict this man some years later, after which his difficult personality made them file several requests aiming to control the consequences of his actions.[92] His course through the itineraries of madness is further revealed by the fact that some years before his interdiction, he was tried for *stupro* (rape) and was later imprisoned for an adulterous relationship.[93]

Wrongly oriented affections and deviant sexual practices appear in descriptions of prodigals, *dementi* and *pazzi furiosi*, illuminating the dynamics of the itineraries of madness. For instance, Lorenzo Baldinotti, whose mental derangement is registered throughout the four interdictions that affected him between 1725 and 1755, caused repeated trouble for his family and the authorities on account of his disordered sexual behavior. He faced rape charges in 1729, and in 1755 was still creating trouble due to his "dissolute" behavior, "illicit pleasures," and "public sensuality."[94] In the case of Lorenzo Baldinotti's son, said to have inherited the "brain and character" of a father "whose extreme extravagance was notorious," his lasciviousness took the form of homosexual tendencies. Said to have shown early signs of extravagance and a behavior similar to that of a *discolo*, Antonio Baldinotti faced criminal charges of sodomy in 1765, when he was in his early twenties, which were left open due to a lack of evidence.[95] All the same, 3 years later there were once again rumors about him, this time saying he had developed an "irrational passion" (*irragionevole passione*) for a man he kept living with him as a lackey in the same countryside villa that had witnessed his father's scandals.[96] Following a request by his relatives, Antonio was sent back to Florence by order of the Auditore Fiscale to be kept under direct surveillance while his interdiction was being approved. Antonio's next of kin not only requested the interdiction, but also solicited his banishment in Volterra or Portoferraio.[97]

The discreet and efficient action of the authorities to conceal a behavior that had by then achieved much publicity speaks of Antonio's privileges before the law, but aristocratic privileges in this case constitute only the first and most evident layer of a much more complex problem when we take into account a wider context. The Baldinotti family had suffered the consequences of mad behavior and had made use of the mechanisms available to control it for at least half a century. At the same time, this provided them with the ability to make convenient use of mechanisms such as incarceration, confinement in a hospital, home restraint, banishment, interdiction, and criminal prosecution. Without the need to settle clear boundaries between reality and fiction, what the Baldinotti case underpins is a social awareness of the characteristics of madness and how certain behaviors and emotional reactions were considered its most definitive indications. In the case of Antonio's sodomitical tendencies, his weakness for same-sex relationships was unanimously singled out as caused by the mental disturbance he inherited from his father, as he was "a young man of little brain and poor conduct."[98]

A similar approach had been taken by the relatives of a man convicted of sodomy when they pleaded for exemption from guilt on account of his "fatuity and foolishness."[99] We have seen how the criminally insane were held not to be responsible for their actions. By the same token, insanity diminished the responsibility of the individual for indulging in vices and moral corruptions such as sodomy. Madness accounted for their "vicious" tendencies at the same time as it exculpated them for indulging them. This is not to say, however, that sodomy on its own was considered to be a kind of madness. In the cases where sodomy appears connected to the argument of diminished responsibility by reason of insanity, there is nothing to suggest that homosexual practices were considered to be the symptom of madness. On the contrary, the argument was that, because the suspect was considered to be mad, he could not restrain himself from committing the crime. As pointed out by critics of Michel Foucault's contention that homosexuality was included in the categories of madness in the eighteenth century, we must bear in mind that homosexuality was "fiercely punished" by law, while madness exculpated individuals on account of their diminished responsibility.[100]

So long as madness presupposed the incapacity to perform rational actions and take rational decisions, the mentally ill were characterized as particularly prone to sexual deviances such as the ones practiced by Lorenzo and Antonio Baldinotti. For instance, a man committed to Santa Dorotea whose sentence had been suspended on account of his insanity was released from the hospital when his *pazzia furiosa* turned into a "mixture of stupidity and *demenza*." To illustrate his current mental condition, the hospital's physician said he "is not furious, and neither disturbs the peace of those around him nor falls into lascivious acts, but has simply become a little imbecile of mind and foolish [*stoliduccio*]."[101]

These notions of madness can thus be read as part of a more general campaign to discipline sexual and moral behaviors which began at the end of the seventeenth century with a strong religious mark but which became progressively secularized during the eighteenth century; materialized, among other measures, in the enforcement of the office of the Auditore Fiscale.[102]

Measures taken to ensure the maintenance of the *buon governo* and preserve the good morals of the inhabitants were conflated with mechanisms to neutralize the consequences of madness. Nonetheless, even if madness and moral depravation produced similar consequences, we must be cautious. Not every morally reprehensible act was considered to be the expression of a deranged mind, nor vice versa. But, the fact remains that insanity could constitute a disruption of public peace and morality.

Although madness was not thought to necessarily entail criminality, they certainly appear connected in the records examined here. What comes to the fore is that the same people who were convicted of a crime, imprisoned for being *discolo*, or admonished for their licentious behavior could later be interdicted or committed to Santa Dorotea. The connection between sexual crimes and interdiction sentences and the fact that interdicted men appear involved in diverse criminal activities broadens the picture of how madness was perceived and handled. On the one hand, it shows how problematic men denounced for mental incapacity could become for public life and to what extent their families turned to the authorities seeking their help. But, on the other hand, it also shows how the indicators of madness changed and adapted from one context to another.

Women's sexual scandals also appear connected to extravagance and to indicators of madness and were the object of a different set of measures to control the problem, but of not so different arguments to condemn the behavior. Cases involving women denounced for their bad reputation disclose how disreputable female behavior could be taken to be the outcome of an altered state of mind. Cases related to elite women who were confined in either of the two Florentine custodial institutions that held women of ill repute, the Conservatorio dei Mendicanti and the Malmaritate, are particularly illustrative. These institutions were used as a temporary solution for matrimonial conflicts that prevented the use of more definitive solutions through ecclesiastical justice.[103] The involvement of the Auditore Fiscale served as a discreet measure to silence the dishonor these women allegedly brought upon their husbands. They were confined at their request for being *donne fiere* (fierce women), that is, because they would not obey their commands. Among the reasons adduced by husbands, we find claims that their spouse had disreputable friendships or that she refused to obey him, having fled from the matrimonial home.

These denunciations of female libertinage and unruliness also made use of the descriptors and languages of madness. One was sent to the Conservatorio dei Mendicanti by request of her husband because she had had various adventures with different men, behaved too intimately with her escorts (*cicisbei*) in public, incurred growing debts buying expensive gifts for them, allowed them to spend the night in her house, and used words of "foolish love [*sciocco amore*]" to speak with them.[104] Another was denounced by her husband because she had fallen under the effects of an immoderate passion (*sregolata passione*) for a surgeon, which "blinded" her, "obscuring her judgement."[105]

Spaces and itineraries of madness 155

A third case presents a more straightforward association between persistent licentious behavior and madness. Angiola della Renna, married to a *cavaliere* and noble herself, was first confined in one of their residences in the outskirts of Florence and later sent to the Mendicanti on account of her persistent and scandalous libertinage. The usual features are present here as well: excessive liberty in her interactions with men, their staying overnight at her residence, and the public scandal her behavior caused in the surrounding population. The ways in which the authorities described her character further support my point here. They said that her "wicked manner" was "to a large extent the consequence of a kind of madness that makes her trespass every obligation," and spoke of "the extravagance combined with the foolishness [*stoltizia*] that agitates the heart of this woman." This "foolishness" and "kind of madness" justified her confinement for 4 years, despite the fact that she sent various petitions with eloquent promises of amendment. Three years after her release, the Auditore Fiscale informed the Council of Regency that Angiola "either not understanding reason or not intending to follow it, seems to be obstinate in her strange way of thinking."[106]

Notions of mental disturbance in family litigation

Many of the private requests that the office of the Auditore Fiscale had to attend to were related to family conflicts, as we have seen, among which matrimonial disputes were prominent. Accusations of licentious behavior and a lax sense of matrimonial fidelity were exchanged by spouses. As was the case in interdiction procedures, in the matrimonial contentions disclosed to the Auditore Fiscale, patrimonial concerns were blended into denunciations of behaviors that were held to reveal a disordered state of mind. These disputes demonstrate particularly well how litigants resorted to the vocabulary of madness to illustrate their accusations against each other and to justify the intervention of the authorities. This instrumental use of the languages of madness at a lay level allows us to elaborate further on the social notions of mental derangement.

In these narratives, mental disturbance appears in close connection with notions of virtue, morality, and family roles. Disordered women were usually portrayed in open defiance of their husband's authority. But the obstinacy they showed, and particularly their reluctance to yield to their husband's authority, was many times only part of a more complicated explanation of the nature of their disorder. Characterizing women's unruliness or libertinage as an indicator of a "disordered disposition" (*animo sregolato*) or stating that they made "utterly extravagant declarations" and only followed their "caprices" served to suggest that their minds were compromised. A clue to the connection asserted between their disordered behavior and a distorted mind is to be found in how the narratives presented and qualified demonstrations of the psychological state that accompanied those acts of unruliness. These women's amorous affections were defined as "foolish" and

156 *Spaces and itineraries of madness*

their passions as "immoderate," their minds and disposition were said to be disordered, and their characters extravagant. The fact that they showed a "disordered disposition" served to justify the need, as the Auditore Fiscale explained regarding a particular case, to be restrained (*sia tenuta a freno*) and persuaded to recognize her duties.[107]

To determine to what extent extravagance and a disordered disposition were associated with mental disturbance, it may be useful to compare the language used in these cases with that used in interdiction procedures. Expressions such as immoderate passions, *animo sregolato*, or extravagance, to name only some, were often employed to argue that a person needed to be interdicted. Analogous notions appear in the cases argued in front of the Auditore Fiscale, where the same arguments were used and similar behaviors were given as examples to support the accusations, but in these cases, the intention was not to interdict a relative but directly to solve a family dispute. In view of the similarities between these notions and the descriptions in interdiction accounts, references to a disordered or extravagant disposition should not be taken as circumstantial. Rather, they suggest that in the private conflicts disclosed to the authorities for arbitration, Tuscan society made use of a shared knowledge that connected immoderate emotions to mental disturbance which, furthermore, appears as an argument that could turn a plea in one's favor.

For instance, Chiara Maria Fondora, who had been confined in the Mendicanti for her wicked character, her behavior toward her *cicisbei*, and, in particular, her shameless manifestations of affection and her foolish love, tried to counter her husband's accusations by attacking him using similar arguments. Relying on the principle that a deranged mind was manifested through odd economic behavior, she accused her husband of "extravagancy," explaining that she had been impelled to live separately from him for over 14 years due to his failure to feed her and their children, to the extent that one of them died from hunger.[108] However, in this dispute between Chiara Maria Fondora and her husband, her fame as a licentious and libertine woman proved to be stronger than her accusations against her husband. The latter's extravagancy was considered less serious in the eyes of the Fiscale compared to the woman's repeated demonstrations of "foolish love" (*sciocco amore*) and scandalous libertinage. If in this case the husband's allegations against his wife were favored, there are plenty of cases that had the opposite outcome. Interdiction procedures that portrayed disordered men through women's accusations offer clear examples of this outcome.

Extravagance and the different forms that madness could assume were not confined to one gender. Accusations of male extravagance also included descriptions of their altered minds and disordered dispositions, but economic behavior was at the very foundation of the model against which male sanity was measured. Male extravagance in economic management was recognized in any behavior that went against the wellbeing of the household from dissipation to being so parsimonious as to withhold the necessary means of maintenance from the family. Prodigality had an antithesis that was seen as revealing as its counterpart of the presence of male mental derangement. For instance, a nobleman involved in a bitter matrimonial dispute was described as a miserly head of family who "moved by violent passions of sordid avarice" (*guidato da violente passione di sordidissima avarizia*) refused to spend on his family's most basic needs, banishing salt and spices for being too expensive and withholding food, clothing, and medical attention from them, to the point of leaving his children to scream with hunger. All these signs, combined with the fact that he insulted and beat his wife in the most indecorous and unfounded way, were said to demonstrate his "disturbed humor" (*torbido umore*) and that he was "disordered in his thinking" (*stravolto nel pensare*), all indicators of an "extravagant head" (*capo stravagante*). Although the local authorities and the wife's kin proposed that the man be interdicted and placed under guardianship, the Auditore Fiscale considered that this was not advisable in this case as it would only lead to further disturbance in the couple's life.[109]

The familial disputes placed under the authority of the Auditore Fiscale for arbitration made use of the behaviors of madness as arguments to support opposing accusations. Violent reactions, dilapidation, sexual misconduct, extravagance, and in general, behaviors that denoted an absence of self-control placed the denunciations in the territory of indicators of mental derangement. These behaviors, more or less explicitly defined as forms of insanity, were used to win the dispute and convince the Auditore Fiscale of one's position. Interestingly, then, the arbitration practiced by the Auditore Fiscale served as a space for the discussion of the boundaries of normal behavior and for the negotiation of what mental disturbance amounted to, which worked in a similar way as that of the Magistrato dei Pupilli. It is also important to note that to speak of mental disturbance in its various gradations had become a recurrent practice to win an argument, drawing from shared conceptions about the dangers madness posed to both private and public lives.

Connecting spaces: the itineraries of madness

The destiny of the insane became a matter of public concern not only when they had transgressed the limits of the law, but also, primarily, on the direct request of family members. Examining the spaces where madness was recorded in the eighteenth century from a comprehensive perspective brings to the fore the fact that there was a web of measures devised to address its consequences. In their quest to curb their mentally afflicted relatives, handle the effects of their behaviors, and above all mitigate the disruption they generated to family life, families moved through the different private and public remedies available, configuring the itineraries of madness. In this respect, as explained in relation to interdiction procedures, requests for incarceration, committal to Santa Dorotea, admonishments, and conscription to serve on a ship's crew were desperate measures to cope with insanity as much as they were mechanisms to introduce a mediator into conflictive family relationships. Families moved from one institution to the other seeking help not necessarily to get rid of their relatives, but in most cases to be able to live with them. At least, that was what was negotiated between families and authorities in a structure that was coordinated by the Auditore Fiscale and the Magistrato dei Pupilli.

The Auditore Fiscale's role in matters related to madness was definitively established during the Regency and officially sealed by the 1750 reforms of Santa Dorotea. But as we have seen, the involvement of the office in matters related to deviance in general, and with madness specifically, went beyond the responsibilities instituted in 1750. In its role of head of police and supervisor of criminal justice, the Auditore Fiscale dealt with madness with the goal of controlling the consequences of deviant behavior in social life in terms of both security and morality. This explains why the office handled not only private requests for institutionalization or incarceration, but also requests soliciting the Fiscale's direct involvement through face-to-face conversations, official reprimands, and other types of admonishments.

The Auditori Fiscali counted on various mechanisms to control the public disorders generated by mental disturbances and at the same time resolve the familial conflicts that came to be entangled with them. The mechanisms ranged from persuasive measures to confinement and exile, all with the goal of restoring social and family order. The ultimate aim was to control the disordered behavior, based on an underlying belief that it could be overturned and, thus, cured. Families resorted to hospital, prison, or interdiction depending upon the particularities of each family group, their past history, and their previous involvement with mental disturbance. In this respect, the dynamics of the itineraries of madness underscore how disciplining the unruly members of society was considered a shared responsibility of families and the state during the Ancien Régime. The destiny of the mentally ill was the result of a series of negotiations between the authorities and their families, which took into consideration issues such as the family's resources, the person's current and chronicled behavior, their level of dangerousness and capacity to disturb, and the need to defend the family honor, among other concerns.

Among the possible courses of action, admonitions and all sort of persuasive strategies were the first to be taken. As seen earlier, families requested the authorities to intervene in their conflicts by acting as mediators in their battles. They could request the Auditore Fiscale to speak with their son so that he would change his behavior, convince their husband to behave properly, threaten a brother that if he continued on the same path he would end up imprisoned, or explain to a wife that her conduct was disrespectful.

Another option was confinement in a fortress, incarceration, or conscription to serve in a ship's crew, intended as a punishment that had the aim of taming (*domare*) disordered men through punishment,[110] "correcting" their mistakes,[111] "moderating" their disobedience,[112] and hopefully keeping them away from a future of crime determined by their bad "inclination" and vicious tendencies.[113] Both could be used to discipline a *discolo*, a *prodigo*, or a man straightforwardly defined as mad, functioning at the same time as a mechanism to protect the rest of the household from their extravagances and violence. Imprisonment could be specifically requested by relatives, both as a security measure and as a way to conceal the crimes committed by a mentally perturbed relative from the view of the rest of society.[114] Forced embarkation, in turn, was usually requested when the imprisonment had proven ineffective or when families could not keep financing or had never been able to finance their confinement, resting upon the principle that the rigors and discipline of maritime life might help curb their ungovernable desires and passions. Requested at different moments in the course of a man's extravagant behavior, they were measures usually taken more than once in a lifetime and were supposed to work in combination with the admonishments of the Auditore Fiscale, who described the harsher punishments that would be inflicted on them if they were to continue on the same path. These measures varied according to age, social origin, and family situation. Conscription to serve on a ship's crew, for example, was not considered suitable for the privileged, in whose case confinement in a fortress was preferred. While the former was intended only for young single men, imprisonment and relegation (*confino*) were the preferred mechanisms to control married men with underage children.

Although confinement behind monastic walls was not a solution used exclusively with women, it is slightly more visible in their cases.[115] The extent to which monasteries were a destiny for the mentally disturbed is hard to assess. The hypothesis that monasteries were the most common refuge for the mentally afflicted whose wealthy families intended to keep them from the indiscreet gaze of neighbors and elite society is poorly documented and does not have a substantial presence in the sources examined here. Although cases of women being confined in a monastery for reprehensible disorders that closely resemble the indicators of madness can be found, the confining of men and women in a monastery on account of madness cannot be taken as a practice. It could, nonetheless, be a stage in the itineraries of madness. For instance, the monastery could be the starting point of the itinerary, as attested by the records of Santa Maria Nuova and Santa Dorotea, which show that both institutions received patients coming from various monasteries in Tuscany. These same records also indicate that on some occasions individuals considered to be mad were temporarily held in a monastery, although these cases are isolated. For instance, in 1748, a man was sent to the Fortezza da Basso in Florence because his frenzies had generated "universal consternation" in the religious community of the monastery in which he was being held. However, he remained there for just a short time. As his "uneasiness" continued to increase, he was sent to the *pazzeria* of Santa Maria Nuova while the authorities waited for his family to pick him up. As this did not happen and there was no one to pay his fee, he was kept there for only 2 weeks until he was finally sent home.[116]

The way in which the administration of justice dealt with the destinations of the criminally insane is also telling with regard to how the itineraries of madness worked. According to Elizabeth Mellyn, until the seventeenth century, the issue of criminal insanity amounted to a problem of guardianship. A sentence of life imprisonment generated a problem of resources that was hard to overcome, since the maintenance of the prisoners had to be paid for by the families. If confinement was not the solution, the criminally insane had to be taken care of by their families, which was a difficulty not easily endured. As a consequence, the problem of what to do with the criminally insane was addressed through a collaborative effort between families, communities, and courts. Until the seventeenth century, Mellyn stresses, the tendency was to send the criminally insane home, which made the family the primary custodial institution. The foundation of Santa Dorotea in 1643, she asserts, changed the destiny of the criminally insane by providing a solution that previously had not existed.[117]

However, the impact of the foundation of Santa Dorotea on the fate of the criminally insane should not be overestimated. After Santa Dorotea was founded, and still during the eighteenth century, the problem of the criminally insane continued to be resolved in a negotiation between families and authorities. Committal was by definition a temporary (and generally brief) measure, as explained before. When criminals were found to suffer a kind of madness that justified their committal to Santa Dorotea, their transfer would be ordered, but this would only last while their condition was dangerous. In some of these cases, the episode of madness was triggered while they were in prison and after they had been sentenced; in others, they were found to be mad during the trial and thus transferred immediately to the hospital. Given that Santa Dorotea was generally overcrowded, its administrative board took special care to ensure that patients were not kept there longer than strictly necessary.[118]

Clearly, then, the problem of how to decide the destination of the criminally insane was only temporarily solved with Santa Dorotea, for once patients were released, the question of what to do with them resurfaced. Their fate was determined by taking into consideration factors such as economic resources, the existence of family networks that could assume their custody, and their physical and mental health and that of their families, among other factors. The itineraries of madness can thus also be observed with regard to the criminally insane. When their madness ceased to be dangerous or if it had never been of a dangerous kind, they could then be sent to prison for a period of time. After this, provided they had relatives who could assume their custody, they could be sent home. Otherwise, they could be sent into exile if they had no family networks and had the physical health to provide for their own maintenance. For instance, Antonio Razzuoli, convicted of theft and sentenced to 5 years of relegation (*confino*) to Grosseto, was caught breaching his sentence. But because he was found to be demented, he was sent to Santa Dorotea, and his sentence was suspended. Nine months later, he was dismissed because his madness had ceased to be dangerous. Given that he also suffered some physical indispositions, it was not considered suitable for him to return to his relegation at Grosseto, so the Auditore Fiscale suggested instead that he be entrusted to the care of his father, who was to be in charge of his custody and responsible for his actions.[119]

Confinement in a ship, a prison, a fortress, or a hospital worked as a measure of last resort. Confinement was often decided upon in combination with other measures, such as official admonitions, home-restraint, or interdiction, sometimes simultaneously and other times as an escalating effort to tame the behavior and control its consequences. An important pattern found throughout early modern Europe is that confinement, regardless of whether it was in a hospital, prison, or monastery, was a temporary and a desperate measure and constituted only part of a much more complicated process.[120] The mentally ill were moved from one place to another. We observe them being relocated from their domestic care to a paid private residence, from confinement in a countryside villa to a fortress, from incarceration to a hospital, and from a hospital to home custody again. As we have seen, the periods of confinement in Santa Dorotea and Santa Maria Nuova were generally short, and the same person could be admitted behind its walls several times. In the end, people could be interdicted while they were being held prisoners in a fortress or be imprisoned by request of their families various times after they were interdicted.[121]

The courses of action taken to address the challenges posed by madness were highly dependent upon social position and economic resources. Families who could afford the necessary maintenance of their relatives in prison or in Santa Dorotea were more likely to obtain the response they expected from the ducal administration. The greater the families' financial resources were, the more mechanisms they could employ, from space and personnel to keep them at home, to legal advice and access to the necessary knowledge to maneuver between the different offices and the judicial structure of the grand ducal administration. In contrast, the situation of poorer people left less space for negotiation. The records suggest, however, that even poor families moved their mentally afflicted members from one place to the other.

Families, magistrates, authorities, and physicians coordinated the series of measures that could be taken to handle and control the consequences of madness, configuring a network in which the Auditore Fiscale often worked as the articulator of the various strategies pursued by families. For instance, the *cavaliere* Francesco del Sera, interdicted for being *pazzo affatto* (entirely mad) and *imbecille di mente* (imbecile of mind), was first ordered to be transferred to a countryside villa and afterwards compelled to receive medical treatment to cure his persistent madness. He was so "obstinately unruly" that he violently rejected any cure or help, on account of which his curator asked the Auditore Fiscale for military help to restrain him and thus force him to receive the cure.[122] His behavior was so difficult that the Fiscale declared he could not be allowed to live in society, for he had persistently disturbed public life with his "extravagances," "frenzies," and his "unusual

162 *Spaces and itineraries of madness*

alteration of spirit."[123] Drawing on the undisputed fact that his *demenza* had become worse over the years, the debate between his distinguished relatives, the Auditore Fiscale, and the Council of Regency was centered on the difficulties of having him secured at home versus the advantages of transferring him to a monastery. The trace of the case disappears until it resurfaces 15 years later, when he was the object of a second interdiction; he was then said to have lucid intervals and was married to a younger woman.[124]

As in this case, the residential situation of the mentally disordered could become a burden that families were often unable to resolve without the intervention of the public authorities, who, in the many cases where family cohabitation proved to be unbearable, had to provide alternative measures. Even if following interdiction, the Pupilli officials were permanently involved in every situation or conflict surrounding their wards, the Fiscale was often required to participate in order to provide for the wellbeing of both the families and the interdicted, ordering, for instance, temporary incarcerations or coordinating the availability of places where they could be taken care of.[125]

Intergenerational and matrimonial conflicts abounded amid the tensions caused by cohabitation with mentally unstable relatives. Temporary marital separation was granted by the authorities in cases of confirmed dangerous madness to which a series of attempts to reunite the couple would follow. For instance, confinement in the Malmaritate or the Mendicanti was used as a temporary measure to contain the effects of a marital conflict in need of being concealed from public sight. As discussed in the previous chapter, during guardianship, conflicts continued to flare up between the interdicted and their relatives, producing further difficulties in the family group. For example, marital violence, often with nearly fatal consequences, could induce the authorities to decide to temporarily separate a couple, either allowing for the wife to reside with her parents or sending her to the Malmaritate or the Mendicanti because of her extravagance and imprudence.[126] In all of these cases, we see how the authorities participated in the family's effort to cope with the collateral damage of mental disturbance.

The Auditore Fiscale and the Pupilli officials, with the help of other eminent state officials and regional authorities, arbitrated in marital disputes, dealt with the larger conflicts that often put the spouses' kin in opposition, and designed strategies of mutual compromise that could secure a peaceful reunion.[127] Conflicts of cohabitation were conflated with the problem of the special care the mentally afflicted often required, not only because familial responsibility over weak members of the family many times had to be enforced by law, but also because the problems that usually accompanied mental afflictions made it difficult to provide permanent solutions, as shown by the case of Lorenzo Maestrini, which began this chapter.

***

Scrutiny of the spaces of madness shows that public responses to mental derangement should be understood as the effect of a collective effort, resulting from a careful negotiation between families, judges, and authorities regarding what it meant to be mentally afflicted, what could be done to cure and/or discipline them, and what were the most suitable remedies that could be applied to mitigate its consequences. Recourse to one or another of the institutional remedies available reveals a social understanding of each of their particular rules, which in turn underscores that the parties involved knew how to maneuver through the legal structure in order to obtain favorable outcomes.

It has been argued here that the characteristics of mental incapacity appearing in interdiction records are echoed in broader institutional scenarios covered by criminal records, admission procedures to Santa Dorotea and the documentation of the office of the Auditore Fiscale. Requests received directly by the latter or through the Otto di Guardia regarding cases of disordered or unruly relatives that made use of the argument of mental instability to differentiate the case from "ordinary" criminal behavior show the pervasiveness of the language of madness in various different social groups. The cases that ended up in the files of the Auditore Fiscale suggest that similar notions of madness were present in different institutional arenas, presenting flexible vocabularies that nonetheless enclosed a similar conception of what it meant to be mentally afflicted. Furthermore, interdiction procedures, the records of Santa Dorotea and the Otto di Guardia, and the special requests handled by the Auditore Fiscale show similar notions regarding what it meant to be mentally disturbed, what were its defining characteristics, and how this affected family life.

The legal categories of mental derangement in the different institutional spaces were flexible and sufficiently undetermined to enclose culturally meaningful notions of madness. For this reason, the picture of the perceptions of madness and the measures taken to cope with it is further nuanced when we bear in mind the different contexts in which madness was disclosed. With definitions that were strongly contextual and relational, accounts and characterizations of mental derangement varied according to the requirements of each new space of appearance. The itineraries of madness reveal the presence of the same indicators and descriptors of madness across different institutions, adapted to the requirements of each space.

Notes

1. ASF, MPAP, *Memoriali*, F. 2300, no. 311, June 1730.
2. ASF, MPAP, *Memoriali*, F. 2300, no. 471, February–March 1734/35; and no. 492, November 1735.
3. ASF, MPAP, *Memoriali*, F. 2300, no. 421, August 1733; and no. 471, March 1734/35.
4. ASF, MPAP, *Memoriali*, F. 2300, no. 471, April 1735.
5. Report of the Magistrato dei Pupilli, MPAP, *Memoriali*, F. 2300, no. 492, November 1735; and Biglietto of Filippo Luci, MPAP, *Memoriali*, F. 2300, no. 483, August 1735.

6 ASF, MPAP, *Memoriali*, F. 2301, no. 56, August 1739; ASF, MPAP, *Atti*, F. 1240, f. 1022, April 1742; and ASF, MS, *Suppliche*, F. 1188, fols. 1091–1112, December 1743.
7 Elizabeth W. Mellyn, *Mad Tuscans and Their Families: A History of Mental Disorder in Early Modern Italy* (Philadelphia: University of Pennsylvania Press, 2014), 9; Lisa Roscioni, *Il governo della follia. Ospedali, medici e pazzi nell'età moderna* (Milan: Bruno Mondadori, 2003), 124–125; Robert Allan Houston, *Madness and Society in Eighteenth-Century Scotland* (Oxford: Oxford University Press, 2000), 30–90; and Roy Porter, *Mind-Forg'd Manacles: A History of Madness in England from the Restoration to the Regency* (London: Penguin Books, 1990), 110–160.
8 On the Stinche as a place of reclusion for the insane following special requests, see Graziella Magherini and Vittorio Biotti, *L'isola delle Stinche e i percorsi della follia a Firenze nei secoli XIV-XVIII* (Florence: Ponte alle Grazie, 1992), 25–59.
9 ASF, SD, *Memorie, Documenti*, F. 23, no. 11, particularly "Del modo di ricevere i Mentecatti."
10 ASF, SD, F. 42, *Istrumenti e ricordi 1642 al 1740*, September 1747, in Graziella Magherini and Vittorio Biotti, *"Un luogo della città per custodia de'pazzi". Santa Dorotea dei Pazzerelli di Firenze nelle delibere della sua congregazione (1642–1754)* (Florence: Le Lettere, 1997), 79.
11 Roscioni, *Il governo della follia*, 236–243 and 257–264.
12 Roscioni, *Il governo della follia*, 116–120.
13 "Copia di Motuproprio di S.M.I. per l'erezione del nuovo Conservatorio di S. Dorotea de 16 novembre 1750," ASF, SD, *Memorie, Documenti*, F. 23, no. 5, inciso 6.
14 Roscioni, *Il governo della follia*, 117 and 138–139.
15 "Copia di Motuproprio di S.M.I. per l'erezione del nuovo Conservatorio," ASF, SD, *Memorie, Documenti*, F. 23, no. 5, inciso 6.
16 ASF, OGB, *Straordinarie*, F. 2661, no. 221, April 1722. For a similar case regarding a *pazza furiosa* who despite being *molesta e molestissima* could not be received in Santa Dorotea because she was unable to pay the fee and could not be admitted to the *pazzeria* of Santa Maria Nuova either, allegedly because there was no space, see ASF, CR, *Fiscale*, F. 755, no. 37, September 1747.
17 The Nove Conservatori del Dominio was the magistracy in charge of the governmental management of most of the dominions of the Grand Duchy of Tuscany and coordinated the relations between the capital and the provinces. On the Magistrato dei Nove in the eighteenth century and relations between the center and the provinces, see Luca Mannori, *Il Sovrano Tutore: Pluralismo istituzionale e accentramento amministrativo nel principato dei Medici (secc. XVI-XVIII)* (Milan: Giuffrè, 1994).
18 Roscioni, *Il governo della follia*, 134–135.
19 The administrative board of Santa Dorotea to the Auditore Fiscale. ASF, SD, *Motupropri, Rescritti . . .*, F. 2, no. 42, December 1756.
20 A similar challenge was faced, for instance, by the administration of Bethlem, the famous English asylum, where restrictive policies of admission were also in place during the eighteenth century. Jonathan Andrews and Andrew Scull, *Undertaker of the Mind: John Monro and Mad-Doctoring in Eighteenth-Century England* (Berkeley: University of California Press, 2001), 38.
21 ASF, SD, *Motupropri, Rescritti . . .*, F. 8, no. 64, September–October 1770.
22 Report of Antonio Lulli, ASF, CR, *Fiscale*, F. 759, no. 11, June 1755. The records of Santa Dorotea show Antonio Lulli explaining with similar arguments why a patient was to be discharged from the institution notwithstanding the requests of their families to keep them inside its walls. Roscioni, *Il governo della follia*, 168–172.

23 Report of the officers of the Magistrato dei Pupilli. ASF, MPAP, *Memoriali*, F. 2303, no. 210, August 1754.
24 Before 1756, Antonio Lulli had been performing occasional visits to the patients of Santa Dorotea and usually gave his medical testimony to assess *pazzia furiosa*. He was the *medico ordinario* of Santa Dorotea until 1788. Roscioni, *Il governo della follia*, 268.
25 Giovanni Targioni Tozzetti (1712–1783), the renowned Florentine physician and naturalist, had been sporadically involved with madness due to his assistance to the Otto di Guardia as *medico fiscale* and his position as official physician of the Stinche prison. Through his involvement with Santa Dorotea, Targioni Tozzetti developed a special concern for mental afflictions which can be observed both in his reports (*perizie*) as *medico fiscale* and in the reports he periodically had to make regarding patients in Santa Dorotea and the mentally afflicted under the care of the Pupilli. This special concern leaves a final mark in his medical consultations (*Consultationes medicae*), which included a section exclusively devoted to hypochondriac and hysterical affections, to epilepsy, and to delirium, among others. BNCF, *Manoscritti*, GTT, no. 234, "Consultationes medicae," cart.2, and no. 235, "Relazioni forensi." Aside from the commentaries of Lisa Roscioni, Enrico Stumpo, and Elena Brambilla, the work of Targioni Tozzetti on madness remains largely unexplored. His role as an "authority" on mental afflictions in the second half of the eighteenth century is examined in Chapter 5. Roscioni, *Il governo della follia*; Enrico Stumpo, "Un uomo per tutte le stagioni: Giovanni Targioni Tozzetti e la polizia sanitaria nella Firenze dei Lorena," in *Relazioni forensi. Ambiente, igiene e sanità nella Firenze dei Lorena*, Giovanni Targioni Tozzetti, ed. S. Pelle (Florence: Le Lettere, 1998), 7–24; and Elena Brambilla, *Corpi invasi e viaggi dell'anima* (Rome: Viella, 2010), 238–241.
26 Lodovico Scutellari was *medico fiscale* between 1756 and 1758.
27 Letter from Niccolò Martelli to the Consulta. ASF, Santa Dorotea, *Motupropri, Rescritti . . .*, F. 2, no. 56, 29 March, 1757; and ASF, CR, *Spedale de Pazzi*, F. 426, no. 3, 24 March 1757.
28 Biglietto of Roberto Pandolfini to the administrative board of Santa Dorotea. ASF, SD, *Motupropri, Rescritti . . .*, F. 3, no. 58, 28 June 1759.
29 Petition sent from the Stinche, signed by Michel'Angelo Mugnaini in the name of the female prisoners, ASF, CR, *Fiscale*, F. 760, no. 21, March 1769.
30 Medical testimony of Giovanni Targioni Tozzetti and Antonio Lulli, ASF, CR, *Fiscale*, F. 760, no. 21, March 1769.
31 Domenico Brichieri Colombi, ASF, CR, *Fiscale*, F. 760, no. 21, March 1769. She was a convicted thief, sentenced to 10 years in the Stinche in 1755, where she had been kept at public expense. We have no information regarding her mental state at the time of the trial, so we should not assume that an insanity plea was put forward in her defense. On the contrary, some suggestions made by the Auditore Fiscale regarding the years after her conviction suggest that her mental affliction developed afterwards or, at least, that it was identified afterwards.
32 In fact, the examination of his *medical perizie* between 1750 and 1788 shows him more than once assuming a position of defense in the interests of prisoners, criminals, and the interdicted against the otherwise inexorable force of the law. See the next chapter for a further discussion.
33 Criminal procedures could be initiated in three ways: through a denunciation by the civic authorities, through private accusation, and on the initiative of the judges (*ex officio*). The case started with the informatory process, during which the criminal courts had to assemble as much evidence as possible and interrogate witnesses to determine if the accusation or suspicion of crime was grounded. When there were sufficient grounds to proceed, the accused was

publicly notified to appear before the court and was given a report of the informatory process that was to be used to build a defense with the help of a *procuratore de' poveri* (procurator of the poor). Once summoned to court, the accused could decide to remain contumacious, fail to attend and disappear, respond to the summons and confess, plea his or her innocence, or appear later with a prepared line of defense, once they had managed to make peace with the offended party. Depending on the seriousness of the crime, the accused could be held in prison during the informatory process. The Tuscan criminal procedure in all its stages, possibilities, and consequences can be seen in Savelli's famous handbook of criminal practice. Marc'Antonio Savelli, *Pratica universale* (Parma: Paolo Monti, 1717), 5–22, first published in 1665, with seven editions until 1748. See also John K. Brackett, *Criminal Justice and Crime in Late Renaissance Florence 1537–1609* (Cambridge: Cambridge University Press, 1992); and Trevor Dean, *Crime and Justice in Late Medieval Italy* (Cambridge: Cambridge University Press, 2007).

34 Savelli, *Pratica universale*, 108.
35 Savelli, *Pratica universale*, 108. He recommended that such cases be avoided and instead advocated for insanity defenses in which the accused could be directly examined by the judges with the support of medical experts, and, although not necessarily imprisoned, he recommended that they be kept under proper custody. Normally, failure to appear before the court after being notified that criminal charges had been brought against them resulted in an "automatic sentence of guilt" with the full statutory penalty.
36 See, for instance, Joel Peter Eigen, *Witnessing Insanity: Madness and Mad-Doctors in the English Court* (New Haven and London: Yale University Press, 1995), 9 and 18–20; and Houston, *Madness and Society*, 72–90 and 113–114. For strategies and collaborative responses to deal with the criminally insane in Tuscany during the previous centuries, see Mellyn, *Mad Tuscans*, 58–93.
37 Taking this into account, my survey of the Otto di Guardia is based on an in-depth scrutiny made for roughly every 3 to 5 years between 1720 and 1770 of the different sections of the archive of the *Otto di Guardia* (namely *Negozi, Negozi dei Rettori, Suppliche, Straordinarie*). Depending on the size of the volumes (*Filze*) and the characteristics of the findings, my soundings covered more than 1 consecutive year. For this reason, the results are not intended to be numerically representative but qualitatively meaningful in terms of the understanding and representations of madness in criminal justice.
38 *Arbitrio* meant that the penalty was decided at the discretion of the judges and was generally used to give a lenient sentence to a crime that, according to the statues, deserved a harsher one. The Otto di Guardia e Balìa was given arbitrary power in 1478, which granted it independence to judge without reference to the statutes. Giovanni Antonelli, "La magistratura degli Otto di Guardia a Firenze," *Archivio storico Italiano* 92 (1954): 3–40; and Brackett, *Criminal Justice and Crime*, 4.
39 Savelli, *Pratica universale*, 107.
40 Paolo Zacchia, *Quaestionum medico-legalium tomi tres* (Nuremberg: Sumptibus Joannis Georgii Lochneri, 1726), Book II, Title I, 112–159. The comprehensive classification of the different variations of madness appearing in Zacchia's *Quaestiones medico legales* (1621–1635) proved to have long-lasting effects in the legal practice of the Italian peninsula: see Mellyn, *Mad Tuscans*, 161–192; and Marco Boari, *Qui venit contra iura. Il furiosus nella criminalistica dei secoli XV e XVI* (Milan: Giuffré, 1983), 70–73. For an overview of Zacchia's work see Alessandro Pastore and Giovanni Rossi, eds., *Paolo Zacchia. Alle origini della medicina legale 1584–1659* (Milan: Franco Angeli, 2008).

41 Carlo Colombero, "Un contributo alla formazione della nozione di malattia mentale: le 'Questioni medico-legali' di Paolo Zacchia," in *Follia, psichiatria e società. Istituzioni manicomiali, scienza psichiatrica e classi sociali nell'Italia moderna e contemporanea*, ed. Alberto De Bernardi (Milan: Franco Angeli, 1982), 317–329.
42 Respectively, ASF, OGB, *Suppliche*, F. 2505, no. 73, 1726; ASF, OGB, *Negozi dei Rettori*, F. 2134, *Negozio* 7275, no. 1, 1730; ASF, OGB, *Straordinarie*, F. 1647, no. 6, 1774; ASF, OGB, *Suppliche*, F. 2542, no. 34, 1767; ASF, OGB, *Suppliche*, F. 2540, no. 195, 1765; ASF, OGB, *Suppliche*, F. 2523, no. 14, 1743; and ASF, OGB, *Suppliche*, F. 2499, no. 74, 1720.
43 Mellyn, *Mad Tuscans*, 58–93.
44 See, for instance, Monica Calabritto, "*Medicina practica, consilia* and the Illnesses of the Head in Girolamo Mercuriale and Giulio Cesare Claudini: Similarities and Differences of the Sexes," *Medicina e storia* 11 (2006): 63–83; Monica Calabritto, "A Case of Melancholic Humors and *Dilucida Intervalla*," *Intellectual History Review* 18, no. 1 (2008): 139–154; Mellyn, *Mad Tuscans*, 167–179.
45 Respectively, ASF, OGB, *Giornale di Negozi*, F. 1071, August 1765, f. 262; and September 1765, f. 282–283.
46 Domenico Brichieri Colombi to the Council of Regency, ASF, CR, *Fiscale*, F. 758, no. 61, December 1754. A *fratello converso* was a lay member of a religious order.
47 The Otto di Guardia was at the center of the criminal system and supervised local courts. The Otto's decisions were in turn supervised by the Auditore Fiscale in the name of the Grand Duke. Antonelli, "La magistratura"; Brackett, *Criminal Justice*, 8–21; and Floriana Colao, "La giustizia criminale come momento di identità dello stato toscano," in *La Toscana in età moderna (Secoli XVI-XVIII). Politica, istituzioni, società: studi recenti e prospettive di ricerca*, ed. Mario Ascheri and Alessandra Contini (Florence: Leo S. Olschki Editore, 2005), 129–175.
48 ASF, OGB, *Negozi dei Rettori*, F. 2134, *Negozio* 7275, no. 1, June 1730. Pleading innocence to the charges of infanticide was a recurrent strategy by women in early modern Italy as a last and, many times, useless effort to conceal the shame of the illegitimate child. See Adriano Prosperi, *Dare l'anima. Storia di un infanticidio* (Turin: Einaudi, 2005).
49 ASF, OGB, *Negozi dei Rettori*, F. 2134, *Negozio* 7254, no. 1, April 1730.
50 ASF, OGB, *Negozi dei Rettori*, F. 2134, *Negozio* 7254, no. 1, April 1730.
51 Judging from the existing studies, inebriation was not as visible in the Tuscan judicial records of the previous centuries. Mellyn, *Mad Tuscans*; and Magherini and Biotti, *L'isola delle Stinche*.
52 It was said regarding two prostitutes, for example, that when they were drunk, "they have less respect than when they are in their brain, although they are always dissolute [*scorrette*] and impertinent." ASF, OGB, *Straordinarie*, F. 2661, no. 49, c. July 1720.
53 ASF, OGB, *Negozi dei Rettori*, F. 2134, *Negozio* 7229, no. 1, February 1729; and ASF, OGB, *Suppliche*, F. 2540, no. 195, November 1765.
54 Respectively, ASF, OGB, *Suppliche*, F. 2537, no. 173, August 1761; ASF, OGB, *Straordinarie*, F. 2679, no. 265, September 1757; ASF, OGB, *Suppliche*, F. 2499, no. 28, December 1720; and ASF, OGB, *Suppliche*, F. 2531, no. 54, September 1751.
55 Savelli, *Pratica universale*, "Delitti," 111.
56 Some of these petitions were signed by the *avvocato dei poveri*; others were directly written by relatives or by the convicted felons themselves. Who wrote

168 *Spaces and itineraries of madness*

the petition and the ability to argue exculpatory circumstances were directly related to the social origin of the petitioners. Poorer prisoners made use of public lawyers; richer ones could write directly themselves and could even afford private legal advice.

57 The extent of the instrumentalization and the space of maneuver given by Italian legal frameworks are a matter of debate. For an overview, see Dean, *Crime and Justice*, 17–28. See also Marco Bellabarba, Gerd Schwerhoff, and Andrea Zorzi, eds., *Criminalità e giustizia in Germania e in Italia. Pratiche giudiziarie e linguaggi giuridici tra medioevo ed età moderna* (Bologna and Berlin: Il Mulino, 2001).

58 In January 1760, Giovanni del Panaio from Lucignano was received in Santa Dorotea as *pazzo furioso*. He had been periodically subject to episodes of frenzy, which came to be associated with the fits of epilepsy he had suffered since early youth. During one of these episodes, he managed to loosen the bonds that secured him to his bed and ultimately managed to beat his wife to death. According to the Auditore Fiscale, Brichieri Colombi, Giovanni's delirium made it impossible to cross-examine him, so the criminal proceedings were interrupted, and he was asked to intervene. Given that the local prison could not hold the "maniac" safely, the only available solution was found to be Santa Dorotea. This case also reveals that pretrial resolutions were an alternative for dealing with these cases of serious and evidently dangerous madness, explaining to some extent the relative scarcity of these kind of cases in the records of the Otto di Guardia. ASF, Nove Conservatori del Dominio, *Memoriali Spediti*, F. 1295, no. 160, January–February 1760.

59 Mellyn, *Mad Tuscans*, 60–61.

60 As Rabin has put it, "The history of the insanity plea documents a tension between a belief in the just exculpation of crimes committed by the insane and the fear of unpunished dissemblers and dangerous lunatics." Dana Rabin, *Identity, Crime, and Legal Responsibility in Eighteenth-Century England* (Basingstoke: Palgrave Macmillan, 2004), 42.

61 A certain Francesco Giani, tried for illegal possession of weapons, was given a mitigated, pecuniary sentence with a term of 1 month with the chance to supplicate for a full pardon because he was 85 years old and "suffered in the brain [*avesse patito nel cervello*]". Accordingly, he was given the *grazie* of his penalty after he petitioned as he had been told. ASF, OGB, *Suppliche*, F. 2505, no. 73, August 1725. Although it was a minor crime, it is nonetheless telling regarding the strategy of avoiding a full acquittal from the beginning. On the laws against the possession of arms, see Brackett, *Criminal Justice*, 103.

62 Giovanni Brichieri Colombi, ASF, CR, *Fiscale*, F. 755, no. 27, July 1747. On the practice of giving official pardons to prisoners on important holy days or special occasions in previous centuries, see Brackett, *Criminal Justice*, 54. "Those not eligible for pardon were private debtors (8.42), the insane (3.42), those held for disobedience to their parents (0.71), those transferred into the prison hospital (2.28), and those who died (4.42 per year)," 54.

63 The records of these special matters handled by the Auditore Fiscale are filed in the archive of the Consiglio di Reggenza, covering 1737 to 1765, which corresponds to the periods of Filippo Luci, Giovanni Brichieri Colombi, and his son Domenico Brichieri Colombi as Auditori Fiscali.

64 The office of the Auditore Fiscale was initially created in 1543 to supervise the fiscal interests of the state in the administration of justice. With time, the Auditore Fiscale increasingly gained importance, acting as the guarantor of the interests of the Grand Duke before the Otto di Guardia e Balìa, whose independence was thus progressively limited. Around 1558, the Otto di Guardia and every other tribunal of Florence or the dominion had to send a copy of

their sentences to the Auditore Fiscale, who had the power of veto over them. Antonelli, "La magistratura degli Otto," 33–36.

65 The powers of the Auditore Fiscale grew stronger during the Regency and were increased further after 1765. From 1768 on, the Fiscale directly managed all Florentine matters relating to public order coming into the Otto di Guardia, which he handled using his power of *arbitrio*. His dual position as supervisor of criminal justice and head of the police came to be regarded with suspicion by Peter Leopold himself, which eventually lead to the suppression of the office in 1784. Alessandra Contini, "La città regolata: polizia e amministrazione nella Firenze leopoldina (1777–1782)," in *Istituzioni e società in Toscana nell'età moderna*, vol. 1 (Rome: Ministero per i beni culturali e ambientali, Ufficio centrale per i beni archivistici, 1994), 456. See also Carlo Mangio, *La polizia toscana. Organizzazione e criteri d'intervento (1765–1808)* (Milan: Giuffrè, 1988), 9–63; and Giorgia Alessi, "Le riforme di polizia nell'Italia del Settecento: Granducato di Toscana e Regno di Napoli," in *Istituzioni e società in Toscana nell'età moderna. Atti delle giornate di studio dedicate a G. Pansini (Firenze 4–5 dicembre 1992)*, vol. 1 (Rome: Ministero per i beni culturali e ambientali, Ufficio centrale per i beni archivistici, 1994), 413–419.

66 Petition signed by the wife of the deranged Francesco del Mazza, reputed to be extravagant and mad, vicious, licentious, and obscene (*sboccato*). ASF, CR, *Fiscale*, F. 758, no. 20, October 1748.

67 Roberto Bizzocchi, *Cicisbei. Morale privata e identità nazionale in Italia* (Roma and Bari: Laterza, 2008), 21–159; Daniela Lombardi, *Matrimonio di antico regime* (Bologna: Il Mulino, 2001), 359–453; Isabel Morant and Mónica Bolufer, *Amor, matrimonio y familia* (Madrid: Editorial Síntesis, 1998), 55–87; Nicola Phillips, *The Profligate Son: Or, a True Story of Family Conflict, Fashionable Vice, and Financial Ruin in Regency England* (Oxford: Oxford University Press, 2013), among others.

68 Catharina Lis and Hugo Soly, *Disordered Lives: Eighteenth-Century Families and Their Unruly Relatives* (Cambridge: Polity Press, 1996), 1–7 and 23–46; Pieter Spierenburg, "Imprisonment and the Family: An Analysis of Petitions for Confinement in Holland, 1680–1805," *Social Science History* 10, no. 2 (1986): 115–146.

69 The *Dizionario della Crusca* defined the *discolo* first as the one who is in constant opposition to everything and cares for nobody else than himself, second as an idiot or illiterate, and third as man of disreputable customs, riotous, and intolerable. See *Vocabolario degli accademici della Crusca* (Florence: Appresso Domenico Maria Manni, 1729–1738), s.v. "discolo," www.lessicografia.it/Controller?lemma=discolo, accessed August 8, 2020.

70 ASF, OGB, *Suppliche*, F. 2530, no. 45, June 1750.

71 For instance, "he lives in idleness, mistreating and beating the supplicants, even threatening that he wants to kill them." ASF, CR, *Fiscale*, F. 759, no. 77, October 1758.

72 When they were denounced by their mothers, as happened with prodigals, the issue of the absence of paternal authority was considered decisive for explaining their misdemeanors and vices.

73 ASF, OGB, *Suppliche*, F. 2523, no. 107, December 1743.

74 This is most clear when we have the possibility of comparing a petition for the conscription to serve in a ship's crew of a *discolo* with a petition for his interdiction years later, as happens in the case of Gaspero Maria Pratesi. ASF, Camera e Auditore Fiscale, *Negozi di Polizia*, F. 2748, no. 148, 1751 for the petition for conscription, and ASF, MPAP, *Memoriali*, F. 2308, no. 11, 1770 for the interdiction procedure.

170   Spaces and itineraries of madness

75 ASF, OGB, *Suppliche*, F. 2531, no. 53, September 1751.
76 Phillips, *The Profligate Son*, xiv–xvii, 139 and *passim*; Lis and Soly, *Disordered Lives*, 23–80.
77 ASF, CR, *Fiscale*, F. 758, no. 64, December 1754. Brichieri Colombi's inquiry determined that the boy had caused his own death, and although the attitude of the mother was found rather negligent for she had not been able to tame him in time, she was considered punished enough by her son's death and did not receive further punishment.
78 ASF, CR, *Fiscale*, F. 761, no. 12, July 1763.
79 ASF, CR, *Fiscale*, F. 761, no. 12, July 1763.
80 ASF, OGB, *Suppliche*, F. 2523, no. 107, December 1743.
81 In order to obtain ecclesiastical separation of bed and board, litigants, mostly women, had to prove that the violence exerted by their husbands was repetitive and life threatening. Although there were other just causes of separation (like adultery, heresy, and contagious diseases), the most recurrent cause was physical abuse (*sevizie*). On this, see Chiara La Rocca, *Tra moglie e marito. Matrimoni e separazioni a Livorno nel Settecento* (Bologna: Società editrice Il Molino, 2009), 245–282.
82 ASF, SD, *Motupropri, Rescritti* . . ., F. 8, no. 75, August 1770.
83 Chiara La Rocca, for instance, examines how male domestic violence could be codified as corrective and deserved by the wife and thus be considered a rational act, provided the correction (generally in the form of *bastonate*) had been controlled and the husband had not let himself be governed by passion. La Rocca, *Tra moglie e marito*, 275–278. See also Elizabeth Foyster, "Male Honour, Social Control and Wife Beating in Late Stuart England," *Transactions of the Royal Historical Society* Sixth Series, 6 (1996): 215–224.
84 ASF, CR, *Fiscale*, F. 760, no. 53, 1760.
85 ASF, CR, *Fiscale*, F. 759, no. 77, October 1758.
86 ASF, CR, *Fiscale*, F. 759, no. 62, January 1760. His troubled mental state led him to being interdicted 10 years later, after his father died and while he was still imprisoned. ASF, MPAP, *Memoriali*, F. 2308, no. 11, March 1770.
87 Petition of Gherardi's relatives, ASF, CR, *Fiscale*, F. 759, no. 37, September 1759.
88 On the religious campaign against premarital relations and mismatched marriages, which during the eighteenth century enjoyed the practical aid of law and the police, see Lombardi, *Matrimonio*, 359–375.
89 ASF, CR, *Fiscale*, F. 758, no. 24, no. 27 and no. 62, 1754.
90 Lombardi, *Matrimonio*, 364.
91 ASF, CR, *Fiscale*, F. 759, no. 41, July 1754; and ASF, MPAP, *Memoriali*, F. 2306, no. 128, October 1764.
92 Report of the Auditore Fiscale referring the words of Orazio Pennetti's father. ASF, CR, *Fiscale*, F. 755, no. 72, July–August 1747. The interdiction, decreed in 1754, can be found in ASF, MPAP, *Memoriali*, F. 2303, no. 179, May 1754. In the following years, the case continues to appear with regards to Pennetti's difficult personality, involving alternatively the Pupilli officials and the Auditore Fiscale. ASF, OGB, *Suppliche*, F. 2537, no. 162, 23 July 1761. Similar arguments were employed to dissolve the marriage of an interdicted man with a lower-ranked woman. ASF, MPAP, *Memoriali*, F. 2302, no. 74, November 1748.
93 ASF, OGB, *Suppliche*, F. 2531, no. 55, September 1751.
94 ASF, OGB, *Negozi dei Rettori*, F. 1729, Negozio 7067, no. 4, 3–8 March 1729; and ASF, CR, *Fiscale*, F. 759, no. 11, July 1755, respectively.
95 ASF, OGB, *Giornale di Negozi*, F. 1071, fols. 220v–221, 17 July 1765.
96 ASF, OGB, *Suppliche*, F. 2542, no. 163, November 1768.

Spaces and itineraries of madness 171

97   ASF, MPAP, *Memoriali*, F. 2307, no. 169, September 1768.
98   Report of Domenico Brichieri Colombi. ASF, OGB, *Suppliche*, F. 2542, no. 163, November 1768.
99   ASF, OGB, *Suppliche*, F. 2523, no. 14, August 1743.
100 Claude Quétel, "Hay que criticar a Foucault?," in *Pensar la locura. Ensayos sobre Michel Foucault*, ed. Elisabeth Roudinesco (Buenos Aires: Paidós, 1996), 67–87 [French edition *Penser la folie. Essais sur Michel Foucault* (Paris: Editions Galilée, 1992)], 73.
101 Antonio Lulli to the Consiglio di Reggenza regarding Antonio Razzuoli, ASF, OGB, *Suppliche*, F. 2542, no. 27, September 1767.
102 See Lombardi, *Matrimonio*, 359–468; Mangio, *La polizia toscana*, 9–80; Alessi, "Le riforme di polizia," and Contini, "La Città regolata."
103 See Daniela Lombardi, *Povertà maschile, povertà femminile. L'Ospedale dei Mendicanti nella Firenze dei Medici* (Bologna: Il Mulino, 1988), 135–215.
104 ASF, CR, *Fiscale*, F. 755, no. 35, 1747.
105 ASF, CR, *Fiscale*, F. 758, no. 64, August 1757.
106 ASF, CR, *Fiscale*, F. 760, no. 26, 1759–1763.
107 ASF, CR, *Fiscale*, F. 758, no. 69, March–July 1755.
108 ASF, CR, *Fiscale*, F. 755, no. 35, 1747.
109 Various testimonies and report of Brichieri Colombi regarding the nobleman Giulio Cocconi. ASF, CR, *Fiscale*, F. 760, no. 69, February 1763.
110 ASF, CR, *Fiscale*, F. 759, no. 77, October 1758.
111 ASF, CR, *Fiscale*, F. 754, no. 56, March 1742.
112 ASF, CR, *Fiscale*, F. 755, no. 11, January 1746/47.
113 ASF, OGB, *Suppliche*, F. 2530, no. 60, June 1750.
114 It was in fact routinely employed as a disciplining measure to reform unruly relatives throughout Europe. Houston, *Madness and Society*, 65. See also Farge and Foucault, *Le Désordre des familles*; Spierenburg, "Imprisonment and the Family," and Lis and Soly, *Disordered Lives*.
115 There is evidence that monasteries were considered as suitable environments for deranged men, particularly for aristocrats. See ASF, CR, *Fiscale*, F. 758, no. 60, 1755; and F. 755, no. 25, 1747.
116 ASF, Santa Maria Nuova, F. 206, ff. 761–769.
117 Mellyn, *Mad Tuscans*, 3, 11, and 196.
118 For instance, in 1753, Benedetto Sezzatini was charged with assault in a brawl, but during the legal enquiries carried out in the informatory process, the judges came to the conclusion that he was *pazzo furioso*, and so he was transferred to Santa Dorotea. ASF, SD, *Motupropri, Rescritti . . .*, F. 1, no. 27, September 1753.
119 ASF, OGB, *Suppliche*, F. 2542, no. 27, September 1767. Commuting prison for exile solved the problem of financing through the felon's own capacity to work.
120 Much has been written to discuss and counterbalance Foucault's main contribution to the history of madness. For an overview, see Porter, *Mind-Forg'd Manacles*; Roscioni, *Il governo della follia*; Roudinesco, *Pensar la locura*.
121 See, for example, Cosimo Casacci, interdicted as *demente* in July 1722 and afterwards alternatively incarcerated for short periods and held under home restraint for many years before he was definitively sent to Santa Dorotea, where he died in 1743. See ASF, MPAP, *Campione di deliberazioni e partiti*, F. 112–138; and ASF, SD, F. 23, no. 3. The same applies for the cases of Lorenzo Baldinotti and Lorenzo Maestrini, discussed earlier in this chapter.
122 ASF, CR, *Fiscale*, F. 755, no. 10, 1746 and 1754.
123 Report of Brichieri Colombi, ASF, CR, *Fiscale*, F. 758, no. 60, June 1755.
124 ASF, MPAP, *Memoriali*, F. 2308, no. 47, August 1770 and no. 333, December 1772.

172 *Spaces and itineraries of madness*

125 The daily accounts of the resolutions and matters affecting each of the minors and incapacitated adults under the authority of the Pupilli attest to this coordination. ASF, MPAP, *Campione di deliberazioni e partiti*, F. 112, 1717 to F. 165, 1770.
126 Case of the interdicted Domenico degl'Albizzi and his wife Maria Caterina Fioravanti. ASF, CR, *Pupillli*, F. 746, no. 12, March 1751.
127 The connection between matrimonial disputes and madness is an understudied aspect of marital life in early modern Tuscany. For example, see the dispute between Caterina Angeloni and her husband Franco Giorgi, ASF, CR, *Fiscale*, F. 760, no. 43, June 1760, and the dispute between Maria Caterina Inghirami and Ferdinando Ginori in ASF, CR, *Fiscale*, F. 754, no. 5, July 1738–December 1739. For similar cases involving interdicted men and their wives, see, for example, the disputes between Maria Caterina Fioravanti and Alfiero Domenico degli Albizi, ASF, CR, *Pupilli*, F. 746, no. 12, 1750–51; Rosa Caterina Pandolfini and Adimaro Adimari, ASF, MPAP, *Memoriali*, F. 2300, nos. 216, 379 and 397, 1727–1732; Giuseppe Rossi and Francesca Arcangeli in ASF, MPAP, *Memoriali*, F. 2300, no. 195, 1726; and Antonio Becciani and Maddalena Palloni in ASF, MPAP, *Memoriali*, F. 2308, nos. 79 and 108, 1771, and ASF, MPAP, *Memoriali*, F. 2309, nos. 147 and 280, 1773.

Bibliography chapter 4

Manuscripts

Archivio di Stato di Firenze (ASF)

- Camera e Auditore Fiscale, *Negozi di Polizia*, F. 2748
- Consiglio di Reggenza (CR)
  - *Spedale de Pazzi*, F. 426
  - *Pupilli*, F. 746
  - *Fiscale*, F. 754–762
- Magistrato dei Pupilli et Adulti del Principato (MPAP)
  - *Campione di Deliberazioni e Partiti*, F. 108–F. 166
  - *Atti e Sentenze*, F. 1144–F. 1362
  - *Suppliche e informazioni: Memoriali e Negozi di Cancelleria*, F. 2299–F. 2318
- Magistrato Supremo (MS)
  - *Suppliche*, F. 1179–F. 1188
  - *Atti e Scritture*, F. 1845–F. 2103
- Nove Conservatori del Dominio, *Memoriali Spediti*, F. 1295
- Ospedale di Santa Dorotea (SD), F. 1–F. 59
- Otto di Guardia e Balìa (OGB)
  - *Giornale di Negozi*, F. 927, F. 956, F. 985, F. 1016, F. 1058, F. 1059, F. 1061, F. 1066, F. 1071

- *Riscontro di Processi*, F. 1433, F. 1438, F. 1442, F. 1471, F. 1478, F. 1557, F. 1558, F. 1670
- *Negozi dei Rettori*, F. 2133–2135
- *Suppliche*, F. 2499–F. 2542
- *Filze Straordinarie*, F. 2654–2690

- Santa Maria Nuova (SMN), F. 206

Biblioteca Nazionale Centrale di Firenze (BNCF)

- *Manoscritti*, Le carte di Giovanni Targioni Tozzetti (GTT), 234–235

Printed sources

Savelli, Marc'Antonio. *Pratica universale del dottor Marc'Antonio Savelli auditore della Rota Criminale di Firenze*. Parma: Paolo Monti, 1717.

Vocabolario degli accademici della Crusca, 6 vols. Florence: Appresso Domenico Maria Manni, 1729–1738. DOI:10.23833/BD/LESSICOGRAFIA, www.lessicografia.it/index.jsp. Accessed August 8, 2020.

Zacchia, Paolo. *Quaestionum medico-legalium tomi tres*. Nuremberg: sumptibus Joannis Georgii Lochneri, 1726.

References

Alessi, Giorgia. "Le riforme di polizia nell'Italia del Settecento: Granducato di Toscana e Regno di Napoli." In *Istituzioni e società in Toscana nell'età moderna. Atti delle giornate di studio dedicate a G. Pansini (Firenze 4–5 dicembre 1992)*, vol. 1, 404–425. Rome: Ministero per i beni culturali e ambientali, Ufficio centrale per i beni archivistici, 1994.

Antonelli, Giovanni. "La magistratura degli Otto di Guardia a Firenze." *Archivio storico Italiano* 92 (1954): 3–40.

Bellabarba, Marco, Gerd Schwerhoff, and Andrea Zorzi. *Criminalità e giustizia in Germania e in Italia. Pratiche giudiziarie e linguaggi giuridici tra medioevo ed età moderna*. Bologna and Berlin: Il Mulino, 2001.

Bizzocchi, Roberto. *Cicisbei. Morale privata e identità nazionale in Italia*. Rome and Bari: Laterza, 2008.

Boari, Marco. *Qui venit contra iura. Il furiosus nella criminalistica dei secoli XV e XVI*. Milan: Giuffrè, 1983.

Brackett, John K. *Criminal Justice and Crime in Late Renaissance Florence 1537–1609*. Cambridge: Cambridge University Press, 1992.

Brambilla, Elena. *Corpi invasi e viaggi dell'anima*. Rome: Viella, 2010.

Calabritto, Monica. "A Case of Melancholic Humors and *Dilucida Intervalla*." *Intellectual History Review* 18, no. 1 (2008): 139–154.

Calabritto, Monica. "*Medicina practica, consilia* and the Illnesses of the Head in Girolamo Mercuriale and Giulio Cesare Claudini: Similarities and Differences of the Sexes." *Medicina e storia* 11 (2006): 63–83.

Colao, Floriana. "La giustizia criminale come momento di identità dello stato toscano." In *La Toscana in età moderna (secoli XVI-XVIII). Politica, istituzioni,* società: studi recenti e prospettive di ricerca, edited by Mario Ascheri and Alessandra Contini, 129–175. Florence: Leo S. Olschki Editore, 2005.

Colombero, Carlo. "Un contributo alla formazione della nozione di malattia mentale: le 'Questioni medico-legali' di Paolo Zacchia." In *Follia, psichiatria e società. Istituzioni manicomiali, scienza psichiatrica e classi sociali nell'Italia moderna e contemporanea*, edited by Alberto De Bernardi, 317–329. Milan: Franco Angeli, 1982.

Contini, Alessandra. "La città regolata: polizia e amministrazione nella Firenze leopoldina (1777–1782)." In *Istituzioni e società in Toscana nell'età moderna*, vol. 1, 426–508. Rome: Ministero per i beni culturali e ambientali, Ufficio centrale per i beni archivistici, 1994.

Dean, Trevor. *Crime and Justice in Late Medieval Italy*. Cambridge: Cambridge University Press, 2007.

Eigen, Joel Peter. *Witnessing Insanity: Madness and Mad-Doctors in the English Court*. New Haven and London: Yale University Press, 1995.

Foyster, Elizabeth. "Male Honour, Social Control and Wife Beating in Late Stuart England." *Transactions of the Royal Historical Society* Sixth Series, 6 (1996): 215–224.

Houston, Robert Allan. *Madness and Society in Eighteenth-Century Scotland*. Oxford: Oxford University Press, 2000.

La Rocca, Chiara. *Tra moglie e marito. Matrimoni e separazioni a Livorno nel Settecento*. Bologna: Società editrice Il Molino, 2009.

Lis, Catharina, and Hugo Soly. *Disordered Lives: Eighteenth-Century Families and Their Unruly Relatives*. Cambridge: Polity Press, 1996.

Lombardi, Daniela. *Matrimonio di antico regime*. Bologna: Il Mulino, 2001.

Lombardi, Daniela. *Povertà maschile, povertà femminile. L'Ospedale dei Mendicanti nella Firenze dei Medici*. Bologna: Il Mulino, 1988.

Magherini, Graziella, and Vittorio Biotti. "*Un luogo della città per custodia de'pazzi*". *Santa Dorotea dei Pazzerelli di Firenze nelle delibere della sua congregazione (1642–1754)*. Florence: Le Lettere, 1997.

Magherini, Graziella, and Vittorio Biotti. *L'isola delle Stinche e i percorsi della follia a Firenze nei secoli XIV-XVIII*. Florence: Ponte alle Grazie, 1992.

Mangio, Carlo. *La polizia toscana. Organizzazione e criteri d'intervento (1765–1808)*. Milan: Giuffrè, 1988.

Mannori, Luca. *Il sovrano tutore: Pluralismo istituzionale e accentramento amministrativo nel principato dei Medici (secc. XVI-XVIII)*. Milan: Giuffrè, 1994.

Mellyn, Elizabeth W. *Mad Tuscans and Their Families: A History of Mental Disorder in Early Modern Italy*. Philadelphia: University of Pennsylvania Press, 2014.

Morant Deusa, Isabel, and Mónica Bolufer Peruga. *Amor, matrimonio y familia*. Madrid: Editorial Síntesis, 1998.

Pastore, Alessandro, and Giovanni Rossi, eds. *Paolo Zacchia. Alle origini della medicina legale 1584–1659*. Milan: Franco Angeli, 2008.

Phillips, Nicola. *The Profligate Son: Or, a True Story of Family Conflict, Fashionable Vice, and Financial Ruin in Regency England*. Oxford: Oxford University Press, 2013.

Porter, Roy. *Mind-Forg'd Manacles: A History of Madness in England from the Restoration to the Regency*. London: Penguin Books, 1990.

Prosperi, Adriano. *Dare l'anima. Storia di un infanticidio*. Turin: Einaudi, 2005.

Quétel, Claude. "Hay que criticar a Foucault?" In *Pensar la locura. Ensayos sobre Michel Foucault*, edited by Elisabeth Roudinesco, 67–87. Buenos Aires: Paidós, 1996. [French edition *Penser la folie. Essais sur Michel Foucault*. Paris: Editions Galilée, 1992].

Rabin, Dana. *Identity, Crime, and Legal Responsibility in Eighteenth-Century England*. Basingstoke: Palgrave Macmillan, 2004.

Roscioni, Lisa. *Il governo della follia. Ospedali, medici e pazzi nell'età moderna*. Milan: Bruno Mondadori, 2003.

Spierenburg, Pieter. "Imprisonment and the Family: An Analysis of Petitions for Confinement in Holland, 1680–1805." *Social Science History* 10, no. 2 (1986): 115–146.

Stumpo, Enrico. "Un uomo per tutte le stagioni: Giovanni Targioni Tozzetti e la polizia sanitaria nella Firenze dei Lorena." In *Relazioni forensi. Ambiente, igiene e sanità nella Firenze dei Lorena*, Giovanni Targioni Tozzetti, edited by S. Pelle, 7–24. Florence: Le Lettere, 1998.

5 Experts and authorities on madness

By the sixteenth century, Italian courts had developed an institutionalized tradition of forensics that stimulated the production of key medico-juridical literature on the legal recourse to expert medical opinion. Physicians gained public recognition in legal proceedings insofar as they could play a significant role in the examination of criminal evidence. Both in legal theory and in legal practice, medical experts were considered the ultimate experts on the body, which led to the emergence of the figure of the *perito fiscale*, who assumed an increasingly visible place at trials in order to determine causes of death and to examine wounds and give their expert opinion on how they had been inflicted or what the prognosis was.[1] However, the success experienced by medical practitioners as expert witnesses in matters of the body was not replicated in the judicial assessment of mental incapacity.

In theory, prodigality and insanity could be proven in civil law by the sworn testimony of close relatives and of two reliable witnesses, but exemption from punishment on the basis of insanity (*furiosi*, *dementi* or *pazzi*) was strictly dependent upon the judgment of medical practitioners. However, in practice, both criminal and civil law procedures carried out in Tuscany during the eighteenth century to determine soundness of mind show that medical opinion played a modest role. The majority of the Tuscan judicial proceedings in which a mental condition was under scrutiny were conducted without recourse to medical testimony, casting doubt on the process of the medicalization of madness in the Tuscan legal practice that according to some scholars characterized the period, postponing it at least until the last quarter of the century.[2] Although legal theory had long called for the introduction of medical practitioners as expert witnesses to identify insanity in court, Tuscan judicial practice still largely relied on lay testimonies. Medical practitioners were neither the only nor the most decisive experts involved in the assessment of mental incapacity.

During the eighteenth century, the ultimate authorities on madness continued to be the families of the afflicted. The identification of mental afflictions first occurred in the domestic space and was discussed among family members. Only when they had reached a conclusion regarding their relative's behavior was the case made known to the authorities, and public provisions devised to address its challenges followed the primary purpose of helping the families. Given the purposes of these remedies, the assessment of madness necessarily had to rely first and foremost on the opinion of those who knew the mentally afflicted. Long-term views and discussions based on familiarity with the defendant were preferred in order to determine the extent to which his or her behavior disrupted domestic and social life or imperiled the familial economy.

This chapter explores the involvement of medical opinion in judicial procedures in which madness was under scrutiny with especial attention to the uses, circulation, and meanings of the languages of madness. It first examines the involvement of medical opinion in the assessment of criminal insanity and mental incapacity and then discusses the involvement of clergymen and the Auditore Fiscale. The chapter elaborates on the weight of medical knowledge in these civil and criminal procedures, with a close examination of the language employed by medical practitioners in their testimonies. It aims to explore how and when they introduced precise medical categories, and to what extent these categories circulated among the different agents participating in a judicial procedure. The chapter argues that medical practitioners disputed their secondary place as authorities over matters of the mind (behind the families), equal with the clergy and ducal officials, among which the Auditore Fiscale assumed an increasingly leading role. The language of madness was thus largely built upon lay notions of mental affliction that were negotiated with the authorities and sometimes ratified by specialists on the mind, a category that comprised medical practitioners and priests on equal footing.

Recourse to medical opinion to assert mental incapacity

To understand the involvement of medical opinion in legal inquiries into mental capacity, we must bear in mind that interdiction procedures were based on the Florentine Statutes, which stated that interdiction requests alleging an incapacity to manage one's affairs needed to be submitted by a close relative and supported by the testimony of two witnesses of good reputation. In other words, the foundational statutes regulating interdiction procedures asserted by omission that medical expertise was unnecessary to assess mental incapacity. These republican statutes were still in use in the eighteenth century and were recurrently recalled by the Pupilli officials in the first period after the 1718 statute reform of the Pupilli office that confirmed its jurisdiction over interdictions and adult curatorship.[3]

While the statutes did not ascribe a role to medical opinion in the assessment of mental capacity, there was a vast legal tradition that pointed toward their involvement, and the Tuscan judicial records of the period attest that magistrates, authorities, and legal practitioners acknowledged that medical opinion had a crucial role in the judicial assessment of any kind of disease, including madness. Following Paolo Zacchia's call for the importance of medical opinion in the judicial assessment of insanity, Tuscan jurists like Marc' Antonio Savelli recommended that criminal insanity be directly scrutinized by judges and further certified by medical opinion in his *Pratica universale*.[4] However, in practice, the Tuscan courts solved matters regarding mental afflictions without recourse to medical opinion. Civil and criminal records show that medical practitioners were seldom called upon to assess mental capacity in an interdiction procedure or to determine liability in a criminal one. However, the scarcity of medical opinion in the Tuscan courts is not necessarily an expression of how medical knowledge on madness was valued in the administration of justice. The practice of civil law over the years had demanded the more regular involvement of medical practitioners in order to provide expert testimony regarding insanity. In 1734, for instance, a report of the Magistrato Supremo voiced the concern that mental incapacity should be assessed by medical practitioners and not be judged based exclusively on the opinion of petitioners and lay testimonies. The latter, the magistrates asserted, could only describe the signs that might or might not entail someone's incapacity, but they could not judge if these signs were enough to declare the person incapable.[5]

The detailed records of interdiction procedures allow us to make an in-depth analysis to understand the role of medical opinion in the Tuscan administration of justice when mental incapacity was involved. Of a total of 201 interdictions on account of *demenza* decreed between 1700 and 1775, only 59 procedures, amounting to 29.3%, included a medical opinion at some point, whether when the interdiction was decreed, during curatorship, or when the interdicted petitioned for its revocation (see Table 5.1). Of these, some were given in the form of testimonies handwritten or only signed by a surgeon or a doctor, and others constitute references in the authorities' reports stating that medical practitioners had been consulted. At least half of the testimonies were written by practitioners who worked in the *pazzeria* of Santa Maria Nuova or in Santa Dorotea. If we measure the incidence of medical opinion against the whole sample of interdictions decreed between 1700 and 1775, we find that the 29.3% decreases to 10%, with a total of 59 procedures involving recourse to medical opinion against 544 interdictions decreed without the involvement of medical expertise. Although an increase can be identified between 1700 and 1775, this growth is markedly slow and shared by the rise of other "experts" on madness, such as the Auditore Fiscale, as will be discussed later on.

The number of medical testimonies increases slightly if we also include the cases in which – after the interdiction was decreed – either the magistrates or the relatives of the interdicted made reference to a past or current committal in either one of the Florentine madhouses (the *pazzeria* of Santa Maria Nuova or Santa Dorotea). In eight interdiction procedures (4%), we find references to one of the *pazzerie*, which added to the 29.3% that included the testimonies of medical practitioners amount to 33.3%. Surprisingly, there are several cases of interdicted men and women who appear in the records

Table 5.1 Involvement of medical opinion in interdiction procedures between 1700 and 1775

Interdictions for demenza		
Reference to mental institution after interdiction decree	8	4%
Recourse to medical opinion	59	29.3%
No recourse to medical opinion	134	66.7%
Total	201	100%

Interdictions for demenza, prodigality, and unspecified incapacity		
Reference to mental institution after interdiction decree	8	1%
Recourse to medical opinion	59	10%
No recourse to medical opinion	544	89%
Total	611	100%

Source: ASF, MPAP, *Memoriali e Negozi di Cancelleria*, F. 2299–F. 2310 and ASF, MPAP, *Campione di Deliberazioni, e Partiti*, F. 112–F. 170.

of Santa Dorotea but whose committal is not mentioned at any point of their interdiction. As explained in the previous chapters, in Tuscany, interdiction and confinement in a mental institution were two completely unrelated legal procedures with no necessary references to each other. This explains why some people whose interdiction was decreed without stating the cause of incapacity, or with no mention of a past or current committal, appear in the records of Santa Dorotea or Santa Maria Nuova. Most notable is the case of a man who was interdicted for prodigality – with no reference to a state of *demenza* – who appears in the records of both of the madhouses in Florence.[6] Thus, although being committed to Santa Dorotea or the *pazzeria* of Santa Maria Nuova was considered to be medical confirmation of *demenza*, the particularities of interdiction procedures made it neither mandatory nor necessary to mention it.

According to the legal foundations of interdiction procedures, the responsibility to provide evidence for the alleged incapacity rested on petitioners. For this reason, medical experts were summoned in the majority of the cases by family members in the form of written statements that were added to the other testimonies supporting their petition of interdiction. In a minority of the cases, it was the magistrates who resorted to medical opinion when they were in the process of verifying the foundations of the petition. Having this in mind, medical testimonies can be divided into four categories: 1) those signed by both a doctor and a surgeon who had been for some time in charge of the health of the defendant; 2) those signed by doctors or surgeons who had been called by the supplicants with the sole purpose of assessing the individual's mental state in order to proceed with a petition for interdiction; 3) those signed by *medici condotti* and *cerusici condotti*, doctors, and surgeons from the provinces officially appointed and paid by the town's administration, who had been consulted by the authorities;[7] and, in the end, 4) those signed by the surgeons or physicians of either of the existing mental institutions, usually at the request of petitioners.

Medical testimonies not only were introduced to support an interdiction petition, but could also be provided later on, even when the interdiction had been decreed without recourse to medical opinion. For instance, medical practitioners could testify for the soundness of mind of a defendant who petitioned for the interdiction to be lifted. Seven out of the 59 interdiction procedures with recourse to medical opinion correspond to this category, in which medical practitioners declared that the person's mental disturbance had abated and that the person was fit to be restored to the normal administration of his or her affairs. Alternatively, they could simply state that the defendant had never been affected by a mental disease.

Medical testimonies could also be introduced by relatives as a response to a petition to revoke the interdiction, in this case to demonstrate that the soundness of mind alleged by the interdicted was not present. For instance, 70-year-old Gaetano Migliorini was interdicted in 1767 for a *demenza* he had allegedly suffered since the age of 24. The petition was made by his daughter-in-law with the support of a collective testimony stating that he "is not and has never been able to administer his possessions, not only because he is demented and has no rational understanding, but also because he is unable to distinguish his interests, and is prodigal."[8] No further proof of his mental incapacity was required by the Pupilli officials to declare him interdicted, and at this stage we find no record of medical involvement of any kind. However, when Gaetano himself petitioned for the interdiction to be lifted, his daughter-in-law argued against his petition and produced a note from Santa Dorotea declaring that Gaetano Migliorini had been committed there.[9] The testimony just declared that his name could be found in the records of the hospital and made no reference to Migliorini's past or current mental condition. Even so, the fact of his past committal was considered a sufficient ground to not revoke the interdiction.

In the end, there was also indirect recourse to medical opinions, which can be found in the second-hand transmission of oral medical testimonies, a usual situation when the defendant lived outside of Florence. In these cases, inquiries were conducted via the local administrative authorities, who, when requested to investigate the mental condition of a defendant, sometimes made reference to a medical opinion without presenting it directly. As explained in previous chapters, local authorities were asked to make further enquiries regarding denunciations of mental incapacity even when petitioners had already provided the two statutory testimonies. To respond to this request, they generally made a summary of their investigation indicating that they had questioned several credible witnesses (*degne di fede*) to corroborate the denunciation, among whom medical practitioners were sometimes included. We also have to take into account that they could have consulted medical experts without this being stated in the report. In any case, the inquiries conducted by the provincial authorities generally compared the information that had been gathered with their own experience with the information gathered from the defendant and their families, regardless of whether medical practitioners had been consulted.

Why a medical practitioner had been contacted to give his testimony on the defendant's state of mind is not always revealed, but there are some clues to explore in this regard. On the one hand, the records suggest that, as a medical opinion was not mandatory to determine mental capacity in interdiction procedures, medical practitioners were called in cases that were contested by the defendants or by other family members who were against the procedure or in cases that the authorities were or could be reluctant to concede. In fact, medical testimonies usually appear in particularly well-documented procedures that happen to have more testimonies than the two mandatory ones. On the other hand, recourse to medical opinion might have been determined by the previous contacts of the family with medical practitioners. For instance, medical testimonies were used to a greater degree to attest physical ailments with damaging mental consequences, such as apoplexy and epilepsy, or in cases where the families had contacted medical practitioners in the past in order to consult with them or treat the defendant. This is particularly the case with those who had visited most of the different destinations in the itineraries of madness and especially those who had been at a given point committed to Santa Dorotea or the *pazzeria* of Santa Maria Nuova (which did not necessarily coincide with the time at which the interdiction petition was issued). In any case, by and large medical opinion was used at the discretion of the petitioners, only rarely being a direct requirement of the authorities.

Testimonies given by medical practitioners related to the Florentine madhouses allow us to explore this issue further. The existence of cases in which a reference to a past or current committal is only given after the interdiction was decreed leads to the question of why, if medical opinion had been involved, it was not mentioned in the interdiction procedure. Although to have been committed to a madhouse was indisputably considered proof of mental incapacity, it was not necessary to mention it to secure an interdiction decree. Lay witnesses attesting to past or current mental disturbances were proof enough, particularly when these testimonies made the connection between mental state and daily performance in public, professional, and family life. This was something that a testimony from Santa Dorotea or Santa Maria Nuova was simply not able to do. In fact, for most of the period under study here, testimonies from either of the mental hospitals are limited to attesting to someone's committal, only occasionally giving the reasons for the internment. The primary purpose of the certification was to attest that the individual was or had been committed to the mental institution, regardless of how medical knowledge understood the specific mental illness.

Before delving into the role medical opinion had in the development of an interdiction petition, we should note that medical experts might have been involved in the identification of insanity in a larger proportion of cases than the records indicate. For instance, petitioners could have chosen not to include medical testimonies even if they had contacted medical practitioners to treat their mentally afflicted relative. We know this because in some cases, although the interdiction proceedings present no record of the involvement of medical opinion, later proceedings relating to the management of the curatorship reveal that it was otherwise. It can happen that medical practitioners had treated the defendant's mental affliction before the interdiction, or that the interdicted had been committed to Santa Maria Nuova or Santa Dorotea, but nothing of the sort was revealed in the interdiction records. It should also be taken into consideration that the absence of medical opinion might be the outcome of how records were kept rather than of an actual exclusion of medical opinion. For instance, it could be argued that magistrates and judges consulted medical practitioners but did not record their opinions.[10] Either way, both interdiction procedures and later proceedings related to the management of the curatorship attest to the infrequent involvement of medical opinion and to the limited infiltration of medical terminology in the judicial narratives of mental disturbance.

The role of medical testimonies

The terminology employed in medical testimonies, as was the case with all of the judicial accounts of madness, was conditioned by the aims of the legal procedure for which they were produced. Marked by the need to demonstrate that the alleged mental incapacity resulted in economic mismanagement that posed a serious threat to the family patrimony, medical testimonies generally employed nonmedical terms that were closer to legal language than to medical vocabulary. A significant proportion of medical testimonies employed categories such as *mentecatto* and *demente* in combination with more descriptive expressions such as illness of the mind (*infermità di mente*), ill with madness (*infermo di pazzia*), devoid of cognition, judgement, brain or intellect (*privo di cognizione, di senno, di cervello, d'intelletto*), and imbecility of mind (*imbecillità di mente*), to name a few. Among the medical categories that do appear, apoplexy and epilepsy are the most common, followed at some distance by *delirio melanconico* (melancholic delirium), *alterazione di fantasia* (alterations of fantasy), and *fissazioni di mente* (mind fixations).

When medical diagnostic categories were incorporated into Tuscan judicial practice, they were invariably followed by the traditional formula aimed at establishing the defendant's level of estrangement from reason. In this sense, eighteenth-century medical testimonies are striking for their unchanged embeddedness in the medico-legal tradition that had been established since the introduction of the vernacular in the sixteenth century.[11] Medical labels were meaningful so long as they established that an episode of derangement, accident, or long-term disease had left the individual bereft of reason, deprived of cognition, out of his or her wits, or alienated from reason (*privo di intelletto* or *di cervello, privo di cognizione, sbalordito, uscito fuori di sé, tolta la favela, alienato dalla ragione*), thus rendering them *mentecatti* or *dementi*.

Thus, even when medical testimonies provide a diagnostic category, it is accompanied by the usual lexicon employed by lay witnesses and supplicants to legitimize the assessment of mental incapacity. Furthermore, medical testimonies tend to be repetitive, with a deliberate tendency to simplify medical references, hardly ever delving into the causalities behind the diagnostic category and sometimes not even making reference to its defining features.[12] In this regard, it should be recalled that the tendency to repeat terms of patients is not something specific to judicial medical testimonies of mental illnesses but commonly appears in physicians' descriptions of diseases when communicating with their patients, as has been argued in studies on epistolary medical consultations or studies on medical case books.[13] During the early modern period, physicians tended to follow their patients' choices of terms and diagnosis when labeling their ailments. Thus, medical testimonies also address the negotiation of the authority of medical knowledge over matters of the mind. Medical practitioners had to serve the interests of their patients, and at the same time they had to give importance to themselves by pointing out new areas where they had exclusive expertise.

In judicial practice, medical practitioners, like any witness, were supposed to predict the connection between the alleged mental incapacity and the likelihood of financial ruin. The precise kind of mental illness, its symptoms, or physiological foundations were secondary in comparison to how it affected the individual's life, or for how long it had lasted. As a consequence, there are many cases in which the difference between a testimony signed by a medical practitioner and the rest of the testimonies supporting the petition for interdiction is not discernible. Given the absence of specialized medical terminology, the expertise of the medical gaze seems to have rested on the common sense and respectability of the signers, which could account for the practice of stating their profession even if their account was not framed in medical terms.

Bearing witness to the role played by medical testimonies in the identification of mental incapacity, many medical practitioners not only shared their place as key witnesses with priests, but also their signature was sometimes inserted between other signatures on a collective testimony.[14] Testimonies supporting an interdiction petition generally consisted of an account of the defendants' misdeeds and economic mismanagement, some with descriptions of their deviant behavior, others with straightforward references to their allegedly disturbed mental state. The amount of detail varies greatly from one case to another, and some are evidently statements written by the petitioners themselves or their procurators and were only given to the deponents to sign. In these cases, medical practitioners sometimes added a further comment next to their name, but it was only slightly different from the main text of the testimony and was usually written using the same legal, nonmedical terms.

For instance, Maria Maddalena Scardigli from Empoli was interdicted in 1749 on the request of her nephews, who claimed she suffered from "dementia and madness" (*demenza e pazzia*). The interdiction petition was accompanied by two testimonies, one signed by various persons and the other by a priest and a *medico condotto*. While the former made reference to Maria Maddalena's poor economic situation, aggravated by her solitude and "incapacity to make a living for she is deprived of reason and mad," the testimony signed by the priest and the physician stated that she had been for many years "devoid of reason and almost completely *impotens sui*," and as she was "incapable of reason," her "*pazzia*" had "reduced her to misery."[15] As proves to be the case in the majority of the testimonies signed by medical practitioners, nothing particularly medical was revealed in this testimony. Not only was it also signed by a priest, but it was also written using the conventional legal terminology employed in judicial practice when mental incapacity was involved. Thus, the signature of the medical practitioner was equated with that of the priest, their occupations being valued as equally pertinent for the assessment of madness and the specificities of their gazes and terminologies not differentiated.

Medical testimonies did not necessarily have a different role than the testimonies given by neighbors or family members, and this explains why, although medical testimonies are present in 29.3% of interdiction procedures for reason of *demenza*, this number is not really indicative of the influence they had on the decision to issue the interdiction decree. Some differences can be drawn, however, between medical testimonies and the testimonies given by lay witnesses, for the former went further than being just a trustworthy voice on a phenomenon that could be recognized by any observer. In interdiction procedures, the authority of priests and medical practitioners was largely founded on their longstanding acquaintance with the defendant, especially when the testimony was separate and handwritten. In fact, medical practitioners, particularly when appointed surgeons or doctors of the place (*condotti*), framed their testimonies in terms of a lifetime knowledge of their patients, whom they claimed to have treated on several occasions even if exclusively for physical complaints. This could explain why medical practitioners often illustrated their testimonies with remarks on their patient's biography, with expressions such as "he has always been" or has "never been" demented. Even if they did not give a medical opinion on the mental condition in question, medical practitioners could attest to a more intimate familiarity with the defendant, which left them in a privileged position to judge their patients' behavior and the workings of their minds.

Medical testimonies provided in support of petitions to revoke an interdiction played a slightly different role than when they acted as proof of incapacity. In these cases, physicians and surgeons presented a proof of sanity rather than of insanity, serving as witnesses to the absence of an illness whose presence had not been identified by a medical practitioner in the first place. Declaring someone's soundness of mind was even less medically specific than attesting to someone's mental incapacity. Assertions such as "he has never been demented nor deprived of proper cognition, and I have always found him to be of a perfectly healthy mind, though indisposed in body," are not rare.[16] That they had been legally found to be of unsound mind before was not an impediment to declaring that they had always been sound, with an "always" whose duration was as imprecise as when testimonies declared for the contrary. To a greater degree than when attesting for mental incapacity, medical practitioners supporting petitions for an interdiction to be lifted centered their arguments on their patient's ability to perform daily tasks, their impeccable management of their affairs, and, especially in cases concerning old men, their general fitness.[17] After all, mental disturbance, when measured in terms of mental incapacity or criminal insanity, had different levels according to the person's social performance. Men and women could be considered able to manage their affairs even though they presented some degree of mental disability, just as they could be considered liable to punishment for a crime.

There are other interesting features to note with regard to medical testimonies introduced into proceedings for the interdiction to be lifted. Someone who had been interdicted through legal proceedings that employed the usual unspecific references to dissipation and economic mismanagement, with no recourse to either medical opinion or medical categories, could have his or her civil rights restored on the basis of a medical testimony that asserted they were "presently sound of mind and of the whole body, not troubled by any frenzy, and thus capable of dealing with and managing any of his most important interests."[18] Implicitly, therefore, the proceedings to end the interdiction and curatorship could reveal that an interdiction had really been decreed for a suspected *demenza* in cases that had been based solely on narratives suggesting economic mismanagement and classic prodigality.

Medical testimonies could be similar to other testimonies, they could be medically unspecific, and they could share their place with other testimonies, but they did produce a precise outcome. Although recourse to medical opinion was not the general practice in civil or criminal procedures, when it was involved it was generally taken as indisputable proof. It is rare to find occasions when medical testimonies were contradicted by the magistrates, but some exceptions do exist. The most common type is when medical testimonies asserting someone's soundness of mind were not considered sufficient grounds for the interdiction to be lifted. But there are a few cases in which the information first gathered to support an interdiction was later considered to have been wrong, either because of new inquiries carried out by the Pupilli, or because the medical practitioner himself reconsidered his first assessment.[19] In the end, there are also cases in which the same medical practitioner first attested to someone's unsoundness of mind only to later declare that this person's mind worked fine and was (and had always been) consequently perfectly capable of managing his affairs.[20]

The employment of medical categories

The diversity of medical practitioners giving their testimonies in the Tuscan courts attests to the lack of specialization in diseases of the mind that characterized Europe during the period. Expertise on mental afflictions was not settled within the medical profession, and for most of the period under study here, both physicians and surgeons were considered equally qualified to testify the presence of mental disturbance.[21] Furthermore, it is not possible to distinguish a qualitative difference between testimonies signed by doctors and those signed by surgeons. Most of the time, doctors and surgeons signed either two different testimonies that were, however, written using similar terms, or both signed the same testimony. Hence, during the whole period not only did medical practitioners compete with the clergy for their status as the most suitable experts for assessing madness, but also questions of status inside the medical profession itself were unsettled. In fact, the patients of Santa Dorotea were under the custody of a surgeon until 1756, when the hospital was assigned its first permanent physician with the appointment of Antonio Lulli. Still, physicians and surgeons disputed their roles as medical authorities in forensic affairs, including the assessment of madness.

It is well known that early modern medical experts in madness made their appearance hand in hand with the development of specialized spaces for the treatment and the cure of the mentally afflicted and the consolidation of the mad business.[22] In Tuscany, the institutional changes brought by the Regency, particularly the new admission procedure to Santa Dorotea, were the signs of an initial shift in the balance between surgeons and doctors. As explained in the previous chapter, since 1750 *pazzia furiosa* had to be certified by a doctor (not a surgeon), and since 1756 Santa Dorotea had a permanent physician in charge of admissions, treatments, and discharging patients. Moreover, the increasing number of petitions for committal made it necessary to appoint two additional physicians as the official public experts (*periti fiscali*) to determine which patients merited committal.

These changes, in combination with the growing number of petitions for interdiction and committal toward the mid-eighteenth century, contributed to the emergence of new medical experts in madness. Physicians such as Giovanni Targioni Tozzetti, Antonio Lulli, and Francesco Antonio Viligiardi developed a practical expertise on mental diseases through their contact with and treatment of patients in Santa Dorotea and their roles of *periti fiscali* in the civil and criminal courts of the Duchy.[23] The names of these physicians start to stand apart from the rest of the medical testimonies in the records of the Pupilli both because they were called more frequently and because they tended to use more specific medical terminology. This is paralleled by a slight increase in medical testimonies. Of the 59 interdiction procedures for *demenza* carried out between 1700 and 1775 with the use of medical opinion, 33 were decreed after 1750, with groupings of 10 and 11 between 1755–1760 and 1770–1775, respectively. The emergence of Vincenzo Chiarugi and the reforms at San Bonifazio hospital, which took the place of Santa Dorotea in 1788, suggests that the tendency continued during the following decades. This change was accompanied by a steady increase in interdiction sentences during the last decades of the century.

The lack of specificity in medical testimonies should not be taken as an indication of how madness was conceptualized and treated among the Tuscan medical community. In fact, the medical writings of the Tuscan physicians Giuseppe del Papa (1648–1735), Antonio Cocchi (1695–1758), and Giovanni Targioni Tozzetti (1712–1783) demonstrate the existence of a much more varied medical language than the one recorded in the judicial records of the period.[24] In this context, it has been argued that the lack of specific medical terms to categorize mental disturbance in judicial practice was motivated by the possible reluctance of physicians and surgeons to use labels that might be dishonorable to their clients.[25] However, the Tuscan sources suggest something different. It has been shown in previous chapters that petitioners and witnesses had no reluctance to employ straightforward labels of madness, such as *demente, pazzo*, or *mentecatto*, all of which left no doubt as to the association with mental disturbance. Thus, it seems that medical practitioners asked to give a judicial testimony should not have been particularly worried about their clients being offended by a straightforward association with mental disturbance. Rather, the lack of medically specific terms has more to do with the specifics of the interdiction procedure. As has been argued here, medically specific terms made no difference to the outcome of the procedure. On the one hand, *demenza* had to be proven by observable evidence, and this was found in behavior and actions, regardless of the medical diagnosis. On the other hand, as descriptors such as *fissazioni* or *turbazioni di fantasia* started to be employed following the institutional changes that gave physicians such as Targioni Tozzetti and Lulli an official authority over the medical diagnosis of madness, it seems that the choosing of categories might have had more to do with those physicians' new power than with a reluctance to offend their clients.

Regarding the possible stigma of having a relative publicly labeled mad, we have to bear in mind that interdictions themselves entailed publicity, as the decree had to be published so that it was widely known that the individual was not able to make a contract and that any debt would be declared void. Dishonor had already come from having a family member declared prodigal or demented, although we should not discard the possibility that withholding the precise details would be less harmful. This could account for the cases decreed without specification of the causes and, to some extent, for the lack of specificity in the characterization of the behavioral disorder and the state of mind it revealed. However, cases in which precise categories were employed suggest that the choosing of terms had more to do with the circumstances surrounding the denunciation and the purposes of the procedure than with honor and a need to conceal madness.

Epilepsy and apoplexy

Nine out of the 59 interdiction procedures that use medical testimony declare the cause of *demenza* to be epilepsy or apoplexy. This incidence is paralleled in criminal justice, where, for instance, Giovanni Targioni Tozzetti frequently gave his expert opinion as *medico fiscale* on the mental and physical effects of epilepsy and apoplexy to argue for a remission of sentence for health reasons. In other words, madness was certified by medical practitioners mostly when it left clear physical signs. However, precisely because epilepsy and apoplexy had clear physical signs, they were repeatedly employed by petitioners in both criminal and civil courts to craft a petition for interdiction or reduction of sentence without resorting to medical opinion. Its presence was easily recognizable, but at the same time they constituted illnesses for which medical assistance was frequently sought.[26]

The two conditions were not well differentiated, although apoplexy was particularly associated with old age, singled out as a mark of inevitable physical and mental decay. Situated at the interstices between bodily and mental ailments, the etiologies of epilepsy and apoplexy may not have been completely clear to nonspecialists, but their bodily signs and effects on intellectual faculties were indisputable even to a lay observer. The typical events that signaled the presence of epilepsy and apoplexy, such as convulsive seizures, partial or complete paralysis, loss of speech and/or vision, and severe mental confusion, appear to have been widely known to lay petitioners in the criminal and civil courts.[27]

Accounts of epilepsy and apoplexy assume slightly different tones depending on the context and in accordance with the requisites of each legal space. Epilepsy, still widely referred to as *mal caduco*, and strokes resulting in various levels of paralysis were commonly employed by prisoners to justify petitions for the reduction of a sentence, as we have seen. These petitions were generally accompanied by testimonies from the *medico fiscale* or a *medico condotto*. Intended to demonstrate that the convicted felon deserved a lenient sentence, medical testimonies in these cases almost invariably focused on the physical consequences of both conditions. The person's mental state was, consequently, left in the background. Following the principles of criminal law, these medical testimonies had to convince the authorities of the felon's delicate health, which had to be serious enough to prevent him or her from performing hard labor or to require a better environment and special treatment. Medical testimonies that argued for the seriousness of an apoplectic or epileptic condition affecting a convicted felon were not necessarily more generous in their descriptions than the medical testimonies presented in interdiction procedures. As Targioni Tozzetti explained to the Otto di Guardia in 1768, epileptic convulsive seizures, when occurring frequently and at short intervals, could easily give rise to apoplexy and ultimately result in death.[28] The formula could vary, but the quantity of information was equally scant.

Allusions to epilepsy and apoplexy in interdiction procedures were primarily used as evidence of mental incapacity, even if it was a mental incapacity that possessed the clearest physical evidence possible. To understand this connection between physical and mental impairment, we should keep in mind that interdictions were thought to mitigate the consequences of *demenza*, prodigality, and deafness or muteness, so the conflation was at the very core of interdictions. The narratives of interdiction in fact suggest that mental incapacity in its various forms was in many cases merged with various levels of physical impairment, as we have seen. In the particular case of apoplexy and epilepsy, intensifying physical impairment was indisputably correlated with increasing mental deterioration. The purpose of interdiction procedures made it important to highlight the latter, while a criminal context made it pivotal to highlight the former.

Interdiction procedures demonstrate that, notwithstanding the fact that the symptoms of epilepsy and apoplexy were known to lay society, families reported them in a different way than medical practitioners. Medical testimonies generally presented apoplexy and epilepsy as marks of a physiological damage in the person's mental faculties. For instance, the physician Francesco Antonio Viligiardi declared his patient had suffered "fierce epilepsy," a "serious and incurable illness" that had rendered him "*amente*," which together with his advanced age dramatically reduced his possibilities of recovery.[29] Medical testimonies of apoplectic or epileptic episodes would sometimes go a little further, contextualizing the patient's circumstances in terms of mobility, whether they were taken care of and the kind of treatment they received. In contrast, lay petitioners tended to skip the specification of the medical category (which was sometimes even referred to simply as "accidents") and went straight to the mental incapacity caused by a convulsive episode or stroke, on account of which "he has gone so out of himself [*uscito talmente fuori di se*] that he has become *mentecatto*,"[30] or that it had left the afflicted "subject to an almost continual dementia,"[31] "weak of mind,"[32] or "reduced to the level of imbecility of forces and mind."[33]

The sick bodies of the allegedly mentally incapable were generally a matter of concern after the interdiction, when the Pupilli had to figure out the best measures to ensure that they were properly taken care of. At this stage, more accurate accounts regarding their mental and bodily health could be useful. For instance, Xaverio Valloni, a Florentine of advanced age and with no offspring, was interdicted in 1748 at the request of his caretakers, who simply declared he had become demented, without presenting any medical testimony.[34] Along with the interdiction, the petitioners requested that they be appointed as administrators and be put in charge of Valloni's custody and care. However, later proceedings inform us that his condition was framed as "melancholy and [mental] fixations" aggravated by an apoplectic stroke which left him severely physically impaired. Close scrutiny of the labels used, the voices involved, and the situations that prompted the use of one or another term is valuable in examining the principles regulating the languages of madness.

Xaverio Valloni's case resurfaces 2 years later when his 2 sisters, both nuns, initiated litigation against his caretakers over his care and custody.[35] The sisters accused the caretakers, a mother and her son, of misappropriation, opportunistic motives, and ill treatment of the defenseless Valloni, who "had fallen little by little into a fierce melancholy and fixations." The Pupilli's report informs us that on top of the melancholy and mental fixations that had afflicted him for years, "rendering him stupid and *melenso*," Xaverio was suffering from severe physical complications due to a more recent apoplectic stroke. Only now was a medical testimony added to the lay testimonies presented to demonstrate Xaverio's physical condition to argue both that he needed constant care and that he was already receiving it.

This case is interesting for the clues it provides as to how and why medical testimonies were employed. While it had not been necessary to medically certify Xaverio Valloni's alleged melancholy and mental fixations, this step was needed for his apoplexy and its consequences. When the interdiction proceedings began, the caretakers not only had been informally in charge of managing Xaverio's affairs for some time, but had also assumed his custody and attendance to his domestic needs. The assertion regarding his mental incapacity was in fact not under discussion until his sisters intervened. And when they did, what was contested was not the nature of Xaverio's mental affliction, but instead who was to take on his custody and care, given that his sisters were unable to provide these themselves as they were nuns; and also what was to happen to his property. The 2 nuns claimed that their brother's caretakers, who had also been appointed administrators of his patrimony, had come to "dominate him completely," seizing upon his weakness to take advantage of him and consume his patrimony. In proof of this situation, the sisters noted that Xaverio had made a donation to the woman who had assisted him over the years, which his heirs – the 2 sisters and their Monastery – tried to impugn on the grounds of his alleged mental incapacity.[36]

A doctor and a surgeon signed a testimony declaring that they had treated Xaverio Valloni for the past 5 months and that he was "sick with an apoplectic malady, an indisposition which requires, beyond our cure, the continual assistance of a person day and night to care for the said patient."[37] Still not completely convinced of the actual situation of their ward, the Pupilli officers resolved to send a physician to observe Xaverio's condition and his caretakers' behavior.[38] The report that the informer wrote for the Pupilli differs from most medical testimonies in its careful description of the old man's body and mental state. He described that he had found Xaverio "lying on a resting chair [*sedia a riposo*], stupid, astonished, pusillanimous, taciturn and incapable of reasonable discourse," being only able to respond with small and insignificant words to the informant's questioning. He could not recall any past events and continuously answered "I do not remember." When he was asked to stand up, he could hardly get to his feet, showing a "considerable weakness" (*debolezza non lieve*) and loss of energy in his body to the extent that he could not move his legs without help. The informant explained that all these signs indicated that "for some time apoplexy has resided in this imbecile head, and as a fatal and malign guest has left, maybe as its indelible print, the organ of the brain defected, inefficacious and weak," affecting not only his intellectual faculties, but also preventing his animal spirits from distributing movement to his extremities.[39]

This kind of detailed description is atypical in court records, particularly for its insights into the workings of the brain fibers and spirits and into the consequences a change in the brain's substance had on the intellectual operations and in bodily motion. The testimony just quoted made explicit reference to apoplexy as producing irreparable damage to the brain, which in turn affected bodily motion by immobilizing the animal spirits. In the medical testimonies of interdiction procedures, the word brain is not usually used to explain the physiological functioning of the organ from which impulses are sent to the rest of the body to command its functioning but rather to name the seat of the faculty of reason. Doctors and surgeons would only enter into physiological details if there was an argument to be made regarding the physical condition of the defendant, a condition whose irrevocability was in this case fundamental to emphasize. The primary aim of this medical inquiry was to assess the defendant's lack of mobility and need for assistance, so the description addresses aspects that were usually left outside such medical testimonies.

We find a similar situation regarding a troublesome interdicted man who had been confined in the fortress of Volterra, when he requested permission from the Council of Regency to be allowed to return to Florence due to the violent epileptic fits he was suffering from. His petition was supported by an exceptionally elaborate medical testimony. It declared that he was

> frequently subjected to stretching [*stiramenti*] of the nerves and convulsions, and especially during the month of July last year he was afflicted by an inflammatory fever accompanied by grave and dangerous epileptic accidents, on account of which he was on the brink of losing his life.[40]

References to nerves, convulsions, fevers, and other precise indications of physical sufferings are not usually found in medical testimonies. Furthermore, in this case, the basis of the physician's argument in favor of transferring the interdicted back to Florence was that the weather in Volterra was especially harmful to his health. Once again, the focus of the discussion was on the interdicted's physical condition, not on his troubled mind, although we know he had been interdicted for being a riotous, extravagant and uneasy (*inquieto*) mad man (*pazzo*).[41]

Due to their variety and regular appearance across the evidence under scrutiny here, petitions claiming epilepsy or apoplexy in order to argue for mental incapacity with the support of medical opinion are highly valuable for studying the circulation of the vocabulary of madness. On the one hand, the conflation of the physical and mental symptomatology accompanying both conditions explains why petitioners were so at ease in describing their characteristics. Yet, on the other hand, this same conflation explains the involvement of medical opinion in these petitions. Given their commonness and highly disabling physical consequences, we can assume that medical practitioners were consulted more frequently for ailments related to epilepsy and apoplexy than for other mental afflictions, especially when the latter were manifested in forms that were not physically harmful either to the patient or to others, as was the case with many of the interdicted.

Bearing witness to the pervasiveness of medical ideas, legal practice widely accepted the precepts of health and disease that dictated, for example, better air and diet, a change of climate, and the avoidance of situations that generated emotional distress (the so-called *passioni d'animo*). All these conditions, according to the principles of the six non-natural factors that influenced health and disease, were to be carefully managed if one intended to preserve or be restored to health.[42] Epilepsy and apoplexy were no exceptions. As explained by the Italian physician Andrea Pasta (1706–1782) regarding epilepsy, it was "not always derived from humoral causes," but when it was, "it is undeniable that the *scosse d'animo* [shaking or agitation of the soul] can frequently control it and make it disappear."[43] This explains why the authorities considered the argument of epileptic or apoplectic felons valid who requested that their penalties be mitigated or pardoned. Similarly, the Pupilli officials usually supported requests for a "change of air," better living conditions, or a change of diet. The principles of the six non-naturals, still strongly present as the primary preventive mechanism for health preservation, were applied not only to apoplexy and epilepsy, but also in general to all physical or mental distempers.

Other medical categories

The more medical testimonies left the realm of the body and its physical evidence to explore the signs of mental disturbance, the more prominence was given to references to altered psychological states, specifically to descriptions of alterations of judgement in connection with emotional disruptions. With the appearance of new authorities on mental illnesses following the appointment of Antonio Lulli as permanent physician of Santa Dorotea and of figures such as Giovanni Targioni Tozzetti as consultant physician, medical testimonies started to add to the traditional *mentecatto*, *frenesia*, and "bereft of cognition" concepts such as *delirio*, *fissazioni*, *alterazioni* or *turbazioni di fantasia*, and *demenza ipocondriaca*. Contrasting with the plain, unspecialized, and generic testimonies of other medical practitioners, Lulli and Targioni Tozzetti explained the mental incapacity of their patient by making reference to their perturbed fantasies, their deliriums, and their mental fixations.

In this scenario, the term "melancholy" has a limited appearance compared to the previous centuries. According to Elizabeth Mellyn, melancholy was the preferred term to categorize madness in the civil and criminal court records of Tuscany during the sixteenth and seventeenth centuries, and lay society demonstrated the capacity to argue for its signs and characteristics without the direct help of medical practitioners.[44] Scholars have engaged in vast discussions about the European fascination with this mental affliction, regarded at the same time as a fashionable disease and as a pitiable malady, associated not only with artistic geniality, intellectual occupations, and the elite, but also with deep suffering and suicide. With religious, political, and cultural meanings that shaped its form by turns, melancholy was probably the most commonly used term to classify mental affliction in the sixteenth and seventeenth centuries. Its characteristics, meanings, and medical explanations were widely available and pervaded a wide spectrum of early modern European society.[45]

Nevertheless, from being the most used term to describe mental incapacity in Tuscany in the previous centuries, melancholy had now been dissolved into the even more generic *demenza* both in lay narratives and in medical testimonies, appearing in only 4 out of 611 interdictions. When we do find the term, it is as descriptor or qualifier of the concepts *fissazioni* and *delirio*.[46] The same happens in the records of Santa Dorotea, where we find the term used only in the phrases melancholic delirium or melancholic fixation. That the delirium or the fixation was melancholic indicated, on the one hand, the proximity between melancholy and frenzy and, on the other, that suicidal thoughts were involved. The presence of an altered fantasy, a fixation, or a delirium served to differentiate melancholy conceived as an emotional disposition from melancholy that entailed serious mental derangement, which could easily turn into mania or which could lead its victim to make an attempt against his or her own life.[47] However, cases of suicidal or murderous behavior were generally framed simply as *pazzia furiosa* by the authorities in the admission records of Santa Dorotea.

We need to consider that these observations are conditioned by the sources under study here. Melancholy, in fact, was at the intersection between sanity and insanity, for it did not necessarily imply loss of cognition or the complete compromising of one's mental faculties. Thus, it could be argued that with the normalization of interdiction procedures over the centuries, melancholy by itself ceased to be a category accountable for interdiction, even less for criminal insanity, for the compromising of the mental faculties was debatable. From this point of view, the relative decline in the citing of melancholy can be interpreted as the result of the requirements of judicial practice rather than as a reflection of its actual disuse as a diagnostic category to frame and explain mental disturbance at a social level. Nonetheless, even if it was in response to changes in judicial practice, the fact is that while melancholy seems to have been the preferred category to frame the mental incapacity of a relative during the sixteenth and seventeenth centuries in Tuscany, by the eighteenth it no longer prevailed.

There are further considerations to take into account. Mental fixations (*fissazioni*) or alterations of fantasy (*alterazioni di fantasia*) had been part of previous conceptions of melancholy, and thus it might seem striking that they were not employed in the medical testimonies of the first half of the eighteenth century. In this regard, changes in the medical lexicon of madness can also be explained as part of a cultural change. As will be argued in the next chapter, the focus of conceptions of madness was changing from economic performance to emotional displays, and so it makes sense that medical practitioners would also introduce expressions that pointed to the inner disposition of the defendant. What seems remarkable is the introduction of specific terms to depict altered mental or emotional states in medical testimonies that had predominantly been built around economic performance and deviance from behavioral norms. Despite their being accompanied by the indispensable *demente*, *melenso*, and *mentecatto*, the terms *fissazioni di mente*, *turbazioni di mente/fantasia*, or *alterazioni di mente/fantasia* were introduced to describe the individual's state of mind as proof of mental incapacity. This change is closely connected to the identification of emotional anguish or emotional perturbations (*angustie d'animo* or *turbazione d'animo*) as both triggers and signs of mental derangement.

Medical practitioners generally did not disclose the contents of their patients' mental fixations or the images produced by their altered fantasies. Most times we are left only with the declaration that the person was subjected to a "melancholic delirium that seriously affected his fantasy," or that he had "fallen into some mental fixations."[48] But sometimes they slipped in comments regarding the object of the delusional symptoms and mind fixations of their patients. One was prone "to conceive false ideas of a suspicion of being poisoned," another suffered "false persecutory ideas," and yet another was "subject to many extravagancies of fantasy, expressed with impious and obscene words."[49] Fixations led one to believe that he owned a house that he had in fact rented for many years, and in another case they made him believe that he was a nobleman who had been promised in marriage to the Princess of Wales.[50] "Alterations of mind" could also be present in the form of an "amorous passion" in which the "delirious intellect" of the patient would be "fixated on the object of her madness."[51]

There are two other categories employed in medical testimonies that should be examined here. One is *demenza ipocondriaca* and the other *affezioni nervose*. Contrary to what might be expected, the century's fashionable "nervous affections" and their paramount diseases, male hypochondria and female hysteria, are not represented in the Tuscan court records.[52] When we take into account the range of diseases covered by any volume of medical consultations published in the eighteenth century, mental afflictions are predominantly represented by hysteric and hypochondriac affections. Second in the list are epileptic or apoplectic fits. Other types of mental disorders, such as melancholic delirium or some unspecified "mental perturbations," appear in a clear minority compared to the other three.[53]

Nervous diseases came into fashion in elite European societies and, judging from Italian medical consultations, the Italian Peninsula seems to have been no exception. However, as Jonathan Andrews has warned us, the configuration of nervous complaints was a matter of contention in the medical profession during the eighteenth century, particularly regarding the boundaries between sanity and insanity, and whether nervous diseases could be considered as sufficient cause, for instance, to determine the necessity of someone's confinement.[54] In this context, it is not strange that nervous complaints were not employed to argue mental incapacity or an insanity defense. Nervous complaints were categories still too undetermined to be raised before a court of law. For instance, of the 59 medical testimonies introduced in interdiction procedures, only 1 framed the defendant's condition in terms of *demenza ipocondriaca* and 1 as *affezioni nervose*. While the former gave no details further than to declare that the defendant's "reasoning" was "unstable" (*raziocinio non stabile*), the latter gave sufficient details as to explore how these kinds of afflictions might have been regarded in the Tuscan courts.[55]

In 1764, the Florentine physician Francesco Antonio Viligiardi characterized a defendant's mental condition as *affezzioni nervose* caused by a combination of inveterate diarrhea and "the many vexations of soul [*vessazioni dell'animo*] he suffered," which caused him "strong and frequent convulsions of head and chest." In one of the rare occasions in which a medical testimony resembles the line of argument usually employed in medical consultations, Viligiardi described other symptoms such as the patient's difficulty sleeping and frightened awakenings in which the patient suffered "trepidations and intermittencies of heart and oppressions of breath." That is, he employed the category of nervous disease but accompanied it with physical signs that gave demonstrable facts to it. In this context, his nervous distempers were identified as the consequence of his "weak machine" and a "mediocre health," a condition he could certify, as he declared, for he had been his attending physician for 7 years. The testimony was intended to emphasize that the defendant was completely unable to attend to his affairs and pay his debts, to which end Viligiardi placed the accent on the patient's sick and disabled body, which would be restored to health only if the patient abstained from any serious occupation.[56]

Medical languages in context

As we have seen, the medical languages of madness were flexible and adaptable to the different requirements imposed on medical practitioners. When one examines these terms in the contexts, it can be observed to what extent petitioners, witnesses, and defendants reshaped and resignified them according to their needs. The representation of the mental sufferings of Antonio Corsini, interdicted and committed at least twice to Santa Dorotea, is particularly remarkable.[57] In December 1756, Giuseppe Nardi, cousin of Antonio Corsini, made two parallel requests to the Grand Duke, one to interdict him and place him under the curatorship of the Magistrato Supremo, and the other one to confine him in Santa Dorotea. The vocabulary used in both petitions was remarkably plain: one spoke of Antonio's *demenza*, the other of his *pazzia*.[58] Nonetheless, the supporting testimonies and further enquiries undertaken in response to the interdiction petition employed a wider range of categories. Although he was admitted to Santa Dorotea in early December, his interdiction was only decreed at the beginning of April 1757. Antonio's "unhealthy state of mind" (*poco sano stato di mente*) was not doubted by the authorities, but its consequences, and who was to be entrusted with the administration of his patrimony, generated months of discussion. The Pupilli argued that they had jurisdiction for overseeing the curatorship (instead of the Magistrato Supremo, as the petitioner requested), and at the same time they strongly opposed the appointment of Giuseppe Nardi as the administrator.

Two physicians were involved in the interdiction procedure: a local physician from Prato and Antonio Lulli from Santa Dorotea in Florence. The first diagnosis that we know of was made by the physician of Prato, who reported in November 1756 that for 6 months he had seen Antonio Corsini affected by "a melancholic delirium without fever" accompanied "by a grave fear and a profound sadness caused by mournful [*funesti*] thoughts and the imaginary dangers that his altered fantasy represents in his mind, which together with obstinate fixation, become the continual occupation of his spirit." With the intention of proving to the state officials the necessity of his interdiction, the physician reported that Antonio had strongly refused any kind of treatment or care and rejected medical advice. Contravening the doctor's indications, he refused to practice the physical activities recommended for the improvement of his mental and physical health, such as riding or maintaining an active social life. On the contrary, he preferred solitude, had slept in his clothes for weeks, and had even refused to eat to the extent that it had been necessary "to make him eat by force, so that he would not perish."[59]

In a remarkably lengthy testimony, the local physician spoke of Antonio's altered state of mind without giving a physiological explanation for it. Instead, he was concerned with its signs, which he presented contextualized in precise situations. His attention was centered on the extent to which his patient contravened the principles of the six non-naturals, according to which attention to physical and social activities, diet, and sleep were considered essential to preserve health and counteract diseases. The testimony explained that Antonio Corsini defied the expected codes of behavior by living deprived of amusements, by refusing to eat and take care of his health, and by being indifferent to his domestic affairs. The physician identified the key to Antonio's mental state in his mournful thoughts and "altered fantasy," which subjected him to suicidal thoughts and imaginary fears. Following the traditional importance attributed to the imagination in the etiology of melancholy, the physician explained that his altered fantasy produced mind fixations that moved him to reject food, avoid people, and behave oddly. He explicitly said that he had been consulted several times by the family in order to treat Antonio, despite the patient's open defiance to his indications.

By contrast, the testimony sent by Santa Dorotea's physician, Antonio Lulli, was concise and lacked any description of symptoms. It simply declared that Antonio Corsini was "demented and incapable to attend to his own interests given the considerable depravation [*depravazione*] of the mind."[60] Although it conveyed the idea of a damaged brain by using the word "corruption," the description was limited to the minimum of information required to attest to his *demenza* in an interdiction procedure. The admission record is even more scant, as it only declared that Antonio had been received in the institution because he had fallen into madness (*dato in pazzia*).

As Antonio Corsini's madness unfolded, new concepts were recorded. After Antonio had spent just a couple of months at Santa Dorotea, the physician and surgeon of the institution wrote a report to discharge him, claiming that "although he has suffered in the past from mental alienations and disturbances of his fantasy originated by anguishes of the soul [*angustie d'animo*], for some time now he has nevertheless become greatly recovered, and enjoys continued lucid intervals for most of the day," on account of which a full recovery could be expected.[61] More attuned this time to the description given by the physician from Prato, the testimony provided insight into Corsini's madness by referring to his anguish as the origin of his mental alienation. The change is interesting, as it introduces the concept of *angustie d'animo*, which is common in other medical sources of the period such as the *Consulti medici*, but which is not that common in the medical testimonies presented in interdiction procedures.[62] This was the same anguish that the physician from Prato had framed as mournful thoughts, altered fantasy, and mental fixation.

The prospect of lucid intervals posed a delicate problem for legal provisions regarding insanity, as their episodic nature called any standardized response into question. However, this issue was more relevant for determining the level of accountability of the criminally insane than in assessing mental incapacity. Compared to the difficulty of determining if a person had experienced a lucid interval while committing a crime, given that interdiction was a temporary measure, the likelihood of lucid intervals only entailed that the person could more easily be released from curatorship.

Antonio Corsini himself made a reference to his lucid intervals as grounds for his plea for protection against his ill-intentioned relatives. Writing while still confined in Santa Dorotea, he chose to use the category of lucid intervals to argue that he was lucid enough so as to have a say in the selection of a suitable administrator. But at the same time, he sought to blame his mental affliction on the iniquities of his relatives, for which purpose it served him better to highlight the depth of his affliction rather than its episodic nature. And so, instead of denying his mental incapacity, he declared that he suffered from mental disturbances (*turbazioni di mente*) accompanied by lucid intervals, which placed him, all the same, in need of an "expert and honest administrator" who could protect his patrimony and defend him against his relatives.[63]

To illustrate his mistrust of his relatives, Antonio dwelt upon the details of his mental disorder, disclosing how he conceived and made sense of it, in which his biography and his family played a major part. His petition can thus be taken as a re-elaboration of the medical diagnosis to support his claim against his relatives. Giuseppe Nardi was the son of his former tutor, a man whom he did not trust and probably feared. Having become an orphan while underage, Antonio's guardianship had been entrusted to Domenico Nardi, who was married to his paternal aunt, following his father's testamentary dispositions. The Nardis were the only family left to Antonio, and, as such, they had intervened in his economic affairs even after he had come of age.[64] Although it seems that he lived alone in Florence for a while, by the time Giuseppe Nardi made his petitions, Antonio resided with the Nardis in Prato, where he had been affected by the *delirio melanconico*, as the local physician framed it.

Antonio Corsini, whose primary interest was to keep the Nardis as far away from his affairs and his patrimony as possible, chose the terms employed by the physician of Santa Dorotea to explain his mental sufferings but ascribed them new meaning. Building upon his biography, Antonio enumerated in his petition the situations that had led to the "anguished disposition" (*animo angustiato*) that ultimately produced the "fixation, and perturbations of mind and fantasy" (*fissazione, e turbazione di mente, e fantasia*) that had affected him.[65] Corsini decided to frame his "mental perturbations" as being triggered by the anguish his adverse familial situation generated for him. As he saw it, he had not only been left under the guardianship of a greedy and dishonest uncle while underage, but the man had also extended his authority after he had come of age, first withholding from him the usufruct of his patrimony and refusing to give accounts of his administration, and afterwards persuading him to sign dubious contracts, which caused Corsini to incur considerable debts that he did not know how to settle.

Antonio Corsini framed his mental illness as caused by the *angustie d'animo* that these concrete adverse circumstances produced in him, as did many other interdicted persons and prisoners. It is not rare to find eighteenth-century defendants and patients signaling wrong or inexpert economic performance and potential bankruptcy as sources of anguish that led to mental derangement. Together with ongoing family conflicts, marriage disputes, and love affairs, economic setbacks were frequently cited not only by the Tuscan sufferers, but also by other European patients and defendants as well.[66] The novelty here, then, is not so much the connection between these sources of anxiety and madness but the vocabulary employed and the legal context of its appearance. Antonio Corsini was able to coordinate his personal agenda and experience with the possibilities of interdiction procedures and contemporary medical terminology, for he did not stop at the anguish he felt because of these events, but presented them as the antecedents of his subsequent "fixation" and "disturbance of mind and fantasy." Furthermore, he was able to employ these medical categories on his own behalf, for the evidence suggests that he actually managed to keep the Nardis at a distance from himself and his patrimony.[67]

As in many other interdiction procedures, the accounts of Antonio Corsini's mental affliction acquired more precise vocabulary as the family conflict behind the interdiction petition was unraveled, evolving from the unspecific *demente* and *pazzo* to the more defined *delirio melanconico, turbazione di fantasia*, and *ostinata fissazione*. This case illustrates how the introduction of a more precise terminology of mental disturbance responded to a complex series of events that were not always connected with the actual mental condition they were supposed to describe, or to its evolution, but much more to the agency of the involved parties. Categories were not only flexible, but their use was also carefully considered. Antonio Corsini understood that he could build a better case if he presented himself as the victim of the abusive schemes of his relatives, which had caused him to fall into the "fixations, and perturbations of mind and fantasy" that led him into the hospital. In contrast, his uncle, who had been acquainted with the different doctors who had assessed Antonio's state of mind when he made the interdiction petition, decided not to include any of the precise medical categories that they used to describe his nephew's sufferings.

Judging from this case, the incorporation of medical categories seems to have been strongly dependent on the frequency with which those employing them had been exposed to medical notions, which went hand in hand with the perceived seriousness of the mental condition under examination. But that was not the only factor causing these categories to be used. This issue is discussed further in the next chapter, but for now it is important to note that characteristics of the narratives where there is no direct involvement of medical opinion suggest that litigants and authorities had a background of their own to turn to when they wanted to define and characterize mental disturbance. This background was built upon centuries of litigation that required the exercise of reflecting on what constituted mental incapacity, how mental disturbance could be identified, and which were its most important indicators. This knowledge transmitted across generations might also have been influenced by the increasing circulation of books of medical advice destined for a lay public, as well as could be the outcome of a popular knowledge of mental diseases.[68] Additionally, the context and biography of the sufferer strongly conditioned how their mental condition was framed and the words chosen to describe it. For instance, recurrent private resort to medical practitioners to treat mental ailments was a luxury which only the privileged could afford, but the characteristics of the family group or the household composition, among other circumstances, also played their part. The narratives of madness in judicial records are in this way a re-elaboration of the personal and family biography using the setting provided by public institutions, legal framework, and medical knowledge.

Categories were actively chosen to secure specific outcomes in close accordance with the context and circumstances that surrounded the denounced deviant behavior. The problem of assessing the level of permeation of medical understanding of madness in lay society lies precisely in the contextual nature of the languages of madness, their malleability, and the ability demonstrated by petitioners to adapt their language to the circumstances. However, this reveals the agency of petitioners and underpins their capacity to move the strings of the institutional apparatus to achieve their aims. When petitioners needed to make a strong argument regarding the nature of mental afflictions, they almost invariably demonstrated their ability to describe them using current medical terms.

The instrumental choosing of categories

Medical practitioners introduced the vocabulary of madness in accordance with the purposes of each legal procedure. Their language, instead of acting as fair mirror of the mental condition they were supposed to describe, responded to the context of the disclosure of madness, as we have seen. This was not because the choice was arbitrary or the mental condition had been invented by the witness in complete disconnection from the behavior he was supposed to be labelling; rather, as in the case of lay testimonies, medical practitioners decided how much they would reveal and in what way, precisely in accordance with the purposes and aims they were supposed to serve. Whether to support a petition for interdiction, a defendant's contention of sanity, or a criminal's claim of insanity, the vocabulary with which testimonies were composed was the outcome of careful considerations.

In July 1752, the wife and brother of Domenico Cugi requested his interdiction, claiming that for a long time he had been "bereft of cognition, and as a demented [person], he is unable to attend to his own interests."[69] In support of Domenico's relatives, we find a testimony signed by the *medico condotto* and the local priest, which repeated the same formula and was equally unspecific, save for a note the physician added after his signature. Assuring the reader of the veracity of his testimony because of his long-term knowledge of the patient's medical history, the doctor added to his signature that he was the "physician of the city of Prato and attending physician of the household of the Signori Cugi."[70] The petition was thus crafted by recourse to the usual terms and was found to be enough to prove Domenico's "defect of unsound mind" (*difetto di sana mente*) and that consequently he was stupid and *melenso*.[71]

Strikingly, only 6 months after the interdiction was decreed, the original supplicants turned again to the authorities but this time to request that Domenico's interdiction be revoked. The petition was supported by a testimony from the same physician, who now attested to his sanity of mind employing a completely different set of terms. The state of "being completely bereft of cognition," on account of which the doctor declared Domenico could not "distinguish what he does or says," was now said to have been caused by a "continual fixation." While the first testimony had been framed following a formula that emphasized the person's long-term incapacity as revealed by his daily performance, the second testimony was framed in much more precise medical terms. The physician explained that Domenico

> had been for a long time in a state of not being able to attend his own interests due to a continual fixation that had alienated him from reason, [but] it can now be said that he has cleared [*sgombrata*] his mind from the said fixation.[72]

Not only was he declared sound of mind by the same medical practitioner who only a few months earlier declared he had been bereft of cognition for 8 years, but also that state of severe mental impairment had changed into a mental fixation. That is, from being a characteristic not likely to change (a "defect," as the Pupilli officers framed it), Domenico's mental condition was transformed into a phase from which he had been able to emerge. How could such a serious and apparently permanent condition have abated in just months?

As in many other cases, the choice of terms here responds more to the desired outcome than to an intention to provide accurate descriptions of a precise mental condition. The interdiction had been secured by the assertion that he suffered a mental incapacity that was framed as a long-term intellectual impairment, giving the impression it was irreversible. Conversely, for the interdiction to be lifted, the implication that it was irreversible had to be changed so as to suggest instead that it had been a temporary state. To this end, the term fixation was especially suggestive. Notwithstanding the fact that the physician chose the expression of "continual fixation," references to mental fixations were usually employed to describe episodic madness rather than permanent intellectual impairment. Mental fixations gave space for lucid intervals, which were considered grounds enough for the Pupilli to lift an interdiction, even if temporarily, regardless of whether it meant that it would have to be imposed anew once the individual fell into madness again.

It is possible to formulate a plausible hypothesis as to what happened between Antonio Cugi's interdiction and its removal. Taking into account how other interdiction procedures developed and what changed in the 6 months that elapsed since the interdiction was decreed probably had less to do with Domenico's mental condition and more to do with the household dynamics, particularly the relationship between the two brothers and the role played by Domenico's wife. Similarities with other cases suggest that the first description had been simplified in order to fit the requirements of the legal script. Many interdiction procedures were argued by using simple labels, concentrating the debate on more practical matters, such as the individual's economic performance, his or her deviation from behavioral norms, and their general resemblance to the stereotypes of mental incapacity. It is only in cases that were contested by the defendants or in those involving complicated family tensions that would not abate once the interdiction was decreed that we are given further details on how the given mental affliction was perceived, framed, and explained.

The change in the configuration of Domenico Cugi's mental affliction not only reveals the strong agency of litigants behind interdiction procedures, but it also suggests that the categories employed were carefully and collectively chosen. By and large, court records show that medical practitioners had to adapt their language both to the constraints imposed by the judicial system and to the demands set forth by litigants. How much a doctor would elaborate on the characteristics of a given mental affliction depended not only on the requirements of the institution, but also on the specific circumstances surrounding each case. It is a general rule regarding the shaping of the languages of madness that the more complex the familial situation, the greater the need for more precise terms and for longer characterizations.

The capacity to adapt to the context and shape testimonies in accordance with the circumstances can be observed in the writings of eminent physicians such as Giovanni Targioni Tozzetti, whose narratives and lines of argument tend to change according to the audience (and institution) to which they were directed. His testimonies in the Otto di Guardia focused on physical characteristics, responding to the necessity to demonstrate that, for example, the life of a prisoner was at serious risk if he was not transferred to a better environment.[73] But, in general, he chose not to elaborate on the nature of the mental afflictions he had identified. Furthermore, categories such as *delirio melanconico* or *fissazioni di mente* are, to my knowledge, generally absent from Targioni Tozzeti's testimonies to support supplications for the reduction of penalties. On the contrary, his *Relazioni in casi di demenza*, which comprised his expert opinion on the admission procedure to Santa Dorotea and several assessments of the mental condition of people held in prison, are framed in much more precise medical terms and blend detailed information on their mental condition with descriptions of its physical effects.[74] By the same token, the categories he used to attest to mental incapacity before the Magistrato dei Pupilli are generally different from the ones he employed to frame *pazzia furiosa* in the admission procedures to Santa Dorotea.[75] While the former categories point to the degree to which the intellectual faculties of the person were involved, latter categories stressed the person's level of dangerousness. Similarly, categories that he frequently employed to frame mental disturbances in his *Consulti medici* are almost absent from his legal assessments. Significantly, *affezioni isteriche* and *affezioni ipocondriache*, two distinct diagnostic categories of mental affliction that appear in the consultations he attended, appear very rarely in the court records of the period, as mentioned before. Also responding to their contexts and purposes, his medical consultations delved into the physiological bases of the mental diseases he was consulted about, giving more precise diagnostic categories than the ones he employed in front of the Tuscan courts.[76]

Experts of the soul

Most legal procedures to determine mental capacity were argued without the involvement of medical practitioners. In the debate over the boundaries between sane and insane behavior, family members held the primary authority, followed by members of the clergy, medical practitioners, and ducal officials. In this scenario, while medical practitioners were seldom called upon to testify for someone's mental condition, priests often gave their personal accounts regarding the behavior of the defendants and were generally included among the signers of collective testimonies. Testimonies signed by members of the clergy were not only considered essential to corroborate interdiction petitions, but were also preferred by the interdicted to demonstrate their soundness of mind in their petitions for the interdiction to be lifted.

The roles played by priests as witnesses in cases relating to the state of someone's mind attest to the enduring role of the Catholic Church as the ultimate supervisor of moral behavior. Still attuned to the counter-reformist principles, the Church continued to aspire to enforce the compliance to the Catholic patterns of expected behavior and spiritual life, and this is clear in the testimonies signed by priests. These testimonies were generally centered on the defendants' social performance, moral qualities, and observance of Catholic precepts. According to most of the priests testifying, mental disturbance was revealed through the defendant's reluctance to attend Church on a weekly basis, in his or her failure to follow the rules regarding confession and Holy Communion, and even in their refusal to pay the tithe.[77]

Priests' testimonies had a unique quality, stemming from their role as guardians of morality. The way priests' testimonies were crafted suggests they were testifying as experts on the person's soul, which only they were in a capacity to judge. Given their training and privileged position, priests were held to be the direct recipients of the hidden secrets of moral life. The inclusion of a testimony signed by a member of the clergy did not automatically result in a favorable response, especially when there were conflicting testimonies. But, in general, the testimony of a priest counted as proof of truth, with the assertion being cast in the tones of a moral authority that was difficult to contradict.

Priests not only testified as experts over the matters of the soul and spiritual life, but they also acted as witnesses whose credibility was widely considered incontrovertible. This is why someone who had been interdicted for a medically certified mental incapacity could later succeed in obtaining its revocation based solely on the defendant's and clergymen's assertion of his or her soundness of mind. In these cases, medical testimonies could even be contradicted, as the case of Maria Maddalena Panfi, interdicted in 1743 at the request of her two sons, shows. The interdiction petition claimed that she was not only the victim of certain "corporal indispositions," but also that she had lately "suffered many accidents," which rendered her in a state of "mental obfuscation and deprived of memory." Her sons' contention was supported by medical testimony which explained Maddalena had suffered an "epileptic accident, which proved to be very serious, and rendered her confused of mind [*imbarazzata di testa*] the whole day, as happens on most occasions with these accidents."[78] In other words, the case was built upon a medical language that identified very precise physiological origins of the defendant's inability to manage her affairs. For even if the medical testimony spoke only of one "epileptic accident," according to the supplicants she would likely suffer more seizures, which accounted for a condition that was likely to continue over time. Based on what was asserted by witnesses at the *viva voce* on her dissipation, and especially taking into account the fact that the medical testimony demonstrated that she "suffers from epileptic accidents that cause her great heaviness [*molta gravezza*] and mental obfuscations," the officials of the Pupilli considered Maddalena Panfi liable for interdiction.[79]

Two years later, Maddalena petitioned for her interdiction to be lifted, alleging it was completely false that she was not, nor ever had been, of unsound mind.[80] To prove her claim, she presented the testimonies of various priests attesting that she had always been of sound body and mind, which was considered by the authorities as enough to prove her claim and thus grant her request. The interesting issue lies in the fact that Maddalena Panfi's argument for revocation was not that she had been cured from her previous ailment, but instead that she had never suffered from a disease that affected her mind. Furthermore, she chose to support her claim with the testimony of clergymen, without recourse to medical opinion. The evidence provided by the clergymen regarding her soundness of mind was considered proof enough for the Pupilli to revoke the interdiction, as if there had been no medical testimony involved in the initial assessment. The Pupilli's decision here demonstrates once more that the criteria that predominated in these matters were practical ones. If the clergymen could confirm that Maddalena was of right mind, and provided the patrimony was of modest proportions and she herself demonstrated the necessary will to resume her administration, they were willing to grant the petition.[81]

Although testimonies written by clergymen sometimes repeated the categories employed by petitioners or other witnesses, they often made no reference to the defendant's mental state. Clergymen assessed mental capacity using a different measure. A defendant who according to the medical testimony suffered from a melancholic delirium with epileptic fits could be defined simply as a *mentecatto* who "is not capable of managing his own affairs, being indisposed in bed, and is incapable of receiving the Holy Sacraments."[82] In this case, not only was the medical category completely unrelated to the cleric's testimony, but the model against which the person's mental capacity was measured also differed. His state of mind, from the point of view of the priest, was so altered that he could no longer receive the Holy Communion, sufficient grounds to attest that he was indeed mentally incapacitated.

In addition to Christian behavior, priests evaluated the defendant's social performance in accordance with the established gender roles.[83] Men were assessed in their capacity of heads of family, based on whether they acted as virtuous educators, whether they set a moral and rational example to their children, whether they demonstrated the capacity to control themselves, and whether they complied with family hierarchies and exerted the proper amount of power (for instance, that they were not ordered around by their wives). In turn, women's mental capacity was assessed in terms of how they performed their maternal or wifely duties, whether they behaved virtuously, and how they raised their children. The usual line of argumentation in these cases is illustrated by the testimony given by a priest to explain why a 65-year-old man, widely reputed as *pazzo*, prodigal, disturbed, violent, and extravagant, deserved interdiction. The priest declared "he has always been a man whose behavior is not only of little advantage for his house and family, but also of an unchristian character." The priest recounted that the defendant had ruined his family with his dissipation, litigations, and robberies; that he had been imprisoned on many occasions; and that his "mad behavior" had also caused him to be committed twice to the madhouse. He concluded by declaring that "he lives very badly, having no devotion to God, and during this present year of 1768 to this day he has not fulfilled his Easter precept" or paid the fifth, so that "it is clear, that such a man is not good, neither in his soul nor in his body."[84]

These testimonies also shed light on the extent to which Church efforts to discipline the family and promote certain values were negotiated alongside lay notions and family demands, such as those disclosed in interdiction procedures. In this sense, the clergy's authority on mental derangement can also be explained by taking into account their prerogatives over family life. Priests acted as guardians of the institution of the family, they were the undisputed mediators in family conflicts, and were the first source of aid to turn to in times of trouble. This role, at the forefront not only of matrimonial litigation, for instance, but also of "infra-judicial" negotiations to resolve conflicts at community levels, also comes to the fore in the social and familial management of mental afflictions.[85] As petitioners repeatedly stated, they resorted to interdiction only after all other strategies to convince the defendants to change their behavior had failed, among which they generally recalled how local priests or personal confessors had unsuccessfully tried to exert their influence.

The expertise of the Auditore Fiscale

In a context of growing interest in the characteristics and consequences of mental derangement, the records suggest that the Auditori Fiscali developed a practical knowledge of madness through their repeated interventions to control its public consequences. They were in continual contact with families, physicians, and other state officials to decide the destiny of the mentally afflicted. Furthermore, their role as mediators between family concerns, defense of the principles of *buon governo* (the eighteenth-century principle behind police practice), and medical conceptions of insanity positioned them as a point of convergence for the negotiation of the understandings of madness. In their management of mental afflictions, the Auditori Fiscali combined their legal training with more practical knowledge gathered in the exercise of their duties. To a large extent, the circulation of language took place through the office of the Auditore Fiscale, where different social backgrounds and disciplines met.

In the context of changeability that characterized the itineraries of madness, public institutions such as the office of the Auditore Fiscale and the Magistrato dei Pupilli provided a sense of stability. There was a difference, however, in the way these two institutions exercised their steady control. While the officials of the Pupilli practiced a close surveillance of the lives and interests of the mentally afflicted for extended periods, the task was generally undertaken by the magistracy as a whole, without it being assigned to a particular magistrate. In contrast, the Auditori Fiscali engaged personally with the mentally afflicted and their families. Furthermore, given that the office was not subject to the continual changes experienced by the Tuscan magistracies,[86] the Auditore Fiscale offered a permanence that the rest of the provisional measures lacked. During the period under scrutiny here, only three men held the office. Filippo Luci was the Auditore Fiscale between 1737 and 1746, followed by Giovanni Brichieri Colombi until 1753, and then by the latter's son, Domenico, who held the office until 1784, when it was abolished. The characteristics of the office and the detailed records kept by the Tuscan administrations allowed for a transmission of this practical knowledge from one Auditore Fiscale to the next, and across the ducal administration.

Cases of recurrent episodes of madness such as the kind that affected Lorenzo Maestrini and Lorenzo Baldinotti, both discussed in previous chapters, usually called for the involvement of the Auditore Fiscale. Cases of markedly troublesome individuals could even be dealt with by two or three different Auditori Fiscali, most notably in the case of Lorenzo Baldinotti, which was handled by the three Auditori Fiscali of the period under study (Filippo Luci, Giovanni Brichieri Colombi, and Domenico Brichieri Colombi). Between 1725 and 1755, Lorenzo Baldinotti was alternatively imprisoned, under house arrest in Florence and in one of the properties the family possessed in the Tuscan territory. He was committed to both Santa Maria Nuova and Santa Dorotea for short periods and resided in several public and private places, including his brother's parish and a family residence in the outskirts of Florence.

The role of the Auditore Fiscale as the authority that evaluated and authorized committal in the name of the Grand Duke is further elucidated when we bear in mind that his involvement with madness went further. In fact, many of the people committed to Santa Dorotea were old acquaintances of the office. Furthermore, given that the mentally ill were generally only accepted for short periods at a time, when they were released from the hospital, the Auditori Fiscali continued their intervention through their roles as mediators, judges, and supervisors of the person's behavior on the request of family members or by direct command of the Council of Regency. The continuity of their involvement with the mentally disturbed and their families made the Auditori Fiscali a prominent figure in the configuration of the languages of madness, and, in addition, it positioned them at the intersection of medical and lay knowledge.

The principle behind the definition of a *pazzo furioso*, which differentiated those in need of being committed from those whose custody was a family responsibility, was certainly not enough to solve the problem madness posed for both private and public lives. Even if the patient ceased to present signs of mania at Santa Dorotea, this was no guarantee that his or her problematic behavior would come to an end. People subject to recurrent episodes of raving madness followed by periods that according to the medical gaze entailed no danger to public life often continued to create trouble to their families while in their periods of sanity. The criterion applied to deal with such cases was not unanimous, but, when public safety was concerned, the Auditore Fiscale held the final word. For instance, Lorenzo Maestrini had been released in 1735 from Santa Dorotea during a lucid interval, against the opinion of the Magistrato dei Pupilli. The Pupilli's authority covered only Lorenzo's guardianship and the administration of his patrimony, while his care, because it concerned public order, fell under the jurisdiction of the Auditore Fiscale.[87]

The permanent need to make space for new patients forced the administration of Santa Dorotea to release from their custody any "maniac" who gave proof of a "notable recovery."[88] This happened with Giorgio Jacquet, a French citizen, who was released from Santa Dorotea in 1757 because he ceased to give "manifest signs of madness" once he had been committed. In the eyes of the hospital authorities, this proved that "the furious excesses committed against his own wife and children are the effect of inebriation."[89] However, this was precisely the difficulty with Giorgio's madness, for he was repeatedly "subject to some melancholic delirium, that he most of the times foments with his immoderate habit of drinking wine and liquor."[90] As a consequence, although he was released from Santa Dorotea in 1757 with the special recommendation of the administrative board that Domenico Brichieri Colombi was to instruct his father of the need to provide proper custody for his son and particularly to ensure he was "kept completely distant" from wine,[91] Giorgio Jacquet continued to seriously disturb social life, forcing both his family and the authorities to resort to committal at various times. But neither Santa Dorotea nor the Fortezza da Basso in Florence was a successful solution for his problem. Wine, viewed as the source of all the inconveniences that his mental disturbance occasioned, continued to produce the same results.

Demonstrating the depth of his engagement with the problem, Brichieri Colombi not only supervised Giorgio Jacquet's committals to Santa Dorotea, but also mediated between him and his desperate wife, who strongly insisted on the impossibility of cohabiting with her violent husband. In 1758, after a second period in Santa Dorotea, Brichieri Colombi coordinated Jacquet's arrest and confinement in the Fortezza while he once more tried to convince the father to assume responsibility for his son. All the same, the problem persisted, and in 1761 we find him once more in the hospital, from where the administrative board intended to discharge him once he ceased to give signs of his recurrent frenzies.[92]

As on other occasions, Brichieri Colombi's narratives both repeat the concepts used by petitioners, medical experts, and magistrates to describe Giorgio Jacquet's mental condition and assign new meanings to them. The reports of the Auditori Fiscali describing the characteristics and consequences of mad behavior are therefore to be examined as acts of synthesis and recreation, as the product of the accumulation of different gazes and the result of their own interpretation. They voiced the concerns and perceptions of family members, which were usually not expressed in written form but in oral conversations, which they combined with the written reports of medical practitioners and ducal officials.

Although in this case, we have access to the medical reports from Santa Dorotea, the commands given by the Council of Regency, and the petitions from Jacquet's father, it is in Domenico Brichieri Colombi's narratives that we find the most telling details. The medical category of *delirio melanconico* employed in his reports is combined with descriptions of Giorgio's frenzies, used by the Fiscale to explain the real danger posed by his frantic behavior to the Council of Regency. Giorgio Jacquet's melancholic delirium was recognized in the "extravagances" he continually committed and in his habit of walking around armed and attacking people indiscriminately, even snatching food from villagers with "sword in hand."[93] His frenzy, Brichieri Colombi noted, was of a "delicate kind," so long as it was "fomented by his excessive drinking."[94] While the medical authorities in charge of Santa Dorotea were concerned with the symptoms and possible cures of madness, the Auditore Fiscale dealt directly with its consequences, resorting to mechanisms of control and disciplining that were commonly employed in police matters.

The Auditori Fiscali developed a sort of practical specialized knowledge of madness due to their close involvement with cases of episodic madness that frequently called for their intervention. For instance, in the case of Lorenzo Maestrini discussed at the beginning of the previous chapter, the officials of the Pupilli consulted the expert opinion of the Auditore Fiscale Filippo Luci to expand on the particulars of the case. The Auditori Fiscali had become "authorities" on the characteristics and dangers of madness, and their view was considered crucial to devise the appropriate measures for handling it. Sometimes they were in contact with physicians and the *medici fiscali*, but many cases were handled without recourse to medical opinion. The authority of the Auditore Fiscale over madness grew from the second half of the eighteenth century onward, in part due to the office's involvement in the admission procedure to Santa Dorotea. The intensification of their involvement is accompanied by a rise in cases of deviant behavior openly or obliquely connected to madness disclosed directly to the office of the Fiscale. By 1770, Domenico Brichieri Colombi, who had headed the office since 1753, had acquired a reputation as an expert in madness within the grand ducal administration, so it was only logical that he was consulted on the state of mind of people denounced for mental incapacity to the Magistrato dei Pupilli.

Madness was an object of police interest, regardless of whether it made its appearance in civil procedures, criminal prosecutions, or private petitions that did not go to trial. Nonetheless, the involvement of the Fiscale was no longer limited to order and control, and he had begun to play a more decisive role as an expert on madness. His gradually accumulated knowledge was therefore integrated with his previous power to imprison and acquit individuals based on criteria of order and good government. In a characteristic more evident in Domenico Brichieri Colombi than his predecessors, we see the Fiscale skillfully resorting to categories and notions of madness gained through his practical involvement with mental deviance, to the extent of providing precise categorizations that closely resembled medical diagnosis. We thus observe him giving straightforward judgments regarding the mental state of people who had only been vaguely described in previous testimonies.

A close examination of the evolution of the categories used to describe the mental incapacity of Cosimo Cambellotti is indicative of the role that the Auditori Fiscali came to play in determining legal mental incapacity. He was interdicted for the first time in 1768, at 65 years old, followed by a second interdiction 7 years later, both times at the request of his son. The main focus of both petitions, as usual, was Cosimo's advanced age and economic mismanagement: his inveterate lack of economy, negligent administration, and compulsive selling of household goods had resulted in repeated incarcerations.[95] The connection between bad administration and mental derangement was made explicit in the supporting testimonies, which gave a more nuanced description of Cosimo's mental state. In the first interdiction, the son's allegation was supported by two testimonies signed by two priests and several acquaintances, stating he was known to be "not only of weak head, but also half mad" (*capo debole* and *mezzo pazzo*), so that due to his "mad conduct" (*pazza condotta*) he had not only reduced himself to a miserable state, but had also been incarcerated several times, and even committed to hospital on two occasions.[96]

No further information was required to decree the interdiction in 1768. However, in 1775, Cosimo Cambelloti was again denounced by his son, who now described the family's precarious economic situation as a result of his father's "advanced age," "extravagances," and violent reactions. On this occasion, the authorities resorted to the Auditore Fiscale to gather further information. Domenico Brichieri Colombi, who at that point had over two decades of practical experience with cases of madness, gave a testimony that was not limited to confirming the economic mismanagement and public disorder caused by the defendant. Testimonies had asserted that Cosimo was a "disturbed, violent and uneasy man" (*uomo torbido, violento ed inquieto*) who lived "arbitrarily" and hampered the cultivation of his lands, "moved only by his extravagant ideas and his uneasy spirit."[97] In the eyes of Brichieri Colombi, the defendant's behavior, "as it tends to the destruction of his own possessions and that of the petitioner, his son, seems to be that of a person who has an altered fantasy," which combined with his "disturbed, violent and uneasy nature" and the four criminal prosecutions carried out against him hitherto were more than enough to declare his mental incapacity and order the interdiction.[98] The Fiscale's testimony was both the synthesis of the different gazes involved in the case and the creation of new diagnostic categories nurtured by his previous involvement in similar cases, as seen in the inclusion of the idea of an altered fantasy to explain Cosimo's wild behavior.

* * *

Throughout the century, authority over madness continued to be in the hands of those who had traditionally held it –that is, families and priests. Study of the parties involved in the assessment of mental incapacity suggests that medical practitioners and the Auditori Fiscali tried to establish an authority over matters of the mind that had traditionally been occupied by families and priests. Their success was not even, however. On the one hand, the evidence suggests that the introduction of medical knowledge in the Tuscan courts was as slow, as it was in other European societies. Medical testimonies were neither necessary nor sufficient to assess mental incapacity or criminal insanity in the eighteenth-century courts of law. In contrast, the office of the Auditore Fiscale became more relevant to the legal assessment of mental affliction. The records show them exerting increasing influence on the decisions of the authorities and in the resolution of conflicts involving madness.

Physicians and priests adjusted their vocabulary to the needs and concerns of petitioners, resulting in a language that was predominantly simple and concentrated on practical indicators of deviant behavior. Thus, it was not only petitioners and lay witnesses who changed their lexicon according to the context in which they spoke, but also medical practitioners and priests. This careful choice of language is paralleled by the authorities, who similarly employed their categories according to each context, adapting their languages to the requirements of each institutional space. This is particularly clear in the vocabulary of the Auditori Fiscali, who through their increasing involvement with madness, were able to construct a language of their own that changed according to whether they were acting in their capacity as chief of police; as regulators of the admission procedure to the mental hospital; as supervisors of criminal justice; or as mediators between the families, the central administration, and the mentally afflicted.

Any assessment of who were the recognized authorities and experts on madness, and of how their insight was valued, must take the agency of petitioners into account. The introduction of testimonies signed by priests or medical practitioners, or recourse to the authority of the Auditore Fiscale underscores the agency of the parties involved and the strategies employed by family members to resolve their private conflicts. Even the figure of the Auditore Fiscale, who apparently personifies the progressive concentration of executive power of the Ancien Régime,[99] can be seen negotiating with family members, intervening in private conflicts, and being called as an expert on matters of the family and the mind by the Magistrato dei Pupilli. Medical practitioners and priests played the role requested by family members, whether to prove someone's sanity or assert his or her insanity. For this reason, the involvement of medical testimonies in the legal assessment of mental disturbance reflects more the strategies adopted by families to litigate their cases than the absence of a recognized authority over matters of the mind.

That said, although medical practitioners had little impact in the Tuscan institutional and legal management of madness, there is sufficient evidence in the records to assert that a specialized medicine of the mind had started to develop (and to be recognized as such). This change is observed in the introduction of more precise medical lexicons toward the second half of the century, when Tuscan judicial practice begun to ascribe a certain place to medical practitioners as the new experts on the mind, exemplified by the roles assumed by Antonio Lulli and Giovanni Targioni Tozzetti. In the end, it should be taken into account that the relatively low impact of medical testimonies in interdiction procedures and criminal justice cannot be taken as proof of the lack of prestige of the medical profession in Tuscan society. In other words, when assessing the involvement of medical knowledge in the shaping of notions of insanity, we must bear in mind that litigation and the public management of madness constitute a source that gives only a partial view of the phenomenon. The fact that in some cases, after years of litigation, we are informed that medical practitioners had been in contact with both the litigants and the authorities is particularly revealing. The institutional spaces of madness, accessed through legal records and supplication narratives, simply did not require the direct involvement of medical knowledge.

Notes

1 The development of legal medicine and the growing importance acquired by medical practitioners as expert authorities on the body in early modern Italian courts have been the subject of the studies carried out by Alessandro Pastore and Silvia de Renzi. See Alessandro Pastore, *Il medico in tribunale: La perizia medica nella procedura penale d'antico regime (secoli XVI–XVIII)* (Bellinzona: Casagrande, 1998); Silvia De Renzi, "La natura in tribunale. Conoscenze e pratiche medico-legali a Roma nel XVII secolo," *Quaderni Storici* 108, no. 3 (2001): 799–822; and Silvia De Renzi, "Medical Expertise, Bodies and the Law in Early Modern Courts," *Isis* 98, no. 2 (2007): 315–322. For a European overview, see Michael Clark and Catherine Crawford, eds., *Legal Medicine in History* (Cambridge: Cambridge University Press, 1994).
2 Graziella Magherini and Vittorio Biotti, "Madness in Florence in the 14th–18th Centuries: Judicial Inquiry and Medical Diagnosis, Care and Custody,"

International Journal of Law and Psychiatry 21, no. 4 (1998): 362; and Graziella Magherini and Vittorio Biotti, *L'isola delle Stinche e i percorsi della follia a Firenze nei secoli XIV–XVIII* (Florence: Ponte alle Grazie, 1992). Elizabeth Mellyn has also challenged the notion of the leading role played by medical knowledge and medico-legal treatises like Zacchia's in the shaping of lay notions of insanity discussed in the Tuscan courts. See Elizabeth W. Mellyn, *Mad Tuscans and Their Families: A History of Mental Disorder in Early Modern Italy* (Philadelphia: University of Pennsylvania Press, 2014), Chapter 5. The legal assessment of insanity in criminal and civil courts during the eighteenth century continued to be a matter of common sense not only in Tuscany, but largely throughout Europe. See Robert Allan Houston, "Courts, Doctors, and Insanity Defences in 18th and Early 19th Century Scotland," *International Journal of Law and Psychiatry* 26, no. 4 (2003): 339–354; Robert Allan Houston "Professions and the Identification of Mental Incapacity in Eighteenth-Century Scotland," *Journal of Historical Sociology* 14, no. 4 (2001): 441–466; and Joel Peter Eigen, *Witnessing Insanity: Madness and Mad-Doctors in the English Court* (New Haven and London: Yale University Press, 1995), 95.
3 See, for instance, ASF, MPAP, *Memoriali*, F. 2300, no. 249, July 1728, no. 399, October 1732 and no. 457, November 1734.
4 Paolo Zacchia, *Quaestionum medico-legalium tomi tres* (Nuremberg: Joannis Georgii Lochneri, 1726), Book II, Title I, 112–159; and Marc'Antonio Savelli, *Pratica universale* (Parma: Paolo Monti, 1717), 107–108.
5 Report of the Magistrato Supremo regarding the petition to interdict Diacinto Cicci, not granted. ASF, MS, *Suppliche*, F. 1185, fol. 375v and fol. 388, June 1734.
6 This is the case of Geri Gori, interdicted for prodigality in 1750. See ASF, MPAP, *Memoriali*, F. 2302, no. 198, July 1750; ASF, SMN, F. 206, fol. 808, when he was transferred to Santa Dorotea in 1754; ASF, SD, *Motupropri, Rescritti* . . ., F. 1, no. 67 and no. 74, 1755, when he was discharged from Santa Dorotea and interned again months later. However, the majority of patients committed to Santa Dorotea do not appear in the records of the Pupilli, attesting for the complete dissociation between interdiction and confinement. After the changes to the legal framework in Tuscany at the end of the eighteenth century, interdiction and confinement came to be united in the same procedure.
7 The practice of appointing a medical practitioner from the community (called *medico condotto* or *cerusico condotto*) was designed to provide a medical cure for those who could not pay for it privately. According to the studies of Carlo Cipolla, inquiries carried out by the Grand Duchy in times of epidemics suggest that the number of medical practitioners throughout the territory was surprisingly high. See Carlo Cipolla, *Contro un nemico invisibile. Epidemie e strutture sanitarie nell'Italia del Rinascimento* (Bologna: Il Mulino, 1985), 287.
8 ASF, MPAP, *Memoriali*, F. 2307, no. 2, March 1767.
9 ASF, MPAP, *Memoriali*, F. 2307, no. 22, April 1767.
10 This is the case when we only have access to the decrees of interdiction but not to its documentary basis or when the procedure was initiated directly before the court and not through written petitions, thus leaving less information.
11 The evidence studied by Elizabeth Mellyn, mostly from the fifteenth and sixteenth centuries, is striking for its similarity in many aspects with the eighteenth-century lexicon. Part of the terminology, which is most deeply entrenched in the Roman legal tradition, was falling into disuse. But by and large, reference to the effects of madness in terms of making the individual devoid of reason, alienated from reason, taking them out of their senses (*lo cavano del cervello, lo cava del sentimento*), which formed the basis of the judicial treatment of madness in the previous centuries, is still at the core of the medical argumentation in the eighteenth century. Mellyn, *Mad Tuscans*, 39–40, 44 and *passim*.

12 The same argument is made by Lisa Roscioni regarding the *medical perizie* that preceded committal to Santa Dorotea. See Lisa Roscioni, *Il governo della follia. Ospedali, medici e pazzi nell'età moderna* (Milan: Bruno Mondadori, 2003), 269.
13 Jonathan Andrews and Andrew Scull, *Customers and Patrons of the Mad-Trade: The Management of Lunacy in Eighteenth-Century London* (Berkeley: University of California Press, 2003), 45–48; Barbara Duden, *The Woman Beneath the Skin: A Doctor's Patients in Eighteenth-Century Germany* (Cambridge: Harvard University Press, 1998), 62–71, 94–95 and *passim*; Robert Weston, *Medical Consulting by Letter in France, 1665–1789* (London and New York: Routledge, 2016), 93–112; Michael Stolberg, *Experiencing Illness and the Sick Body in Early Modern Europe* (Basingstoke: Palgrave Macmillan, 2011), 68–76; among others.
14 Although customary practice dictated that two credible testimonies supporting a petition for interdiction were sufficient, many of these testimonies were signed by more than 10 people. Among the names, servants, kin, authorities, priests, and medical practitioners were mingled in no clear order. When witnesses could not write their names, a note was added stating that the testimony had been signed by another in the deponents' presence, at their request and after its content had been read to them. Some of these names had an individual comment added to the signature with the same characters, that is, handwritten by the signee.
15 ASF, MPAP, *Memoriali*, F. 2302, no. 129, July 1749.
16 ASF, MPAP, *Memoriali*, F. 2300, no. 235, January 1727/28.
17 For example, there is the testimony of Leonardo Berti, surgeon from San Gaudenzio, attesting to Gaspero Pratesi's fitness and capacity to administer his affairs. The surgeon specified that despite his advanced age, Gaspero was in possession of a healthy body and was consequently still active and successful in the public world. Pratesi had been interdicted because he had allegedly "gone childish" (*rimbambito*), but when he petitioned immediately afterwards for the interdiction to be lifted, the magistrates considered that his successful businesses and the testimonies he provided proved that he was neither prodigal nor imbecile. ASF, MPAP, *Memoriali*, F. 2306, no. 262 and no. 284, August 1766.
18 ASF, MPAP, *Memoriali*, F. 2302, no. 113, June 1749.
19 ASF, MPAP, *Memoriali*, F. 2304, no. 70, October 1756.
20 ASF, MPAP, *Memoriali*, F. 2306, no. 262, July 1766 and no. 284, August 1766.
21 Doctors had a university education and were from the upper classes. On the contrary, surgeons were generally of lower status and started to receive practical training in hospitals only in the seventeenth century. Considered artisans, surgeons theoretically could only work on the external surface of the body. Elena Brambilla, "La medicina del Settecento: dal monopolio dogmatico alla professione scientifica," in *Storia d'Italia, Annali 7, Malattia e medicina*, ed. Franco della Peruta (Turin: Einaudi, 1984), 5–81; and Cipolla, *Contro un nemico invisibile*, 270–324.
22 See, for instance, Roscioni, *Il governo della follia*; Roy Porter, *Mind-Forg'd Manacles: A History of Madness in England from the Restoration to the Regency* (London: Penguin Books, 1990); Andrews and Scull, *Customers and Patrons*; Jonathan Andrews and Andrew Scull, *Undertaker of the Mind: John Monro and Mad-Doctoring in Eighteenth-Century England* (Berkeley: University of California Press, 2001).
23 Antonio Lulli was the physician of Santa Dorotea between 1756 and 1788. Giovanni Targioni Tozzetti was first the physician of the Stinche prison and was then appointed *medico fiscale* in 1758. In 1757, he was in charge of the official assessment of *pazzia furiosa* in the admission procedure of Santa Dorotea together with Lodovico Scutellari. Francesco Antonio Viligiardi was appointed substitute *medico fiscale* in 1758. Their involvement in the treatment and

214 *Experts and authorities on madness*

assessment of madness has been studied by Roscioni, *Il governo della follia*, 265–292 and *passim*.

24 Giuseppe Del Papa, *Consulti medici*, vols. 1–2 (Rome: Appresso Giovanni Maria Salvioni, 1733), Antonio Cocchi, *Consulti medici*, vols. 1 and 2 (Bergamo: Vincenzo Antoine, 1791), and BNCF, *Manoscritti*, GTT, nos. 234–235. For the conceptualization of mental diseases in Italian medicine before the eighteenth century, see Roscioni, *Il governo della follia*, 217–243; Alessandro Dini, ed., *Il medico e la follia. Cinquanta casi di malattia mentale della letteratura medica italiana del Seicento* (Florence: Le Lettere, 1997); and Rita Mazza, "La malattia mentale nella medicina del Cinquecento: tassonomia e casi clinici," in *Follia, psichiatria e società. Istituzioni manicomiali, scienza psichiatrica e classi sociali nell'Italia moderna e contemporanea*, ed. Alberto De Bernardi (Milan: Franco Angeli, 1982), 304–317.

25 For instance, according to Houston, the lack of straightforward words like "mad" or "madness" in documents from the civil courts of Scotland responds to the intention to avoid terms that could be taken as offensive by defendants. Robert Allan Houston, *Madness and Society in Eighteenth-Century Scotland* (Oxford: Oxford University Press, 2000), 341.

26 Epilepsy and apoplexy were frequent complains in medical consultations by letter of the period in the Italian peninsula and in other parts of Europe as well. See, for instance, Del Papa, *Consulti medici*; Antonio Felici, *Consulti medici*, vols. 1–2, Wellcome Library, MS.2344–2345; Giacomo Bartolomeo Beccari, *Consulti medici*, vols. 1–2 (Bologna: Dalla Stamperìa di San Tommaso d'Aquino, 1777). For some studies on the topic, see Weston, *Medical Consulting*; and Andrews and Scull, *Customers and Patrons*, among others.

27 For example, according to Stolberg, "The dangers of a stroke appear to have been widely known among the general population, and the more technical synonym 'apoplexy' was commonly used," and even more, "It seems that laypeople thought about apoplexy and its causes in much the same way as physicians." Similarly, epilepsy, he states, was not only widely known but especially feared. Stolberg, *Experiencing Illness*, 92–93 and 52, respectively.

28 Giovanni Targioni Tozzetti on the prisoner Giuseppe Martini, charged with murder and sentenced to 10 years in prison. His original penalty had already been commuted to a lighter one on account of his epilepsy, but, almost 2 years later, he petitioned again for the *grazia* "to be liberated from prison, or his penalty to be commuted to a lenient one that would keep him alive." ASF, OGB, *Suppliche*, F. 2542, no. 130, July 1768.

29 Interdiction of Rinaldo Tedaldi. ASF, MPAP, *Memoriali*, F. 2305, no. 150, August 1761.

30 ASF, MPAP, *Memoriali*, F. 2304, no. 54, July 1756.

31 ASF, MPAP, *Memoriali*, F. 2305, no. 150, August 1761.

32 ASF, MPAP, *Memoriali*, F. 2304, no. 71, January 1757.

33 ASF, MPAP, *Memoriali*, F. 2304, no. 59, October 1756.

34 The interdiction decree only stated that he had become "demented" based on the "testimonies and justifications" presented in court. When the justifications to support a petition for interdiction were made in person, they were usually recorded in the *Atti* of the Magistrato Supremo, which for the months in question unfortunately are not available for consultation. A copy of these testimonies, nonetheless, was provided in 1750 in ASF, MPAP, *Memoriali*, F. 2302, no. 202, June 1750, and thus we know that Valloni's mental incapacity was assessed without recourse to medical opinion. The interdiction decree can be found in ASF, MPAP, *Memoriali*, F. 2302, no. 29, May 1748.

35 ASF, MPAP, *Memoriali*, F. 2302, no. 178, March 1750.

36 ASF, MPAP, *Memoriali*, F. 2302, no. 202, June and July 1750.

37 ASF, MPAP, *Memoriali*, F. 2302, no. 178, February 1750.
38 The informant signed only with his name but was referred to as *dottore* by the Pupilli officials. In general, physicians used the titles of *medico fisico*, *dottore in medicina*, or *membro del Collegio dei Medici*; however, the accurate medical details provided by this report suggest that he was a doctor of medicine.
39 ASF, MPAP, *Atti e sentenze*, F. 1280, June 1750, fol. 994. The spirits, according to the Hippocratic–Galenic explanatory framework, were the connectors between body and soul, and the animal spirits were located in the brain and acted as mediators commanding cognitive functions, perceptions, and bodily functions. Mechanistic explanations conceptualized the movement of animal spirits as commanded by the brain through a network of fibers, which was to become the nervous system.
40 Testimony of Girolamo Ricci, "First Physician" of Volterra on Francesco del Mazza's health condition. ASF, CR, F. 758, no. 20, May 1753. No medical testimony had been required to assess his madness when he was interdicted and confined in the Fortezza 5 years earlier.
41 ASF, CR, F. 758, no. 20, October 1748.
42 According to humoral theory, there were six non-natural factors that governed health and disease: air, sleep and waking, food and drink, excretion and retention, movement and rest, and the accidents of the soul. Several studies have explored how this theory marked the experience of health and the body. Among them, see Sandra Cavallo and Tessa Storey, eds., *Conserving Health in Early Modern Culture* (Manchester: Manchester University Press, 2017); Joël Coste, *Les éscrits de la souffrance. La consultation médicale en France (1550–1825)* (Seyssel: Champ Vallon, 2014); Sandra Cavallo and Tessa Storey, *Healthy Living in Late Renaissance Italy* (Oxford: Oxford University Press, 2013) and Séverine Pilloud and Micheline Louis-Courvoisier, "The Intimate Experience of the Body in the Eighteenth Century: Between Interiority and Exteriority," *Medical History* 47 (2003): 451–472.
43 Andrea Pasta, *Dei mali senza materia* (Bergamo: Stamperia Locatelli, 1791), 17.
44 Mellyn, *Mad Tuscans*, 149–150.
45 For a sample of this fruitful scholarship, see Angela Groppi, "La malinconia di Lucrezia Barberini d'Este," in *I linguaggi del potere nell'età barocca*, vol. 2, *Donne e sfera pubblica*, ed. Francesca Cantù (Rome: Viella, 2009), 197–227; Angus Gowland, *The Worlds of Renaissance Melancholy: Robert Burton in Context* (Cambridge and New York: Cambridge University Press, 2006); Magdalena S. Sánchez, "Melancholy and Female Illness: Habsburg Women and Politics at the Court of Philip III," *Journal of Women's History* 8, no. 2 (1996): 81–102; H.C. Erik Midelfort, *A History of Madness in Sixteenth-Century Germany* (Stanford, CA: Stanford University Press, 1999); Michael MacDonald, *Mystical Bedlam: Madness, Anxiety, and Healing in Seventeenth-Century England* (Cambridge: Cambridge University Press, 1981). Recent historiography has cast doubt on the extent to which melancholy occupied the attention of physicians in sixteenth- and seventeenth-century Italy. Cavallo and Storey, *Healthy Living*, 179–208.
46 Probably not coincidentally, one of the four interdictions that employed the term is a remarkably well-documented one. The case is discussed at length in the next chapter.
47 For instance, ASF, CR, *Spedale de Pazzi*, F. 426, Ins. 7; ASF, SD, *Motupropri, Rescritti . . .*, F. 1, no. 45, January 1754; and BNCF, *Manoscritti*, GTT, no. 235, vol. III, "Relazioni in casi di demenza," fol. 208. On the medical use of *delirio*, *fissazioni*, and *fantasia alterata* as symptoms of eighteenth-century Tuscan madness, see Roscioni, *Il governo della follia*, 171–276. On the Renaissance conceptualization of madness as melancholy, frenzy, and mania, see Gowland's useful overview in *The Worlds of Renaissance Melancholy*, 33–97.

48 Respectively, ASF, CR, *Spedale de Pazzi*, F. 426, no. 7, March 1759; and ASF, MPAP, *Memoriali*, F. 2303, no. 245, February 1755.
49 Respectively, ASF, SD, *Motupropri, Rescritti* . . ., F. 3, no. 41, December 1758, and no. 39, October 1758; and ASF, SD, *Motupropri, Rescritti* . . ., F. 8, no. 72, January 1771.
50 Respectively, ASF, SD, *Motupropri, Rescritti* . . ., F. 8, no. 90, April 1771; and ASF, CR, *Fiscale*, F. 756, no. 7, July 1760.
51 Testimony of Francesco Viligiardi regarding Antonina Perini. ASF, MPAP, *Memoriali*, F. 2309, no. 114, July 1773. Antonina Perini was confined and interdicted on account of her *furore erotico* and *pazzione amorosa*. Her case has been examined in Roscioni, *Il governo della follia*, 3–18.
52 Diseases of the imagination were not new to the eighteenth century. For a call to a reconsideration of the chronology of hypochondriac melancholy, see Yasmin Haskell, "The Anatomy of Hypochondria: Malachias Geiger's *Microcosmus hypochondriacus* (Munich, 1652)," in *Diseases of the Imagination and Imaginary Disease in the Early Modern Period*, ed. Yasmin Haskell (Turnhout: Brepols, 2011), 275–299.
53 See the work of Tuscan physicians such as Giuseppe del Papa, Antonio Cocchi, and Giovanni Targioni Tozzetti, paralleled by the publications of other Italian physicians. Del Papa, *Consulti medici*; Cocchi, *Consulti medici*; BNCF, *Manoscritti*, GTT, no. 234, "Consultationes medicae," cart.2, fasc. X, *Consulti per affezioni ipocondriache ed isteriche*; Armillei, Gaetano, *Consulti medici di vari professori*, vols. 1–2 (Venice: Presso Giuseppe Corona, 1743–1745); Niccolò Cirillo, *Consulti medici*, vols. 1–2 (Venice: Presso Francesco Pitteri, 1770), among others.
54 Jonathan Andrews, "'In Her Vapours . . . [or] Indeed in Her Madness'? Mrs Clerke's Case: An Early Eighteenth-Century Psychiatric Controversy," *History of Psychiatry* 1, no. 1 (1990): 125–143.
55 ASF, MPAP, *Memoriali*, F. 2303, no. 67, December 1752; and ASF, MPAP, *Memoriali*, F. 2306, no. 140, December 1764.
56 ASF, MPAP, *Memoriali*, F. 2306, no. 140, December 1764.
57 As a result of their different nature, the records of his committal are far briefer than the records of the interdiction procedure, which contain exceptionally detailed accounts of Corsini's mental affliction. See ASF, MPAP, *Memoriali*, F. 2304, no. 87, December 1756–April 1757, and no. 223, January 1759, compared with ASF, SD, *Motupropri, Rescritti* . . ., F. 2, no. 40, December 1756, and F. 3, no. 11, April 1758, and no. 44 February 1759.
58 Respectively, ASF, MPAP, *Memoriali*, F. 2304, no. 87, December 1756; and ASF, SD, *Motupropri, Rescritti* . . ., F. 2, no. 40, December 1756.
59 Testimony of the physician Giovanni Torello Leoni, ASF, MPAP, *Memoriali*, F. 2304, no. 87, November 1756.
60 ASF, MPAP, *Memoriali*, F. 2304, no. 87, December 1756.
61 Testimony signed by Antonio Lulli and Antonio Sani, respectively, physician and surgeon of Santa Dorotea, ASF, MPAP, *Memoriali*, F. 2304, no. 87, March 1757.
62 *Angustia* was defined as "*Miseria, Affanno, Afflizione, Travaglio*," coming from the Latin "*Anxietas, solicitudo, angustia*," with a second meaning "*istrettezza, brevità*." *Vocabolario degli accademici della Crusca* (Florence: Appresso Domenico Maria Manni, 1729–1738), s.v. "angustia," www.lessicografia.it/Controller?lemma=ANGUSTIA, accessed August 8, 2020.
63 ASF, MPAP, *Memoriali*, F. 2304, no. 87, March 1757. In fact, following Corsini's request, the administration of his patrimony was entrusted to a third party.
64 According to Antonio Corsini's recounting, Domenico Nardi was his testamentary tutor for 4 years, in which position he continued unofficially for a further 9 years. He was, then, at least 27 years old when interdicted and confined to Santa Dorotea.

Experts and authorities on madness 217

65 ASF, MPAP, *Memoriali*, F. 2304, no. 87, March 1757.
66 MacDonald, *Mystical Bedlam*, 72–11; Andrews and Scull, *Customers and Patrons*, 110–112; and Houston, *Madness and Society*, 281–287.
67 In 1758, Antonio Corsini appears again at Santa Dorotea, from where he was discharged in 1759 after a testimony signed by Giovanni Targioni Tozzetti recommended "fresh air" and the joys of the countryside as the best course of treatment, provided he were to be under "the custody and direction of a wise person" who could "dominate him, supervise his behavior in the future" and regulate his diet and general regimen. ASF, SD, *Motupropri, Rescritti . . .*, F. 3, no. 11; ASF, MPAP, *Memoriali*, F. 2304, no. 223, February 1759, and BNCF, *Manoscritti*, GTT, no. 235, "Relazioni in casi di demenza," fols. 203–204v, respectively.
68 Roy Porter, ed., *The Popularization of Medicine, 1650–1850* (London and New York: Routledge, 1992). Unfortunately, the cultural impact of books of medical divulgation and domestic medicine, which were an editorial success during the century, has not been studied, to my knowledge, in the Italian Peninsula. For the impact of health regimens during the sixteenth and seventeenth centuries in Italy, see Cavallo and Storey, *Healthy Living*.
69 ASF, MPAP, *Memoriali*, F. 2303, no. 50, July 1752.
70 ASF, MPAP, *Memoriali*, F. 2303, no. 50, June 1752.
71 ASF, MPAP, *Memoriali*, F. 2303, no. 50, August 1752.
72 ASF, MPAP, *Memoriali*, F. 2303, no. 84, December 1752.
73 For instance, ASF, OGB, *Suppliche*, F. 2532, no. 15, August 1752, or ASF, OGB, *Suppliche*, F. 2542, no. 130, July 1768 and no. 186, January 1769.
74 BNCF, *Manoscritti*, GTT, no. 235, "Relazioni in casi di demenza," fols. 202–260.
75 For instance, ASF, MPAP, *Memoriali*, F. 2303, no. 245, February 1755; and ASF, MPAP, *Memoriali*, F. 2304, no. 223, February 1759.
76 BNCF, *Manoscritti*, GTT, no. 234, "Consultationes medicae," cart. 2, fasc. X, *Consulti per affezioni ipocondriache ed isteriche*.
77 It should be noted that references to these issues served more to demonstrate that the person's general behavior was at odds with societal norms than to suggest that un-Catholic behavior was madness *per se*.
78 ASF, MPAP, *Memoriali*, F. 2301, no. 201, September 1743.
79 "Gravezza" could also mean affliction, trouble, or anguish. See *Vocabolario*, s.v. "gravezza," www.lessicografia.it/Controller?lemma=GRAVEZZA, accessed August 8, 2020.
80 ASF, MPAP, *Memoriali*, F. 2301, no. 164(2°), May 1745.
81 The contention that the patrimony was too scant to afford the interdiction fees and the involvement of the Pupilli was a common argument made by the interdicted when they petitioned to regain their civil rights. The Pupilli's response varied according to the particulars of each case, but it was generally agreed that what mattered most was the conservation of economic resources, so if the interdiction proved to be more detrimental than the allegedly poor administration of the interdicted, the latter was considered the lesser evil.
82 ASF, MS, *Atti*, F. 1914, December 1730, fol. 1000.
83 Elisa Novi Chavarria, "Ideologia e comportamenti familiari nei predicatori italiani fra Cinque e Settecento. Tematiche e modelli," *Rivista Storica Italiana* 100, no. 3 (1988): 704–705.
84 ASF, MPAP, *Memoriali*, F. 2307, no. 147, June 1768.
85 For instance, Chiara La Rocca has argued that priests were behind strategies to solve matrimonial crises before a couple would resort to the *separatio thori*. Chiara La Rocca, *Tra moglie e marito. Matrimoni e separazioni a Livorno nel Settecento* (Bologna: Società editrice Il Molino, 2009), 315. The role of priests as mediators between social actors and institutions in the administration of justice is at the core of Ottavia Niccoli's study on the meanings of forgiveness in

judicial practice. See Ottavia Niccoli, *Perdonare. Idee, pratiche, rituali in Italia tra Cinque e Seicento* (Rome: Laterza, 2007).
86 R. Burr Litchfield, *Emergence of a Bureaucracy: The Florentine Patricians, 1530–1790* (Princeton, NJ: Princeton University Press, 1986).
87 ASF, MPAP, *Memoriali*, F. 2300, no. 471, February–March 1734/35.
88 Note of the Council of Regency to Brichieri Colombi referring to the situation as reported by the administrative board of Santa Dorotea, October 1757. ASF, CR, *Spedale de Pazzi*, F. 426, Ins. 4.
89 ASF, CR, *Spedale de Pazzi*, F. 426, October 1757.
90 Note of Brichieri Colombi to the Council of Regency, October 1758. ASF, CR, *Fiscale*, F. 759, no. 76.
91 Note of the Council of Regency to Brichieri Colombi referring to the situation as reported by the administrative board of Santa Dorotea, October 1757. ASF, CR, *Spedale de Pazzi*, F. 426, Ins. 4.
92 In August 1761, the administrator of Santa Dorotea wrote to the Council of Regency informing them once more of Giorgio Jacquet's ongoing situation. The issue was that when committed he would cease to experience his frenzies caused by excessive alcohol consumption but invariably, once released, would relapse into them. ASF, CR, *Spedale de Pazzi*, F. 426, Ins. 4, August 1761.
93 ASF, SD, *Motupropri, Rescritti* . . ., F. 3, no. 1, January 1758.
94 ASF, CR, *Fiscale*, F. 759, no. 76, October 1758.
95 See, respectively, ASF, MPAP, *Memoriali*, F. 2307, no. 147, December 1767; and ASF, MPAP, *Memoriali*, F. 2310, no. 237, March 1775.
96 ASF, MPAP, *Memoriali*, F. 2307, no. 147, April–May 1758.
97 ASF, MPAP, *Memoriali*, F. 2310, no. 237, testimony dated 22 March, 1775.
98 Report of Domenico Brichieri Colombi, ASF, MPAP, *Memoriali*, F. 2310, no. 237, June 1775.
99 Alessandra Contini, "La città regolata: polizia e amministrazione nella Firenze leopoldina (1777–1782)," in *Istituzioni e società in Toscana nell'età moderna*, vol. 1 (Rome: Ministero per i beni culturali e ambientali, Ufficio centrale per i beni archivistici, 1994), 426–508; and Carlo Mangio, *La polizia toscana. Organizzazione e criteri d'intervento (1765–1808)* (Milan: Giuffrè, 1988).

Bibliography Chapter 5

Manuscripts

Archivio di Stato di Firenze (ASF)

- Consiglio di Reggenza (CR)
  - *Spedale de Pazzi*, F. 426
  - *Pupilli*, F. 746
  - *Fiscale*, F. 754–762
- Magistrato dei Pupilli et Adulti del Principato (MPAP)
  - *Campione di Deliberazioni e Partiti*, F. 108–F. 166
  - *Atti e Sentenze*, F. 1144–F. 1362
  - *Suppliche e informazioni: Memoriali e Negozi di Cancelleria*, F. 2299–F. 2318

- Magistrato Supremo (MS)
  - *Suppliche*, F. 1179–F. 1188
  - *Atti e Scritture*, F. 1845–F. 2103
- Ospedale di Santa Dorotea (SD), F. 1–F. 59
- Otto di Guardia e Balìa (OGB)
  - *Suppliche*, F. 2499–F. 2542
- Santa Maria Nuova (SMN), F. 206

Biblioteca Nazionale Centrale di Firenze (BNCF)

- *Manoscritti*, Le carte di Giovanni Targioni Tozzetti (GTT), 234–235

Wellcome Library

- Felici, Antonio and others, *Consulti medici*, vols. I–II. MS.2344–MS.2345
- Scovolo, Giacomo, and others. Archival material. *Consulti medici*. MS4472

Printed sources

Armillei, Gaetano. *Consulti medici di vari professori spiegati con le migliori Dottrine Moderne, e co' le regole più esatte della scienza meccanica*, vols. 1–2. Venice: Presso Giuseppe Corona, 1743–1745.
Beccari, Giacomo Bartolomeo. *Consulti medici*, vols. 1–2. Bologna: Dalla Stamperìa di San Tommaso d'Aquino, 1777.
Cirillo, Niccolò. *Consulti medici*, vols. 1–2. Venice: Presso Francesco Pitteri, 1770.
Cocchi, Antonio. *Consulti medici*, vols. 1–2. Bergamo: Vincenzo Antoine, 1791.
Del Papa, Giuseppe. *Consulti medici*, vols. 1–2. Rome: Appresso Giovanni Maria Salvioni, 1733.
Pasta, Andrea. *Dei mali senza materia*. Bergamo: Stamperia Locatelli, 1791.
Savelli, Marc'Antonio. *Pratica universale*. Parma: Paolo Monti, 1717.
Vocabolario degli accademici della Crusca, 6 vols. Florence: Appresso Domenico Maria Manni, 1729–1738. DOI:10.23833/BD/LESSICOGRAFIA, www.lessicografia.it/index.jsp. Accessed August 8, 2020.
Zacchia, Paolo. *Quaestionum medico-legalium tomi tres*. Nuremberg: Sumptibus Joannis Georgii Lochneri, 1726.

References

Andrews, Jonathan. "'In Her Vapours . . . [or] Indeed in Her Madness'? Mrs Clerke's Case: An Early Eighteenth-Century Psychiatric Controversy." *History of Psychiatry* 1, no. 1 (1990): 125–143.
Andrews, Jonathan, and Andrew Scull. *Customers and Patrons of the Mad-Trade: The Management of Lunacy in Eighteenth-Century London*. Berkeley: University of California Press, 2003.
Andrews, Jonathan, and Andrew Scull. *Undertaker of the Mind: John Monro and Mad-Doctoring in Eighteenth-Century England*. Berkeley: University of California Press, 2001.

Brambilla, Elena. "La medicina del Settecento: dal monopolio dogmatico alla professione scientifica." In *Storia d'Italia, Annali 7, Malattia e medicina*, edited by Franco della Peruta, 3–147. Turin: Einaudi, 1984.

Cavallo, Sandra, and Tessa Storey, eds. *Conserving Health in Early Modern Culture*. Manchester: Manchester University Press, 2017.

Cavallo, Sandra, and Tessa Storey. *Healthy Living in Late Renaissance Italy*. Oxford: Oxford University Press, 2013.

Chavarria, Elisa Novi. "Ideologia e comportamenti familiari nei predicatori italiani fra Cinque e Settecento. Tematiche e modelli." *Rivista Storica Italiana* 100, no. 3 (1988): 679–723.

Cipolla, Carlo. *Contro un nemico invisibile. Epidemie e strutture sanitarie nell'Italia del Rinascimento*. Bologna: Il Mulino, 1985.

Clark, Michael, and Catherine Crawford, eds. *Legal Medicine in History*. Cambridge: Cambridge University Press, 1994.

Contini, Alessandra. "La città regolata: polizia e amministrazione nella Firenze leopoldina (1777–1782)." In *Istituzioni e società in Toscana nell'età moderna*, vol. 1, 426–508. Rome: Ministero per i beni culturali e ambientali, Ufficio centrale per i beni archivistici, 1994.

Coste, Joël. *Les éscrits de la souffrance. La consultation médicale en France (1550–1825)*. Seyssel: Champ Vallon, 2014.

De Renzi, Silvia. "La natura in tribunale. Conoscenze e pratiche medico-legali a Roma nel XVII secolo." *Quaderni Storici* 108, no. 3 (2001): 799–822.

De Renzi, Silvia. "Medical Expertise, Bodies and the Law in Early Modern Courts." *Isis* 98, no. 2 (2007): 315–322.

Dini, Alessandro, ed. *Il medico e la follia. Cinquanta casi di malattia mentale della letteratura medica italiana del Seicento*. Florence: Le Lettere, 1997.

Duden, Barbara. *The Woman Beneath the Skin: A Doctor's Patients in Eighteenth-Century Germany*. Cambridge: Harvard University Press, 1998.

Eigen, Joel Peter. *Witnessing Insanity: Madness and Mad-Doctors in the English Court*. New Haven and London: Yale University Press, 1995.

Gowland, Angus. *The Worlds of Renaissance Melancholy: Robert Burton in Context*. Cambridge and New York: Cambridge University Press, 2006.

Groppi, Angela. "La malinconia di Lucrezia Barberini d'Este." In *I linguaggi del potere nell'età barocca, vol. 2. Donne e sfera pubblica*, edited by Francesca Cantù, 197–227. Rome: Viella, 2009.

Haskell, Yasmin. "The Anatomy of Hypochondria: Malachias Geiger's *Microcosmus hypochondriacus* (Munich, 1652)." In *Diseases of the Imagination and Imaginary Disease in the Early Modern Period*, edited by Yasmin Haskell, 275–299. Turnhout: Brepols, 2011.

Houston, Robert Allan. "Courts, Doctors, and Insanity Defences in 18th and Early 19th Century Scotland." *International Journal of Law and Psychiatry* 26, no. 4 (2003): 339–354.

Houston, Robert Allan. *Madness and Society in Eighteenth-Century Scotland*. Oxford: Oxford University Press, 2000.

Houston, Robert Allan. "Professions and the Identification of Mental Incapacity in Eighteenth-Century Scotland." *Journal of Historical Sociology* 14, no. 4 (2001): 441–466.

La Rocca, Chiara. *Tra moglie e marito. Matrimoni e separazioni a Livorno nel Settecento*. Bologna: Società editrice Il Molino, 2009.

Litchfield, R. Burr. *Emergence of a Bureaucracy: The Florentine Patricians, 1530–1790*. Princeton: Princeton University Press, 1986.

MacDonald, Michael. *Mystical Bedlam: Madness, Anxiety, and Healing in Seventeenth-Century England*. Cambridge: Cambridge University Press, 1981.

Magherini, Graziella, and Vittorio Biotti. *L'isola delle Stinche e i percorsi della follia a Firenze nei secoli XIV-XVIII*. Florence: Ponte alle Grazie, 1992.

Magherini, Graziella, and Vittorio Biotti. "Madness in Florence in 14th–18th Centuries: Judicial Inquiry and Medical Diagnosis, Care and Custody." *International Journal of Law and Psychiatry* 21, no. 4 (1998): 355–368.

Mangio, Carlo. *La polizia toscana. Organizzazione e criteri d'intervento (1765–1808)*. Milan: Giuffrè, 1988.

Mazza, Rita. "La malattia mentale nella medicina del Cinquecento: tassonomia e casi clinici." In *Follia, psichiatria e società. Istituzioni manicomiali, scienza psichiatrica e classi sociali nell'Italia moderna e contemporanea*, edited by Alberto De Bernardi, 304–317. Milan: Franco Angeli, 1982.

Mellyn, Elizabeth W. *Mad Tuscans and Their Families: A History of Mental Disorder in Early Modern Italy*. Philadelphia: University of Pennsylvania Press, 2014.

Midelfort, H.C. Erik. *A History of Madness in Sixteenth-Century Germany*. Stanford, CA: Stanford University Press, 1999.

Niccoli, Ottavia. *Perdonare. Idee, pratiche, rituali in Italia tra Cinque e Seicento*. Rome: Laterza, 2007.

Pastore, Alessandro. *Il medico in tribunale: La perizia medica nella procedura penale d'antico regime (secoli XVI-XVIII)*. Bellinzona: Casagrande, 1998.

Pilloud, Séverine, and Micheline Louis-Courvoisier. "The Intimate Experience of the Body in the Eighteenth Century: Between Interiority and Exteriority." *Medical History* 47 (2003): 451–472.

Porter, Roy. *Mind-Forg'd Manacles: A History of Madness in England from the Restoration to the Regency*. London: Penguin Books, 1990.

Porter, Roy, ed. *The Popularization of Medicine, 1650–1850*. London and New York: Routledge, 1992.

Roscioni, Lisa. *Il governo della follia. Ospedali, medici e pazzi nell'età moderna*. Milan: Bruno Mondadori, 2003.

Sánchez, Magdalena S. "Melancholy and Female Illness: Habsburg Women and Politics at the Court of Philip III." *Journal of Women's History* 8, no. 2 (1996): 81–102.

Stolberg, Michael. *Experiencing Illness and the Sick Body in Early Modern Europe*. Basingstoke: Palgrave Macmillan, 2011.

Weston, Robert. *Medical Consulting by Letter in France, 1665–1789*. London and New York: Routledge, 2016.

6 Emotional disturbances and the circulation of the languages of madness

Scholars generally concur that emotions acquired a new visibility during the eighteenth century. Although there is less agreement on whether this defines the eighteenth century as the age of sensibility, scholarly opinion agrees that the century witnessed a renewed debate on the role of emotions in social life, family relationships, religious practice, economic practices, and politics.[1] William Reddy has argued that in revolutionary France, "for a few decades, emotions were deemed to be as important as reason in the foundation of states and the conduct of politics. After 1794, not only was this idea rejected, even its memory was extinguished."[2] In contrast and taking issue with the approach to the period as the age of sentimentalism, Thomas Dixon has claimed that it "was not merely an 'Age of Reason,' but nor was it merely an 'Age of Passions.' It was an age of reason, conscience, self-love, interests, passions, sentiments, affections, feeling and sensibility."[3]

During this century, medical, legal, and lay cultures of knowledge debated the connection between emotions and health and particularly between disturbed emotions and mental disease. This chapter aims to explore the correlations that can be found between medical, legal, and lay conceptions of madness and the role each ascribed to emotional disturbances. It argues that during the eighteenth century, displays of emotional distress were increasingly presented as evidence of mental affliction in Tuscan judicial records. This process was paralleled by the attention paid by contemporary medical literature to anguish, passions, agitations, or perturbations of the soul (*animo*) in the conceptualization of mental disease. Considered as both a cause and symptom of mental disturbance, emotions played a crucial role in eighteenth-century narratives of madness. Judicial descriptions of mad behavior at the beginning of the century were primarily focused on financial mismanagement and breaches of codes of behavior. Toward the second half of the century, descriptions paid increasing attention to psychological states and to the person's patterns of emotional reactions as a way to prove, describe, or illustrate mental affliction.

The eighteenth-century Tuscan provisions to cope with madness served as a space to debate the limits of acceptable emotional displays and the implications of disturbed emotions. In this sense, the language of madness and the role attributed to emotional disturbances as its most determinant indicators are an inherent part of the debate about acceptable behavior. Lay society transferred to this debate wider anxieties about the changing values of family life, intergenerational conflicts, and gender relations, all framed within an overarching concern about financial behavior and patrimony administration. Emotions came to be crucial for distinguishing rational behavior from the indicators of a disturbed mind. Negotiating forms of appropriate emotional display presupposed exploring how emotional reactions affected a person's mind, in which situations certain forms of emotional excess could be accepted, and in which others they had to be condemned. Furthermore, careful considerations had to be taken to establish how these forms of divergent emotional display were to be controlled, disciplined, differentiated, or punished.

This chapter attempts to chart the connection between madness and emotional disturbances by studying the languages of distressed emotional states that were singled out as evidence of mental affliction. It explores the uses and meanings of terms denoting emotional displays that were thought to indicate its presence by paying particular attention to the network of words that accompany them, following the idea that the context that surrounds a term affects, shapes, and conditions its meaning.[4]

I employ the terms "emotions" and "emotional disturbances" being well aware that they are extemporaneous to the eighteenth-century Italian language.[5] The word *emozione* was not in use during the century, but the terms "sentiment," "passion," and "affections" are not more fruitful. The word *sentimento* continued to be used chiefly to mean rational opinion, in the manner of a belief, commonly employed by authorities when they gave their final position on a particular matter. The *Vocabolario degli accademici della Crusca* published in 1729–1738 defined "sentimento" as "sense, intellect, judgement" (*senso, intelletto, senno*), alternatively as "significance, excellence and beauty of a conception," and as "concept, thought, opinion." In fact, expressions such as *uscir del sentimento* and *esser fuor del sentimento* were still used to mean "lose one's senses, become mad, be mad" (*perdere il senno, impazzare, esser pazzo*).[6] Neither *senno* (which meant intellect, wisdom, knowledge, and judgement) nor the derivations from *sentimento* (*sensibilità, sensibile*) had a connection to emotions at the beginning of the eighteenth century in the Italian language. Likewise, the word *affetto* was not employed to mean affections as psychological state in general but exclusively as affection toward another person – in particular, maternal or paternal affection.[7] In the end, the word "passion" (*passione*) was critical for medical language and criminal records during the period but it hardly appears in interdiction records. Thus, framing emotional disturbances under the medical "passions of the soul" was also deemed inadequate.

References to emotional displays are grouped in lay narratives around concepts such as *animo* and *spirito*. Neither of the two terms was disentangled from traditional religious and humoral notions of the soul, but was increasingly employed to mean psychological disposition or emotional state.

To reflect the estrangement from reason in which the person found him or herself, these terms were coupled with *passione, stravagante, inquieto, volubile*, or *irregolare*. It is to translate these compound terms that I employ the concept of "emotional disturbances" to convey the idea that lay, medical, and legal languages considered the manifestations of a disturbed, irregular, changeable, or unstable disposition as the key to a disordered mind.

The forms of emotional disturbance under examination here shed light on how individuals, their families, authorities, and medical or legal professionals reflected on, interpreted, valued, or condemned certain forms of emotional expression. Given that I am interested in contemporary people's evaluation and interpretation of emotions, the problem of how they were felt or even whether they were actually felt is not relevant here. This is not to say that the narratives under study constitute fictions that were completely detached from the reality they were supposed to be describing – in fact, the characteristics of the negotiation between authorities and families sometimes entailed that some denunciations were indeed considered to be deliberate lies, or simply exaggerations, misinterpretations, or partial truths, to the same extent that others were judged to be accurate descriptions. But the focus here is different. For the purpose of elaborating on how certain forms of emotional display were increasingly considered to provide evidence of mental disturbance, the mere allusion to the indicators of these types of emotional display proves the point, regardless of their veracity. In this sense, the scope of this chapter is to assess the instrumental value of denouncing a person for manifesting indicators of emotional disturbance, which simultaneously attests to how emotions were regarded and how certain types of deviant forms of emotional reaction came to be connected with madness. Thus, the very weakness of the sources – their instrumental nature – provides an entry into how families and authorities understood and negotiated forms of accepted behavior and emotional reactions.

Medical approaches to emotional distress

Disturbing emotions were not a new cause in the etiology of madness. As the sixth non-natural or external factor that could affect a person's health – together with air, bodily excretions, diet, sleep, and exercise – passions of the soul could alter the humoral balance, thus affecting the functioning of the body and producing disease.[8] Psychological disturbances – that is, excessive passions or affections – were themselves diseases.[9] As movements of the soul with capacity to mutate the brain, the connections between emotional disturbances (*passioni* or *angustie d'animo*) and mental diseases were entrenched in early modern medical discussions regarding the causes and symptoms of melancholy and mania.[10]

During the eighteenth century, causalities such as emotional disturbances, strong emotional experiences, and life-changing events were discussed by Italian physicians as both cause and symptom of mental disease. Three useful terms to examine the place of emotional perturbations in this discussion are *angustie d'animo*, *agitazioni d'animo*, and *turbazioni d'animo* (anguishes, agitations, and perturbations of the soul). Anguish could be used to mean that the heart or the lungs were under pressure as well as to mean the psychological experience of oppression (*angustia d'animo*).[11] The fact that *trasporti* (transports) were defined as *agitazione* and *commozione d'animo* also points to the fact that *animo* in these contexts was employed to mean disposition or mood rather than the intellective part of the rational soul, or one's thinking, discourse, will, and desire, which were the other definitions given to the word.[12] Agitations, anguish, and perturbations of the soul as a psychological state could be caused, for instance, by "internal passions," "occupations that are disquieting," and "serious and intense affairs" combined with the abuse of liquor.[13] They could also be the effect of the "afflictions and disquiet" suffered due to the long sickness of a spouse[14] or be caused by the "mistreatments" inflicted by a husband, manifested through weight loss, fevers, and uneasiness (*inquietezza*).[15]

The physician Andrea Pasta claimed in his *Dei mali senza materia*, published posthumously in 1791, that *angustie d'animo* or perturbations of the mind/soul had the power to "mutate and correct the structure of the brain and of the nerves."[16] *Angustie d'animo*, regardless of whether they were triggered by real or imagined events, could cause illnesses such as hysteria and hypochondria but could also cure them when treatment was properly conducted. He explained that these diseases were caused "not from excess or vice in the humors, but from a disorder and disturbance in the nervous system" produced by *perturbazione dell'animo* or the *guai dell'animo* such as fear, anger or indignation, sadness, or efforts of the mind. The brain, explained the physician from Bergamo, was particularly sensible to the stimulus of the passions of the soul.[17] In the words of Antonio Felici, a physician from Macerata, "there is no bigger enemy for the membranous and nervous system than the affections of the soul."[18]

According to the Florentine physician Giovanni Targioni Tozzetti, when combined with the individual's predisposition to "excessive agility and irritation of the nerves" and to the "excess of saline and stimulant particles dispersed in the general mass of his humors," the *passioni d'animo* conspired to "overturn his whole nervous system, and especially that of the head."[19] Targioni Tozzetti declared in one of his medical consultations of 1765 that, due to his occupation as *medico fiscale*, he was "obliged to visit and examine almost every [person] diseased with *demenza*" in Tuscany, and he counted up to 80 a year. Of these 80 mentally afflicted patients, he declared that 95% suffered from melancholic delirium caused by emotional disturbances (*deliranti melancolici, per motivo di angustie d'animo*). He explained that, although the numbers were high, the important thing to bear in mind was that at least 90% of these patients would recover completely in a few weeks.[20]

Medical consultations by letter constitute a useful tool to examine how the role played by *turbazioni* or *agitazioni d'animo* was conceived in the

226 *Emotional disturbances*

development and cure of mental derangement. Emotional disturbances were in fact incorporated in the etiology of mental afflictions in the narratives of both the solicitors of medical consultation and in the physician's responses.[21] The key to the understandings of the connection between emotional disturbances and mental disease is found in the characterization of melancholic and manic deliriums or in the symptomatology of hysteric and hypochondriac affections. During the eighteenth century, physicians in their responses to medical consultations frequently incorporated the "diverse and frequent passions of the soul and mental agitations,"[22] "mental fixation on unhappy thoughts,"[23] "a long and dark passion of the soul," accompanied by "obstinate wakefulness" and "disquieting dreams,"[24] or even a "great passion of fear"[25] in their evaluation of the causes and symptoms of mental disease. The symptoms of emotional disturbances ranged from excessive sensibility to external stimuli (*scuotimenti ad ogni piccola sorpresa*) and the tendency to be easily disturbed (*facilità a turbarse nell'animo*), to fear and uneasiness (*inquietudine*) when in darkness, insomnia, and confusion.[26] For instance, patients consulting for what physicians classified as hysteric and hypochondriac affections were said to have a "lively fantasy which apprehends too easily each thing, even if minimal, as if it were big, to the point that every cloud of suspicion, every simple idea of fear terrifies and arouses her."[27] In this state, "only one thought suffices, and a simple imagination of a thing serves in a word to put into agitation her heart and blood and all the animal spirits, and in sum to disturb her whole animal economy."[28]

In another case, a woman's hypochondriac affection, caused by a serious fright (*spavento*), caused her to suffer "great consternations of the soul and apprehension of any disgrace, even of sudden death, especially in the time of the night, and every time she leaves her body free to her troublesome melancholic ideas."[29] "Mental fixations in unhappy thoughts"[30] were also combined with emotional instability, which could turn a melancholic delirium into mania. Someone suffering a melancholic delirium could become "furious almost as maniacs,"[31] or the "altered imagination [*fantasia*]" of another could lead him to

> such a mental instability that at times he cried and at times he laughed... at times he was in bead and at times over a canapé, at times always dressed and at times undressed, at times loaded with fears and at times light, despite the season.[32]

Emotional instability was often accompanied by *inquietudine*. The term was mostly used to convey the feeling and psychological state of disquiet or uneasiness, which would many times come together with physical restlessness, manifested as involuntary movements, spasms, or physical agitation. *Inquietudine* was an inner state closely connected to *perturbazioni d'animo* and anxiety. In these cases, the alteration of "the nervous juices" would become "offensive to the fibers which serve the vital and natural movement of the same [internal] organs, [from which] emerges that internal mad uneasiness [*smaniosa inquietudine*], that is called anxiety [*ansietà*]."[33] The term *inquietudine* is especially interesting given that, although it also appears in medical consultations, it was mostly employed in lay narratives.

Since *angustie d'animo* could cause mental derangement, they were to be avoided at any cost in order to restore health. The contents of Italian medical consultations of the eighteenth century illustrate the extent to which the precepts of the doctrine of the six non-natural factors were still present. Among the indications given to patients consulting for mental and nervous ailments, physicians recommended first and foremost "to escape as if they were poison" any "disturbance" or "forced application of the spirit" that could "disconcert the quietness of the soul" and "to observe a good life regiment with respect to the other five non-natural things."[34] As triggers of mental diseases, patients were advised to avoid *passioni d'animo* at all costs in order to be restored to health. Hence, the importance was ascribed to seeking "cheerfulness of the soul" (*ilarità dell'animo*)[35] through a regulated and well-balanced life, indulging in joyful activities, favoring social life over solitude, and practicing physical exercise. The goal was to achieve the necessary state of "quietness" and "tranquility" (*quiete d'animo* and *tranquillità d'animo*), "far away from any fear."[36] Given that the predominant source of these diseases was emotional disturbances, the best way to control and cure them was for patients to learn how to manage them. During the eighteenth century, therapeutics were moving away from the traditional bleeding and purgatives but still operated within the framework of the six non-naturals. The combination of weather, diet, environment, and emotions were still the key elements in use to counterbalance and hopefully restrain the effects of mental afflictions.[37]

Circulation and re-elaboration of the languages of emotional distress

The attention given to emotional disturbances in the medical literature is also reflected in lay accounts of mental derangement, which suggests an interesting convergence between medical, legal, and lay cultures of knowledge. Interdiction and criminal records and, in general, the accounts given to characterize madness throughout its itinerary reveal that the incapacity to exert control or management over one's emotions was singled out as evidence of a disease whose source was in the mind. This sheds light on the problem of the connections between lay and medical knowledge from an interesting angle, as these narratives suggest that medical theories circulated among the laity and that the flow was not just in one direction. Influences ran in multiple directions; acting among various layers; producing a common resource that litigants, judges and magistrates, medical practitioners, and priests could resort to in order to find a suitable formula to describe mental affliction. Instability, uneasiness, abrupt fits of anger, and any emotional display seen to systematically breach accepted norms are common features in the languages of madness.

Narratives involving defendants who had been interdicted several times or whose families had been involved in various interdiction procedures during the century are especially useful to examine in order to understand the dynamics of the circulation of languages of madness and the interplay between medical, legal, and lay perceptions of insanity. Given that these cases shed light on the experience and management of madness over extended periods of time, they become particularly valuable to study the language used to characterize mental disorder, and how it changed with time. By the same token, they enable us to examine the involvement of medical knowledge and medical explanations in the process of identifying and denouncing a family member for mental incapacity. They also allow us to track the process by which a family, after identifying a mental disturbance, explored different strategies to make sense of the disorder and manage its consequences.

Any attempt to assess the foundations of the lexicon used to describe mental incapacity and its meanings must take into account the contacts that petitioners and family members may have had with medical knowledge prior to the interdiction petition. Previous interdictions in the family, as well as past illnesses or long-term mental afflictions of family members may have resulted in a medical practitioner being contacted. In any case, it must be borne in mind that studies of the treatment of madness outside mental institutions in early modern Europe show the same patterns as the treatment of diseases in general: patients sought medical advice after they had already identified what was wrong with them, asserted a diagnosis, and attempted self-treatment.[38] Furthermore, there was a wide literary spectrum for accessing medical knowledge, from health regimes and books of domestic medicine to compendiums of the art of medicine and surgery published for a nonspecialized public – or which were originally written for medical practitioners but reached a wider audience.[39]

As discussed in the previous chapter, when medical practitioners were involved in interdiction procedures, their testimonies did not always disclose whether their assessment of the patient's condition was based on a single visit or long-term treatment. Further, doctors and surgeons *condotti* often gave their testimony more in their capacity as privileged social witnesses rather than as expert medical practitioners with a particular knowledge of the mental condition under examination. In other words, recourse to medical testimonies does not automatically mean that the defendant had been in previous contact with medical practitioners, and if they had been, we do not necessarily have access to that information. It is possible, however, to find some hints regarding the contacts that the family might have had with medical practitioners before the interdiction, as some of the cases that will be examined here demonstrate.

The evidence suggests that neither a familiarity with the procedure for interdiction and its requirements nor a previous recourse to medical treatment necessarily entails a more precise medical lexicon of mental incapacity. When we know that medical practitioners had been involved in a case, the tendency is for petitioners and defendants to incorporate, reshape, and re-signify medical categories. For instance, in 1761, the relatives of 72-year-old Francesco Rossetti said he had been assaulted by a *furore maniaco* many years before, which his relatives had been forced to treat medically "with great expenditure to the house." Afterwards, he had suffered "a similar mania more, and more times."[40] In this case, the category of mental incapacity used to sustain the interdiction petition is a medical one, but it is employed in a way that is detached from its symptoms, which are not described. When the case reappears later in the records, however, this medical category is not employed. Instead, the only reference to Francesco's mental condition was the mention of his "decrepitude" and of his "capricious" – thus, illogical and irrational – act of abandoning his son's residence, guided by what was seen as an insubstantial desire for "being better."[41] The medical category of *furore maniaco* had been replaced by the more culturally meaningful reference to his unstable and capricious character, which, combined with his advanced age, was held sufficient to illustrate his mental incapacity.

The use of medical terminology was not necessarily conditioned by the direct involvement of medical practitioners. We have seen how in the cases of Lorenzo Baldinotti and Lorenzo Maestrini, both from the first half of the century, their mental disorders were largely characterized with lay and legally embedded terms, even though they had been treated by medical practitioners. A different situation is exemplified by the case of Angiolo Barchesi, interdicted five times between 1735 and 1754. On the one hand, his interdictions were decreed with the involvement of medical opinion. On the other hand, the accounts of the parties involved, including his own, demonstrate an interesting appropriation and re-elaboration of the medical terms employed in the expert testimonies.

Angiolo Barchesi's first interdiction was decreed in November 1735, based on a testimony from Santa Dorotea, which attested that he was in the hospital afflicted by a semi-manic insanity (*insania semimaniosa*).[42] Additional characteristics and the behavioral signs of his insanity were disclosed only in the second interdiction, decreed in May 1737, this time without recourse to medical opinion. While in the first interdiction, we have access only to the testimony given by the keeper of Santa Dorotea, who employed a category rarely used in the hospital records, in the second interdiction we only have access to the description given in a testimony signed by Angiolo's mother, some neighbors, and a priest. In this lay testimony, the technical term "semi-manic insanity" was diluted into plain *demenza*, *pazzia*, and the description of mad actions. The testimony explained that although he had regained his soundness of mind for a while, he had relapsed into his *demenza*, "doing diverse things of a man of unsound mind, such as [signing] contracts with great and evident prejudice" to his interests, accompanied by illogical violence, which made him attack people for no reason.[43] Based upon these signs

230 *Emotional disturbances*

and perhaps taking into account the expert testimony given in 1735, the interdiction decree of 1737 declared that the lay testimony revealed Barchesi "had become completely demented and furious."[44] The interdiction decree made a compound from the lay testimonies, the official category, and the medical label, replacing furiousness with the medical manic insanity (the medical term for the institutional *pazzia furiosa* that described cases susceptible to committal) and combining it with the unavoidable legal term of *demente*.

The narratives describing Angiolo Barchesi's mental afflictions changed over the years, introducing the dimension of emotional affliction. While the two following interdiction procedures were built upon the unspecific categories of *infermo di pazzia* (third interdiction with testimony of the physician of the *pazzeria* of Santa Maria Nuova, 1740)[45] and *demenza* (fourth interdiction, based on the information that he had been sent again to the *pazzeria*, 1746),[46] from 1753 onwards the narratives incorporated more precise categories to describe his mental condition. The change in the lexicon is even more interesting if we take into account how Angiolo himself presented his illness.

We have access to Angiolo Barchesi's voice only after four interdiction procedures and at least four committals.[47] During the time that elapsed between 1735, when the first interdiction was requested, and 1753, when Angiolo sent a written testimony giving his side of the story, his family group had changed. While the first procedures were conducted by Angiolo's mother, by 1753 he had married and his wife and in-laws had taken on that role. His recurrent episodes of madness were disclosed in accordance with the changes in his domestic sphere, as his position of weakness inside the family structure passed from him being the responsibility of his mother to that of his wife. Angiolo's petitions centered precisely around this issue, arguing that the involvement of his wife's male kin and her behavior toward him oppressed him in such a way as to induce him to break his silence and make his voice heard.

According to Angiolo Barchesi's recount, the third episode of mental disturbance that sent him once more to Santa Maria Nuova had been triggered by the profound distress his wife's "cruelties" (*sevizie*) had caused him. She had "capriciously" left the matrimonial residence to live with her father, "on account of which the informant thus troubled [*tribolato*], had a fierce oppression of spirits [*soppressione di spiriti*] that took him out of himself," causing him to be committed, yet again, to the madhouse.[48] But his tribulations went beyond his episode of derangement, for after "heaven gave him the grace after a few months to turn him back to his senses [*ritornarlo in se*]," he had to face a long confrontation with his brother-in-law, who had been appointed administrator of his patrimony during his interdiction. In Angiolo's eyes, his in-laws had taken advantage of his situation, making ill use of his resources, refusing to hand over the accounts of their administration, and obstructing his business as librarian. Once he had regained his soundness of mind and had his civil rights restored, Angiolo initiated litigation against his in-laws, demanding that they pay the numerous debts they had incurred during their administration. Although the authorities sided with Angiolo, his debtors pulled every available string to delay the payment for as long as possible, which ultimately resulted in further unbearable distress for Angiolo, who appears a year later interdicted once more, this time "afflicted by a continual delirium," as reported by the keeper of the *pazzeria* of Santa Maria Nuova.[49]

Over the years, what had initially been framed in terms of a deviant economic performance and a tendency to furious reactions evolved into emotional anguish provoked by a combination of familial conflicts and economic setbacks. It is striking and eloquent that the transition was voiced by the sufferer himself, demonstrating a clear awareness of his recurrent mental disturbances, of what triggered them and of his capacity to overcome them after some months. He could have chosen to deny his past insanity, as many other interdicted men and women did, but instead he chose to use it in the civil litigation against his in-laws to his advantage. Attesting once more to the awareness litigants demonstrate of the consequences of the vocabulary they chose and the situations they disclosed to the authorities, Angiolo Barchesi decided to highlight the emotional distress that the cruelties and subsequent "capricious" abandonment by his wife had inflicted on him. Furthermore, he explicitly connected his emotional distress with insanity and demonstrated an ability to explain it without using any specific medical category.

The transformation at work in the characterization of Angiolo Barchesi's insanity should not be interpreted as necessarily connected to an actual change in the manifestation of his mental disturbance. One possible interpretation is that in 1735, Angiolo suffered a violent outbreak of madness that placed him under what in those times was typified as mania and frenzy, which later evolved into anguish and anxiety, and finally resulted in a (melancholic) delirium. But this is not necessarily the case, and it does not shed sufficient light on how his madness was perceived and understood by him and his relatives. Rather, I propose to interpret the categories employed as being the result of various factors in which the influence of medical knowledge and the course of the affliction mingle with cultural notions, private concerns, agency, and circumstantial developments. The case shows the extent to which insanity was depicted according to the contexts of its disclosure, adapting to the unfolding of the family history, and assuming the forms that most suited the purpose of each litigation.

While the depiction of Angiolo Barchesi's madness was contingent upon his family situation, the line of argumentation chosen by litigants attests to wider changes in the perceptions and attitudes to madness. In this sense, it is not a coincidence that only after 1750 did they refer to the emotional disruptions his familial conflicts caused him, but not before. The same applies to the narratives of Antonio Corsini and Lorenzo Baldinotti, discussed in the previous chapters. The connection between emotions and madness and particularly the role attributed to emotional disturbances as determinant indicators of madness became particularly visible in the second half of the century.

Emotional disturbances in context: venting family conflicts

Particularly in the second half of the century, interdiction procedures involving people who recurrently lapsed into a state of mental incapacity tend to incorporate more eloquent descriptions when the cases are argued anew. Over time and with the experience gained in each litigation, the narratives of mothers, wives, brothers, and sons begin to acquire additional complexity. The more intricate the litigation became and the more frequently relatives turned to the authorities for mediation, the more nuanced the meanings of mental incapacity and the more complicated the scope of its reported consequences become. Initial descriptions that were mainly centered around economic mismanagement or dissipation are complemented in subsequent petitions with new insight into the familial and emotional dimensions of the alleged mental affliction, with narratives delineating with increasing detail the consequences it caused to family life. Similarly, the testimonies produced by the sufferers themselves also tend to acquire a richer vocabulary, depending on their relapses, and so does the reported level of familial conflict surrounding them. The dynamics of family discord and the course of the given mental disorder also played a part in the shaping of the languages of mental incapacity.

Probably no case exemplifies the dynamics and depths of the shaping of a vocabulary of madness better than that of Antonio Becciani, whose mental disturbance was characterized differently as the familial conflicts surrounding him unfolded. Antonio Becciani, from Barberino di Mugello, was first interdicted in 1764 for allegedly being "foolish, stupid and almost mad [*melenso, stupido, e quasi mentecatto*]" and then interdicted a second time in 1771 because for some years he had been under "a profound melancholy, stupid and macilent." Subsequently, he was said to suffer a "dangerous imbecility" and a "melancholic humor," being prone to commit various extravagancies and having a tendency to be overpowered by his "overheated fantasy."[50] The interdiction procedures of Antonio Becciani and the recurring litigations surrounding them conceal, as in many other cases, profound discords, strong animosities, and conflicting agencies in a family that had been strained by the presence of insanity for more than a generation. The leading voices, as on other occasions, were those of two women – Antonio's mother and his wife.

Until 1771, we find no trace of emotional disturbance in the narratives of Antonio Becciani's mental incapacity, and, in fact, if we were to set aside the later developments of his case, we would be tempted to catalogue these procedures as one more example of the apparent predominance of explanations that presented intellectual impairment as a cause of mental incapacity. In 1764, Antonio Becciani's mother, Caterina Puccini, had declared him to be foolish and stupid to the extent of not being able "to distinguish between what was useful and what was harmful." Similarly, on that occasion, the supporting testimonies claimed that even though he was 30 years old, he was unable to manage his affairs on account of his "diminished discernment."[51] However, later proceedings presented Antonio's condition as episodic and with stronger emotional connotations than is revealed in these initial proceedings. His foolishness became a state provoked by a profoundly disturbed inner state, built upon a sense of betrayal by his mother, which caused him deep vexation and recurrent episodes of anguish and aggressive agitation. At least that is how Antonio and his wife depicted his affliction.

Only a few months after the first interdiction had been decreed, Antonio petitioned for it to be lifted, arguing that it was not true that he was the *stolido* and prodigal his mother had made him out to be, although his mother had not used either of those labels. He claimed that the interdiction had been machinated by his mother who, motivated by her preference for her second-born son, aimed to deprive Antonio of the patrimony and give it instead to her other son, so that he could have the prospect of a better marriage.[52] Antonio's petition accomplished its purpose, and he was freed from the interdiction; but 3 years later his mother and brother succeeded in their aims when they managed to secure a semi-interdiction that restricted Antonio's economic management by placing him under the supervision of local authorities, followed by a full interdiction in 1771.

In the interdiction petition of 1771, Antonio's mother and brother still presented his mental incapacity by claiming that he had been "for some years now . . . imbecile and *mentecatto*."[53] The core of their argument still rested on the assessment that he suffered a combination of lack of experience and "weakness of spirit." But the petitioners now provided a new testimony, signed by priests, neighbors, and local authorities, stating that Antonio was subject to " . . . a profound melancholy, [and was] stupid and macilent."[54] As explained in previous chapters, the language of madness and mental incapacity was flexible and overarching, so the imbecility and stupidity denounced by Antonio Becciani's relatives in the second interdiction procedure did not exclude the melancholy identified by the witnesses. Melancholic or not, Antonio continued to be considered in a state of diminished understanding, except that the source of it was now attributed to his emotional sufferings.

Terms were carefully chosen in framing petitions for interdiction. This becomes particularly clear if we take into account the fact that Antonio Becciani's father had also been interdicted in 1747, so the Becciani family was familiar with the practices of the Magistrato dei Pupilli long before Antonio's interdiction. Consequently, we can assume that they were perfectly aware of what was required to secure an interdiction, which would explain their insistence on the labels *imbecile* and *mentecatto*. Interested in concealing the conflictive relationships that surrounded the case, they did not describe the particulars of Antonio's behavior.

The script of the interdiction proceedings of Antonio Becciani was remarkably similar to the one that had been employed to interdict his father 20 years before. Giovan Battista Becciani's interdiction had been decreed in

234 *Emotional disturbances*

1747 after some unidentified relatives claimed he was *mentecatto*, and the authorities' enquiries demonstrated that he was "so imbecile and of little soundness of mind [*poco sano di mente*]" that nobody believed him capable of properly managing his affairs.[55] The fact that Antonio was also said to be *mentecatto* and *imbecile* suggests his mother as the probable deviser of the line of argument, since she was familiar with interdiction procedures. In 1747, the petitioners, witnesses, and authorities agreed that Giovan Battista's wife, Caterina, was not only equally incapable of assuming the management of her husband's affairs, but she was even held responsible for the perilous state of the patrimony. Given that everyone considered Giovan Battista to be imbecile, the economic mismanagement was primarily attributed to Caterina, who lived separately from her husband and was said to dissipate his patrimony to satisfy her "splendid" tendencies, while she even withheld money from him. Consequently, it is particularly interesting to note that around 20 years later, she decided to denounce her son for economic mismanagement, resorting to almost the same arguments raised against her spouse when he had been interdicted – and indeed the same arguments that had been raised against her.

Hereditary mental disturbance was a visible and acknowledged reality in the eighteenth century, and so when Caterina Puccini decided to frame her son's incapacity in terms similar to those used in her husband's interdiction, she was relying on this awareness. The economy of words has, thus, a twofold explanation: the categories *stupido*, *mentecatto*, or *melenso* were generally sufficient when backed up by reliable witnesses, but, further, the precedent of a father interdicted for a similar mental condition was by itself convincing. However, later developments in the story suggest that the terms initially chosen to describe Antonio Becciani's mental incapacity give an incomplete picture of the discursive resources his family had available to characterize a mental illness. In what proves to be a pattern rather than an exception, standardized narratives often conceal nuanced conceptions of what mental incapacity amounted to, what its consequences were beyond the risk posed to the patrimony, and how emotional instability was becoming a decisive sign. Further, families demonstrate a clear awareness of the implications attached to how mental incapacity was characterized and of the possibility to direct these characterizations according to one's goals.

The disclosure of more nuanced perceptions of mental incapacity is tied to changes in the familial dynamics that led its members to resort to interdiction in the first place. The narratives in this case delve into the depths of the defendant's mental sufferings in response to the flaring up of familial disputes around him, bearing witness to the extent to which madness was framed as a contextual and relational reality. Shortly after the second interdiction, Antonio Becciani's wife, Maddalena Palloni, wrote a petition to be appointed administrator of her husband's patrimony, claiming he had been declared *melenso* by her in-laws with the sole purpose of taking advantage of him. The woman's argument was that her husband was neither "imbecile of mind" nor "the mad person [*non è quel mentecatto*] depicted by Benedetto his brother." She acknowledged that her husband was a "man by nature weak in cognition and spirit, [and] prone to be seduced," but this only made him unable to defend himself against his brother's schemes.[56]

In the petition, Maddalena declared that Benedetto's machinations were also directed against her, accusing him of resorting to all sorts of strategies, even to physical attacks, to try to keep her away from her husband and the administration of his patrimony.[57] She was referring to a period in which Antonio, persuaded by his kin, felt a strong animosity toward her. As a result, he had sent a petition to the Pupilli requesting them to send her away from him, declaring that Maddalena had inflicted "insufferable abuses" on him. The episode reveals a long-term conflict between Maddalena and her brother-in-law who, she claimed, had always hated her and opposed her marrying Antonio. Her narratives depict Benedetto as violent and capable of any scheme in pursuit of his abusive intentions. In contrast, Benedetto tried to attack her credibility by accusing her of marrying for money, of dissipating her husband's resources, and of maintaining dishonorable friendships with various men. His testimony is striking for its obvious similarities with the line of accusation made against Caterina Puccini when the late Giovan Battista Becciani had been interdicted in 1747.

The claim that Antonio was not as mad as his brother had intended make him seem, but was still of a weak cognition and spirit, changed into statements about his "dangerous imbecility" and "melancholic humor" in Maddalena Palloni's subsequent petitions. Becciani, who had initially been depicted as of weak character and suffering a certain degree of mental impairment, was in 1773 described as prone to suffering outbursts of anger that put his wife's life in serious danger. One of these aggressive episodes was considered so serious that the officers of the Pupilli were moved to order the provisional separation of the couple. All the efforts by the officials "to procure peace and reunite the couple" had proved unsuccessful in overcoming "the imbecility and extravagance of Anton Luigi Becciani, his cruelties against his wife and the abuses she has suffered, the unwise and disrespectful behavior of Benedetto Becciani, the indiscretion of Caterina Puccini, and her mistreatment of her daughter-in-law."[58]

About a month later, Maddalena requested that she be allowed to resume her life at her husband's side, claiming that, notwithstanding his past abuses and mistreatments, she did not fear the "dangerous imbecility of her spouse, which makes him fall sometimes into extravagances." She explained that, although Becciani's "melancholic humor" could not be "controverted," she had "not the least fear," judging from the "practice she [had] acquired of his nature in the many years they lived together." If her husband had committed "some extravagances" against her (i.e., if he had reacted aggressively by attacking and beating her with various objects), this was due to his mother's and brother's instigation. They, she said, "oppressed" Becciani and "overheated his fantasy" with ill-intentioned insinuations against her.[59]

This "dangerous imbecility" moved her to take a parallel course of action, when her brother-in-law raised questions about the authenticity of her affections for Antonio. According to Benedetto, before she made the request to resume cohabitation with Antonio, Maddalena herself had attempted to send her husband to Santa Dorotea, but her petition was not granted as he was not found to suffer the kind of madness that was liable to committal; moreover, she had attempted at various times to secure his imprisonment through supplications made to the Auditore Fiscale.[60] Thus, the case also illuminates the itineraries of madness and how families maneuvered through them, taking recourse to one or the other as the events unfolded. The authorities were thus placed at the center of the battlefield of the disputes of the families who followed long litigations in their attempts to solve their private conflicts.

In the numerous petitions Maddalena Palloni sent to the Pupilli, we see her ability to define and fluently elaborate on her husband's mental condition and her instrumental incorporation of concepts in accordance with the goal of the narrative. Antonio Becciani's mother and brother alleged his imbecility and stupidity to obtain the two interdiction decrees. Maddalena Palloni, for her part, raised concerns about his "weakness" and natural tendency to be oppressed by his relatives' machinations, his tendency to suffer melancholic episodes during which he became violent, and his irritable and easily influenced imagination, among other things, to explain Antonio's irascible reactions toward her. It is worth noting her use of the terms "melancholy" and "melancholic humor," which she framed as a "temporary bad humor" or "the critical moments when her husband is seized [*sorpreso*] by some melancholy." She explained that these critical moments were engineered by "their common enemies" who "know how to disconcert . . . his spirit." Furthermore, during the period they lived apart from Antonio's relatives, he was free of these episodes, and they had been able to spend their time harmoniously.[61]

Given that Antonio Becciani was already interdicted, the issue under contention was not whether he was indeed mad, but rather how he related to his relatives and how they treated him. In their effort to convince the authorities of their opposing versions, Maddalena Palloni and Benedetto Becciani characterized Antonio's ailments as being caused by the other's actions. According to Maddalena, Antonio's melancholy had originated from his brother's ill-intentioned comments, which disconcerted his spirit. Conversely, Benedetto argued that his brother's madness was a response to Maddalena's licentious practices, on account of which "seized by a strong passion [*forte passione*], being thus sick he had to be in bed for a period of almost two years."[62]

Maddalena's explanations are particularly interesting here as they underscore a shift in the ways mental afflictions were described in the Tuscan courts of law by lay society during the second half of the eighteenth century. The concept of recurrent episodes of melancholy was, of course, not new and neither was her characterization of the disease.[63] But the difference here, compared to previous accounts of mental incapacity based mostly on economic mismanagement, is how she explained her husband's disease in connection with his character, his biography, and his relationships. Maddalena employed the phrases "disconcert his spirit" and "bad humor," characterizing Antonio as mentally disturbed by the overflowing emotional instability that had overcome him, when she was trying to explain why he needed to be separated from his brother. These fluctuations of temperament were said to have originated, as explained before, in the disturbing events he had had to endure.

Thus, Maddalena's lexicon reflects the shift that, according to Michael Stolberg, can be observed in the letters of eighteenth-century French and German patients regarding the meanings of the terms "temperament" and "humor." According to Stolberg, references to a bad, lively, or fluctuating humor during this century were related more to what we today understand as mood or disposition than to the balance between the four humors.[64] This assertion can be taken further if we consider the role Maddalena ascribed to Antonio's inner disposition.

An altered imagination or disturbed fantasy constitutes a *topos* in the etiology of melancholy,[65] and Maddalena's narratives center on Antonio's distorted ideas and on his overheated fantasy. The accusations made by Benedetto about Maddalena's supposed dishonorable friendships were so powerful that just the possibility of her infidelity clouded his judgement and disturbed his mind, as she explained. His exacerbated jealousy was held to have such a pernicious effect on his susceptible fantasy that it isolated him from reality and made him reject their new-born son, convinced as he was that he was illegitimate. Maddalena's narrative made use of entrenched medical understandings of melancholy and its most characteristic signs, but she adapted them so as to prove her point regarding the decisive role exerted by his brother in the course of his illness. Further, her depiction of her husband's mental affliction served to expose the depths of the family conflict that led its members to disclose Antonio Becciani's illness to the authorities in the first place. Her descriptions were given not to prove his madness, but to resolve the dispute with her in-laws. That is, her goal was not to convince the authorities that he was mad (Antonio was already interdicted), but to seek help in what she framed as a defense of her husband from his relatives' iniquities.

Maddalena's line of argument was shared by the other accounts in the proceedings. The local authority from Barberino di Mugello had in fact testified that Antonio's disturbed fantasy had been triggered by jealousy resulting from the rumors, inflated by his brother and mother, regarding Maddalena's alleged infidelities. Siding in this with Antonio's kin, he claimed that his "greatest passions and *turbazioni d'animo* come from his wife's sociability."[66] Although the official from Mugello introduced a story that differed from what Maddalena Palloni had asserted, he agreed with her on the nature and main source of Antonio's mental disturbance. Whether labeled as passions, *turbazioni d'animo*, overheated fantasy, or melancholic humor, the cause of Antonio's mental affliction was identified by all the parties involved as the disturbing effects his familial situation exerted on his mind.

There is one more issue to examine regarding the lexicon of Antonio Becciani's mental affliction. We observe expressions such as that he was "infuriated" (*infuriatosi*), that "his fantasy was overheated" by his relatives (*essergli stata riscaldata la fantasia*), that he mistreated and inflicted "cruelties" against his wife (*strapazzi* and *sevizie*), or that he manifested a "dangerous imbecility," illustrated with references to an occasion when Maddalena had been forced to escape from the matrimonial residence, running to desperately seek protection from her husband's fury. Thus, Becciani's story suggests that lay society conceived the connection between low spirits and mania as a natural consequence of the shifting emotional disturbances that characterized a deranged mind. Furthermore, it shows that emotional agitation and shifting moods were at the center of the cultural understanding of madness. Demonstrating the existence of a lay understanding of the various characteristics of melancholy, these narratives made use of them to seek the intervention of the authorities in their widening disputes. In this sense, we have to bear in mind that, whereas this case is one of the rare ones in the eighteenth century in which lay narratives made use of the concept of melancholy to frame mental incapacity, the fluidity ascribed to his emotional instability is common in interdiction procedures of the second half of the century. The employment of the concept in this case may be taken to be exceptional, but not its characterization nor its connotations.

Physicians frequently warned the authorities that a melancholic delirium could easily turn into a furious one, as attested by many of the Santa Dorotea records.[67] In the Becciani story, we do not see the term delirium, *furioso*, or mania, but nonetheless the symptomatology and medical categories appear translated into un-medicalized contexts that suggest a very similar conceptualization. Likewise, although his altered fantasy was very much discussed, there is no recourse to contemporary medical terms such as mental fixations (*fissazioni*) or mind/fantasy perturbation (*perturbazioni di mente/fantasia*).

In Antonio Becciani's case, neither in the interdiction proceedings nor in the records of his curatorship do we find any evidence that medical opinion was involved. In fact, neither of the interested parties seemed to need expert opinion on a matter that could be observed and sufficiently argued by those around the sufferer. The lexicon they employed was neither particularly medical nor necessarily new, but its terms, such as "melancholic humor" and "overheated fantasy," were reshaped to fit the new concerns of the eighteenth century. The family, with its conflictive relationships, had been placed at the center of attention. These new social concerns made room for more individualistic representations of mental disturbance that saw in emotional displays the privileged indicators of the workings of the mind. The narratives of Becciani's mental disturbance defined the characteristics of his disorder by following a new purpose.

We have seen that since their origins, interdiction procedures were primarily aimed at protecting patrimony from the consequences of mental incapacity. Thus, requests were mainly argued in relation to property and economic behavior. Excessive expenditure, growing debts, and engagement in wrong or counterproductive economic transactions had played a leading role as indicators of mental incapacity. In this regard, Elizabeth Mellyn has suggested that between the sixteenth and seventeenth centuries in Tuscany, notions of mental incapacity pathologized economic mismanagement.[68] Although this tendency was still present during the eighteenth century, explanations shifted from external and practical behaviors to the manifestations of emotional instability and its repercussion in familial relationships.

Given that Antonio Becciani's mental incapacity was never challenged, the narratives were not bound to economic behavior. As happens with many other defendants during the eighteenth century, Antonio's case continues to be litigated not in relation to patrimony administration but because of the relational effects and emotional dimensions of his mental disturbance. The issues under discussion in this case and in general in the interdiction records of the second half of the century were how and where the mentally afflicted were supposed to live; who was to take care of them; what were the responsibilities of their next of kin; and what measures could be taken to discipline them, cure them, and manage them. To determine and solve these questions, more accurate descriptions were necessary, for the conventional legal categories of mental incapacity had proved to be insufficient.

Narratives acquired more nuanced tones the moment they left the realm of economic behavior to enter the realm of relationships and emotions. Maddalena Palloni spoke of herself and her expectations with regard to her marriage to a man she knew to be profoundly sick but whose mental disturbances she had nonetheless accepted, in what can be interpreted as a mixture of genuine affection and a more practical concern to ensure she was not separated from her children. Wives raising their voices and using this mixture of emotional and practical lines of argumentation are commonly found in eighteenth-century records. The possibility of losing one's children often forced women to accept cohabitation with a mentally afflicted husband, and this was among the standard issues negotiated between women and the authorities in interdiction procedures. But they received something valuable in exchange: the Pupilli usually placed them as administrators of their husband's patrimony, and even if a third person was entrusted with this task, they were generally the preferred mediators between the ducal administration and the interdicted. Maddalena Palloni was the ultimate authority on Antonio Becciani's mental condition, and the state officials relied mostly on her to build their opinion of it. Thus, this case allows us also to observe the extent to which women played a leading role in the management of madness. In this disclosure of domestic space through the voice of women, we see male irrationality under their control, since women were being placed in the position of rational agents in the household – a position that was promoted and ratified by the authorities.

Emotional disturbances as indicators of mental derangement

What unifies the different spaces in which madness was disclosed during the eighteenth century is the increasing visibility acquired by emotional disturbances as evidence of mental derangement. Although, as explained in the previous chapter, medical terminology generally did not penetrate the civil and criminal courts, examination of the languages of madness suggests that there were shared meanings and common understandings, particularly regarding the role attributed to emotional distress. The uses, contexts, and meanings of the lexicon of emotional distress constitute a crucial aspect to understand the problem of the circulation of languages, the permeation of lay notions in medical knowledge, and the social appropriation of medical categories. Rather than "colonizing" the realm of the mind, medical professionals were ascribing names to realities that had been first brought to their attention by the sufferers and their families. The study of the linguistic resources of litigants and witnesses to name and describe emotional disturbances allows us to question the top-down model of the popularization of medicine, presenting the process instead as the result of a crisscrossing of conceptions and languages.[69]

Furious reactions as sign of mental derangement

Crimes that were motivated by feelings of anger, hate, revenge, or jealousy are common in the records of the Otto di Guardia, the majority of which were sentenced with the ordinary penalty.[70] However, in some cases, the crime was found to have been committed while in a perturbed state of mind caused by a strong passion. Guided by the principles established by Roman law, the Tuscan criminal system considered that strong emotions had the power to alter one's judgement and capacity of discernment. Strong passions were held to be extenuating circumstances, provided it could be proven that they had left the suspect deprived of full discernment.[71]

Anger, regardless of whether it stemmed from unrequited love, jealousy, or a just desire for revenge, appears in criminal procedures as the quintessential passion that "blinded," overpowered, and transported the accused far from the realm of reason. While the power of passions to shatter one's reason was widely accepted, judges often differed with petitioners when it came to decide whether the presence of passions entailed that their consequences could be condoned. Diminished responsibility was not determined only by an assessment of the extent to which passions had disturbed the person's mind. Although reacting violently to a serious offence was considered justified anger, this could change if the anger had been controlled and only later evolved into a calculated revenge. So, in the case that a desire of revenge moved the offended to attack days later, the crime changed from unpremeditated murder to attempted murder, for it showed intent, motivation, and premeditation.[72]

The definitive signs that the line of sanity had been crossed were found in the events that led up to the crime. A finding of insanity was contingent on the possibility of proving that the crime had been unpremeditated or fortuitous and that it had been caused by justified reasons, but it also depended on the nature and intensity of the passion and the person's biography. An insanity plea in these cases was pertinent only if they could prove that they had a tendency to lose their temper to the point of irrationality.

Episodes of frantic anger are frequently put forward as arguments to reduce a sentence.[73] Even if these petitions did not always result in a favorable response, they are indicative of the interpretations given to these emotions and the extent to which they were taken to have the power to alter a person's mind. The key to how lawyers and judges assessed the emotional reaction under scrutiny is provided by the words used to describe the aforementioned psychological states. Sometimes, anger is only termed as *avutosi a male*, *revocatosi all'animo*, or a *mal animo*, expressions for a feeling of resentment and indignation caused by a certain event that eventually led to the need to be vented (*sfogare*), but which did not necessarily entail a temporary loss of reason. However, in other cases, it was said that the accused acted "seized by passion and blinded" (*presso dalla passione, ed accecato*),[74] in "the heat of anger" and the "heat of passion" (*calore dell'ira* and *calore della passione*),[75] or "seized by anger" (*preso dall'iracondia*).[76]

Excessive displays of rage were frequently said to have been accompanied by inebriation, which theoretically served to prove further that the person had been bereft of reason when committing the crime. Drunkenness, it was widely agreed, weakened one's ability to control one's temper. Petitioners in fact tried to attenuate their responsibility using the argument that while "overheated with wine" (*riscaldati dal vino*), they had been "seized with anger" (*sorpreso dalla collera*)[77] or "seized with a violent passion and insurmountable anger" (*sorpreso da violenta passione, e da insuperabile collera*).[78]

Furious and violent reactions could be taken to be the cause of a temporary mental derangement or could be its symptom. For instance, in 1756, a man prosecuted for contumacy for firing his arquebus at his paternal uncles attempted to reduce his culpability by claiming he suffered from the "great misfortune" that "many times, particularly when agitated by some passion, he remains completely bereft of cognition, and totally demented and unable to understand his duty."[79] His petition was accompanied by the testimony of his uncles in which they confirmed their nephew's assertion by saying he was widely reputed to be *pazzo* and *scemo di cervello*. The interesting issue here is how the petitioner linked his fits of madness with his tendency to be agitated by passions. Attesting to this new concern that can be observed in interdiction records in the second half of the century, the petition characterized the crime as an episode of temporary madness produced by a disturbing emotion. The petition made use of the ancient legal tradition that attributed the power to cloud a person's judgement to passions; only here it was placed in a context of a person who was reputed to be mad. In other words, it was not that a sudden overpowering rage had moved him to act but that he was overpowered by rage only because he was mentally ill.

Much as Natalie Davis has pointed out regarding sixteenth-century pardon tales, I have not found any cases where the disturbing powers that anger exerts over the mind were cited in order to diminish the responsibility of women for committing a crime.[80] Women are arraigned for crimes of murder, assault, and slander, but their anger is generally not used as either a mitigating or an aggravating factor. In cases of quarrels and altercations that ended in physical violence, women were also said to have "taken it badly" (*avutosi a male*) when somebody had insulted them or their families, and so they threw a stone in response, for instance.[81] Female and male violence stemmed from similar motives: defense of honor, self-defense, jealousy, animosity, and resentment, to name a few. Responding with insults, blows, throwing stones, or any other violent reaction that could eventually lead to the death of an adversary was a possible reaction for both genders. However, in general terms, female anger was not used as evidence of a temporary state of mental obfuscation. Extenuating circumstances for their physical violence or murderous actions were more likely to be found in the principles of self-defense and honor, on the one hand, or a lack of full discernment or plain simplicity (*semplicità* or *sciocchezza*), on the other, rather than in an uncontrollable fit of rage.[82]

When we leave the domain of criminal justice to enter interdiction procedures and special requests to denounce a disordered relative, the association between unfounded outbursts of rage and mental disturbance is not only gender specific, but also age specific. While emotional instability was identified as evidence of both female and male mental disturbance, violent and particularly irascible reactions are almost invariably associated with men. Different gradations of men's mistreatments (*strapazzi*) of others or physical and verbal abuse were frequently introduced as evidence of the disorder in which mentally disturbed men found themselves. Their actions were attributed to their being of an "unruly nature and a quarrelsome disposition" (*natura poco docile e d'animo rissoso*) or of a "ferocious nature" (*naturale feroce*).[83] They were said to have the tendency to become incandescent (*da in escandescenze*), be transported by outbursts of fury (*furiosi trasporti*) for the most unexpected reasons, and to fall into frenzy (*esser solito dare in frenesia*), or to be frequently driven by a mad fury or "excesses of fury" (*furibondo, frenetico*, and *eccessi di furia*).[84]

While irascible reactions were given as evidence of male mental incapacity throughout the adult lifecycle, irascibility and the tendency to let themselves be overwhelmed by surges of anger were more frequently associated with old age. In interdiction procedures, a series of undesirable and reprehensible actions were said to have been committed by elderly men in the "heat of anger" or "under the impetuosity of indignation and anger."[85] Judging from these examples, it can be said that Tuscan society considered that when men reached a "decrepit age" – roughly in their 70s and 80s – they were particularly prone to emotional instability, which often assumed the form of uncontrolled and illogical bouts of fury.[86]

Although emotional disturbances in old age remain a largely unexplored field, studies on the experience and the cultural meanings of early modern old age have suggested that low spirits were the most common emotional affliction of the elderly.[87] In fact, humoral theory tended to view old age as a stage in life mostly governed by melancholy and phlegm, tending to passivity rather than to aggressiveness. According to studies of eighteenth-century medical literature on old age which have touched upon the emotional disturbances of this age group, the authors of these books saw the elderly as no longer troubled by unwanted passions, for mental and physical decline was thought to bring on a "weakening of sensations, appetites and passions."[88] Against this background, the connection that emerges in interdiction procedures between old age and growing irascibility seems remarkable.

When examining this issue in interdiction procedures, we need to bear in mind that the disruptions of family life caused by prodigality and *demenza* changed according to the age of the defendant and that this in turn shaped the characterizations of mental and emotional disturbances. While in the case of young men the issues at stake were their future families and the authority of their elders and for middle-aged men, the administration and care of a current family, in the case of the elderly their offspring were already grown up, so it was a matter of legacy and inheritance. It could be argued, therefore, that the family conflicts surrounding the elderly made the interdiction narratives denouncing both old men and old women more open to descriptions of the emotional realm. But, besides these considerations, what comes to the fore is that old age was held to produce an inability to control one's emotions, together with the mental decay it entailed.

Interdiction procedures and trials involving criminal insanity provide a different perspective on intense emotions and their power to cloud one's judgment – different from that attained through studies of family history. Insults and verbal abuse, physical violence, and death threats were part of the family disputes disclosed to early modern courts and were the most common cause for matrimonial litigation. As scholars have pointed out, the fact that anger and violent reactions appear almost invariably associated with male behavior has more to do with the uses and requirements of justice than with an actual gendered differentiation.[89] For a request of separation to be successful, petitioners – predominantly females – had to present plausible stories and strong motives, among which *sevizie* (cruelties) and physical threats that put their life in danger were among the most effective.[90] In this context, there is nothing particularly remarkable in the frequent allusions to mistreatment and aggressive behavior portrayed in interdiction procedures, except that they were presented in front of the courts with a different aim and argued as evidence of mental incapacity. That is, violent reactions were used not only to prove the need to live separately from a husband, but also to explain why a father, husband, or son was thought to be subject to mental disorder.

Complaints about spousal violence have been mostly examined from the point of view of expectations about marriage, the emergence of the so-called romantic family, power relations, and behavioral norms.[91] However, scholars have generally not read these disputes from the point of view of the history of madness, thus missing the opportunity to elaborate on how litigants conceived of emotional distress, how it was thought to affect the mind, and how they used evidence of emotional distress to turn a litigation to their favor. The sources under consideration here illuminate the problem of references to matrimonial violence from a different perspective. The fact that ungrounded or intensely violent outbursts were increasingly used as evidence of mental incapacity suggests interesting conclusions in this regard. It portrays women making use of shared cultural codes about what constituted mental disturbance and how it affected one's emotional displays. It also suggests that the notion that disturbed emotional reactions served as evidence of altered states of mind could have played a role in the change in the way matrimonial disputes started to be settled toward the end of the century.[92]

Passions

In criminal records, passions are predominantly framed as a sudden feeling of rage or as a tendency to experience fits of fury that clouded a person's rational faculties. However, notwithstanding the frequent references to passions as a powerful force capable of disturbing judgement in the criminal proceedings and supplications to the Otto di Guardia, the term "passion" makes few appearances in the records of the Magistrato dei Pupilli. The phenomenon is worth examining, taking into account that "passion" is singled out by scholars as the most common term in the early modern world for making reference to emotions, particularly when they were associated with irrationality.[93] In particular, passion was still a prominent term in eighteenth-century medical literature to make reference to disturbed emotions, the *passioni d'animo* that were capable of irritating the nerves and producing – or aggravating – mental afflictions, as discussed before.

"Passion" in the records of the Pupilli is mostly employed to refer to the vital force guiding the behavior of a young prodigal. What drove them to dissipate was either the "passion" to gamble, the need to "satisfy their passions," or the "passion that governs him."[94] Passion appears in this context as a force that took control over the individual, commanding his thoughts and actions, inducing unhappy consequences. The passion to spend, gamble, sell goods, or indulge in the pleasures of lavishness, women, and alcohol was portrayed as a compelling force rather than as an overpowering feeling, albeit with the same effect.[95] The disturbing powers of the passion to gamble assumed particularly exacerbated levels when the gambler was confronted by his relatives. In one case, it was said that the desire to gamble turned into a "mad passion" (*forsennata passione*) driving him to engage in "excesses of fury" (*eccesi di furia*) and causing him to experience fierce transports (*fieri trasporti*) to the extent of "frenzy," all signs that, according to this man's wife, proved his "uncertain temperament and humor."[96]

Alternatively, though to a lesser degree, "passion" was employed to mean amorous affection, lust, or occasional suffering, without implying a force capable of disturbing the mind. But it could also be considered strong enough as to alter a person's judgment. A "disordered passion" (*sregolata passione*) could be an amorous affection that obscured a woman's rational faculties rendering her insane. It could entail the consideration that her head had been taken hostage by passion or that it had dazzled her (leaving her *acciecata*), a condition that could equally affect both sexes.[97] Particularly in old age, love was considered capable of entering people's head (*gl'amori, che gli sono entrati in testa*), engulfing them (becoming *ingolfato*) and thus leaving them in a state of mental incapacity.[98] Passion in the sense of excessive love preoccupied early modern societies for numerous reasons, starting with the strains it put on the inheritance line and family decorum. The battle against dishonest love was blended, here, with the new conflicts of the eighteenth-century family. When it affected the elderly, a clear-cut association was made between passionate affections and insanity under the idea that advanced age rendered the elderly helpless before the effects of the passions that assaulted them.[99] Accordingly, love affairs and late remarriage (mostly of men in this case) were often used as arguments for the interdiction of an elderly parent.

However, in general, the employment of the word *passione* in accounts of mental incapacity is rare. Expanding the discursive resources of emotional disturbances, interdiction narratives employed a quite rich and varied range of terms to allude to emotional turmoil. Instead of turning to *passioni d'animo* (which I have been able to find only once in the records of the Pupilli), litigants and state officials preferred to attach the adjectives of irregular, unstable, uncertain, uneasy, and extravagant (*irregolare*, *volubile*, *incerto*, *inquieto*, and *stravagante*) to the nouns used to make reference to the psychological state (*capo*, *temperamento*, *umore*, *spirito*, or *animo*).

Emotional instability and unpredictable emotional reactions

Frantic fits of fury were at the core of the traditional image of madness. The raving mad running amok in the streets was a part of the social fears that were responsible for the development of strategies such as confinement and interdiction to deal with the problem since Antiquity. We have seen that the *furioso* was a Roman category that had survived in the Tuscan judicial framework until the eighteenth century, even if it had fallen into disuse. In turn, the *pazzo furioso* was the legal category that justified committal to the mental hospital, termed *mania furiosa* in medical language. However, violent reactions are not the most noticeable emotional display cited as

246 *Emotional disturbances*

evidence of mental incapacity in interdiction proceedings or in the records of the office of the Auditore Fiscale. Emotional disturbances included a wide variety of displays, ranging from rage and extreme irascibility to low spirits, with various forms of emotional instability in between. But what seems even more important to note is that divergent forms of emotional distress were associated with the same individual. Violent fits of anger and frenzy could easily coexist or alternate with low spirits and melancholy. People categorized as mentally ill were said to change unexpectedly from laughter to tears or show alternate periods of dejection with periods of hyperactivity, extreme irritability, and compulsive behavior. The manic condition was also unstable and did not suppose a constant state of frenzy. As a husband said in petitioning for his wife's committal in 1760, "she is mad [*pazza*], and many times goes from a cheerful madness [*pazzia allegra*] to a frenetic madness [*pazzia frenetica*]."[100]

At the core of these narratives is the perception that the key to ascertaining the presence of mental incapacity, instead of fury or persistent low spirits, was emotional instability, favoring the image of shifting moods as their preferred evidence for mental incapacity. Extravagant and irregular characters, unpredictable or illogical reactions, and uneasiness abound in the narratives of interdiction procedures, repeated in descriptions of perturbed states of mind, reported through other channels to the authorities of the Grand Duchy. Furthermore, if we take into account the expectation that a good *paterfamilias* or a virtuous administrator would be "well moderated in his actions" (*ben regolato nelle sue operazioni*),[101] it becomes clear that the lack of regulation over actions and emotions meant deviance.

Behind this understanding of self-government, we find long philosophical and medical traditions. Renaissance culture had praised the self-government of passions and appetites, producing a vital discussion that emphasized the importance of balanced life regimes not only for health, but also for social life and politics.[102] Similarly, humoral theory was structured on the importance of regulation and balance. The importance of equilibrium was still at the core of the management of improper passions during the eighteenth century, which gave a particular attention to willpower, rational faculties, and the workings of the brain as the main factors responsible for emotional imbalance. The various forms of unpredictable reactions and emotional instability that were presented as the main symptoms of mental affliction in eighteenth-century medical literature were similarly employed with increasing frequency as evidence of mental disturbance in lay social circles, albeit using a different lexicon.

The medical recommendations given to patients complaining of mental afflictions or nervous complaints such as hysteria or hypochondria invariably point toward the importance of balance. Patients had to control their lives and follow regulated life systems, with a convenient amount of exercise and rest, a balanced diet and a proper combination of intellectual activities, domestic affairs, and social amusements. Excess and lack of regulation were, in this sense, equated with unhealthy lives, and any patient who intended to counteract the disease had to undertake serious changes to regulate his or her life. In particular, a well-equilibrated life was the only way to avoid the damaging effects of *angutie d'animo* (anguishes of the soul), which were often responsible for triggering mental disease. The Tuscan physician Giovanni Targioni Tozzetti, for instance, used to argue for the importance of regulation, control, and authority as an effective way of curing madness in his medical consultations and expert legal opinions.[103] The importance of equilibrium and, particularly, the damaging effects of emotional instability and emotional excess can similarly be traced in the legal records under study here, forming an important layer of the lay narratives of mental disturbance.

The inability to control one's temper and appetites was a major concern for Tuscan families. Ascriptions of inner turmoil and lack of self-control, we have seen, were commonly employed to describe, and thus prove mental derangement; the same was true of shifts of temper, which denoted a lack of self-government and awakened a fear of social disorder. As the eighteenth century progressed, petitioners increasingly tended to center their claim of mental incapacity on the observation that their relatives manifested a persistent instability, indicated by their recurrent shifts of ideas, purposes, or moods. That their expenditure and debts were capricious was only one aspect of a disorder that, on the level of relationships, was primarily perceived as consisting in an unpredictable character. Concomitant with the incapacity to follow rules and conform to expected behavior, petitioners singled out the defendant's inconsistent or "irregular" (*irregolare*) "character."[104] Their personalities were perceived as uncontrollable, not only because they refused to be tamed, but even more because no patterns could predict their behavior. The resolutions, affections, and animosities of these people could shift unexpectedly to any imaginable end at the slightest provocation.

The conception of the disrupted emotional state identified in prodigals and the demented is best summarized under the term *inquietudine* (uneasiness or restlessness), which presupposed a lack of internal peace with physical and emotional manifestations. Allegedly mentally incapacitated men and women were often described by their relatives as *inquieto* or *inquieta*, demonstrating a *spirito inquietissimo* or a *naturale inquieto*. *Inquietudine* was defined as *travaglio, passione, tribolazione* in Italian, which mean affliction, passion, tribulation.[105] In the sources under study here, the term was employed to define the emotional and physical sensation of feeling uneasy, disquieted, anguished, emotionally agitated, and disturbed. It was usually accompanied by descriptions of the actions that indicated this state of disturbance, which served both to illustrate and categorize the type of mental affliction under observation. Many of the terms employed for emotional disruption are words that also have very precise physical meanings. In the case of *inquietudine*, it meant physical restlessness and the feeling of disquietude at the same time.

Inquietudine could affect a person's mind in various ways and was evidenced through a gradation of emotional displays, from fickleness, volatility, and instability, to frenzy. It was employed to indicate the emotional state

248 *Emotional disturbances*

that accompanied a deranged behavior, conveying the feeling of uneasiness that frequently vexed the mentally disturbed and compelled them to behave and react oddly. At the same time, it alluded to the relational consequences of this emotional state. In fact, the term was employed not only to describe perturbed states of mind, but also to characterize the "disquieting" influence these behaviors exerted on surrounding family members.

The elasticity observed in the meanings and applications of *inquietudine*, shared by most of the judicial categories examined in this book, circumvented the need to employ more straightforward terms to name mental disturbances. This is of particular interest when we examine the hidden meanings of the term, comparing them with the different contexts in which they could be employed. For instance, husbands often describe their wives as being of a *spirito inquietissimo* or a *naturale inquieto* to argue for their wife's confinement in an institution such as the Conservatorio dei Mendicanti or the Malmaritate.[106] In both cases, the resemblance with the common features of mental affliction, with its implications of extravagance, unruliness, and instability, comes to the fore. These conservatories of female virtue were repositories of women denounced for diverse behavioral disorders in which sexual misconduct and mental derangement came together, concealed between prostitution, adultery, and their allegedly being women in danger (*donne pericolanti*). When we direct special attention to the vocabulary employed to describe these women's disorders, we observe that the male evaluations of feminine normativity and their rejection of women's defiance of decency and masculine authority were mixed with appreciations of their state of mind. The key to understanding this mixture is the use of the word *inquietudine*, as the case of a woman confined for allegedly being a "very uneasy woman" (*inquietissima donna*) who manifested "an extraordinarily uneasy nature" (*naturale inquieto fuori di modo*) and was "hardly capable of adapting to any plan."[107] For *inquietudine* indicated instability, and this in turn was held to be a sign of mental disturbance. Women of "uneasy spirits" would change their minds for no reason or would have a *fervido umore*, that is, a turbulent, intense, and boiling disposition.[108]

In other cases, *inquieto*, particularly when applied to men, was coupled with "stupid in the brain" (*scemo di cervello*), "weakness of mind" (*debolezza di mente*), "signs of an unsound mind" (*segni di non sana mente*), or *furioso*, in which cases the link between the inner turmoil denoted by the word *inquieto* and mental illness was straightforward.[109] Moreover, the very presence of the term *inquieto*, when used in connection to other categories such as "prone to fall into frenzy" (*solito dare in frenesia*), "fantastical man" (*uomo fantastico*), and "madness" (*pazzie*), was a sufficient evidence to support an accusation of *demenza*.[110]

The gender differentiation disclosed by the two examples presented before is not fortuitous. Although *inquietudine* was employed in descriptions of both men and women, its connotations and ambit of application were gender specific. In women, it denoted a difficult temper and reprehensible demeanor and indicated a passionate or unstable character. While women's *inquietudine* was generally shown in their changing decisions and what was perceived as their misguided affections and unfounded sufferings and vexations, men's *inquietudine* was often connected with displays of anger and periods of agitated hyperactivity. They were restless and anxious, constantly moving, unable to sleep at the recommended hours, and continuously changing their location or activity. They were never satisfied, unable to yield and accept the rules, and unable to settle down. Their inherent uneasiness at times made them irritable and frantic and at times excessively driven by a particular sensation, feeling, or idea. Thus, it also made them stubborn and fixed on irrational purposes or improper affections. Their *inquietudine* drove them to engage in futile and expensive litigations, which could be against their relatives, their creditors, or whoever was opposed to their goals.[111] In the end, it made them very resistant to the commands of the Magistrato dei Pupilli, driving them to send petition after petition, or sometimes presenting themselves personally before the officials to try to get their way.

Again the key to grasping the meanings ascribed to these terms lies in the ways they are combined. One who was said to demonstrate a "rather uneasy and resentful nature" (*naturale alquanto inquieto e risentito*) was also described as having an *inquietissimo naturale*, becoming in his advanced age "a character so irregular that dealing with him becomes impossible for everyone, and he sometimes gives signs of an unsound mind."[112] Thus, the inner instability that characterized someone as *inquieto* was also linked to a character considered irregular (*irregolare*), unstable (*volubile*), and uncertain (*incerto*).

The two extremes of this instability received unequal attention in the narratives, with a greater focus on the violent and angry manifestation. This does not mean that the low-spirited phase was not perceived but rather that it caused far less disturbance in family life. There are some exceptions, nonetheless. One is when dejection led to suicidal intentions, in which case the low-spirited state was described using the proper medico-legal lexicon for admission to Santa Dorotea (most times through the plain *pazzo/a furioso/a* and on a few occasions using *delirio melanconico*).[113] The other exception is when dejection affected the financial performance of the sufferer, manifested through a profound insecurity or weakness of character that made him incapable of making decisions or unable to stick to any plan (a characteristic termed *volubile*). Remarkable in this regard are the letters written by one interdicted man in which he disclosed his total impotence with regard to the management of his property, describing his desperation and the recurrent urges he had to disappear and leave everything behind (including his wife and children) "because I cannot live like this any longer." In the eyes of the officials of the Pupilli, these letters demonstrated his *volubilità* and complete incapacity to regulate his affairs.[114]

The unstable disposition that characterized a state of *inquietudine* indicated both that the person was governed by his or her emotional turmoil, which oscillated between two extremes, and that he was unable to act in

250 *Emotional disturbances*

accordance with behavioral norms. For this reason, *inquietudine* was also equated to an "irregular head" (*capo irregolare*) responsible for behaviors that were both improper and extravagant.[115] A *capo irregolare* was also someone of an "extravagant humor," who had shown himself to be "indocile," lived "irregularly" (meaning both beyond the law and with instability), committed "unreasonable arbitrary [actions]," abused his wife, and was, thus, "half mad" (*mezzo matto*).[116] The adjective *irregolare* highlighted not only that the person lived outside social rules, was disorderly (in these cases, coupled with *sregolato*, used also to indicate the licentious activities of the prodigal), but also particularly that this disorder came from an irregular head. A *capo irregolare* was very similar to an "extravagant brain" (*cervello stravagante*) and, in general, to the states corresponding to other phrases in which the same word *irregolare* describes a person's nature, humor, behavior, etc.

Another term employed to convey emotional instability was "extravagant." Extravagance has been frequently pointed to as a characteristic that subsumed the manifold transgressions committed by the mentally ill. In early modern Europe, madness was strongly associated with being extravagant, behaving extravagantly, doing extravagant things, or displaying extravagant emotions.[117] In the eighteenth-century Tuscan records examined here, extravagance was an overarching term frequently employed to characterize the behavior, actions, and emotional reactions of the allegedly mentally incapable. Petitioners and authorities often summarized the problem of someone held to be mentally incapacitated by labelling their behavior, mind, and disposition as extravagant. Like the majority of the terms examined here, *stravagante* served to indicate the illogical workings of a deranged mind, the emotional turmoil that many times accompanied the former, and how these two were manifested through abnormal behavior. A concept that was sufficiently broad as to comprise various forms of deviation, extravagance was used to indicate the degree into which a given behavior, practice, and emotional display diverged from the boundaries of normality.

The semantics of the term are rather imprecise, and it had manifold uses and interpretations. *Stravagante* was defined as "fantastical, deformed, out of ordinary use."[118] Something extravagant was something strange and different, which could not be reduced to standard forms and did not conform to accepted rules. An extravagant person was fantastical, which was also to be *falotico* and *intrattabile*, that is, abstract in the sense of detached from reality and intractable.[119] When the word was used to characterize a person's behavior or personality, the breaching of rules and standards it implied was closely related to madness and the realms of fantasy and imagination. Extravagance then provided a dimension of strangeness and lack of moderation, and at the same time, it conveyed the idea of emotional and mental instability.

The use of the term "extravagant" in the sources examined here covers a wide range of contexts and discloses interesting meanings. It mostly appears after 1750, and, although we encounter both female and male extravagance, the concept appears largely associated with middle-aged and elderly men. In the few cases in which young men were described as extravagant, the concept was primarily used to catalogue the prodigal's excessive expenditure, his fondness for grandeur, sociability, diversions, and vices. The debauchery that we have seen as concomitant to prodigality and the unruly *discoli* was indeed a form of extravagance, which served both to demonstrate their flouting of the accepted rules of behavior and their "irregular head" (*capo irregolare*).[120] They acted outside the rules and their behavior could not be predicted – as suggested by the terms "extravagance" and "irregular" – and they could reach undesirable extremes, such as making improper marriage proposals.[121]

Contrary to what can be observed in descriptions of older men and women, extravagance in young men appears particularly connected with eccentricity, not only because their behavior was unconventional, but also because their oddness expressed itself in a compulsive need to spend in excess of their means, their need for luxuries, and constant diversions. These common features of prodigality could assume more serious forms, as in the case of a certain 19-year-old nobleman who intended to marry a lower-born woman with neither dowry nor respected relations, had participated in the last carnival in a most improper way, and had even attempted to sell most of the family paintings to build a comedy theatre in his villa.[122] These "eccentricities" revealed an "extravagance" which provided clear signs of an altered state of mind. Further, they conveyed an inner disposition toward disorder and instability in a man who was governed by his need to spend and show off.

If we examine this tendency against what was argued before regarding the role attributed to emotional turmoil in perceptions of mental incapacity, the degree to which prodigality constituted a mental disorder in eighteenth-century Tuscany becomes clearer. As was argued in previous chapters, the excessive expenditure by the young generations and their lack of respect for certain values that had ruled their fathers' lives are not features unique to Tuscany and were certainly not automatically associated with madness. Despite the fact that the descriptions of young prodigals were deeply entrenched in a growing conflict between younger and older generations regarding the value of social position and how the latter was concomitant with a certain financial management, older members of the family usually saw the recklessness of youth as pure madness.

The conflicts that characterized the relations between fathers and sons toward the end of the eighteenth century have been beautifully examined by Nicola Phillips in her study of a profligate son whose father, at first desperate and then litigious, in the end could do nothing other than write a memoir to narrate his son's descent into financial ruin, delinquency, and moral depravity. Although her study is not concerned directly with the connection that can be drawn between perceptions of profligacy and perceptions of madness, her study illuminates how the clash of moral values between two generations also entailed a particular conception of a disordered mind. This father described his young son's mind using terms very similar to those examined here. The young man's debauchery indicated he had lost his rational self-control and was governed by the pernicious effects of "irregular and intemperate passions."[123] His father explained his squandering as "some form of insanity" and his sexual promiscuity as "a sign of his irrational and profligate nature" and thought he needed to be brought "back to reason."[124] Madness was evidenced not only in the son's reckless expenditure – which was not new in the eighteenth century – but also in the emotional turmoil behind it.

The meanings ascribed to "extravagance" are further revealed by words it was used with, which, when applied to describe middle aged and old men denounced for mental incapacity, included behavior (*contegno*), character (*carattere*), humor (*umore*), nature (*naturale*), and brain (*cervello*). The financial mismanagement and excessive expenditure that were the starting point of every interdiction petition were accompanied in these cases by expressions that described the defendant's disturbed emotional state. Extravagance infused the brain, spirit, humor and thinking and was accompanied with expressions denoting disturbed forms of emotional display, such as *inquieto*, furious, frenetic, uncertain temperament (*temperamento incerto*), and disconcerted fantasy (*sconcertata fantasia*). Extravagant behavior was mainly associated with three causes in men: a disordered mind, disturbed emotions that were nonviolent and frequently assumed the form of emotional instability, and disturbed emotions that were violent. The latter two were generally accompanied by the first, with expressions that pointed toward the head or mind/brain (*capo* or *cervello*) and thinking or ideas (*sentimento* or *idee*). Thus, we have *cervello stravagante, capo irregolare, volubilità dei suoi sentimenti, stravaganza del suo pensare*, and *stravagante idee*.

The case of one Gaetano Giorgi well exemplifies this issue. Denounced by his wife, Gaetano Giorgi followed the patterns of a prodigal but manifested the kind of prodigality that closely resembled insanity. The core of his disturbance lay in his "passion" for gambling, which moved him to abuse his wife; act extravagantly; and demonstrate his frenetic, mad, and uneasy temper whenever she, or other relatives, denied him money for his vice. He fell into fits of rage, which made him capable of all kinds of indiscretions, extravagances, and excesses. Among his extravagances, his wife listed his gambling like a "mad and stupid man" (*forsennato* and *stolto*), which made him lose huge amounts of money. She also singled out his mistreatment of her as extravagant, with an escalating aggressiveness and innumerable iniquities toward her. According to the wife's account, he was "fierce" (*feroce*) with her, had fits of "frenzy," and continuously demonstrated his "uncertain temperament and humor" and "extravagant humor." One night, when he was "more furious [*foribondo*] and menacing than usual, after having given several signs of disconcerted fantasy," he started to quarrel with his wife and had an outburst of fury against her that ended with him expelling her from the house despite the fact that it was a "rainy day," declaring that she was not to come back ever again. As she recounted it, his threats this time were uttered in such an "extravagant way" that made her fear for her safety and escape.[125]

Extravagant behavior comprised the usual features of defiance of the precepts that guided family life, seen in these men's neglect of their role of heads of family, their lack of self-regulation in their daily lives, and their capricious financial decisions.[126] It is worth mentioning here that the term "extravagance" was for the most part employed by state officials and much less by petitioners. The nuanced descriptions of emotional turmoil recounted before, with their corollaries of instability, imprudence, and the capricious and disordered (*sregolato*) behaviors of the allegedly mentally afflicted were summarized by the authorities by recourse to the term "extravagance." For instance, the officials of the Pupilli described the kind of *demenza* suffered by Lorenzo Baldinotti by referring to his "furious, extravagant and uneasy nature," thus encapsulating the various assessments his relatives had given of his disorder.[127]

***

Conceptions of and terms for madness circulated fluidly between medical, legal, and lay languages in a flux that was highly contingent upon each circumstance, the institution where it was disclosed, and the purpose for so doing. To approach the history of how mental disturbances were experienced, labeled, and treated as a collective process presupposes that those discourses and practices were culturally and "equally" constructed by the actors involved (physicians, authorities, family members, and the mentally disturbed). Study of Tuscan civil and criminal litigation of the eighteenth century demonstrates the existence of a shared knowledge between lay, legal, and medical communities regarding the meanings of mental disturbance, its defining features, and most pressing effects on social and family life. Furthermore, throughout the century, the different perceptions of madness concur on the increasing importance attributed to manifestations of disturbed emotions as indisputable indicators of its presence.

As has been shown here, during the eighteenth century, emotional disturbances played an increasingly determinant role in the ways petitioners, witnesses, authorities, and medical practitioners understood madness. Although in most cases, there is no evidence of the involvement of expert medical opinion in judicial records, lay narratives concur with contemporary medical writings regarding the role attributed to disturbed emotions as an important indicator of mental disturbance. Records of civil and criminal courts demonstrate that certain forms of emotional display were considered as key evidence that the defendant had a disordered mind. The notion that strong feelings could disrupt the mind was a consensus that can be traced in a wide variety of contexts and across various social groups. Legally, it could serve as grounds to argue for diminished responsibility for committing a crime due to the power of passion to temporarily disrupt the rational faculties. Similarly, medical knowledge ascribed increasing importance to strong emotions, referred to as *passioni d'animo*, for their capacity to trigger mental afflictions. In the end, forms of emotional distress were also placed at the center of lay narratives, a centrality that was shared and acknowledged by judges and civil authorities. These narratives were increasingly concerned with how certain behaviors and reactions denoted a disturbed disposition, referred to with the terms *inquietudine, volubile, irregolare,* and *stravagante.*

The new attention given to emotional disruptions as indicators of mental affliction was accompanied by a growing awareness of the emotional dimension of familial relations. Families were paying increasing attention to the emotional displays that characterized mental incapacity because they were preoccupied in defining sane emotional displays as well. Better put, narratives of madness and mental incapacity shed light not only on discussions about proper and improper emotional reactions, but also on the role of emotions in social relations and family life, determining nuanced sets of rules about accepted codes of reaction depending on the space and situation. In this process, notions about what it meant to be mentally disturbed mixed with conceptions about social life, family roles, and personal expectations regarding interpersonal bonds, and in particular, relationships within a family group.

Notes

1 Among this rich historiography, of particular interest to this study are Anne C. Vila, *Enlightenment and Pathology: Sensibility in the Literature and Medicine of Eighteenth-Century France* (Baltimore and London: Johns Hopkins University Press, 1998); Tiziana Plebani, *Un secolo di sentimenti. Amori e conflitti generazionali nella Venezia del Settecento* (Venice: Istituto Veneto di Scienze, Lettere ed Arti, 2012); Henry Martyn Lloyd, ed., *The Discourse of Sensibility: The Knowing Body in the Enlightenment* (Cham: Springer, 2013); and Dana Rabin, *Identity, Crime, and Legal Responsibility in Eighteenth-Century England* (Basingstoke: Palgrave Macmillan, 2004), among many others.
2 William Reddy, *The Navigation of Feeling* (Cambridge: Cambridge University Press, 2001), 143.
3 Thomas Dixon, *From Passions to Emotions: The Creation of a Secular Psychological Category* (Cambridge: Cambridge University Press, 2003), 66.
4 On the contextual nature of the interpretations of emotions, the performative nature of emotions, and the interplay between the cultural context and individual agency, see Reddy, *The Navigation*, 96–111; Dixon, *From Passions*, 5; and Barbara Rosenwein, *Emotional Communities in the Early Middle Ages* (Ithaca and London: Cornell University Press, 2006), 16–25.
5 Thomas Dixon traces the appearance of the term "emotion" in English language of psychological thought back to between 1800 and 1850. Dixon, *From Passions*, 4.
6 *Vocabolario degli accademici della Crusca* (Florence: Appresso Domenico Maria Manni, 1729–1738), s.v. "sentimento," www.lessicografia.it/Controller?lemma= SENTIMENTO, accessed August 8, 2020.
7 This notwithstanding the fact that *affetto* was defined as "passion of the soul born from the desire of good or hate of what is bad," "desire," and in the sense of "benevolence." *Vocabolario*, s.v. "affetto," www.lessicografia.it/Controller?lemma=AFFETTO, accessed August 8, 2020.

8 On medical conceptualization of passions and their role in diseases and the restoration of health, see Sandra Cavallo and Tessa Storey, *Healthy Living in Late Renaissance Italy* (Oxford: Oxford University Press, 2013), 179–208; Elena Carrera, ed., *Emotions and Health, 1200–1700* (Leiden and Boston: Brill, 2013), especially the articles of Elena Carrera, 95–146, and Angus Gowland, 185–219; and Stephen Pender, "Subventing Disease: Anger, Passions, and the Non-Naturals," in *Rhetorics of Bodily Disease and Health in Medieval and Early Modern England*, ed. Jennifer C. Vaught (Burlington, VT: Ashgate, 2010), 193–218.
9 Angus Gowland, *The Worlds of Renaissance Melancholy: Robert Burton in Context* (Cambridge and New York: Cambridge University Press, 2006), 47.
10 For an overview into the discussion of the Italian medical literature of the seventeenth century regarding these issues, see Alessandro Dini, ed., *Il medico e la follia. Cinquanta casi di malattia mentale della letteratura medica italiana del Seicento* (Florence: Le Lettere, 1997).
11 *Angustia* and *angustiato* were employed in at least three contexts in the eighteenth century. The word "anguished" (*angustiato*) could be applied to patrimony and the effects produced by debts: a patrimony was anguished when it was at risk of bankruptcy; someone was anguished by creditors if he or she felt oppressed by them. Additionally, *angustia* was used in medical language not only for psychological anguish (*angustie d'animo*), but also to describe physiological events, such as the contraction or distress of an organ (as *angustia di petto, angustia alla gola, angustie del respiro, sostanza del cervello . . . angustiata*), which entailed a "sensation" of distress. This is one of the pieces of evidence identified by Lisa Smith in French and English medical consultations for the overlap between the mind and body in "'An Account of an Unaccountable Distemper': The Experience of Pain in Early Eighteenth-Century England and France," *Eighteenth-Century Studies* 41, no. 4 (2008): 463. For examples on usage of these expressions in medical literature, see Del Papa, *Consulti Medici*, vol. 2, Consultations 30, 44, and 56.
12 *Vocabolario*, s.v. "trasporto," www.lessicografia.it/Controller?lemma=trasporto and "animo," www.lessicografia.it/Controller?lemma=animo, accessed August 8, 2019.
13 Alessandro Pascoli, *Delle risposte ad alcuni consulti su la natura di varie infermità, e la maniera di ben curarle*, vol. 1 (Rome: Rocco Bernabò, 1736), 40.
14 BNCF, *Manoscritti*, GTT, no. 234, "Consultationes medicae," cart. 2, fasc. X, *Consulti per affezioni ipocondriache ed isteriche*, 114.
15 Testimony of the physician Gaspero Felizio Paver regarding a woman petitioning the Auditore Fiscale to live separated from her husband. ASF, Camera e Auditore Fiscale, *Negozi di Polizia*, F. 2748, no. 38, 1751.
16 Andrea Pasta, *Dei mali senza materia* (Bergamo: Stamperia Locatelli, 1791), 18.
17 "Io tengo che i mali nervosi di questa schiatta non dipendano da ridondanza, nè da vizio di umori, ma da sregolatezza e scomposizione del sistema nervoso, e che tale sconcerto de' nervi e stravagante dissonanza della loro irritabilità proceda interamente da precedute afflizioni, perturbazioni o intensioni smodate e forzose dell'animo. E uno che voglia seriamente razzolare addentro di questi mali, troverà che la sorgente ne suol esser l'animo passionato, o intensamente applicato sia agli studi, sia agli affari politici, militari, o economici; che le morbose impressioni fatte dagli oggetti sì esterni che interni nella sostanza midollar del cervello, e propagate a quella de' nervi che n'è una continuazione e un allungamento, no si distolgono nè si scancellano colle missioni di sangue . . . " Pasta, *Dei mali senza materia*, 50–57.
18 Antonio Felici and others, *Consulti medici*, vol. 1, MS.2344, f. 6.

19 BNCF, *Manoscritti*, GTT, no. 234, f. 114.
20 BNCF, *Manoscritti*, GTT, no. 234, f. 158v.
21 Research on medical consultation by letter has mainly focused on the experience of the body, the patient–physician relationship, the development of medical practice in terms of diagnosis and cures, and the construction of medical networks. The general characteristic of this genre in Europe is that letters were sent by socially privileged people to famous physicians (as is the case of the medical consultations examined here). These letters were not necessarily written by patients themselves but by relatives or by the patient's physician. It should be borne in mind, however, that what has survived was the correspondence that involved elite patients, although, as Steinke and Stuber observe, "we cannot exclude that consultation by letter was also practiced on a more local level by country doctors." Hubert Steinke and Martin Stuber, "Medical Correspondence in Early Modern Europe: An Introduction," *Gesnerus* 61, no. 3/4 (2004): 146. The study by Barbara Duden, *The Woman Beneath the Skin* (Cambridge: Harvard University Press, 1998), attests to this possibility. See also Séverine Pilloud and Micheline Louis-Courvoisier, "The Intimate Experience of the Body in the Eighteenth Century: Between Interiority and Exteriority," *Medical History* 47 (2003): 451–472; Smith, "An Account"; and Robert Weston, *Medical Consulting by Letter in France, 1665–1789* (London and New York: Routledge, 2016).
22 Gaetano Armillei, *Consulti medici di vari professori spiegati con le migliori Dottrine Moderne, e co' le regole più esatte della scienza meccanica*, vol. 2 (Venice: Presso Giuseppe Corona, 1743–1745), "Affezione Scorbutico-melancolica," 97.
23 Antonio Cocchi, *Consulti medici*, vol. 1 (Bergamo: Vincenzo Antoine, 1791), "Ipocondria," 96.
24 Armillei, *Consulti medici*, vol. 2, "Affezione isterico-ipocondriaca," 163.
25 This "grande passione di timore" was followed by "perturbati fantasmi, e sogni spaventevoli," which affected the patient's brain in such a way that it caused him to suffer a complicated epileptic disorder, causing organic failure in the brain that explained the persistence of the ailment. Cirillo, *Consulti medici*, vol. 2, Consulto XL, "Epilessia Idiopatica da Timore. Per l'Ecc. Sig. Aloisio Manini Nobile Veneziano," 89
26 Antonio Cocchi, *Consulti medici con un' appendice d'altri scritti in parte inediti* (Milan: Società tipogr. de' classici italiani, 1824), "Affezione scorbutica e ipocondriaca," 83.
27 BNCF, *Manoscritti*, GTT, N. 234, f. 121r.
28 BNCF, *Manoscritti*, GTT, N. 234, f. 121r.
29 Consultation to Giovanni Targioni Tozzetti, BNCF, *Manoscritti*, GTT, N. 234, f. 124.
30 Cocchi, *Consulti medici con un'appendice*, "Ipocondria," 102.
31 BNCF, *Manoscritti*, GTT, 235, *Relazioni forensi*, "Relazioni in casi di demenza," f. 208.
32 BNCF, *Manoscritti*, GTT, N. 234, f. 96.
33 Antonio Ponticelli, *Di tre specie di affezione isterica, e ipocondriaca. Trattato teorico-pratico e consulti* (Lucca: Per Vincenzo Giuntini, 1759), 35.
34 BNCF, *Manoscritti*, GTT, N. 234, "Consultationes medicae," cart.2, fasc. X, *Consulti per affezioni ipocondriache ed isteriche*, f. 107r.
35 Cirillo, *Consulti Medici*, vol. 2, "Affezione Convulsiva Ipocondriaca," 53.
36 Armillei, *Consulti Medici*, vol. 2, Consulto XLIII, "Affezione isterico-ipocondriaco spasmodica con disposizione all'idrope," 87 and Consulto XLIV, "Affezione ipocondriaca vera," 89, respectively.
37 For a discussion on the available therapeutic methods in use at Santa Dorotea and more widely in Europe during the eighteenth century, see Lisa Roscioni, *Il*

governo della follia. Ospedali, medici e pazzi nell'età moderna (Milan: Bruno Mondadori, 2003), 217–292; and Roy Porter, *Mind-Forg'd Manacles: A History of Madness in England from the Restoration to the Regency* (London: Penguin Books, 1990), 169–228.

38 Patients could resort to a wide range of healers depending on their concerns, their motivations, and economic resources. Charlatans, unlicensed healers, priests, officially appointed surgeons and doctors (*cerusici condotti* and *medici condotti*), private surgeons or doctors called in specific circumstances, or personal physicians called recurrently were among the options. For the Italian context, see David Gentilcore, *Medical Charlatanism in Early Modern Italy* (Oxford: Oxford University Press, 2006); and Gianna Pomata, *La promessa di guarigione: malati e curatori in antico regime: Bologna XVI-XVIII secolo* (Rome: Laterza, 1994). Similar conclusions regarding the process that led to medical help being sought for mental afflictions were made by MacDonald and, more recently, Andrews and Scull. Self-diagnosis and diseases first identified by families were also combined with diseases whose existence and identification were mentioned by doctors, as it was in their interest to expand the scope of their practice and make it more profitable. Jonathan Andrews and Andrew Scull, *Customers and Patrons of the Mad-Trade: The Management of Lunacy in Eighteenth-Century London* (Berkeley: University of California Press, 2003), 45–51; and Michael MacDonald, *Mystical Bedlam: Madness, Anxiety, and Healing in Seventeenth-Century England* (Cambridge: Cambridge University Press, 1981), 113–114.
39 On this literature, see Cavallo and Storey, *Healthy Living*; and Roy Porter, ed., *The Popularization of Medicine, 1650–1850* (London and New York: Routledge, 1992).
40 ASF, MPAP, *Memoriali*, F. 2305, no. 131, June 1761.
41 ASF, MPAP, *Memoriali*, F. 2307, no. 95, December 1767.
42 Testimony of Francesco Giampieri, *cameriere* (keeper) of Santa Dorotea, ASF, MS, *Atti*, F. 1214, 18 November 1735, f. 1432.
43 ASF, MS, *Atti*, F. 1983, 29 April 1737, f. 377.
44 ASF, MPAP, *Memoriali*, F. 2300, no. 547, May 1737.
45 ASF, MS, *Atti*, F. 2016, 15 November 1740, f. 125.
46 ASF, MPAP, *Memoriali*, F. 2301, no. 206(2°), 20 May 1746. In this case, the interdiction was directly initiated by the Pupilli officials.
47 I have not been able to find records of Angiolo Barchesi's committals in Santa Dorotea or Santa Maria Nuova. Before 1750, the records of Santa Dorotea have lacunae, and those of the *pazzeria* of Santa Maria Nuova are nearly non-existent.
48 ASF, MPAP, *Memoriali*, F. 2303, no. 118, July 1753.
49 ASF, MPAP, *Memoriali*, F. 2303, no. 229, October 1754.
50 See, respectively, ASF, MPAP, *Memoriali*, F. 2306, no. 120, August 1764; F. 2308, no. 79, January 1771; and F. 2309, no. 280, October 1773.
51 ASF, MPAP, *Memoriali*, F. 2306, no. 120, August 1764.
52 ASF, MPAP, *Memoriali*, F. 2306, no. 162, November 1764.
53 ASF, MPAP, *Memoriali*, F. 2308, no. 79, January 1771.
54 ASF, MPAP, *Memoriali*, F. 2308, no. 79, January 1771.
55 ASF, MPAP, *Memoriali*, F. 2301, no. 285, June 1747.
56 ASF, MPAP, *Memoriali*, F. 2308, no. 108, February 1771.
57 Disputes between women and their brothers-in-law are a common ingredient of the familial conflicts disclosed to the Pupilli for mediation. See Giulia Calvi, *Il contratto morale. Madri e figli nella Toscana moderna* (Rome: Laterza, 1994), 87–105.
58 Report of the officials of the Magistrato dei Pupilli, ASF, MPAP, *Memoriali*, F. 2309, no. 147, August 1773.

258 *Emotional disturbances*

59 Petition of Maddalena Palloni. ASF, MPAP, *Memoriali*, F. 2309, no. 280, October 1773.
60 Information sent by Benedetto Becciani. ASF, MPAP, *Memoriali*, F. 2309, no. 280, January 1774.
61 ASF, MPAP, *Memoriali*, F. 2309, no. 280, October 1773.
62 Petition of Benedetto Becciani. ASF, MPAP, *Memoriali*, F. 2309, no. 147, July 1773.
63 For instance, Gowland, *The Worlds of Renaissance Melancholy*; Monica Calabritto, "A Case of Melancholic Humors and *Dilucida Intervalla*," *Intellectual History Review* 18, no. 1 (2008): 139–154; and Monica Calabritto, "Tasso's Melancholy and its Treatment: A Patient's Uneasy Relationship with Medicine and Physicians," in *Diseases of the Imagination and Imaginary Disease in the Early Modern Period*, ed. Yasmin Haskell (Turnhout: Brepols, 2011), 201–227. Elizabeth Mellyn has examined fifteenth- and seventeenth-century Tuscan judicial narratives depicting melancholy, which although they maintain the basic vocabulary used by Maddalena Palloni, do not place their focus on emotional disturbances and their relational consequences nor present the specification and differentiation of voices that can be observed in Becciani's case. Elizabeth W. Mellyn, *Mad Tuscans and Their Families: A History of Mental Disorder in Early Modern Italy* (Philadelphia: University of Pennsylvania Press, 2014), 128–160.
64 Michael Stolberg, *Experiencing Illness and the Sick Body in Early Modern Europe* (Basingstoke: Palgrave Macmillan, 2011), 88.
65 See Gowland's discussion regarding the role of the imagination and of disturbing events in Robert Burton's theory of melancholy. Gowland, *The Worlds of Renaissance Melancholy*, 43–72.
66 ASF, MPAP, *Memoriali*, F. 2309, no. 147, August 1773.
67 For instance, ASF, SD, *Motupropri, Rescritti . . .*, F.3, no. 39, October 1758.
68 Mellyn, *Mad Tuscans*, 128–160.
69 For an overview of the top-down model of the popularization of medicine, see Porter, *The Popularization*.
70 Honor, anger, and revenge appear to be the common factors of the early modern criminal prosecution. See John K. Brackett, *Criminal Justice and Crime in Late Renaissance Florence 1536–1609* (Cambridge: Cambridge University Press, 1992), 101–117. For an overarching view, see Trevor Dean and K.J.P. Lowe, eds., *Crime, Society and the Law in Renaissance Italy* (Cambridge: Cambridge University Press, 1994).
71 Marc'Antonio Savelli, *Pratica universale* (Parma: Paolo Monti, 1717), 107.
72 Savelli, *Pratica*, 111.
73 See, for instance, the case of a man who committed murder while he had "the blood upside down" by reason of his wife's insults and arguments. Since the attack had been unpremeditated and he had not been in control of himself while he committed it, he was spared the death sentence. ASF, OGB, *Suppliche*, F. 2511, no. 8, April 1730.
74 ASF, OGB, *Suppliche*, F. 2537, no. 93, January 1761.
75 ASF, CR, *Fiscale*, F. 754, no. 60, July 1743.
76 ASF, OGB, *Suppliche*, F. 2530, no. 95, July 1750. Descriptions here draw on the usual physical changes that were thought to accompany an outburst of rage to highlight the degree to which the feeling had clouded the suspect's judgement. On the physical signs accompanying anger, see Elena Carrera, "Anger and the Mind-Body Connection in Medieval and Early Modern Medicine," in *Emotions and Health. 1200–1700*, ed. Elena Carrera (Leiden and Boston: Brill, 2013), 95–146; Kristine Steenbergh, "Green Wounds: Pain, Anger and Revenge in Early Modern Culture," in *The Sense of Suffering: Constructions of Physical*

Pain in Early Modern Culture, ed. Jan Frans van Dijkhuizen and Karl A.E. Enenkel (Leiden: Brill, 2009), 165–188; and Fay Bound Alberti, "'An Angry and Malicious Mind'? Narratives of Slander at the Church Courts of York, c.1660–c.1760," *History Workshop Journal* 56, no. 1 (2003): 59–77.
77 ASF, OGB, *Suppliche*, F. 2537, no. 173, August 1761.
78 ASF, OGB, *Suppliche*, F. 2537, no. 202, August 1761. Because there always was a concern for discipline, men who pointed to their inebriation to explain their irascible reaction were not likely to see their sentence commuted. The circumstances surrounding the crime and the individual's past history were fundamental in determining to what extent they deserved a *grazia*.
79 ASF, OGB, *Suppliche*, F. 2534, no. 113, April 1756.
80 Natalie Zemon Davis, *Fiction in the Archives* (Stanford: Stanford University Press, 1987), 81–82. It is well known that more men than women were prosecuted for violent behavior in the early modern courts. However, as Garthine Walker suggests, "This interpretative model of men's violence as 'normal' and women's as numerically and thus culturally insignificant is inadequate." Garthine Walker, *Crime, Gender and Social Order in Early Modern England* (Cambridge: Cambridge University Press, 2003), 75.
81 ASF, OGB, *Giornale di Negozzi del Banco di Città*, F. 985, fol. 6, November 1749. Female violence was exerted not only between women, but also against men.
82 See, for instance, the case of a woman tried for infanticide who claimed she had committed the crime to defend her honor and out of her "semplicità e sciocchezza" (simplicity and foolishness). ASF, OGB, *Suppliche*, F. 2499, no. 74, November 1720.
83 ASF, MPAP, *Memoriali*, F. 2302, no. 286, September 1752; and F. 2302, no. 231, February 1751.
84 ASF, MPAP, *Memoriali*, F. 2300, no. 249, July 1728; F. 2304, no. 133, August 1757; F. 2302, no. 73, January 1748/49; and F. 2306, no. 293, August 1766, respectively.
85 ASF, MPAP, *Memoriali*, F. 2301, no. 218, April 1744.
86 I have examined this topic in "The Emotional Disturbances of Old Age: On the Articulation of Old-Age Mental Incapacity in Eighteenth-Century Tuscany," *Historical Reflections/Réflexions Historiques* 41, no. 2 (2015): 19–36; and "Cuando la mente se oscurece y el cuerpo se debilita. El dolor de la ancianidad en el Gran Ducado de Toscana, siglo XVIII," in *Homo Dolens. Cartografías del dolor: sentidos, experiencias, registros*, ed. Rafael Gaune and Claudio Rolle (Santiago: Fondo de Cultura Económica, 2018), 293–314.
87 David G. Troyansky, *Old Age in the Old Regime* (Ithaca, NY: Cornell University Press, 1989), 118–124; and Lynn A. Botelho, "The 17th Century," in *The Long History of Old Age*, ed. Pat Thane (London: Thames & Hudson, 2005), 131.
88 Troyansky, *Old Age*, 119. See also Daniel Schäfer, "'That Senescence Itself Is an Illness': A Transitional Medical Concept of Age and Ageing in the Eighteenth Century," *Medical History* 46, no. 4 (2002): 538.
89 Laura Gowing, *Domestic Dangers: Women, Words, and Sex in Early Modern London* (Oxford: Oxford University Press, 1996), 180–231.
90 Chiara La Rocca, *Tra moglie e marito. Matrimoni e separazioni a Livorno nel Settecento* (Bologna: Società editrice Il Molino, 2009), 251–265.
91 The bibliography is too vast to be cited here. For a comprehensive survey, see Silvana Seidel Menchi, "I processi matrimoniali come fonte storica," in *Coniugi nemici. La separazione in Italia dal XII al XVIII secolo*, ed. Silvana Seidel Menchi and Diego Quaglioni (Bologna: Il Molino, 2000), 15–94.
92 According to Daniela Lombardi, physical and verbal forms of abuse started to be considered an acceptable cause of separation even when life was not

in danger toward the end of the century. Daniela Lombardi, "L'odio capitale, ovvero l'incompatibilità di carattere. Maria Falcini e Andrea Lotti (Firenze 1773–1777)," in *Coniugi nemici. La separazione in Italia dal XII al XVIII secolo*, ed. Silvana Seidel Menchi and Diego Quaglioni (Bologna: Il Molino, 2000), 335–367.
93 For an overview of this discussion, see Dixon, *From Passions*, 1–19.
94 ASF, MPAP, *Memoriali*, F. 2302, no. 128, April 1749; ASF, MPAP, *Memoriali*, F. 2303, no. 15, December 1751, and no. 59, August 1752, respectively. The term appears employed in this sense in few more cases, see ASF, MPAP, *Memoriali*, F. 2305, no. 92, September 1760; ASF, MPAP, *Memoriali*, F. 2306, no. 265, April 1766, and no. 293, August 1766.
95 The compulsion driving the actions of the eighteenth-century prodigal strongly resembles the driving force of a bipolar person during a manic episode, with hyperactivity and an aggressive obstinacy that grew stronger as his gambling was impeded. According to the *Diagnostic and Statistical Manual of Mental Disorders*, a manic episode is characterized by "a distinct period of abnormally and persistently elevated, expansive, or irritable mood and abnormally and persistently increased goal-directed activity or energy," accompanied by at least three to four of the following symptoms: "1. Inflated self-esteem or grandiosity, 2. Decreased need for sleep . . ., 3. More talkative than usual or pressure to keep talking, 4. Flight of ideas . . ., 5. Distractibility . . ., 6. Increase in goal-directed activity (either socially, at work or school, or sexually) or psychomotor agitation (i.e., purposeless non-goal-directed activity), 7. Excessive involvement in activities that have a high potential for painful consequences (e.g., engaging in unrestrained buying sprees, sexual indiscretions, or foolish business investments)." In the case of the eighteenth-century Tuscan interdicted, symptoms 1, 2, 5, 6, and 7 are recurrently reported, particularly the last one. American Psychiatric Association, *Diagnostic and Statistical Manual of Mental Disorders*, fifth edition (*DSM-5*) (Washington, DC: American Psychiatric Association, 2013), 124.
96 Accusations of Angiola Mori against her husband Gaetano Giorgi in her interdiction petition, which was not granted. ASF, MPAP, *Memoriali*, F. 2306, no. 293, September 1766. Notwithstanding these denunciations, he was interdicted only 6 years later. The case appears again in ASF, MPAP, *Memoriali*, F. 2309, no. 78, May 1773.
97 Margherita Roselli, a widow from Arezzo. ASF, CR, *Fiscale*, no. 64, August 1757.
98 ASF, MPAP, *Memoriali*, F. 2300, no. 182, April 1735; and ASF, MPAP, *Memoriali*, F. 2307, no. 46, August 1767.
99 Labarca, "The Emotional Disturbances."
100 ASF, SD, *Motupropri, Rescritti . . .*, F. 3, no. 91, 1760.
101 ASF, MPAP, *Memoriali*, F. 2304, no. 70, December 1756.
102 I am thinking here not only on the predicaments of Galenic medicine but, in general, about conduct manuals or the humanist praising of the virtuous citizen. These premises are at the core of the *vir virtutis* studied by Quentin Skinner, for instance, in the self-discipline of Norbert Elias' civilizing process, and in the self-examination and scrutiny promoted by the Protestant and Catholic Reformations, to name some of its facets. Quentin Skinner, *The Foundations of Modern Political Thought*, vol. 1 (Cambridge: Cambridge University Press, 1978), 88–101; Norbert Elias, *The Civilizing Process* (Oxford: Blackwell, 2000), chapter 2; Adriano Prosperi, "Diari femminili e discernimento degli spiriti: le mistiche della prima età moderna in Italia," *Dimensioni e problemi della ricerca storica* 2 (1994): 77–103; and Françoise Lebrun, "The Two

Emotional disturbances 261

Reformations: Communal Devotion and Personal Piety," in *A History of Private Life*, vol. 3, ed. Roger Chartier (Cambridge, MA: Belknap Press, 1989), 69–109.
103 See his recommendations regarding Antonio Corsini, who was subject to fixations and melancholic delirium. BNCF, *Manoscritti*, GTT, N. 235, vol. III, "Relazioni in casi di demenza," fols. 203–204v.
104 ASF, MPAP, *Memoriali*, F. 2307, no. 19, May 1767.
105 *Vocabolario*, s.v. "inquietudine," www.lessicografia.it/Controller?lemma=inquietudine, accessed August 8, 2020.
106 On this argument, see Daniela Lombardi, *Povertà maschile, povertà femminile. L'Ospedale dei Mendicanti nella Firenze dei Medici* (Bologna: Il Mulino, 1988), particularly 135–215.
107 ASF, MPAP, *Memoriali*, F. 2305, no. 25, October 1759.
108 ASF, MPAP, *Memoriali*, F. 2303, no. 76, 24 February 1753. *Fervido* came from *fervente*, meaning *bollente* (boiling) and *intenso, veemente* (intense, vehement). See the entries for "fervido" and "fervente" of the *Vocabolario*, www.lessicografia.it/Controller?lemma=fervido and www.lessicografia.it/Controller?lemma=fervente, accessed August 8, 2020.
109 See ASF, MPAP, *Memoriali*, F. 2304, no. 32, June 1756; ASF, MPAP, *Memoriali*, F. 2307, no. 19, May 1767; and ASF, MPAP, *Memoriali*, F. 2303, no. 210, August 1754, respectively.
110 ASF, MPAP, *Memoriali*, F. 2302, no. 73, January 1748/49.
111 See, for instance, the cases of Vincenzio Coletti, Giuseppe Buonamici, or Pietro Marracci in ASF, MPAP, *Memoriali*, F. 2302, no. 44, 1748, and no. 106, 1749; and ASF, MPAP, *Memoriali*, F. 2306, no. 265, 1766, respectively. Litigiousness was also coupled with extravagance and capriciousness. The evidence examined here suggests that litigiousness was perceived as an anomaly, although it did not receive, to my knowledge, a medical categorization. The limited scholarship on the subject suggests that pathological litigious behavior, although it had classical roots, was categorized as the "litigants' delusion" by German psychiatry around the mid-nineteenth century, a term that assumed different connotations according to the psychiatric schools of the twentieth century. Benjamin Lévy, "From Paranoia Querulans to Vexatious Litigants: A Short Study on Madness between Psychiatry and the Law. Part 1," *History of Psychiatry* 25, no. 3 (2014): 299–316.
112 ASF, MPAP, *Memoriali*, F. 2307, no. 19, May 1767.
113 See the admission records of Santa Dorotea. ASF, SD, *Motupropri, Rescritti . . .*, F.1–15.
114 Interdiction proceedings of Egidio Pieri, ASF, MPAP, *Memoriali*, F. 2305, no. 7, August 1759, and no. 81, July 1760; ASF, MPAP, *Lettere*, F. 2522, 21 and 26 February 1760, n/f. See also the interdiction proceedings of Giacinto Torsi, denounced by his relatives for his *volubilità dei sentimenti* and "the extravagancy of his operations." ASF, MPAP, *Memoriali*, F. 2304, no. 60, 1756.
115 ASF, MPAP, *Memoriali*, F. 2303, no. 27, May 1752.
116 ASF, MS, *Suppliche*, F. 1209, June–August 1761, fols. 402–411v.
117 The notion of extravagance, nonetheless, has not received particular attention. Traces of its pervasiveness can be found in the studies of Robert Allan Houston, *Madness and Society in Eighteenth-Century Scotland* (Oxford: Oxford University Press, 2000), 174 and 194; Laurent Cartayrade, "Property, Prodigality, and Madness: A Study of Interdiction Records in Eighteenth-Century Paris," (PhD diss., University of Maryland, 1997), 402–405; Joel Peter Eigen, *Witnessing Insanity: Madness and Mad-Doctors in the English Court* (New Haven and London: Yale University Press, 1995), 91–93; and Andrews and Scull, *Customers and Patrons*, 7, 66–69, and 110.

118 *Vocabolario*, s.v. "stravagante," "Add. Fantastico, sformato, fuor del comune uso. Lat novus, absurdus, insolitus," www.lessicografia.it/Controller?lemma=stravagante, accessed August 8, 2020.
119 *Vocabolario*, s.v. "fantastico," www.lessicografia.it/Controller?lemma=fantastico, accessed August 8, 2020.
120 See the interdiction of Pietro Gaspero Cicatti, denounced by his brother for his *contegno improprio e stravagante*, which to his eyes needed prompt repair. ASF, MPAP, *Memoriali*, F. 2303, no. 52, September 1752.
121 See interdiction of Ignazio Giuliano Fiorilli, ASF, MPAP, *Memoriali*, F. 2303, no. 191, May–July 1754.
122 ASF, MPAP, *Memoriali*, F. 2303, no. 191, June 1754.
123 Nicola Phillips, *The Profligate Son: Or, a True Story of Family Conflict, Fashionable Vice, and Financial Ruin in Regency England* (Oxford: Oxford University Press, 2013), 62.
124 Phillips, *The Profligate Son*, 148, 50 and 63, respectively.
125 ASF, MPAP, *Memoriali*, F. 2306, no. 293, 1766.
126 For instance, the interdicted Agostino de Paola, father of seven children, was considered extravagant because he unjustifiably expelled his children from home, dissipated his patrimony with his capricious selling of goods, and showed a complete lack of self-regulation. ASF, MPAP, *Memoriali*, F. 2303, no. 164, March 1754.
127 ASF, MPAP, *Memoriali*, F. 2303, no. 210, Agosto 1754.

Bibliography chapter 6

Manuscripts

Archivio di Stato di Firenze (ASF)

- Camera e Auditore Fiscale, *Negozi di Polizia*, F. 2748
- Consiglio di Reggenza (CR), *Fiscale*, F. 754–762
- Magistrato dei Pupilli et Adulti del Principato (MPAP)
  - *Atti e Sentenze*, F. 1144–F. 1362
  - *Suppliche e informazioni: Memoriali e Negozi di Cancelleria*, F. 2299–F. 2318
  - *Filza Lettere e Responsive*, F. 2480–F. 2519
- Magistrato Supremo (MS)
  - *Suppliche*, F. 1179–F. 1188
  - *Atti e Scritture*, F. 1845–F. 2103
- Ospedale di Santa Dorotea (SD), F. 1–F. 59
- Otto di Guardia e Balìa (OGB)
  - *Giornale di Negozi*, F. 927, F. 956, F. 985, F. 1016, F. 1058, F. 1059, F. 1061, F. 1066, F. 1071
  - *Riscontro di Processi*, F. 1433, F. 1438, F. 1442, F. 1471, F. 1478, F. 1557, F. 1558, F. 1670
  - *Negozi dei Rettori*, F. 2133–2135
  - *Suppliche*, F. 2499–F. 2542
  - *Filze Straordinarie*, F. 2654–2690

Biblioteca Nazionale Centrale di Firenze (BNCF)

- *Manoscritti*, Le carte di Giovanni Targioni Tozzetti (GTT), 234–235

Wellcome Library

- Felici, Antonio and others, *Consulti Medici*, vols. I-II. MS.2344-MS.2345
- Scovolo, Giacomo, and others. Archival material. *Consulti Medici*. MS4472

Printed sources

Armillei, Gaetano. *Consulti medici di vari professori spiegati con le migliori Dottrine Moderne, e co' le regole più esatte della scienza meccanica*, vols. 1–2. Venice: Presso Giuseppe Corona, 1743–1745.
Beccari, Giacomo Bartolomeo. *Consulti medici*, vols. 1–2. Bologna: Dalla Stamperìa di San Tommaso d'Aquino, 1777.
Cirillo, Niccolò. *Consulti medici*, vols. 1–2. Venice: Presso Francesco Pitteri, 1770.
Cocchi, Antonio. *Consulti medici*, vols. 1–2. Bergamo: Vincenzo Antoine, 1791.
Cocchi, Antonio. *Consulti medici con un'appendice d'altri scritti in parte inediti*. Milan: Società tipogr. de' classici italiani, 1824.
Del Papa, Giuseppe. *Consulti medici*, vols. 1–2. Rome: Appresso Giovanni Maria Salvioni, 1733.
Pascoli, Alessandro. *Delle risposte ad alcuni consulti su la natura di varie infermità, e la maniera di ben curarle*, vols. 1–2. Rome: Rocco Bernabò, 1736.
Pasta, Andrea. *Dei mali senza materia*. Bergamo: Stamperia Locatelli, 1791.
Ponticelli, Antonio. *Di tre specie di affezione isterica, e ipocondriaca. Trattato teorico-pratico e consulti*. Lucca: Per Vincenzo Giuntini, 1759.
Savelli, Marc'Antonio. *Pratica universale*. Parma: Paolo Monti, 1717.
Vocabolario degli accademici della Crusca, 6 vols. Florence: Appresso Domenico Maria Manni, 1729–1738. DOI:10.23833/BD/LESSICOGRAFIA, www.lessicografia.it/index.jsp. Accessed August 8, 2020.

References

Alberti, Fay Bound. "'An Angry and Malicious Mind'? Narratives of Slander at the Church Courts of York, c.1660-c.1760." *History Workshop Journal* 56, no. 1 (2003): 59–77.
American Psychiatric Association, *Diagnostic and Statistical Manual of Mental Disorders*, fifth edition (DSM-5). Washington, DC: American Psychiatric Association, 2013.
Andrews, Jonathan, and Andrew Scull. *Customers and Patrons of the Mad-Trade: The Management of Lunacy in Eighteenth-Century London*. Berkeley: University of California Press, 2003.
Botelho, Lynn A. "The 17th Century." In *The Long History of Old Age*, edited by Pat Thane, 113–161. London: Thames & Hudson, 2005.
Brackett, John K. *Criminal Justice and Crime in Late Renaissance Florence 1536–1609*. Cambridge: Cambridge University Press, 1992.

Calabritto, Monica. "A Case of Melancholic Humors and *Dilucida Intervalla.*" *Intellectual History Review* 18, no. 1 (2008): 139–154.
Calabritto, Monica. "Tasso's Melancholy and Its Treatment: A Patient's Uneasy Relationship with Medicine and Physicians." In *Diseases of the Imagination and Imaginary Disease in the Early Modern Period*, edited by Yasmin Haskell, 201–227. Turnhout: Brepols, 2011.
Calvi, Giulia. *Il contratto morale. Madri e figli nella Toscana moderna.* Rome: Laterza, 1994.
Carrera, Elena. "Anger and the Mind-Body Connection in Medieval and Early Modern Medicine." In *Emotions and Health: 1200–1700*, edited by Elena Carrera, 95–146. Leiden and Boston: Brill, 2013.
Carrera, Elena, ed. *Emotions and Health: 1200–1700.* Leiden and Boston: Brill, 2013.
Cavallo, Sandra, and Tessa Storey. *Healthy Living in Late Renaissance Italy.* Oxford: Oxford University Press, 2013.
Davis, Natalie Zemon. *Fiction in the Archives.* Stanford: Stanford University Press, 1987.
Dean, Trevor, and K.J.P. Lowe, eds. *Crime, Society and the Law in Renaissance Italy.* Cambridge: Cambridge University Press, 1994.
Dini, Alessandro, ed. *Il medico e la follia. Cinquanta casi di malattia mentale della letteratura medica italiana del Seicento.* Florence: Le Lettere, 1997.
Dixon, Thomas. *From Passions to Emotions: The Creation of a Secular Psychological Category.* Cambridge: Cambridge University Press, 2003.
Duden, Barbara. *The Woman Beneath the Skin: A Doctor's Patients in Eighteenth-Century Germany.* Cambridge: Harvard University Press, 1998.
Eigen, Joel Peter. *Witnessing Insanity: Madness and Mad-Doctors in the English Court.* New Haven and London: Yale University Press, 1995.
Elias, Norbert. *The Civilizing Process.* Oxford: Blackwell, 2000.
Gentilcore, David. *Medical Charlatanism in Early Modern Italy.* Oxford: Oxford University Press, 2006.
Gowing, Laura. *Domestic Dangers: Women, Words, and Sex in Early Modern London.* Oxford: Oxford University Press, 1996.
Gowland, Angus. *The Worlds of Renaissance Melancholy: Robert Burton in Context.* Cambridge and New York: Cambridge University Press, 2006.
Houston, Robert Allan. *Madness and Society in Eighteenth-Century Scotland.* Oxford: Oxford University Press, 2000.
Labarca, Mariana. "Cuando la mente se oscurece y el cuerpo se debilita. El dolor de la ancianidad en el Gran Ducado de Toscana, siglo XVIII." In *Homo Dolens. Cartografías del dolor: sentidos, experiencias, registros*, edited by Rafael Gaune and Claudio Rolle, 293–314. Santiago: Fondo de Cultura Económica, 2018.
Labarca, Mariana. "The Emotional Disturbances of Old Age: On the Articulation of Old-Age Mental Incapacity in Eighteenth-Century Tuscany." *Historical Reflections/Reflexions Historiques* 41, no. 2 (2015): 19–36.
La Rocca, Chiara. *Tra moglie e marito. Matrimoni e separazioni a Livorno nel Settecento.* Bologna: Società editrice Il Molino, 2009.
Lebrun, Françoise. "The Two Reformations: Communal Devotion and Personal Piety." In *A History of Private Life*, vol. 3, edited by Roger Chartier, 69–109. Cambridge, MA: Belknap Press, 1989.

Lévy, Benjamin. "From Paranoia Querulans to Vexatious Litigants: A Short Study on Madness between Psychiatry and the Law: Part 1." *History of Psychiatry* 25, no. 3 (2014): 299–316.

Lloyd, Henry Martyn, ed. *The Discourse of Sensibility: The Knowing Body in the Enlightenment*. Cham: Springer, 2013.

Lombardi, Daniela. "L'odio capitale, ovvero l'incompatibilità di carattere. Maria Falcini e Andrea Iotti (Firenze 1773–1777)." In *Coniugi nemici. La separazione in Italia dal XII al XVIII secolo*, edited by Silvana Seidel Menchi and Diego Quaglioni, 335–367. Bologna: Il Molino, 2000.

Lombardi, Daniela. *Povertà maschile, povertà femminile. L'Ospedale dei Mendicanti nella Firenze dei Medici*. Bologna: Il Mulino, 1988.

MacDonald, Michael. *Mystical Bedlam: Madness, Anxiety, and Healing in Seventeenth-Century England*. Cambridge: Cambridge University Press, 1981.

Mellyn, Elizabeth W. *Mad Tuscans and Their Families: A History of Mental Disorder in Early Modern Italy*. Philadelphia: University of Pennsylvania Press, 2014.

Muir, Edward. *Mad Blood Stirring: Vendetta in Renaissance Italy*. Baltimore: Johns Hopkins University Press, 1998.

Pender, Stephen. "Subventing Disease: Anger, Passions, and the Non-Naturals." In *Rhetorics of Bodily Disease and Health in Medieval and Early Modern England*, edited by Jennifer C. Vaught, 193–218. Burlington, VT: Ashgate, 2010.

Phillips, Nicola. *The Profligate Son: Or, a True Story of Family Conflict, Fashionable Vice, and Financial Ruin in Regency England*. Oxford: Oxford University Press, 2013.

Pilloud, Séverine, and Micheline Louis-Courvoisier. "The Intimate Experience of the Body in the Eighteenth Century: Between Interiority and Exteriority." *Medical History* 47 (2003): 451–472.

Plebani, Tiziana. *Un secolo di sentimenti. Amori e conflitti generazionali nella Venezia del Settecento*. Venice: Istituto Veneto di Scienze, Lettere ed Arti, 2012.

Pomata, Gianna. *La promessa di guarigione: malati e curatori in antico regime: Bologna XVI-XVIII secolo*. Rome: Laterza, 1994.

Porter, Roy. *Mind-Forg'd Manacles: A History of Madness in England from the Restoration to the Regency*. London: Penguin Books, 1990.

Prosperi, Adriano. "Diari femminili e discernimento degli spiriti: le mistiche della prima età moderna in Italia." *Dimensioni e problemi della ricerca storica* 2 (1994): 77–103.

Rabin, Dana. *Identity, Crime, and Legal Responsibility in Eighteenth-Century England*. Basingstoke: Palgrave Macmillan, 2004.

Reddy, William. *The Navigation of Feeling*. Cambridge: Cambridge University Press, 2001.

Roscioni, Lisa. *Il governo della follia. Ospedali, medici e pazzi nell'età moderna*. Milan: Bruno Mondadori, 2003.

Schäfer, Daniel. "'That Senescence Itself Is an Illness': A Transitional Medical Concept of Age and Ageing in the Eighteenth Century." *Medical History* 46, no. 4 (2002): 525–548.

Seidel Menchi, Silvana. "I processi matrimoniali come fonte storica." In *Coniugi nemici. La separazione in Italia dal XII al XVIII secolo*, edited by Silvana Seidel Menchi and Diego Quaglioni, 15–94. Bologna: Il Molino, 2000.

Shoemaker, Robert B. "The Taming of the Duel: Masculinity, Honour and Ritual Violence in London, 1660–1800." *The Historical Journal* 45, no. 3 (2002): 525–545.

Skinner, Quentin. *The Foundations of Modern Political Thought*, vol. 1. Cambridge: Cambridge University Press, 1978.

Smith, Lisa Wynne. "'An Account of an Unaccountable Distemper': The Experience of Pain in Early Eighteenth-Century England and France." *Eighteenth-Century Studies* 41, no. 4 (2008): 459–480.

Steenbergh, Kristine. "Green Wounds: Pain, Anger and Revenge in Early Modern Culture." In *The Sense of Suffering: Constructions of Physical Pain in Early Modern Culture*, edited by Jan Frans van Dijkhuizen and Karl A.E. Enenkel, 165–188. Leiden: Brill, 2009.

Steinke, Hubert, and Martin Stuber. "Medical Correspondence in Early Modern Europe: An Introduction." *Gesnerus* 61, no. 3/4 (2004): 139–160.

Stolberg, Michael. *Experiencing Illness and the Sick Body in Early Modern Europe*. Basingstoke: Palgrave Macmillan, 2011.

Strange, Carolyn, Robert Cribb, and Christopher E. Forth, eds. *Honour, Violence and Emotions in History*. London: Bloomsbury, 2014.

Troyansky, David G. *Old Age in the Old Regime*. Ithaca, NY: Cornell University Press, 1989.

Vila, Anne C. *Enlightenment and Pathology: Sensibility in the Literature and Medicine of Eighteenth-Century France*. Baltimore and London: Johns Hopkins University Press, 1998.

Walker, Garthine. *Crime, Gender and Social Order in Early Modern England*. Cambridge: Cambridge University Press, 2003.

Weston, Robert. *Medical Consulting by Letter in France, 1665–1789*. London and New York: Routledge, 2016.

Conclusion

Analysis of the itineraries of madness in the preceding pages has allowed us to generate a more complete picture of how madness was understood, explained, and experienced than could be appreciated through study of records from just one of the spaces in which it was recorded during the eighteenth century. Mental disturbances were a present and increasingly demanding reality for Tuscan families, forcing them to resort to the various different institutional mechanisms that were available to help deal with a mentally afflicted relative. We have also seen that madness was increasingly employed as an argument in front of the authorities to settle a dispute or to make sense of odd behavior. Thus, although we cannot ascertain that mental disturbances were identified more frequently in the eighteenth century than in the previous centuries, and we certainly should not conclude that there was a rise in the incidence of mental illness during the century, the fact remains that madness acquired a new visibility.

By and large, Tuscan narratives of madness reveal the capacity of early modern Tuscans to adapt their language to the needs and requirements of each institutional context, whether an interdiction petition, a criminal defense, a petition for mitigation of a sentence by reason of insanity, a petition for confinement, or a particular request sent to the office of the Auditore Fiscale. Entrenched in notions about proper behavior and inserted into family dynamics, notions about madness were further shaped by the requirements of each of the spaces in which madness was disclosed, conditioning its lexicon, typologies, and meanings. Petitioners, witnesses, state officials, and medical practitioners knew how to adjust their language to each context, and every party involved knew how and when it was desirable to introduce certain concepts instead of others.

The generic legal categories of madness and mental incapacity encompassed a wide scope of cultural meanings. This was particularly clear in interdiction procedures, which during the eighteenth century came to accept a broader spectrum of behaviors as being characteristic of madness. Against a backdrop of a constant rise in interdiction petitions, narratives started to introduce familial and personal situations that were no longer exclusively related to patrimony, such as intergenerational conflicts, matrimonial disputes, and altercations with the extended family. The argument of mental incapacity served, then, not only to prove economic mismanagement, but also to argue in favor of one or another side in a familial conflict, to give evidence supporting the need to change household arrangements or legitimize the need to end a co-residence. Changes in social life, the appearance of new expectations of family life, and conflicting agencies inside families were the conflating factors that explain why madness comes to appear more frequently in the eighteenth-century records. The new ways in which intergenerational and matrimonial disputes were managed during the century find an interesting parallel in inquiries into mental capacity, the records of Santa Dorotea, and special requests to control mental derangement. In following the itineraries of madness, litigants resorted to a new language to argue and settle their disputes, where notions about mental disorder played a crucial role.

By the end of the century, emotional agitation and shifting moods were at the center of the cultural notions of madness, present both in medical and lay society. If during roughly the first half of the eighteenth century, mental incapacity was first and foremost recognized in financial behavior, speech, and demeanor, toward the end of the century, it was increasingly evidenced by and illustrated with the person's emotional displays. Although the effects that emotional disturbances could exert on physical and mental health were not a new discovery, the fact remains that the records evidence a shift with regard to how mental incapacity was argued in judicial procedures. Shifts intrinsic to the judicial procedures and the administration of the records are intermingled here with changes in the general administration of the Grand Duchy – the mid-eighteenth century has been identified as the epoch when the changes brought about by the new dynasty became evident – and with deeper cultural movements.[1]

The eighteenth century witnessed the introduction of a new set of concerns regarding familial roles. This change can be traced in the manifestation of intergenerational conflicts implicit in the condemnation of unequal marriages, the tightening of measures to control juvenile unruliness, sexual misbehavior and debauchery, and the spread of religious discourse condemning passionate behavior and proclaiming the virtues of emotionally controlled familial roles. On the other hand, the century brought new spaces of sociability that were accompanied by unprecedented forms of self-determination and by what were perceived as stricter codes of moral behavior. The efforts to control familial disorder that have been examined in this book were concentrated around this contradiction between agency and norms – between a stricter paradigm of rationality and the continual outbursts of uncontrolled passions. Thus, the marked increase of interdiction procedures and the disclosures of mental derangement in general can be placed within a broader context of social and cultural change through which the family disorders described in these records take on a new light.

The languages of madness played a crucial role in the explosion of private life into the public arena. A symptomatic example of the new lens through which behaviors and emotional displays were being codified by the end of the century can be found in Jacopo Riguccio Galluzzi's *Istoria del Granducato di Toscana sotto il governo della casa Medici*, published in 1781.[2] In his depiction of the dramatic end of the Medici rule, Galluzzi characterized the behaviors and state of mind of the Medici family by resorting to the same lexicon of the languages of mental and emotional disturbances that inspired the disclosure of mental derangement through the itineraries of madness. Involved in passionate scandals and licentious practices, the last members of the Medici family were unsuccessful in their efforts to provide an heir and were consequently forced to watch helplessly as Tuscany fell into foreign hands. The pages Galluzzi dedicated to the last members of the Medici family in his *Istoria del Granducato di Toscana* are filled with negative commentaries on their behaviors and emotional disturbances. Most significantly for us here, he applied to Cosimo III, his wife Margherite Louise d'Orléans, their son Gian Gastone and the rest of the family a series of adjectives that disclose both a rejection of and compassion for their perturbed minds and tormented personalities. Inaugurating a trend that was to be followed later by first Gaetano Pieraccini and subsequently by Lord Acton, his descriptions of Cosimo portray him as "naturally melancholic," subjected to passions, furor, and perturbing agitations (*smanie*). Galluzzi talks of the lacerating sorrow (*amarezze*) that besieged his spirit, describing him as permanently anguished (*angustiato*) and in perpetual agitation (*perpetua agitazione*), subject to a jealousy that made him mad (*smanie della gelosia*) as he suffered the iniquities and public rejection at the hands of his wife.[3]

On her side, Margherite Louise was portrayed as utterly "voluble" (*volubile*) and "extravagant," with a "sick spirit" prone to furor and frenzy that made everyone fear that she would decide to put an end to her life. Generating profound uneasiness (*inquietudine*) all around her, especially on her husband, she was subject to passionate fits, showing capricious behavior and a complete disrespect and open disdain for her husband. Her scandalous abandonment of her husband and children before the eyes of the public was the culmination of the disruption of her expected gender role as mother and wife, attributed by Galluzzi to the effects of her perturbed mind. Not only was she excessively extravagant and the source of her husband's endless deep anguishes (*angustie* and *inquietudini*) but also, above all, she exhibited a character that was too unstable to be considered rational. Her relentless "extravagances" (*stravaganze*) and her frequent "agitations" (*trasporti*) were nothing but the inexorable consequence of her "uneasy spirit" (*spirito inquieto*), an expression that by the eighteenth century had come to convey all the perils of having a disordered mind.[4]

The distorted image of womanhood that Margherite projected is paralleled by her sons' lack of manliness, in their weakness, their inability to produce any offspring, and their irresoluteness and passivity. While her elder son sought refuge in the arts and chose a musician as his confidant, her younger son Gian Gastone was as tormented as his parents by all sorts of emotional disturbances. His "spirit" was portrayed by Galluzzi as "agitated," "oppressed by sadness," "anguished by violent passions," and often in a "violent state," as he sought refuge in debauchery and prodigality.[5] Like his father, Gian Gastone was the helpless victim of an unstable woman, who was as extravagant as his mother – Gian Gastone described her as manifesting a *bisbetico naturale* – and alternately subject to periods of "introspection, tears and eternal angers" (*musi, pianti, e rabbie eterne*).[6] The end of the family is symbolized through the pathetic figure of the alcoholic Gian Gastone, confined to his bed for the last 8 years of his life.

Galluzzi's depiction of the failure of the Medici family, their disturbed minds, and tormented characters bears a close resemblance to how familial conflicts were codified in interdiction procedures and in criminal records. The echoes can be found in both the records of Santa Dorotea and in the special requests handled by the Auditore Fiscale. Cosimo III's perturbed mind, furor, and mad reactions; Margherite Louise's capricious and unbalanced spirit; and the prodigal and vicious tendencies of Gian Gastone and the other male members of the Medici family echo of the languages and representations of the Tuscan judicial records. The disorder of the grand ducal family mirrors the disorders of private Tuscan families in their public revelations, in their dynamics, and in their distorted individualities and tormented personalities.[7] They also concur in the attention given to emotional turmoil as a defining feature of insanity.

A close examination of the language used by Galluzzi in his condemnation of the moral excesses manifested by the last Medici is indicative of the special concern developed during the eighteenth century regarding certain forms of emotional disturbance. The relationship between Cosimo III and Margherite Louise was marked, on the one hand, by her extravagances, caprices, and her uneasy and turbulent spirit and, on the other hand, by his weakness of spirit, his personal dose of melancholy, and uncontrolled passions. Their son was similarly portrayed as "a sensible man" (*un uomo sensibile*) consumed by the "violent passions" that continually "anguished" him, his prodigality, and his uneasy character (*carattere inquieto*).[8] In other words, the vocabulary we see employed again and again to portray their disturbed dispositions is in perfect consonance with the vocabulary of mental incapacity we see employed in contemporary civil and criminal records of the Grand Duchy. *Stravaganza, carattere inquieto, pazzie, trasporti*, and *agitazioni* are all terms we see employed to describe the emotional disturbances that tormented the mentally afflicted. We can thus see how the concern over emotional disturbances was not restricted to interdiction procedures or special requests to confine a family member.

Particularly by the second half of the eighteenth century, Tuscan society saw emotional disturbances as the source of familial conflict and mental affliction. *Inquietudine, carattere irregolare, umore stravagante*, and other forms of emotional instability increasingly came to the fore in discussions about deviant behavior. Changing concerns and expectations about family life were intertwined with debates about behavioral norms and expected patters of emotional display. The shaping of notions about and attitudes toward madness and the role attributed to emotions as its most defining signs are thus entrenched in the history of the family. In this sense, the debate about proper emotional reactions, what constituted a normal emotional life, and when emotional reactions breached the frontiers of sanity connect us with the negotiated systems of feelings within Tuscan families.

Notes

1 Mario Ascheri and Alessandra Contini, eds., *La Toscana in età moderna (secoli XVI–XVIII) Politica, istituzioni, società: studi recenti e prospettive di ricerca* (Florence: Leo S. Olschki Editore, 2005); Marcello Verga, *Da "cittadini" a "nobili." Lotta politica e riforma delle istituzioni nella Toscana di Francesco Stefano* (Milan: Giuffrè, 1990); Furio Diaz, *I Lorena in Toscana. La Reggenza* (Turin: UTET, 1988), and R. Burr Litchfield, *Emergence of a Bureaucracy: The Florentine Patricians, 1530–1790* (Princeton, NJ: Princeton University Press, 1986).
2 Jacopo Riguccio Galluzzi, *Istoria del Granducato di Toscana sotto il governo della casa Medici*, 5 vols. (Florence: Gaetano Cambiagi, 1781).
3 Galluzzi, *Istoria del Granducato*, vol. 4, 152, 212, 228–231, and *passim*.
4 Galluzzi, *Istoria del Granducato*, vol. 4, 152–154, 163–164, 172, 212–222 and *passim*.
5 Galluzzi, *Istoria del Granducato*, vol. 4, 348–349.
6 Galluzzi, *Istoria del Granducato*, vol. 4, 333.
7 See Harold Acton, *The Last Medici* (London: Methuen and Co. Ltd., 1958); Gaetano Pieraccini, *La stirpe de' Medici di Cafaggiolo*, vol. 2 and vol. 3 (Florence: A. Vellecchi, 1925); Maria Pia Paoli, "Gian Gastone I de' Medici, Granduca di Toscana," in *Dizionario biografico degli Italiani*, vol. 54 (2000), www.treccani.it/enciclopedia/gian-gastone-i-de-medici-granduca-di-toscana_%28Dizionario-Biografico%29/; and Maria Pia Paoli, "Margherita Luisa D'Orléans, Granduchessa di Toscana," in *Dizionario biografico degli Italiani*, vol. 70 (2008), www.treccani.it/enciclopedia/margherita-luisa-d-orleans-granduchessa-di-toscana_%28Dizionario-Biografico%29/, accessed August 28, 2020.
8 Galluzzi, *Istoria del Granducato*, vol. 4, 220 and 230.

Bibliography conclusion

Printed sources

Galluzzi, Jacopo Riguccio. *Istoria del Granducato di Toscana sotto il governo della casa Medici*, vol. 4. Florence: Gaetano Cambiagi, 1781.
Pieraccini, Gaetano. *La stirpe de' Medici di Cafaggiolo*, vol. 2 and vol. 3. Florence: A. Vellecchi, 1925.

References

Acton, Harold. *The Last Medici*. London: Methuen and Co. Ltd., 1958.
Ascheri, Mario, and Alessandra Contini, eds. *La Toscana in età moderna (secoli XVI-XVIII) Politica, istituzioni, società: studi recenti e prospettive di ricerca*. Florence: Leo S. Olschki Editore, 2005.

Diaz, Furio. *I Lorena in Toscana. La Reggenza*. Turin: UTET, 1988.
Litchfield, R. Burr. *Emergence of a Bureaucracy: The Florentine Patricians, 1530–1790*. Princeton: Princeton University Press, 1986.
Paoli, Maria Pia. "Gian Gastone I de' Medici, Granduca di Toscana." In *Dizionario biografico degli Italiani*, vol. 54, 2000, www.treccani.it/enciclopedia/gian-gastone-i-de-medici-granduca-di-toscana_%28Dizionario-Biografico%29/.
Paoli, Maria Pia. "Margherita Luisa D'Orléans, Granduchessa di Toscana." In *Dizionario biografico degli Italiani*, vol. 70, 2008, www.treccani.it/enciclopedia/margherita-luisa-d-orleans-granduchessa-di-toscana_%28Dizionario-Biografico%29/.
Verga, Marcello. *Da "cittadini" a "nobili". Lotta politica e riforma delle istituzioni nella Toscana di Francesco Stefano*. Milan: Giuffrè, 1990.

Index

Note: Page numbers in *italics* indicate a figure and page numbers in **bold** indicate a table on the corresponding page.

abuse 128, 132, 134, 199, 235; insufferable 235; of liquor 225; physical 242; verbal 242, 243
accountability: of criminally insane 197; diminished 144; for interdiction 193
administrator (*attore*) 7, 33
adolescent prodigals 59–67
adult curatorship 25–26, 32; see also curatorship/guardianship (*cura/curatela*)
adultery 248
adult guardianship (*curatela*) 25; see also curatorship/guardianship (*cura/curatela*)
adult prodigals 67–73
affections (*affetto*) 146, 155–156, 222–224; amorous 245; authenticity of 236, 239; hysteric and hypochondriac 194, 226; misguided 249; nervous 194, 225; passionate 152, 245
affective bonds 146
affezioni ipocondriache 202
affezioni isteriche 202
affezioni nervose (nervous affections) 194, 195
agency 40, 199–202, 210–211
agent (*attore*) 29 see also *attore*
agitations (*agitazioni d'animo*) 222, 225–226, 233, 249, 270
alcohol 142–143, 244
alcohol consumption: by elderly prodigals 76; by young prodigals 70–72; by the demented 97

alterazione di fantasia (alterations of fantasy) 182, 193–194, 196, 197, 238
alterazioni di mente 194
amente 189
Ancien Régime 158, 211
Andrews, J. 195
anger 225, 240–243, 246; abrupt fits of 227–228; frantic 241; *inquietudine* 249; by offences, provocation 143; old age 242; outbursts of 235; against parents 150; women 242; see also emotions
anguished disposition (*animo angustiato*) 198
anguishes (*angustie d'animo*) 225–226, 227, 228, 247; and aggressive agitation 233; anguished disposition 198; and anxiety 231; emotional 194, 231; of soul 197, 247; sources 198
angustie d'animo see anguishes (*angustie d'animo*)
animal spirits 191, 226
animo 222, 223, 225; *angustie d'animo* 194, 197, 198, 225–226, 227, 247; *commozione* 225; *guai dell'animo* 225; *ilarità dell'animo* 227; *mal animo* 241; *perturbazione dell'animo* 225; *perturbazioni di* 226; *quiete d'animo* 227; *revocatosi all'animo* 241; *scosse d'animo* 192; *sregolato* 155, 156; *tranquillità d'animo* 227; *turbazione d'animo* 194, 199, 225–226, 237; *turbazioni d'animo* 225, 237
animosity 242

Index

anxiety (*ansietà*) 198, 223, 226, 227, 231, 249
apoplexy 99, 181, 182, 188–192
arbitrary penalties 137, 142–143
arbitrio 137
Asylums (Erving Goffman) 12
attenuating circumstances 142
attore, attori (administrator) 7, 33, 34
Auditore Fiscale 7, 10, 15, 35, 101, 128, 129, 140; Brichieri Colombi, Domenico 135, 206, 207–210; Brichieri Colombi, Giovanni 206; Council of Regency 144, 145, 155, 158, 162; criminal sentences, supervision 145; *discolo/discoli* 147, 148–149; expertise of 205–210; family conflicts 155–157, 158; Filippo Luci 206, 208; head of police and public order 131–132, 158; intervention 146; and Otto di Guardia e Balìa 147, 163; role 158

balance, importance of 246
Baldinotti, A. 152–153
Baldinotti, L. 1–4, 6, 105, 110, 133–134, 152–153, 206, 229, 231
Barberino di Mugello 232, 237
Barchesi, A. 229–231
Barni, M. 114
Becciani, A. 232–239
Becciani, G. B. 233–234, 235, 236
Bergamo 225
Bini, Z. 149, 150
Biotti, V. 27
Bizzocchi, R. 94
Blackstone 46
Boari, M. 31
Brichieri Colombi, D. 135, 206, 207–210
Brichieri Colombi, G. 206
British society and mental incapacity 44–46
brothers 42, 232
buon governo, principles of 205–206

Calvi, G. 39–40
Cambellotti, C. 101, 209–210
capo irregolare 250, 251, 252
Cartayrade, L. 42–44, 115
Castiglion Fiorentino 63
Catholic Church, role 203
certification: medical 130, 132, 134, 135; purpose 181
cerusici condotti 179–180
Ceuli, G. 65–66

Chiarugi, V. 187
childish (*rimbambito*) mind 98–99
civil incapacity 31
civil justice 25, 48
civil rights 44–46
clergymen 177, 186, 203–205
Cocchi, A. 187
cognition 46, 138, 142; bereft of 192, 200, 201, 241; devoid 182, 183, 185; loss 193; weak 235
Commissions of lunacy 41, 46
compassion 144–145
compulsive behavior 246
confinement 5–6, 35, 131; criminally mad 144, 145; finance 159; forms of 145; in France 44; justified 129, 132, 155; in Malmaritate/Mendicanti 154, 155, 156, 162; persuasive measures 158; petitions for 132, 149; for security reasons 144; in ship, prison, fortress, or hospital 158–161
confino 143
conflicts: of co-habitation 146, 162; family 147, 155, 162, 198, 199, 205, 211, 232–240, 243; intergenerational 146, 162, 223; matrimonial 129, 146, 154, 155–157, 162; resolution of 205, 210; testimonies 203; younger and older generations 251
confusion 226
conscience 222
conseil judiciaire, France 42–43
Conservatorio dei Mendicanti 154, 155, 156, 162, 248
consilia 138
Consulta 134, 145
consulti medici (medical consultations) 183, 194–195, 197, 202, 225–227, 247
continual fixation 200, 201
continual frenzy 128
contumacious/contumacy 136–137, 142, 241
convulsive seizures 188, 189
corporal indispositions 203–204
Corsi, A. 95–96
Corsini, A. 195–199, 231
Council of Regency 134; in 1747 144; and Auditore Fiscale 145, 155, 158, 162; command of 207, 208; violent epileptic fits 191
Council of State 145
crime(s): drunkenness at moment of 142–143, 241; examination of

events 139; feelings of anger, hate, revenge, or jealousy 240; intent and motivation for 136; motive for 141; murder 139, 141, 193, 241, 242; power of passion 253; responsibility for 140; sexual 153–154; of violence 142
criminal insanity 136–145, 146, 160, 193; accountability 197; assessment of 177, 210; destinies 157, 160; different levels 185; diminished responsibility 136, 153; interdiction procedures and trials 243; medical opinion in 177, 178; Santa Dorotea 160
criminal justice: head of police and supervisor 158; proceedings of 151; studies on 143; Tuscan 129, 141; see also Otto di Guardia e Balìa
criminal procedure 136, 176, 185; exemption from punishment in 129; extenuating circumstances 240, 242; medical knowledge in 177; for suspected suicide 139
criminal proceedings 138, 140, 142, 144, 244
cronscription to serve in ship's crew (forced embarkation) 129, 149, 157–158, 159
Cugi, D. 200–202
Cugi, S. 200
cultural anxiety 11
cura see curatorship/guardianship (*cura/curatela*)
curatore (guardian) 24, 29
curatorship/guardianship (*cura/curatela*) 7, 130, 157, 162; adult 177; Antonio Becciani 238; Antonio Corsini 195, 196, 198; of the dumb and deaf 26; and interdiction 178, 185; Magistrato Supremo 195, 196; management of 182; problem of 160
custodial arrangements 4–5, 6, 31, 89, 100, 105, 116, 128, 129–133, 135, 140, 160, 161, 186, 189, 190, 207

daughters 39, 75, 76–77, 89–90, 104, 106, 110–111, 115
Davis, N. Z. 242
deafness 189
death penalty 142, 143, 144
death threats 147
debauchery 147, 151, 251, 252, 268, 270; economic and sexual 148

debole di mente (weak of mind) 92–93, 95, 96, 106
debts 154, 195, 230, 239, 247
Dei mali senza materia 225
del Feo, F. P. 104
deliriums (*delirio*) 12, 134, 138, 192, 193, 231; delirious intellect 194; manic 226; *see also* melancholic delirium (*delirio melanconico*)
della Renna, A. 155
del Papa, G. 187
del Sera, F. 161–162
delusion 194
demente/dementi (demented) 9, 10, 11, 26, 32, 59, 78, 90, 92–93, 96, 100, 134–135, 136, 138, 149, 150, 152; medical testimonies 182, 187, 194, 199
demenza (dementia) 29–30, 32, 65, 78, 134, 137–138, 141, 162, 184, 189; account of 178; Antonio Corsini 196, 197; category 138; cause of 188; configuration of 146; consequences of 189; *demenza ipocondriaca* 192, 194, 195; disruptions of family life by 243; emotional disturbances 225, 229, 230, 248; generic 193; interdiction procedure 178–180, 184, 185, 186, 187, 195, 197; possible variants for 138; *Relazioni in casi di demenza* 202; in Tuscany 43; use 138
demenza, interdictions procedures for 86–117; and age 87–90; categories of **91**; defendants and petitioners 87–90; domestic circumstances of madness 100–112; and family roles 87–90; and gender 87–90, 112–116; meanings and judicial uses of 90–93; representations of mental incapacity 93–100
demenza ipocondriaca 192, 194, 195
denunciation of mental incapacity 29
desires 159, 225, 229, 240–241, 245
determinations (*sentimenti*) 96
deterrent effect 144
deterrent sentences 142–143
Diacceti, A. G. 111–112
diarrhea 195
diet 192, 196, 224, 227, 246
dilapidatori (dissipaters) 29, 57, 90
dilemma 137, 142, 144
diminished liability, assessment of 136–145
diminished responsibility 136, 142, 153, 240, 253

276   *Index*

discolo/discoli 147–149, 150–151, 152, 159, 252
dishonor 145, 148, 154, 187, 235, 237
disobedience 11, 147–151
disordered disposition 155–156
disputes, matrimonial 129, 146, 154, 155–157, 158, 162
disquietude 247, 248
distress, emotional *see* emotional disturbances/distress/instability
disturbed humor (*torbido umore*) 150, 157
Dixon, T. 222
domestic theft 149
domestic violence 149
drunkenness (inebriation) 70–72, 76, 97, 142–143, 207, 241

eccentricities 251
economic management/mismanagement 43, 46, 62, 70, 72
economic resources 130, 131, 133, 161
economic subsistence 37
elderly *see* old age
emotional anguish/perturbations (*angustie d'animo* or *turbazione d'animo*) 194
emotional disturbances/distress/instability 222–254; *agitazioni d'animo* 225–226, 270; *angustie d'animo* 227; circulation and re-elaboration of languages 227–231; family conflicts 232–240; furious reactions 240–244; indicators of mental derangement 240–253; *inquietudine* 226, 227, 247–250; irascible reactions 236, 242–243; medical approaches 224–227; overview 222–224; passions 244–245; *perturbazioni d'animo* 226; symptoms 226; *turbazioni d'animo* 225, 237; unpredictable emotional reactions 245–243
emotional instability 78, 91, 95, 226, 234, 243; damaging effects of 247; extravagance 250; forms of 246, 252, 270; identification 242; by *inquietudine* 226–227; manifestations of 239; overflowing 237; persistent low spirits 246; and unpredictable emotional reactions 245–253
emotions 222–223; control 227, 243; disturbed 222, 224, 244, 252, 253; evaluation and interpretation 224; extravagant 250; immoderate 156; intense 243; lack of regulation 246; and madness 231; management over 227; prodigality 58, 67, 70, 77; *see also* anger
Empoli 128, 184
England 88
English law and mental incapacity 44–46
enlightened sociability 146
environment 135, 188, 202, 227
epilepsy 99, 181, 182, 188–192, 189
exculpatory circumstances 142, 143
exercise 224, 227, 246
expenditure: excessive 239, 247, 251–252; public 135
experts and authorities on madness 176–211; Auditore Fiscale 205–210; clergymen 177, 186, 203–205; medical opinion 177–202; overview 176–177; priests 132, 184, 200, 203–205, 209, 210–211
extravagance/extravagancy(ies) 94–95, 250–253; *capo irregolare* 250; *dementi* and *pazzi furiosi* 152; and disordered disposition 156; eccentricities 251; emotional disturbance 232, 235, 245, 246; emotional instability 250; extravagant brain (*cervello stravagante*) 150, 250, 252; extravagant head (*capo stravagante*) 157, 252; of fantasy 194; foolishness and 155; humors 250, 252; *imbecille di mente* (imbecile of mind) 161–162; implications of 248; *inquietudine* 250; male extravagance 156–157, 159; and melancholic delirium 208; *pazza condotta* 209–210; signs of 152; women's sexual scandals 154

family(ies): conflicts 34, 39–40, 65, 147, 155, 198, 199, 205, 211, 232–240, 243; conflicts of co-habitation 1–4, 146, 162; disputes 105–110, 155–157, 158; domestic arrangements 87–88; emotionally regulated 147; father 90, 146–147, 244, 251–252; financial resources 161; intergenerational conflicts 12–13, 89–90, 129, 146, 162; lines 9, 34, **41**, 65, 89; litigation, mental disturbance in 155–157; maintenance fee 130; marriage conflicts 89, 129, 146, 154, 155, 162;

medical practitioners 181; mental disturbance, signs of 146; mothers 89–90, 232; new concerns 146; parenting and matrimony, issues 146; roles 146; social backgrounds 147; strategies and dynamics 40; violent behavior 149–150
fantasy (imagination) 198, 199; alterations of 182, 193–194, 196, 197, 238; disconcerted 252; disturbances of 197, 237; extravagancies of 194; lively 226; overheated 232, 235, 237–238; perturbation 238; realms of 250; susceptible 237
fathers 90, 146–147, 251–252
fatuitas 138
Faubert, M. 113
fear 225
fee to the magistrate 34–35
Felici, A. 225
female insanity 112, 113; *see also* women
females *see* women
fevers 191, 196, 225
fickleness (*leggerezze*) 152, 247
fidelity, matrimonial 154–155
financial mismanagement *see demenza*; prodigality
financial resources 130, 131, 133, 161
Firenzuola 141
fissazioni di mente (mind fixations) 182, 194, 202
fixations: continual 200, 201; *see also* mental fixations (*fissazioni*)
Florence 145, 152, 155, 191, 198, 206; college in 140; Fortezza da Basso in 159, 207; madhouses in 179; Otto di Guardia in 141; *see also* Santa Dorotea
Florentine Republic 32, 39
Fondora, C. M. 156
forced embarkation 159
Forenzani, A. 102
Fortezza da Basso 159, 207, 208
Foucault, M. 5–6, 153
France 8, 41–44, 58, 88, 222
fratello converso 139
frenetic behavior 97–98
frenzy (*frenesia, frenesie, frenetico*) 93, 138, 159, 161, 185, 192; and anger 246; continual 128; extent of 245; fall into 242, 248; fits of 140, 252; *inquietudine* 247–248; insufferable 128; and mania 231; and melancholy 193; recurrent 208
Frulli, M. 100
furiosi (furious or raving mad) 31–32, 90, 130
furioso 29, 138, 245, 248, 249; *see also pazzo furioso*
furious reactions 240–244
furore 137–138
furore maniaco 229
fury 242–243, 244, 245, 246, 252

Gaci, L. M. 114
galleys 142, 143, 144
Galluzzi, J. R. 269–270
Gambassi, L. 134, 135, 136
gambling 252
gender: identities 146; *inquietudine* 248–249; and interdiction 112–116; relations 223; roles 146–147, 204; violent reaction 242
Giacchi, R. 37
Giorgi, G. 252–253
giudizio universale di concorso dei creditori 34
Goffman, E. 12
Grand Duchy of Tuscany 195, 246, 268, 270; Lorraine reforms 24, 33
Grand Duke 26, 133, 137, 144, 195, 206
grazia 133, 137
Greve 133
Groppi, A. 74–75
Grosseto 160, 161
guardian (*curatore*) 24, 29
guardianship *see* curatorship/ guardianship (*cura/curatela*)

half mad 131, 209, 250
hate 240
hereditary mental incapacity 110
Histoire de la folie (Michel Foucault) 5
homicide 143
homosexuality 152, 153
honesty 133, 135
honor/dishonor 145, 148, 154, 187, 235, 237, 242
Houston, R. A. 7, 12, 39, 46–47, 101, 115
humoral theory 243, 246
humors 225, 236, 237, 245, 250, 252; disturbed 150, 157; extravagant 250, 252; melancholic 232, 235, 236, 237–238

Index

hyperactivity 246, 249
hypochondria 194, 225, 226, 246
hysteria 194, 225, 246

idiocy 45–46, 93
illness of mind (*infermità di mente*) 182
imbecility 138, 191, 233–236, 238; dangerous 232, 235–236; of mind (*imbecillità di mente*) 99, 153, 161, 182, 189; and stupidity 233–236
impunity 144
incerto (uncertain) 245, 249, 252
incorrigibility 148, 149, 150
indecency 97–98
indignation 225
indiscipline among young prodigals 63
individual ownership 47
inebriation (drunkenness) 70–72, 76, 97, 142–143, 207, 241
infanticide 140
Ingram, A. 113
injury, self-inflicted 139
inquietudine (uneasiness) 95, 159, 225, 226, 227, 246–250
insanity 176; among young prodigals 64; categories 138; defense 137, 140–141; expert testimony regarding 178; finding of 241; in France 41–43; identification 182; pleas 136–137, 138, 142–144, 241; and property 47; protecting 42; semi-manic 229; *see also* criminal insanity
insomnia 226
instability 96; *see also* emotional disturbances/distress/instability
insufferable frenzies (*frenesie insoffribili*) 128
intellectual disability (*melensaggine*) 99
intellectual impairment 144
interdiction petition (*supplica*) 29, 38, 39–41, 59, 65, 67, 73, 87–90, 147, 203, 228, 229, 252; development of 182; Domenico Cugi 200; medical testimonies 180, 182, 183, 184, 196, 199
interdiction procedures 28, 30, **41**, **91**, 157, **179**; abuse of 37–39; acquiring familiarity with 110–112; age 9, 13, 25, 87–90; aim of 36; authority of priests 184; bereft of cognition 200, 201, 202; committal to mental hospital 136; concern for madness 129; *demenza* 138, 178–180, 184, 185, 186, 187, 195, 197; *discoli* in 150; epilepsy and apoplexy in 188, 189; and family disputes 105–110; as a family matter 39–41, 228; on Florentine Statutes 177; and gender 9, 13, 39, 87–90, 112–116; inquiries 7–9, 29, 39, 41–48; and judicial procedures 143, 177–178; language in 156; matrimonial contentions 155–157; medical opinion in 177–202; and medical practitioners 228–230; medical testimonies of 191, 197, 199, 200; *melensi* and *mentecatti* in 132; mental fixations 190; mental incapacity 138–139, 163, 177–178, 189; mentally disturbed recorded in 146; normalization 193; parameters set by 130; revocation 1, 2, 41, 43. 73, 99, 109–110, 114–116, 178, 179, 180, 184, 200, 203; strategies of 37–39
interests 222
intergenerational conflicts 100
irascible reactions 236, 242–243
irrational passion (*irragionevole passione*) 152
irregolare (irregular) 224, 245, 247, 249, 250, 251, 252
irregular head (*capo irregolare*) 250–251
irritability, extreme 246

Jacquet, G. 207–208
jealousy 237, 240, 242
Jesuit college of San Giovannino 139
judicial assessment, medical opinion in 176, 177–202
justified rage 142
Justinian's Digest 31
juvenile prodigals 147
juvenile unruliness 268

lack of discernment 139
legal administrators (*attori*) 102
legal capacity, suspension of 35
legal guardianship 60; *see also* curatorship/guardianship (*cura/curatela*)
legal incapacity 58
legal language, of criminal and civil procedures 135
legal procedure, medical opinion 177–202
Leopold, P. 33
liability 15, 178; diminished 136–145
licentious behavior 151–155

Index   279

life imprisonment 160
love 245; dangers of 151–152; foolish 154, 156; in old age 245; self-love 222; unrequited 240
low spirits 238, 243, 246, 249
Luci, F. 206, 208
lucid intervals 138, 162, 197, 201, 207
Lulli, A. 134–135, 186, 192, 196, 197, 211
lunacy 45–46, 93

Macerata 225
madness: case study 1–4; and family 12–13; flexible categories 9–12; itineraries of 4–7; nuanced conceptions 9–12; as police matter 145–157; and property 47; *see also demente/dementi* (demented); *pazzia furiosa*; *pazzo/pazzi*
madness, domestic circumstances of 100–112; interdictions, acquiring familiarity with 110–112; interdictions to solve family disputes 105–110; rhythms of family life 103–105; time frames 101–103; *see also demente/dementi* (demented); *pazzia furiosa*; *pazzo/pazzi*
Maestrini, L. 128, 129, 130, 206, 207, 208, 229
Magherini, G. 27
Magistrato dei Pupilli 24–30, 28, 128; commands of 249; court of 136; curatorship 196; *discolo/discoli* 147, 148; medical testimonies 177, 180, 185, 186, 189, 190, 192, 201, 202; officials of 128, 134, 162, 177, 180, 192, 204, 206, 208, 249, 253; *pazzia furiosa*, framing 202; records of 130, 142; Statute reform of 1680 26–27; Statute reform of 1718 27–28, 32, 177; tutorship 31; *see also* curatorship/guardianship (*cura/curatela*); interdiction procedures
Magistrato Supremo 26–29, 178, 195
Maioli, M. L. 131–132
mal animo 241
mal caduco see epilepsy
malice, lack of 141, 144
mallevadore (administration) 33
Malmaritate, Conservatory of the 104, 154, 162
mania 138, 144, 150, 193, 207; causes and symptoms of 224; characterization 226; emotional disturbances 224, 226, 229, 231, 246; and low spirits 238
mania furiosa 245
marital status and mental incapacity 9, 46, 62, 76–77, 88–91, 104, 106, 151–152
Martelli, N. 134
matrimonial conflicts 129, 146, 154, 155, 162
matrimonial litigation 146, 155–157, 205, 243
matrimonial violence 244
matterelli (mad) 130
matti (mad) 130
matto (mad) 138, 141, 146
medical approaches, to emotional distress 224–227
medical certification 130, 132, 134, 135
medical consultations 183, 194–195, 202, 225–227, 247
medical languages, of madness 195–200
medical literature 3, 4, 15, 96, 135, 222, 227, 243, 244, 246
medical opinion, to assert mental incapacity 177–202
medical practitioners 176–202; Auditori Fiscali 208, 210–211; in interdiction procedures 227–230; testimonies 182–185, 210–211; without 203; written reports of 208
medical testimonies: apoplexy and epilepsy 189; Auditore Fiscale, role 209–210; by clergymen 203, 204; conflicting 203–204; context and shape 202; employment of medical categories 186–195; instrumental choosing of categories 200–202; of interdiction procedures 191, 197; lack of specificity in 187; practitioners 177–197, 211, 228–230; priests' 183, 184, 203–204, 210; principles of criminal law 188; qualitative difference between 186; role 182–185; signers of 203; Targioni Tozzetti's 202; Xaverio Valloni's case 190
medici condotti 179–180
Medici family: Cosimo III de' Medici (Grand Duke) 269, 270; Gian Gastone I de' Medici 269–270; Margherite Louise d'Orléans 269, 270
Medici period 39–40

medico condotto 184, 188, 200
medico fiscale 188, 225
melancholic delirium (*delirio melanconico*) 207, 208; characterization 226; defined 199; by emotional disturbances 225, 226, 238; medical category 208; medical testimonies 182, 193, 194, 196, 199, 204; mental affliction 202; mental disorder 194
melancholic fixations 193
melancholic humor 232, 235, 236, 237–238
melancholy: causes and symptoms of 224; characteristics 238; emotional disturbances 224, 236, 238, 243, 246; etiology 196, 237; framing mental incapacity 238; humoral theory 243; medical testimonies 192, 193, 194, 196; medico-legal category 138; mental confusion by 140; Xaverio Valloni's case 189–190
melensaggine 142
melenso/melensi 132–133, 136, 138, 190, 194, 200, 234
Mellyn, E. 5, 7, 8, 9–10, 27, 32, 58, 94, 144, 160, 192–193, 239
men: anger and violent reactions 243; criminal behavior 142; extravagance 156, 250–252; *inquietudine* 249; mental capacity 204–205; mental derangement 157; mental incapacity 242
mental afflictions 178, 182, 190, 192, 194, 197; Angiolo Barchesi's 230; characteristics 202; classification 193; Corsini's 199; degrees 132; diagnostic categories 202; Domenico Cugi's 202; effects of 227; emotional dimensions 232; etiology 226; expertise on 186; features 248; identification 176; kinds 138, 247; legal assessment 210; long-term 228; management 205, 206; medical recommendations 246; nature 200, 202; notions 177; symptoms of 246
mental capacity, inquiries into 7–9, 40–41
mental confusion 140
mental derangement 146, 149, 155; characterizations 163; emotional disturbances 240–253; legal categories of 163; male 157; public responses to 162–163; territory of indicators of 157
mental deterioration 189

mental disturbance 193, 197, 237–238, 244; association with 187; cause and symptom of 222; characteristics 143, 199; collateral damage of 162; evidence of 246; in family litigation 155–157; framing 202; hereditary 234; identification 199, 228; individualistic representations 238; judicial narratives of 182; in judicial practice 187; lay narratives of 247; legal assessment 211; level of 141; medical practitioners 180, 181, 185, 186, 193, 197; medical testimonies 180, 181; origins and gradations of 137–138; public disorders generated by 158; recurrent 230, 231, 232; signs of 146, 192, 248; terminology 199; unfounded outbursts of 242; weakness for same-sex relationships 153; *see also* emotions
mental fixations (*fissazioni*) 226, 238; medical testimonies 182, 187, 189–190, 192, 193, 194, 201
mental illness 181, 183, 192, 198, 234, 248
mental impairment 139, 142, 189, 201
mental incapacity: assessment 138, 139, 176, 177, 178, 183, 210; Auditori Fiscali, role 209; and body 97–98; categories of 29; category 229, 239; concept of melancholy to frame 238; consequences of 239; convulsive episode or stroke 189; economic transactions 239; emotional disturbances 228, 232–234, 245–247; evidence of 189, 242, 243–244, 246; extravagance 251, 252; form of 129; identification 183; interdiction procedures 138–139, 163, 177–178, 189; legal 138; medical lexicon of 228, 229; medical opinion to assert 177–202; old-age 98–100; reason of 137
mental state, altered 144
mentecatti/mentecatto 29, 90, 130, 132, 133, 136, 138, 144, 182, 187, 189, 192, 194, 204, 233–234
Migliorini, G. 103–104, 180
minors and Roman law 31
monasteries 159
Montanti, E. 111
Montevarchi 135
moods 225, 237, 238, 246, 247
moral behavior, discipline 153

moral depravation 64
moral depravity 58
moral economy 47
mothers 39–41, 60, 61, 89–90, 232
motivation 136, 142, 241
murderous behavior 139, 141, 193, 241, 242
muteness 189

Napoleonic Code 32, 44
Nardi, D. 198
Nardi, G. 195, 196, 198
nervous affections (*affezioni nervose*) 194, 195
nervous complaints 194–195
Nootens, T. 48
Nove Conservatori del Dominio 132

old age: anger 242; apoplexy 188; conflicts 251; custody and care 75–76; decrepitude 75, 98–100, 102, 107, 110; elderly prodigals 73–78; emotional instability in 243; extravagance 250–251; family conflicts 243; interdiction procedures 243; and interdiction procedures 87–90; low spirits 243; medical literature on 243; mental incapacity in 98–100; passions 242, 243, 245; petitions for the interdiction to be lifted 109–110
ordinary penalty 143, 240
ostinata fissazione 199
Otto di Guardia e Balìa 136–137; Auditore Fiscale and 163; crimes judged by 143; *discolo/discoli* 147; epileptic convulsive seizures 188; officials of 141; over local criminal courts 140; records of 143–144; Targioni Tozzeti's testimonies 202

Palloni, M. 234–235, 236, 237, 239
Panfi, F. 110
Panfi, M. M. 203–204
paralysis 188
parricide, attempted 141
partial lifting of the interdiction 35
passions (*passione*) 222–224, 240, 244–245, 247; amorous 194; and crime, extenuating circumstances 240, 242; in criminal procedures 244–245; disordered 245; exculpatory circumstances 143; extenuating circumstances 240, 242; immoderate 154, 156; improper 246; intemperate 252; in interdiction procedure 65–73, 65–74; internal 225; irrational 152; old age 242, 243, 245; power to cloud a person's judgement 242; and prodigality 60–73, 244, 252; self-government 246; of soul 223, 224, 225, 226; stimulus of 225; strong 143, 151, 236, 240; violent 157, 241
Pasta, A. 192, 225
paterfamilias 31, 34, 59, 67–68, 93, 246
Patriarchi, A. 114–115
patrilineal system 60
patrimonial rationality 8, 58, 94
patrimony (*stante la sua demenza, va dilapidando*): importance of 37; mental incapacity and 93–94; *see also demenza*; prodigality
pauperism 135
pazzeria of Santa Maria Nuova 130–136, 159–161; committal to 181, 182; interdiction records 178–179, 182; medical testimonies from 181
pazzia 138, 144, 196–197, 229; *demenza e pazzia* 184; ill with madness (*infermo di pazzia*) 182, 230; *pazzia allegra* 246; *pazzia frenetica* 246
pazzia furiosa 129, 132, 133, 134, 135; certified by doctor 184; deviant sexual practices 152; disordered and violent behavior 150; features of 146; furious fits 149; institutional 230; suicidal or murderous behavior 193; *see also* Santa Dorotea
pazzo/pazzi 10, 11, 92, 95–96, 128, 130, 133–135, 138, 141, 144, 150, 161, 191, 199, 205, 207, 209, 223, 245
pazzo furioso 133–135, 207, 245
penalties 138, 146, 192, 202; arbitrary 137, 142–143; death sentence 143; galleys 142, 143, 144; ordinary 143, 240; prison 130, 141, 144–145, 159–161, 202, 205; statutory 137
Penci, O. 92–93
perturbations of the soul *see animo*
Peruzzi, B. M. 152
Peter Leopold of Habsburg-Lorraine (Grand Duke) 33
Phillips, N. 64, 251
physical abuse 242
physical impairment 99, 100, 189

282 Index

physical violence 242, 243
physicians, as expert witnesses 176–202
physicians *condotti* (*medico condotto*) 179–180
Pia Casa di Santa Dorotea dei Pazzerelli *see* Santa Dorotea
Pieraccini, G. 269
Pisa 131
pity 144–145
pleas: of drunkenness 142–143; insanity 136–137, 138, 143, 144
pleasures 59–67
police matter, madness as 145–157
poor families 131, 133, 134
Portoferraio 152
poverty 131–132, 133, 135
Pratica universale 137
Prato 196, 197, 198, 200
pregnancy 140–141
premeditation 141
priests: and medical practitioners 177, 183, 211, 227; as witnesses 132, 184, 200, 203–205, 209, 210–211
Principate 32
prison 159–161, 202, 205; Stinche 130, 132, 134, 135, 141, 144
prodigality 29, 150, 152, 157, 159; adult prodigals 67–73; in civil law 176; configuration of 146; consequences of 189; and *demenza* 91–92; disrupted emotional state 247; disruptions of family life by 243; elderly prodigals 73–78; excessive expenditure 251; features of 251; in France 41–43; interdictions for 178–179; licentious activities 250; overview 57–59; and passions 244, 252; in Tuscany 43; young prodigals 59–67; *see also* extravagance/extravagancy(ies)
prodighi (prodigals/spendthrifts) 29, 57, 90
property (*sottoposti*), administration of 29
prostitution 142, 248
public expense (*pubbliche spese*) 132
public experts (*periti fiscali*) 186
public honesty 133, 135
public quietness 133, 135
Puccini, C. 232, 234, 235
punishment 129, 137, 143, 144, 158–159, 176, 185; exile 6, 141, 151, 158, 160

Quaestiones medico legales 138
quietness 131, 227

rage 142, 143, 241, 242, 244, 246, 252
rape (*stupro*) 152
raving madness (*pazzia furiosa*) 10, 12; *see also pazzia furiosa*
Razzuoli, A. 160–161
recklessness 113, 150, 251, 252
Reddy, W. 222
reforms (of the Pupilli): 1473 reforms 25; 1565 reforms 26; 1680 reforms 26, 27; 1718 reforms 28, 32, 57; *see also* Magistrato dei Pupilli
Regency, Council of *see* Council of Regency
regulation, importance of 246–247
religion and madness 151, 152, 153, 159, 193, 222, 223
remarriage of elderly prodigals 76–77
Renaissance culture 246
resentment 242
rest 246
restlessness 226, 247, 249
revenge 240–241
revocatosi all'animo 241
Righini, N. 141–142
Rigi, D. 151
Roman law 30–32, 136, 240
Rome 139–140
Roscioni, L. 5, 10, 130
Rossetti, F. 229
Rushton, P. 93

sadness 225
Salvatori, I. 104
San Bonifazio 187
San Gimignano 86
Santa Dorotea 2, 5–7, 10–11, 15, 35, 78, 104, 112–113, 116, 128, 130–136, 195, 198; administration of 130–133; admission procedure 130, 132, 133, 134, 135, 186, 202; Antonio Lulli from 134–135, 186, 192, 196, 197, 211; committal to 149–150, 157, 160, 181, 182; confinement in 159–161; criminally insane 160; discharge from 132–133; fees of 130, 131, 133, 161; foundation of 160; inmates 134; interdiction records 178–179, 182, 186–187; medical testimonies from 181; physicians 130, 131, 133–134; provisions of 1750 131, 133; records of 193; reforms 131, 132, 158
Santa Maria Nuova *see pazzeria* of Santa Maria Nuova
Savelli, M. 136, 137–138, 143, 178

scandalous libertinage 154–155, 156
Scardigli, M. M. 105, 184
scemo 138, 141, 241, 248
scosse d'animo 192
Scotland 41, 46, 58, 88, 93
Scutellari, L. 134
self-control 157, 247, 252
self-defense 242
self-government 246–247
self-inflicted wounds 139, 148
self-injurers 139
self-love 222
self-regulation 246–247, 253
self-treatment 228
semi-manic insanity (*insania semimaniosa*) 229
sensibility 222, 226
sensorial impairments 100
sentiments (*sentimento*) 222, 223, 252
separatio thori (separation of bed and board) 149
sexual behavior: discipline 153; disordered 152
sexual crimes 153–154
sexual misbehavior 248
sexual misconduct 151
sexual permissiveness 11
sexual promiscuity 252
Sgrilli, G. 102
Showalter, E. 113
Signoria, F. 24
simplicity and foolishness (*semplicità e sciocchezza*) 138, 140–141
six non-naturals 192, 196, 227
sleep 224
sociability 58, 63, 92, 94, 146, 237, 251, 268
social awareness 143–144, 152–153
social consequences 145–146
social control 12
social disciplining 12, 147, 150
social role 40, 59, 60, 93, 113
sodomy 152, 153
son(s) 198, 232; familial conflict 158; and father 146–147, 251–252
spaces of madness 128–163; assessment of diminished liability 136–145; criminal insanity 136–145; disobedience and violent behaviors 147–151; licentious behavior 151–155; madness as police matter 145–157; mental disturbance in family litigation 155–157; overview 128–130; *pazzeria* of Santa Maria Nuova 130–136; Santa Dorotea 130–136; special requests *per porre freno a detti disordini* 145–157
special requests *per porre freno a detti disordini* 145–157
spendthrifts: adult 67–73; young 60–67; *see also* prodigality
spirito 223, 245, 247, 248, 269
spirits: alteration of 162; animal 191, 226; and brain fibers 191; forced application 227; low 238, 243, 246, 249; oppression of 230; *spirito* 223, 245, 247, 248, 269; uneasy 210, 248; weakness of 233, 235, 236, 237
spirituality 203
spousal violence 244
squanderer (*dilapidatore*) 57
state guardianship 25
statutes, of Magistrato dei Pupilli 25–26, 177
statutory penalty 137
stealing, uncontrolled 149
stigma, prodigality as 91–92
Stinche prison 130, 132, 134, 135, 141, 144
Stolberg, M. 237
stolido 138, 233
stravagante see extravagance/extravagancy(ies)
strokes 188, 189, 190
stupidity 134, 153, 190, 200, 232–234, 236, 248, 252
stupro (rape) 152
suicide 128, 139, 193, 196, 249
supplica (supplication) 137, 142, 143, 202
surgeons *condotti* (*cerusico condotto*) 228
Suzuki, A. 7, 88

Targioni Tozzetti, G. 134–136, 186, 187, 188, 192, 202, 211, 225, 247
temperament 192, 195, 237, 241, 245, 247, 248, 252
temporary incarceration 39
testimonies: Auditore Fiscale 205–210; clergymen 177, 186, 203–205; collective 203; conflicting 203; in interdiction procedures 29; priests 132, 184, 200, 203–205, 209, 210–211; *see also* medical testimonies
theft 143, 149, 160
tranquility 227
tribulation 230, 247
turbazioni di fantasia 187, 192, 194
turbazioni di mente 194, 197

284 Index

uncertain (*incerto*) 245, 249, 252
uneasiness *see inquietudine*
uneasy nature (*naturale inquieto*) 3, 96–97, 210, 248, 253
uneasy spirit (*spirito inquieto*) 96–97
unpredictable emotional reactions 245–243
unruliness (*indocilità*) 147, 148–149, 154, 155, 248, 268
unstable (*volubile*) 224, 249, 252

Valloni, X. 189–190
Venturini, S. 140
verbal abuse 242, 243
vessazioni dell'animo 195
vexations 233, 249; of imprisonment (*gravità della prigionia*) 145; of soul (*vessazioni dell'animo*) 195
Viligiardi, F. A. 186, 189, 195
Vinattieri, G. B. 110–111
violence 147–151, 159, 161, 205, 207; crimes of 142; domestic 149; epileptic fits 191; fits of anger 246; illogical 229–230; marital 162, 244; outbreak of madness 231; passions 157, 241; *pazzia furiosa* 150; physical 242, 243
violent reactions 157, 209, 240–244, 245–246
Vocabolario degli accademici della Crusca 223
volatility 247
Volterra 152, 191
volubile (unstable) 224, 249, 252

weak of mind (*frenetico* and *debole di mente*) 95–96
weather 227

weight loss 225
widows as privileged interlocutors 40
willpower 246
wives 39–40, 66, 68–70, 72–73, 76–77, 86, 89, 94, 104, 105, 107–108, 114–115, 150, 156–158, 162, 232, 239
women 151–152, 239–240, 242; administrators of their husbands' or sons' patrimonies 239; anger 242; and anger 242; behavioral disorders 248; cohabitation with mentally afflicted husband 239; daughters 39, 75, 76–77, 89–90, 104, 106, 110–111, 115; denouncing husband for prodigality 73; extravagance 250–251; of ill repute 154; inebriated 142; *inquietudine* 249; in interdiction procedures 40–41; as interim heads of family 114, 116; legal powers to 60–61; libertinage 154; and mental capacity 205; and mental incapacity 89–90, 104, 112–116; mothers 89–90, 232; as petitioners 40, 103; power 151; and prodigality 94; sexual scandals 154–155; uneasy spirits 248; *see also* wives
wounds, self-inflicted 139
wrongful intent 139, 142

young prodigality 251; characteristics of 60–61; identification of 60; interdictions 64–65; perceptions of 63–64; reasons behind 64
young prodigals 57–58

Zacchia, P. 137–138, 177–178

Ingram Content Group UK Ltd.
Milton Keynes UK
UKHW022113040523
421267UK00007B/93